UNITED STATES

30°N

Los Angeles

Oʻahu

Hawaiʻi

HAWAIʻI

MEXICO

15°N

Mexico City

North Pacific Ocean

Clipperton

Kiritimati

Line Islands

ds

I

0°   equator

C O O K   I S L A N D S

Marquesas
Islands

F R E N C H

Galapagos
Islands

ERICAN
AMOA

Tuamotu Archipelago

P O L Y N E S I A

15°S

E

Society Islands

Tahiti

Rarotonga

Austral Islands

Gambier Islands

Pitcairn
Islands

th Pacific Ocean

30°S

Rapanui
(Easter)

THE PACIFIC ISLANDS

W   E

155°W   140°W   125°W   110°W   95°W

45°S

Songs from the Second Float

Ariki Avo in full regalia, about to leave his house to officiate at a *tukumai* ritual

Pacific Islands Monograph Series 21

Songs from the Second Float

A Musical Ethnography of Takū Atoll, Papua New Guinea

Richard Moyle

CENTER FOR PACIFIC ISLANDS STUDIES
School of Hawaiian, Asian, and Pacific Studies
University of Hawai'i, Mānoa
UNIVERSITY OF HAWAI'I PRESS • Honolulu

Library of Congress Cataloging-in-Publication Data
Moyle, Richard M.
    Songs from the second float : a musical ethnography of
Takū Atoll, Papua New Guinea / Richard Moyle.
        p. cm.—(Pacific islands monograph series ; 21)
    Includes bibliographical references (p.) and index.
    ISBN 978-0-8248-3175-2 (hardcover : alk. paper)
        1. Music—Social aspects—Papua New Guinea—Tauu Islands.
2. Tauu Islands (Papua New Guinea)—Social life and customs.
I. Title.
    ML3917.P37M69 2007
    781.62'9946—dc22

                        2006035644

✠ Maps by Manoa Mapworks, Inc.

Design by Paul Herr
Printed by The Maple-Vail Book Manufacturing Group

Takū rā ko te vaka, Nukutoa rā ko te ama, arā e ttapa i te
fenua nei ma ko Teamarua—Nukutoa.

Takū Island is like a canoe and Nukutoa is a float,
so this island—Nukutoa—is known here as the
Second Float.
   —Ariki Avo, 1998

In 1891, Takū's small population was forcibly relocated to one of
the atoll's smaller islands. Using the poetic metaphor of the outrigger canoe, that island became a "float" to the "canoe," that is,
their earlier and larger island home. And when in 1930 that same
population moved to their present location, on Nukutoa, their
new island home became a "second float." The title of this book
preserves the poetic metaphor.

Editor's Note

In November 2005, the Center for Pacific Islands Studies joined with Museum of New Zealand Te Papa Tongarewa and the Pacific Studies program at Victoria University of Wellington to cosponsor the international conference, "Culture Moves! Dance in Oceania from hiva to hip hop." The conference evolved from the deep conviction that the arts offer the most dynamic, creative, and visible expression of cultural identity and resilience in the contemporary Pacific. The conveners adjusted the conventional format for an academic gathering to allow troupes and community groups from throughout the region to come together in Wellington, New Zealand, and dance their understandings of themselves and of the world in which they live.

In like manner, Richard Moyle's *Songs from the Second Float: A Musical Ethnography of Takū Atoll, Papua New Guinea* underscores through its detailed and compelling text the prominence of music and dance in the everyday life of a Pacific people. The geographical focus of Moyle's study is Takū, a Polynesian outlier located at the far southeastern border of the Papua New Guinea state.

Takū, as Moyle notes, is vulnerable in multiple ways; its past, present, and future attest to this point. Contact with the European world brought disease, depopulation, displacement, and decades of required labor on a foreign-owned, commercial copra plantation. Despite these deadly, disruptive forces, the people of Takū have persevered, with much of their social structure and religious belief system intact. The retention of this Polynesian heritage has resulted in large measure from their intense commitment to music, dance, and oral tradition. These performative practices lie deeply embedded within the everyday life of Takū; they allow for individual acknowledgment while reinforcing the deep social solidarity that binds the people of the atoll to each other and to their ancestors. The author writes, "the building blocks of Takū society—its survival, strategies, self-sufficiency in material needs, skills in both agriculture and mariculture, practicing a hereditary system of clan-based leadership, enacting interpersonal relationships through egalitarianism and reciprocity, and confronting and managing the unknown through a religious system that incorporates two-way communication and reciprocity—are bound fast by its musicking." In short, music and dance confirm, validate, and give tangible expression to all of these critical, life-sustaining qualities.

Forces at work in the present threaten the integrity of local culture and the communal performances through which it is expressed. The establishment of new forms of representative government has affected the authority of the Ariki, the spiritual leader of the island around whom much of Takū culture revolves. A more immediate challenge to established structures and practices is the growing presence of an evangelical Christian church on the island. Rising sea levels, however, constitute the greatest danger to Takū's future. The consequent erosion of soil and flooding of precious taro gardens could leave the atoll uninhabitable within a relatively short time. It would prove a sad irony, indeed, if this first full ethnography of Takū were also the last.

Richard Moyle's impressive study is the result of extensive residence on Takū as well as an exhaustive search of historical archives and the extant anthropological record. He has produced a comprehensive, integrated work that is interdisciplinary in character and that gives not only agency but prominence and respect to the people of this atoll. Song texts, musical transcriptions, and an effective collection of photographs and maps complement his description and analysis. Of special note is Moyle's attention to how songs are composed and how dances are choreographed. His overall writing evidences an acute sensitivity to the many and layered contexts that inform the creation, performance, and preservation of these art forms. The Pacific Islands Monograph Series is delighted to publish a scholarly work that highlights the centrality of music and dance to expressions of cultural identity and persistence on one Polynesian atoll and, by extension, throughout much of Oceania.

DAVID HANLON

Contents

Illustrations

Photos

Acknowledgments

On Takū itself, the entire project could not have occurred without the approval of Ariki Avo and the community council, and it could not have succeeded without the support and patience of the community itself. To Avo, his wife Samoa, and family, I am most grateful, not just for generous hospitality but also for the many easements into Takū life and their constant interest in the daily research activities.

Several expatriate residents, including Pais Taehu, Kapeatu Puāria, Robert Sini, and Tautai Teneke, were instrumental in smoothing out bureaucratic creases in the offices of the North Solomons Province of Papua New Guinea at a time when no research permits had been issued for many years. Stuart King kindly assisted with practical help and hospitality.

Since the community as a whole approved of my work and daily presence at both mundane and ritual activities, it would be inappropriate to identify individuals. However, I must record with gratitude the cooperation and support of the five clan elders. In addition to Ariki Avo, these included Pure Kīpū, Kikiva Lakoa, Pūtahu Tekapu, and Pāsia Piri (who succeeded his brother Tenehu in 1998).

To John Sione Konga, captain of the MV *Sankamap*, and his crew, I am grateful for more than sixty days of travel made comfortable and even engrossing by stimulating conversation and many acts of kindness on both land and sea.

My first research assistant, Natan Nake, died tragically in 1995, having declined medical treatment in Buka for a heart condition in favor of remaining on the island to assist with the project. Natan's perpetually cheerful disposition and ability to work long hours transcribing song poetry and stories were indispensable assets during the early months of my residence. My second assistant, Tekaso Laroteone, was equally industrious and patient. As the Ariki-designate, Tekaso had unique access to sources of information about much of the community's religious life. During his four months' residence in Auckland in 1998 and 1999, he and I worked on the translation of several hundred songs and exhausted ourselves happily in endless discussions on both specific and abstract aspects of Takū life and music.

I am indebted to Jane Moulin for contributions to the discussion on dance and to Don Niles for logistic support during the fieldwork periods; to both of these colleagues together with Michael Webb I express my additional thanks for their ready agreement to travel to Auckland and relief-teach for me during the period 1998–2000.

Within the Department of Anthropology, I am grateful to Hamish Macdonald for his preparation and repairs of photographs, to Joan Lawrence and Seline McNamee for their preparation of maps and figures, and also to Peter Kerr in the School of Music for expert computer advice. I thank Jane Eckelman of Manoa Mapworks, Inc, in Honolulu, for preparing the final versions of the maps that appear in this work.

I also acknowledge with thanks Margaret Spencer and Len Murray for permission to use photographs of Takū; Sheila Waters for permission to copy material and photographs belonging to her father, E W P Chinnery; and Helen and David Lawrence for supplying archival material from Port Moresby. Tim Bayliss-Smith kindly supplied the results of his measurements of Takū's islands and gardens, based on a set of United States Air Force aerial photographs taken in 1943. I am also grateful to Ann Chowning for her comments on draft chapters.

The Center for Pacific Islands Studies has been unfailingly supportive and practical while this manuscript was in their hands. For her expert editorial smoothing of my linguistic roughness and her patient suggestions for easing the reader into unfamiliar territories, I am grateful to Terre Fisher. And for her devoted eye for detail I am also indebted to CPIS Managing Editor Jan Rensel.

The initial visit to Takū occurred as the final project under the UNESCO-funded Territorial Survey of Oceanic Music program, organized through the Archive of Maori and Pacific Music at the University of Auckland. The second visit was funded with the help of a research grant from the university itself, and three subsequent visits were funded by a grant from the Marsden Fund, the first in Ethnomusicology. A further visit in 2001 was financed by Television New Zealand's *Tagata Pasifika* program. To all these agencies I am most grateful.

More than a mere acknowledgement is due my wife, Linden, and Keri, Stuart, and Philippa. The anguish of two months of lost contact after Rabaul's eruptions in 1994 was followed by a succession of Christmas absences not easily borne, and the completion of this book is testimony to their continued love, support, and resilience.

2005 Postscript

Takū's musical life is an ongoing process of development and reshaping but, of necessity, any written study of that musical life has practical but artificial boundaries of time.

Although this book was completed in 2003, I returned to the island for a further five months in 2004 to find both predictable and unpredictable changes in several areas of social, political, and religious activity; these will be discussed in separate publications. I also noted the ongoing foreshore erosion and the community's desperate appeal to the Australian government for funds to build a seawall right around Nukutoa Island.

In 2002 Kikiva Nukuria, the elder of Hare Māsani clan, died and was succeeded by his brother Hitina. Because of his own senility, Pūtahu Tekapu, the elder of Hare Nāoro clan, has assigned some of his *marae* duties to his son Ahelo. I also note the passing in 2002 of Nūnua Posongat, a man whose immense abilities are merely alluded to in this book, and which are now only the subject of residents' nostalgia. Elsewhere I have written an obituary for Nūnua (Moyle 2002), but one of his comments in 1998 seems apposite now. As external and internal forces continue in ever-changing configurations to influence Takū's secular and sacred activities, Nūnua was confident about the overarching and enduring authority of the Ariki and Pure: *E sē lavā te oti; te paua rā e moe*—Their power is still there; it cannot ever finish.

Preface

Few researchers have spent extended time on Takū. William Churchill (1884) and Richard Parkinson (1885, 1896) visited briefly, as did the Hamburg Museum's South Seas Expedition in 1910 led by Ernst Sarfert (Thilenius 1931). The American linguist Samuel H Elbert spent six weeks on Takū in 1963 studying the language; he subsequently produced a report on living conditions and a brief outline of local customs for the Australian administration (Elbert 1963a). He also made a series of audio recordings, later deposited in the Bernice P Bishop Museum, Honolulu. Another American linguist, (Irwin) Jay Howard, worked on the island in 1964, 1976, and 1978–1979 to produce a dictionary of the Takū language. A preliminary version of this dictionary exists in computer disk form only, and apparently only one publication resulted from Howard's fieldwork (Howard 1981). Arriving first as an assistant to Howard on his final trip, Barbara G Moir returned to Takū in the 1980s as a graduate student in archaeology, researching the cultivation of the giant clam (Moir 1989).

My own fieldwork consisted of six periods of two or three months each, beginning in 1994 and concluding in 2000. I visited briefly again in 2001. During these periods I was a guest of Ariki Avo, who gave me the ancestral name Sauhatu to denote his adoption of me into his own family, a name used in my presence on formal occasions by most people, but on all occasions by the Ariki's mother, Tepuka.

Linguistic Orthography

Several issues of language arise in this work. Illiteracy is confined to older residents who grew up before the present school was established, but younger Takū tend to correspond with one another in an idiosyncratic manner and without any diacritics. In the absence of a uniform orthography, I have tried to present original Takū material in as clear a manner as possible, specifically with respect to double consonants and long vowels. To this end, I consulted with Takū teachers at the community school and with several other adults and linguists.

In written Takū, one letter may commonly represent two different sounds. Thus, the word *ara* in which both vowels are short means "path," but if the second vowel is long—*arā*—the word means "and then." Most of the people who write in Takū use the same /a/ to represent both the /a/ and /ā/ sounds, but when reading aloud from such material, they frequently pause or reread to correctly identify long vowels. Just as there are short and long vowels, there are also single and double consonants. For instance, *kai* (to eat) has a single consonant, but the consonant can be doubled, in which case it forms another word, *kkai* (fable). Double consonants are produced by prolonging the articulation of the respective short consonants. In this work, I mark long vowels with a macron and double consonants by doubling them, as here.

Because of the nature of the material, I have also included a wide variety of vernacular terms in the text; a glossary at the end of the book lists those more frequently used.

Language Change

Takū's spoken language is in a state of flux. For instance, older residents use an /f/ sound *(fare)* while younger Takū prefer an /h/ sound *(hare);* this extends to even personal names. Since it is apparent that use of /h/ forms is increasing as the number of practitioners of the /f/ forms decreases through natural attrition, I use the /h/ form in this present work except, for instance, in songs where the /f/ form is deliberately and consciously retained. One exception is the universal retention of /ff/. Among children and teenagers, the /r/ tends to be trilled, and /h/ is substituted for /s/ in some words *(heai* for *seai)*, in apparent imitation of Nukumanu or Peilau speaking style. Such idiosyncrasies have not been incorporated in this work. Additionally, /l/ and /r/ are used interchangeably among speakers generally, with the exception of /ll/, and many words routinely contain both forms (*laro* "below," *rilo* "out of sight").

Personal Names

Although the names given to infants at birth are retained for life, many residents acquire other names that tend to be used in preference to their birth names. In some instances, the assigned naming occurs at a very young age, and indeed, during the fieldwork period, a few adults discovered their birth names for the first time. Some arrived at the discovery through their own initiative, others from workmates on Nukuria, Bougainville, or elsewhere; several of these names have now become incorporated within local nomenclature to the extent that they recur as birth names in subsequent generations of the same family. The issue of which form of the personal name should be used in this present work is complicated somewhat by my references to song poetry, where either form of the name may appear. My requests for guidance from the community revealed divided opinion.

Accordingly, to accommodate this complex set of circumstances, I use in the book what I believe to be the more common form of a personal name.

Many personal names include the definite article *te*, which, when written, is normally incorporated into the following word to produce a single word. I generally follow this practice, but write articles as separate words when presenting vernacular texts and when identifying geographical locations, the latter because frequently the name constitutes an entire phrase, for example, Te Utua Anuanu (Anuanu's Outcrop).

Musical Orthography

Much of Takū's singing can be represented in notational form using standard orthography, but a few features require special explanation.

Transposition

In instances where a notation has been transposed from the pitch recorded, for purposes of eliminating accidentals or constantly shifting between clefs, I indicate the original pitch at the head of the transcription. Thus "+2" indicates that the original overall pitch was two semitones higher than that transcribed.

Vowel Shifts and Underpinned Texts

For aesthetic reasons discussed elsewhere (see pp. 174–176), most song poetry observes a vowel shift from /a/ to /o/ in some, but not all, words, and I had to make a working decision about the linguistic form in which song poetry should appear. I chose to retain the sung form when underpinning texts to musical notations, indicating a shift by writing a changed /a/ as /ò/, but I revert to the spoken form when discussing texts alone, since the focus here is on the poetry itself rather than its mode of delivery.

Singers occasionally appear to omit one syllable of a word or they were sung too softly to be audible on the recording; in the notations such syllables appear within brackets.

Bar-lines

In the few notations that show metered characteristics, the dotted bar-lines delineate bars. Elsewhere, bar-lines designate larger structural divisions: double bar-lines identify the end of a half verse, refrain and singing stabilizer, and dotted bar-lines occur at the ends of phrases within a half verse.

Abbreviations

For reasons of economy of space, notations carry abbreviated terms denoting song structure or performance features:

hcl   hand clapping
hmh   *hakamauhua* (singing stabilizer), a structural element

Rhythmic Recitation

Several children's game songs are performed in rhythmic recitation. Since precise pitch is irrelevant, I have dispensed with the five-line staff when notating these. Individual notes sung at an indefinite pitch or rhythmically recited are represented, with conventional note-heads replaced by crosses.

Song Structure

Because references to song structure occur in several chapters, I include here a summary of terminology. Indigenous terminology for song structure is precise and applies to all categories of local composition. The most common context for discussions using such terminology is after a singing error has occurred during the rehearsal of newly composed material. The correct material is identified by its poetic content or its structural label or both. Such a corrective procedure is possible because a typical performance presents material in a sequence of named sections: the *vvoro* (opener) is followed by the *hakamauhua* (singing stabilizer) and *hati* (refrain). For each of the subsequent verses of the song, sections are presented as follows: *puku* (first verse-part)—*hakamauhua* (singing stabilizer)—*soa puku* (companion verse)—*hakamauhua* (singing stabilizer)—*hati* (refrain). This structure is typified in the poetry of a *lani* song (table 1) in praise of success in ocean fishing by hand-lining.

Table 1. Typical Structure of a Takū Song

vvoro	*Te hānota i te laki nei.*	I fished in the northwest trade wind.	opener
hakamauhua	*Nimonimo nau e te tahe.*	Spinning around in the current.	singing stabilizer
hati	*Leva hānota i te laki nei.*	My sweetheart fished in the northwest wind.	refrain
puku	*Tele tau hatu ma tau tamana;*	I let down my sinker, uttering my [dead] father's formula;	verse
hakamauhua	*Nimonimo nau e te tahe*	Spinning around in the current.	singing stabilizer
soa puku	*Tele tau hatu ma te Seiana,*	I let down my sinker, uttering Seiana's formula.	companion verse
hakamauhua	*Nimonimo nau e te tahe.*	Spinning around in the current.	singing stabilizer
hati	*Leva hānota i te laki nei.*	My sweetheart fished in the northwest wind.	refrain
puku	*Nau talaki te tuahenua;*	I opened the fishing grounds,	verse
hakamauhua	*Nimonimo nau e te tahe*	Spinning around in the current.	singing stabilizer
soapuku	*Nau talaki o pula malama,*	I opened them with a successful catch	companion verse
hakamauhua	*Nimonimo nau e te tahe.*	Spinning around in the current.	singing stabilizer
hati	*Leva hānota i te laki nei.*	My sweetheart fished in the northwest wind.	refrain
puku	*Hatau aku ika i tau atua;*	With my spirit beside me, I caught my fish;	verse
hakamauhua	*Nimonimo nau e te tahe*	Spinning around in the current.	singing stabilizer
soapuku	*Hatau aku palu e Laputuna,*	With Laputuna beside me, I caught my *palu* fish.	companion verse
hakamauhua	*Nimonimo nau e te tahe.*	Spinning around in the current.	singing stabilizer
hati	*Leva hānota i te laki nei.*	My sweetheart fished in the northwest wind.	refrain

In notations appearing in this book, repetition of the *hati* or the *hakamauhua* or individual verses is indicated at the end of preceding lines, for example:

E ā - ī - ē,   ni mo - mo - e a - ke tò - nò u ru - to - no.

A Chronology of Previous Audio Recordings

Table 2. A Chronology of Previous Audio Recordings

Recorder	Date	Description	Location of Originals
Ray Sheridan[1]	1953	songs	National Archives, Canberra
Margaret Spencer[2]	1960	songs	Archive of Maori and Pacific Music, Auckland
Samuel Elbert	1963	stories, songs	University of Hawai'i, Honolulu
Segaropa (Seg) Pūtuha	1979	songs	unknown
Tekapu Apava	1973	songs, stories	held by recorder
Irwin Howard	1976–1979	stories	unknown
Richard Feinberg	1984	songs	held by recorder

Notes
1. Working on behalf of the Australian Broadcasting Commission.
2. Author of *Doctor's Wife in Rabaul* (1967).

I am unaware of any commercial recordings or published notations of Takū songs, and although several published accounts of visits to the atoll include mention of dance performances, the sole published summary is an encyclopedia article by Barbara Moir (1998).

Issues of Privacy

There are certain types of information I have deliberately excluded from this work for reasons of privacy. Each of the five clan elders *(mātua)* includes in his inventory of ritual utterances a series of invocations *(taku)* intended for performance on the *marae* in the presence of the other elders and the assembled adult population of the community. Their contents cover a variety of topics vital to the physical and spiritual well-being of the people, and performance is intended to enlist ancestral assistance to achieve those ends. The mode of delivery and typical duration of the utterances, however, is such that a casual listener would be unlikely to memorize them and use them for personal purposes, and to that extent, the *taku* constitute private property. Accordingly, when discussing the roles of the clan elders, I refer to this material only in translation.

Men make contact with their ancestors and personal spirits through invocations called *kavai*. These are used most commonly when fishing, to secure supernatural assistance and so increase the likelihood of a successful trip but also occasionally on shore as well. Because knowledge of *kavai* is kept within individual families, a father passing on his repertoire on request to his sons, I do not discuss these invocations further or present them as examples.

Another category of song is excluded from detailed study here for similar reasons. Each clan possesses a *hakapiri henua* ("attaching the death-necklet") song performed as a garland is placed around the neck of a dead fellow clan member shortly before burial. Only those senior clan members standing close by at that moment join in; indeed, only such people are familiar with the song, and even then, only a few may be able to sing it in its entirety. In keeping with the restricted nature of such songs, it was the wish of the community that details about them be excluded from this work.

Companion CD

A companion CD, *Songs from the Second Float,* issued by Ode Records, Post Office Box 37-179, Parnell, Auckland, New Zealand, contains recordings of several songs discussed here. Ordering details can be found online at <http://www.oderecords.co.nz/default.asp>.

Introduction

This book is a musical ethnography of a Polynesian outlier, Takū, an atoll lying off the east coast of Bougainville, politically incorporated in Papua New Guinea but having more cultural affinities with the other outliers far to its southeast, all but one of which is located outside Papua New Guinea. The work arose from a request in 1994 from the island's chief (the Ariki) and council for a tangible means of documenting its performance traditions, in the first instance for the benefit of high school students living away from the island for up to five years and considered to be gaining an academic education at the expense of a cultural education. Additionally I have endeavored to present to a wider readership the pervasiveness of performance in both mundane and ritual life and the parallel pervasiveness of the spirit world in activities on land and sea.

There is on Takū a perception, widely reported elsewhere in the Pacific, that the ever-increasing pace of European cultural presence is beginning to significantly influence thinking away from those values and skills that have formed the nucleus of shared experiences and beliefs binding the island's four hundred residents into a functioning community. Music performance, the act that Christopher Small labels "musicking" (1998), is one such experience, shared because the ability to so engage is assumed to be universal among the residents. Music is also part of a more general belief system because singing opens a pathway of communication with inhabitants of the spirit world, who are held to be as susceptible as humans to the aesthetic appreciation of faultless entertainment. But the sudden and unexpected death in 1994 of the island's last *purotu* performance specialist in the absence of any trained successor, either for himself or for the other specialists, has cast in doubt the village's ability to sustain the level of performance of even a generation ago. Now there is a common perception that the 1960s and 1970s represented something of a Golden Era.

Takū is multiply isolated. A small atoll whose natural resources alone are now insufficient to sustain the present population's material needs, let alone maintain any commercially viable agricultural or aquacultural production program, it has been omitted from provincial and national government development planning as a separate entity, although it is routinely grouped together with what are commonly known as the "Atolls," comprising Nissan, Nukuria (Fead Island), Cartarets, and Nukumanu (Tasman Island). Takū lies at the extreme eastern tip of Papua New Guinea's territorial boundary and thus remains outside coastal maritime routes, receiving nominally monthly visits from the provincial government's sole vessel, MV *Sankamap,* and irregular visits from one other vessel based in Kaveing in New Ireland. And, although the village continues to receive fleeting visits from various government agencies, it had hosted only three researchers before my own arrival—two linguists and an archaeologist—only one of whom subsequently produced an academic publication (Moir 1989). For these reasons, Takū and its culture are largely unknown even within Papua New Guinea, and thus it seemed desirable and necessary to include in this present work information that will serve not only to establish the cultural contexts for music performance but also to portray the broader material and social environments that frame daily life in its secular and ritual modes and impinge in a more general sense on the performing arts. The island community's present cultural and musical circumstances arise from a combination of local initiatives and foreign influences occurring in the eras both before and since contact with Europeans, and songs composed in these contexts continue to function as markers of social achievement or social identity. A survey of the contact with other islands is included in my outline of Takū society generally.

Two events of major significance occurred in the late nineteenth century, and their impact continues to be felt. The accidental introduction of disease reduced the population to an almost unsustainably low level, and this sheer lack of numbers spelled the end of both the oceangoing sailing canoes and the existing social system. While living at reduced numbers, the Takū seem to have unwittingly sold the atoll to a foreigner who subsequently removed its population to a smaller islet. There she effectively denied them access to traditional forms of food gathering and ritual activities, and this brought about rapid changes in religious practice and further social disruption. It was to be a further forty years before a new social order emerged. Significantly— since that emergence was interpreted as vindication of religious belief—the catalyst for change took the form of preemptive ancestral intervention via a spirit medium, Faite Pūtahu. The events of this period in the island's history seemed to herald the present social system on Nukutoa Island, which, through its five-clan structure, embraces the twin principles of reciprocity and egalitarianism.

Even within an egalitarian society, however, a person may acquire social distinction and personal influence through achievement rather than inheritance. Takū's mythology prior to European contact is dotted with accounts of individual men and women whose initiative and actions were deemed laudable because they were undertaken on behalf of the village. The island's founding Ariki, Atui, and Pure leaders reached an enduring agreement about their respective areas of responsibility; one nineteenth-century Ariki used his supernatural powers to drive away European intruders; named castaways from Nukumanu and Peilau introduced new techniques for catching prestige fish; a spirit-child speaking through an early twentieth century woman made significant changes to the social system and material culture; the grandfather of the present Ariki instituted a number of regulations relating to food gathering still in force today; and the achievements of individual fishermen from mythological accounts of the distant past to the present are vicariously relived through use of a first-person poetic perspective. On the level of group activity, egalitarianism is occasionally replaced by its complementary value— competition—in formal events designed to allow individuals to enhance their personal prestige. Of these events, men's fishing competitions are the most common. Such occasions also express the temporary reversal of another cultural attribute, male domestic dominance, for it is the women who organize and control associated onshore events. They, not the other men, deliver sanctioned verbal and physical abuse and humiliation to under-performing male participants; they also require them to display their dancing abilities. On other formal occasions, women may also temporarily suspend the normal brother-sister avoidance and submit men—even the Ariki himself—to the double humiliation of having to dance inside the women's drinking houses and with female relatives. By this sanctioned violation of an essentially segregated activity, women enjoy a measure of redress for perceived social imbalances.

Songs are ascribed either human or supernatural origins. On occasion the distinction may be blurred or even disputed, but there can be no doubt that religious life in general is integral to the way the village operates as a social entity. Even though it is located within Melanesia, Takū is a Polynesian outlier and, as in Polynesia proper, the relationship between the uttered word and religious practice and belief is well attested (see McLean 1999, 371; Kaeppler and Love 1998, 200). Although the extent and precise nature of the relationship varies among island groups, it is evident that the act of singing is a central means of establishing contact with the supernatural world; more specifically, song opens lines of communication with particular local spirits. It should be noted that traditional Polynesian religion, formerly a systematic and coherent set of activities and beliefs in each of its Pacific Island groups, has now been replaced by Christianity with its own many and varied forms. The late twentieth century renewal of interest in Polynesian cultural identity in regions such as Aotearoa and Hawai'i entailed a revival of attention to specific aspects of indigenous religious belief but did not amount to winding back the cultural clock. Takū, however, represents something of an exception since its village leaders have rejected the introduction of Christianity on several occasions. They refused to allow teams of missionary evangelists to land on the island and, up to 1999, successfully prevented the erection of churches.

This is not to suggest that traditional religious practices on Takū have continued unabated throughout the period since European contact. A combination of circumstances, each highlighting in its own way the fragility of atoll existence, combined to decimate the population and break intergenerational lines of transmission for ritual knowledge; events conspired to effectively remove the means of maintaining site-focused acts and processes, and finally in 1973, the untimely off-island death of the community's spiritual head produced a crisis of unprecedented proportions. Despite these difficulties, community leaders maintained as well as they could various forms of private and public contact with a pantheon of spiritual beings who were either known and trusted or only partially known and feared. Two significant features of these survivable catastrophes were their foreign origins and their essentially noncompetitive nature, at least in a religious sense; in sharp contrast, the impetus for adopting Christianity, with its potential to eliminate traditional religious beliefs and practices, has emanated from within the community itself and is essentially and overtly competitive. Ariki Avo is acutely aware of the changes to social structure and secular authority that wholesale conversion to Christianity would probably bring, having witnessed similar developments on the neighboring islands of Nukuria and Nukumanu. In 1995 Avo told me emphatically, "This island is not an island of the church, but of tradition," but by 1998 the number of converts had grown to the point where he had to admit, "Christianity is here now." In this work I present an overview of Takū's religious practices and beliefs in both the historic and present periods, the beliefs underpinning several themes of song poetry, and the activities typically described in that body of poetry. I also sketch out the nature and extent of Christianity's impact.

For a community of some 160 adults, the number of songs in the active repertoire—I stopped recording at a thousand—is impressive. But to ask "Why so many?" is perhaps to miss the point since, for Takū's residents, music is not a abstraction, it is performance (see table 3). The more relevant question therefore is "Why is there so much singing on Takū?" To begin to answer that question, we must try and identify the functions of singing. What the people sing about represents their idealized world—ideal sets of interpersonal relationships, success rates for fishing expeditions and gardening productivity, and even ideal conditions for the activities they hold dear in life, among which dancing figures most prominently. In a small, isolated community constantly living within a few weeks of famine—if weather conditions turn bad and fishing becomes impossible—there is a constant need for reassurance that the relationships binding people into a community still function in the here and now. People need to know they continue to be a recognized and working part of that community, and singing about their relationships is one way they, as a corporate group, can affirm what amounts to a secular creed—not in any prescriptive sense, but rather by detailing the ongoing expression of the principles that underpin society as a whole. Each day presents challenges to the cohesion of the community because of the dangers fishermen face each time they enter the open ocean in small canoes. It is not surprising that one

Table 3. Principal Takū Categories of Song and Dance

Takū Name	Designation	Origin	Occasion	Participants	Instrument	Comments
hula	dance	local or imported	formal or informal	young women	guitars	genre introduced in 1950s
lani	song	local or imported	informal	pairs or groups of men	none	sung in two-part harmony
lū	song	most are spirit-composed	formal	men and women	none	performance venue tightly controlled
mamakoho	dance	spirit-composed	formal	women	*tuki* drum	few in number; rarely performed
paki	dance	imported	formal	men	*tuki* drum	single specimen in repertoire
rue	dance	local or imported	formal or informal	men	ad hoc idiophone	sung slowly before sudden acceleration
sau	dance	spirit-composed	formal	mostly women	occasional hand clapping	few in number
sore	dance	spirit-composed	formal	women	none	few specimens in repertoire
takere	dance	spirit-composed	formal	men	dancers' sticks	two specimens in repertoire
tani	song	local or imported	informal	man or woman	none	songs embedded in *kkai* fables
toha	dance	local or imported	formal or informal	women	none	
tuki	dance and/or song	most are human-composed	formal or informal	men or women, or both	hand clapping for some songs only	much stereotyping of melodies, poetry
uru	song	local	formal	men	none	obsolete

key theme in song poetry is successful and safe ocean fishing, and another is the support of family members back on shore. The constant potential danger posed to social unity is matched and neutralized by constant singing about secure and effective social relationships. And these relationships extend beyond the living to encompass ancestral spirits, whose accessibility and powers of assistance constitute an integral part of activities such as gardening and the capture of prestige fish, whose successful outcomes are believed to lie beyond purely human endeavor.

Death represents the ultimate disunifying element of life, and it seems no coincidence that the greatest number of new songs are composed when someone dies. More than seventy new *tuki* songs were composed in 1996 when thirteen residents died, and almost fifty songs appeared in the following year. But, important as it is to compose and sing these new songs, they have no enduring value in their own right; they are sung only once in public in recognition of the fact of the death, and then may be put aside as the community turns its attention to new events and challenges. The commemoration of a death in the *tukumai* ritual is also the greatest single period of singing generally, since in addition to both new and old *tuki* songs, whole afternoons are devoted to performance of large-scale men's and women's dances.

The act of singing seems to unite people in ways no other group activity does, and the achievement of tight unison without any singing leader or conductor represents the ultimate in egalitarianism—perhaps more than one hundred adults choosing to do exactly the same thing in the same manner and predetermined sequence at the same time and in the same place. Dancing, which adds a visual dimension to the power of the sung word, brings a whole-body avenue of physical expression to the performance. The song poetry speaks principally about people—named, individual fellow islanders: those with whom singers choose to associate in group activities, those to whom they defer in matters of particular expertise (fishing, the enactment of ritual), those for whom singers grieve when they die, and those whom they join on occasions of celebration. Such people do not simply exist in a static or abstract sense; their significance in the poetry derives from the nature of their association with the singers. Interpersonal relationships, and the ways these are defined and articulated, necessarily occupy a large part of everyday life on a small island where—for example—privacy is hard to achieve, and where most residents are directly related to more than a quarter of the population. Relationships also occupy a significant part of song poetry because the poetry idealizes these associations, and the act of uttering this poetry in group singing affirms and teaches about the relationships. In a broader examination of Takū society (chapter 2) I examine the specific relationships that bring residents together as social units, which, as part of their distinct responsibilities, create and perform certain types of songs.

By their attendance and participation at formal events in the ritual arena, residents partake of the concept of collective identity, not in the name of

their island as "Takū" but in the name of their island as "home" *(te henua nei)*.
There is however no assertion of the type "We are Takū, this is our music and
it expresses our culture/politics" because both performer and audience are
Takū and are interchangeable within the performance of even a single item;
in addition, the various song types are theoretically available to composers
from any clan. If "Takū" has any meaning at all for the community, it is to
indicate a group whose identity is stated only indirectly by reference to the
deceased and therefore must be inferred. The term remains, however, a useful convention for the purposes of the present book.

Predictably for an atoll culture, the many aspects of fishing permeate daily
life in both its mundane and ritual modes. Canoe construction and maintenance, ritual and practical preparations, collection of bait, the typically day-
long or nightlong fishing expeditions themselves, and subsequent informal
gatherings to discuss the catch or lack thereof occupy much of the time of
canoe-owning men—virtually all adult males. Unable to sustain itself on garden produce alone, the community acknowledges its dependence on the skill
of its fishermen, and it celebrates publicly and corporately the outstanding
achievements of individual enterprise. In so doing, the community acknowledges that events at sea are not egalitarian, as on land, and that a degree of
unpredictability surrounds most outbound expeditions. For their part, fishermen seek compensation for human uncertainty by appealing to ancestors
and other spirits for assistance in catching bountiful quantities of specific
species. Indeed, the pursuit of shark, tuna, and oil fish in particular is carried
out on the belief that such a partnership is necessary for success. And both
those who go out and those who stay behind join forces and voices to praise
what is considered the outcome of correct adherence to fishing protocol; in
this way they plug gaps in empirical knowledge with a restated belief in a relationship of ritual cause and empirical effect. Devoting more than 80 percent
of their contemporary poetic output to *tuki* songs about canoe building and
fishing, both men and women poets and composers focus on what is clearly a
matter central to their sense of community and their continued presence on
the island. The poetry and performance of *tuki* songs are discussed at several
points in this work.

Like speech, singing is a form of verbal utterance, and the two have structural parallels that center on repetition of earlier material before the introduction of new material. In music, however, the repeated material is unchanging
and forms the *hakamauhua* (singing stabilizer). A limited vocabulary of terms
for song structure is offset by the practice of learning new material through
imitation rather than direct instruction; a system of verbal cueing devices
either called out during performance or embedded within melodic contours
guides the less experienced performers. Although the style of Takū's performing arts has similarities with those of neighboring outliers, there are several
clear identifiers in the singing, such as the strong preference for unison, widespread use of melodic stereotypes, unique categories of song, and a singing

voice that accentuates the ends rather than the beginnings of syllables. There are also differences of degree, by which Takū-composed songs in categories shared by its neighbors can be distinguished. These and other elements of structure and performance are discussed in detail in this volume.

A potential threat to Takū's continued existence now confronts and confounds the community. The effects of rising sea levels and accelerating erosion on the low atoll could conceivably spell the end of the island in just a few years. This ethnography may therefore constitute both the first and last detailed account of life on a multiply vulnerable outpost of Polynesia.

Chapter 1
Geography and History

The Geographical Setting

Takū, a coral atoll some 200 kilometers east of Bougainville in the political territory of Papua New Guinea (maps 1, 2), lies 157°1'12" east longitude and 4°45'12" south latitude.[1] In contrast with much of the rest of Papua New Guinea, Takū is a Polynesian outlier and has cultural and historical links with a loose chain of similar atolls stretching southeast through Solomon Islands and Vanuatu toward Polynesia proper. Two of the atoll's immediate, inhabited neighbors—Nukuria, 160 kilometers to the west, and Nukumanu, 315 kilometers to the east—are also outliers. Almost circular in shape (map 3), the atoll consists largely of reef up to a hundred meters wide and completely covered only at high tide, when canoes can safely travel over it en route to ocean fishing grounds. Three reef channels allow canoe access to the ocean, but only one of these is deep and wide enough to allow the entry of larger vessels. The greatest known depth inside the lagoon is approximately one hundred meters.

Along the eastern edge of the atoll are a series of small islands *(motu)*, and one further island lies at the northwest corner; the ground of each is less than a meter above the high-tide level. Land area totals some ninety hectares.

Place-names on or near Takū Island's eastern shore are prefixed by "Tua" (oceanside) and those on or near the western shore are prefixed by "Tai" (lagoonside); see map 4.

Takū's climate experiences seasonal variation. The southeast trade winds blow from around June to October, and both the period and the wind are known as *te anāke.* From December to May, the prevailing wind is *te laki,* the northwest trade wind, which sometimes blows strongly. By contrast, there appears to be little seasonality in agriculture, and households plant and harvest their taro crops as needed throughout the year. The sole community is currently located on Nukutoa Island (map 5).

The atoll as a whole derives its name from the first person to have died there, according to mythology. In a fourfold compounding of the nomenclature, the founding spirit Takū was buried at a location on an island in the atoll, all of which carry that name.

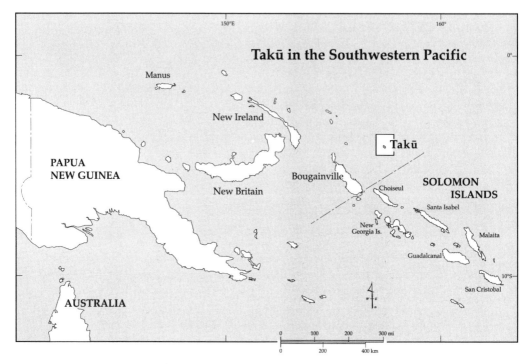

MAP 1

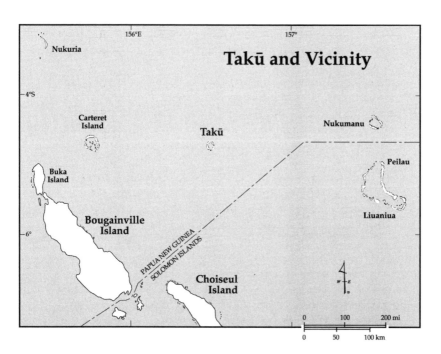

MAP 2

Takū Atoll

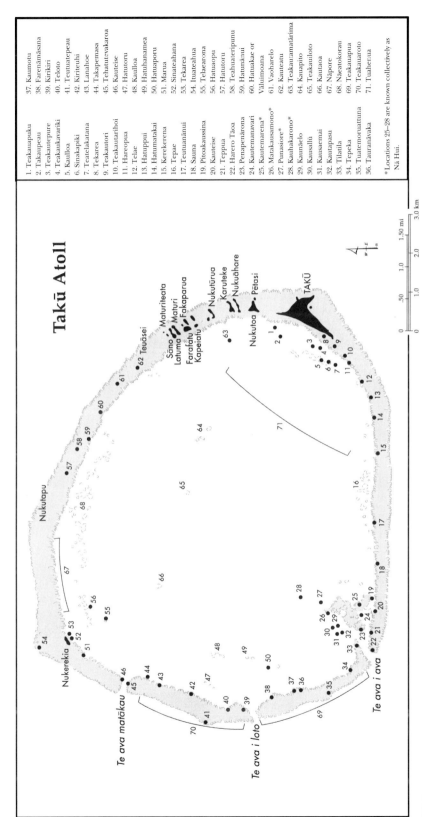

1. Teakauapuku
2. Takaupeau
3. Teakautepure
4. Teakaukavariki
5. Kaulloa
6. Sinakapiki
7. Teatelakatana
8. Tekarea
9. Teakautori
10. Teakautarihoi
11. Hareopua
12. Telae
13. Hatuppui
14. Hatumatakai
15. Kerekerena
16. Tepae
17. Teutunānui
18. Sauna
19. Pitoakaussina
20. Kauteise
21. Teppua
22. Harero Tāoa
23. Penapenārona
24. Kautemanavari
25. Kautemarena*
26. Matakausamono*
27. Punasitore*
28. Kauhakarono*
29. Kaunāelo
30. Kausalli
31. Kausaemai
32. Kautapasu
33. Tilatila
34. Tepeka
35. Tuatemornattuna
36. Tauranāvaka
37. Kaumotu
38. Farenāmasana
39. Kirikiri
40. Teloto
41. Teutuatepeau
42. Kiriteuhi
43. Lanahoe
44. Takapemasa
45. Tehatutevakaroa
46. Kauteise
47. Hatutoru
48. Kaulloa
49. Hatuhanamea
50. Hatuaporu
51. Marua
52. Sinateahana
53. Tekarea
54. Ituateahua
55. Telaearona
56. Hatuaopu
57. Hatutoru
58. Teahuateripumu
59. Hatunānui
60. Hatuakae or Valuimoana
61. Vaoharelo
62. Kauteatu
63. Teakautamatarima
64. Kauapito
65. Teakauloto
66. Kautaoa
67. Nāpore
68. Nāeatokorau
69. Teakauapua
70. Teakauaroto
71. Tuaherua

*Locations 25–28 are known collectively as Nā Hui.

MAP 3

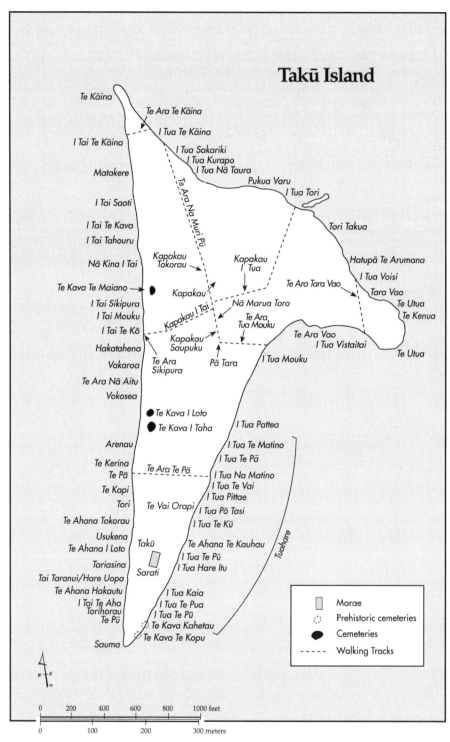

Takū Island

Te Kāina

Te Ara Te Kāina

I Tua Te Kāina

I Tai Te Kāina

I Tua Sakariki
I Tua Kurapo
I Tua Nā Taura

Matakere

Pukua Varu

I Tua Tori

I Tai Saoti

I Tai Te Kava

I Tai Tahouru

Tori Takua

Nā Kina I Tai

Kapakau
Tokorau

Kapakau
I Tua

Hatupā Te Arumana

I Tua Voisi

Te Kava Te Maiano

Kapakau

Te Ara Tara Vao

Tara Vao

Te Utua

Te Kenua

I Tai Sikipura

Nā Marua Toro

I Tai Mouku

Te Ara
Tua Mouku

I Tai Te Kō

Te Ara Vao

Hakatahena

Kapakau
Saupuku

I Tua Vistaitai

Te Utua

I Tua Mouku

Vakaroa

Te Ara
Sikipura

Pā Tara

Te Ara Nā Aitu

Vokosea

Te Kava I Loto

Te Kava I Taha

I Tua Pattea

Arenau

I Tua Te Matino

Te Kerina

I Tua Te Pā

Te Pā

Te Ara Te Pā

I Tua Na Matino

Te Kapi

I Tua Te Vai

Tori

I Tua Pittae

Te Ahana Tokorau

Te Vai Orapi

I Tua Pō Tasi

Usukena

I Tua Te Kū

Te Ahana I Loto

Takū

Te Ahana Te Kauhau

Tariasina

I Tua Te Pū

Tai Taranui/Hare Uopa

Sarati

I Tua Hare Itu

Te Ahana Hakautu

I Tua Kaia

I Tai Te Aha

I Tua Te Pua

Torihorau

I Tua Te Pū

Te Pū

Te Kava Kahetau

Sauma

Te Kava Te Kopu

Te Ara Na Muri Pū

Kapakau I Tai

Tuahare

	Marae
	Prehistoric cemeteries
	Cemeteries
- - - -	Walking Tracks

0   200   400   600   800   1000 feet

0   100   200   300 meters

MAP 4. Takū Island was home to the community until the late nineteenth century.

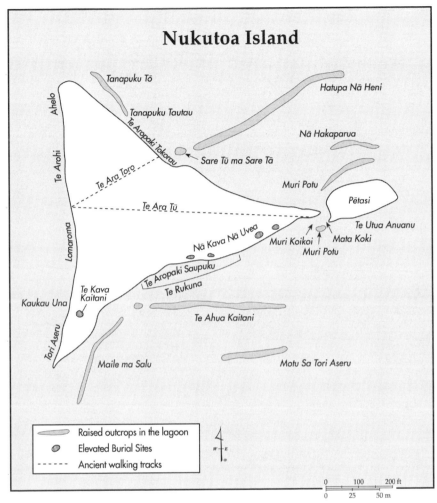

Nukutoa Island

Tanapuku Tō

Hatupa Nā Heni

Ahelo

Tanapuku Tautau

Nā Hakaparua

Te Aropaki Tokorau

Te Arohi

Sare Tū ma Sare Tā

Te Ara Toro

Muri Potu

Pētasi

Te Ara Tū

Te Utua Anuanu

Lomaroma

Nā Kava Nā Uvea

Muri Koikoi   Mata Koki

Muri Potu

Te Aropaki Saupuku

Te Kava
Kaitani

Te Rukuna

Kaukau Una

Tori Aseru

Te Ahua Kaitani

Maile ma Salu

Motu Sa Tori Aseru

Raised outcrops in the lagoon

Elevated Burial Sites

Ancient walking tracks

0   100   200 ft
0   25   50 m

MAP 5. Nukutoa Island is the present location of the community.

Nukutoa–The Physical Setting

Most of the 140 houses on Nukutoa Island are of the traditional type, with thatched roof, woven mat walls, and a doorway at each end. The houses of the five clan elders feature doorways on each side but are otherwise materially identical. Because of space restrictions, only a few houses have an adjacent cookhouse, and virtually all cooking is done outdoors on open fires fueled mainly by coconut shells. Use of earth ovens common elsewhere in the Pacific is restricted to special events because of the additional resources and effort they require. Beside many houses stand tanks fed from shelters with iron roof-

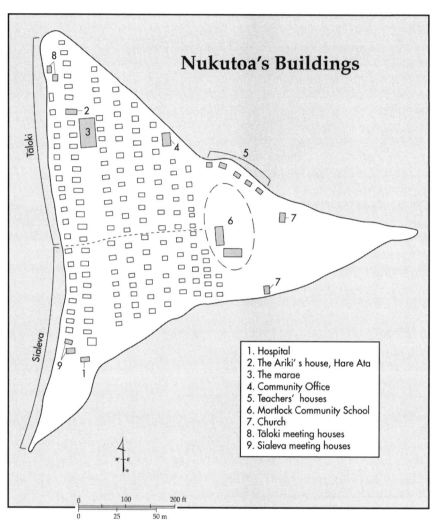

Nukutoa's Buildings

Tāloki

Sialeva

1. Hospital
2. The Ariki' s house, Hare Ata
3. The marae
4. Community Office
5. Teachers' houses
6. Mortlock Community School
7. Church
8. Tāloki meeting houses
9. Sialeva meeting houses

0   100   200 ft
0   25   50 m

Map 6

ing that catches quantities of fresh water. Beside the last row of houses stands
the council office, where the radiotelephone is operated, regular village
meetings are held, and infrequent court sittings occur. Adjacent to the office
stands an abandoned cooperative store, a never-used Catholic chapel, four
houses for teachers, and the school compound. To the rear and southern
side of the schoolyard stand traditional-style houses erected in 1999, where
Seventh-Day Adventist and United Church adherents hold Christian worship.
The total land area is some six hectares.

The houses are arranged in ten lines paralleling the beachfront (map 6),

Photo 1. A southerly view down the "main road" on Nukutoa. The Ariki's house is second from the right and the *marae* ritual arena is the unbounded area immediately to the left of his house. *(Hamish Macdonald)*

the larger distance between the second and third rows constituting the "main road." This wider strip of land accommodates groups of dancers proceeding from the southern end of the village to the *marae*, an unbounded ritual area adjacent to the Ariki's house. The second, third, and fourth rows each contain some thirty houses but, because the central land toward the island's eastern end is occupied by the school, the houses in the last three rows are limited to the small spaces along the edge of the school compound. With the exception of dwellings temporarily vacated for mourning purposes or while a family is off the island, the houses are all occupied.

White coral sand, transported in bags from the beaches of neighboring islands, forms the ground covering around and inside Nukutoa's houses (photo 1). A few banana palms, papaya trees, and shrubs grow among the houses, but the soil is insufficient to support domestic planting; the coral base of the island is covered with only some two meters of sand. Canoes resting on blocks line the island's tips on the lagoon side, and the canoe-building yards at both the southern and eastern tips of the island also function as congregation points. Next to the yard at Sialeva stands a medical clinic and a nurse's house that has never been used. Along most of the lagoon, lengths of sea wall have been constructed against rising sea levels and subsequent land erosion using wire baskets full of coral slabs (in the absence of stone) and sections of coconut palm trunk or branches of other trees. Similar sea walls stand at other points around the island.

The island is encircled by coconut palms, many of which are milked twice daily for the misty white liquid that ferments into *kareve* toddy in a few days. Most men attend drinking sessions each weekend, and women also participate on formal occasions involving the entire island. Prolonged periods of song and dance are normally incorporated into such sessions, and more than a hundred liters of the toddy are painstakingly produced and joyously consumed each week.

In 1998 the island had a total of fifty-two serviceable small canoes called *tamāvaka*, twenty-two tuna-fishing *vaka sī* canoes, and some fifteen aluminum and fiberglass boats. The layout of the larger yard at Sialeva accommodates both storage and construction of canoes. Just above the high-tide mark along the western side stretches a line of some thirty-two *huāvaka* medium-sized canoes, each resting on three blocks. Higher up the beach sit eighteen *vaka sī*, many of them wrapped in plastic sheets for protection against sun and rain. The eastern side is ranged with several dinghies and a large number of canoes in various stages of decay, their inverted position signaling the absence of any plans for immediate use. Next to these vessels, on the flat area of this peninsula, stand as many as ten canoes under construction. Men attend daily to their canoes, bailing them out after rain and checking their leaf or mat coverings on sunny days. Fanned by strong winds and aided by rising sea levels, the tides of January 2000 rose to new levels, forcing men to move the entire fleet at both Tāloki and Sialeva from the beachfront to the level ground at the island points, and in 1999 local government raised the fearsome possibility of relocating the entire population to Bougainville.

Takū Island, covering some sixty-five hectares, lies some 600 meters to the south of Nukutoa. Here the community's gardens occupy an area of some twenty-three hectares excavated to the level of the water table. Since Takū is accessible by foot at low tide, the plots are visited by most families several times each week. Takū Island, a settlement location for many centuries, is also rich in mythological, historical, and religious associations. Several named sites may be approached only by members of the appropriate landowning family, and although, in most instances, the reasons for imposing the access bans have been forgotten, the bans are still respected. Consequently, constructions and objects of apparent antiquity survive, but most people are both ignorant and uninterested in them, and an upturned giant clamshell placed on an access path—understood to be an ancient form of warning—is the sole physical evidence of the existence of potential danger. There continue to be a sufficient number of accidents and illnesses attributable to some misdemeanor occurring on Takū to maintain general belief in the continuing potency of these old prohibitions.

Takū's gardens are wet, lying in an extended excavated area in the northeast of the island. Most gardens, which lie some two meters below a network of elevated paths, are rectangular, bordered with giant taro (*kanokano, Cyrtosperma* sp) and filled with taro (*Colocasia* sp) (photo 2). Men grow giant taro along the outer border of land (*nā keri*) and woman cultivate taro in the inner complex of gardens (*toaha*). This arrangement is a relatively recent phenomenon. In normal weather, the soil is deep and rich enough to plant and cultivate without tools, but most families possess wooden digging sticks for when the soil dries hard. Garden produce is routinely brought to Nukutoa by canoe. Bayliss-Smith (pers comm) estimates that twenty hectares is used for taro and three hectares for giant taro (Boag and Curtis 1959). The remainder of the island is flat and dominated by coconut palms, planted when the European manager ordered existing trees cut down for the creation of a coconut plantation. Other trees have grown back and now serve as a source of timber used in house and outrigger construction, as well as providing firewood. Much of the island is covered in secondary growth, shrubs four to five meters tall. Along the lagoon several small areas lacking coconut palms mark the house sites of clan elders who refused to move to Kapeiatu Island in the 1880s when the atoll was bought by "Queen" Emma Forsayth.

Unseen in the lagoon waters fronting both Takū and Nukutoa Islands lie family-owned gardens of giant clams whose shells were once the source material for adzes and other tools, and whose meat continues to be harvested for large-scale feasts. Takū's mariculture has recently become the subject of Western research (Moir 1989).

The other islets of the atoll are quite small (only eight are larger than one hectare) and are visited principally for their supplies of coconut and pandanus materials. On Kapeiatu Island lie the creeper-entwined ruins of the cement house, copra shed, and water tank belonging to the plantation manager, vacant since the 1930s. The most distant island, Nukurekia, is now a wildlife reserve, where public access is limited to daylight hours, and overnight stays are punishable by a fine. The ban on killing edible seabirds that nest there in large numbers is periodically lifted by the Ariki, and the annual school picnic to the island gives the children a chance to visit this remote location.

Photo 2. The central garden area on Takū Island, individual plots bordered with giant taro. *(Hamish Macdonald)*

Population

Atoll populations, whose limited material culture and small numbers are combined with geographical remoteness, are particularly vulnerable to adverse
weather conditions and introduced disease. Takū's population was devastated
by disease in the late 1800s and subsequently rebuilt with imported personnel; it has experienced extreme fluctuations, from a point perilously close to
extinction to severe overcrowding in the early 1990s. It now appears to have
stabilized at around four hundred.

The earliest date when a resident population figure can even be estimated
is 1843, when Andrew Cheyne visited the island in search of bêche-de-mer
(sea cucumber). The numbers of adult males needed to crew the ten large
canoes Cheyne observed approaching his vessel (Shineberg 1971, 295) suggest that the total population at that time could have been more than one
hundred.[2] That William Churchill (1909, 88) observed several such canoes
at Takū in 1884 suggests an adult male population of at least double figures,
given the labor required to sail them and haul them from the water. However, the adults among the sixty-four individuals he counted at that time
would have been hard put to man the canoes. The dramatic drop in numbers
between 1843 and 1884 may be attributed to the effects of an epidemic that
struck the island during that period (see below). Richard Parkinson visited
the atoll in 1885 and again in 1896, recording the population at "about fifty"
and seventeen, respectively (1911, 517; see photo 3), and in the early 1900s
residents had reached the extraordinarily low figure of twelve "pureblooded"
individuals (Friederici 1912, cited in Moir 1989, 83). Emma Forsayth's introduction of laborers to her copra plantation around this time reversed the
decline and began an extended period of steady population growth. Several
families and occasional individuals left Takū in the 1950s and 1960s to seek
employment elsewhere; most settled on Bougainville Island, in jobs associated with the Panguna Copper Mine. The outbreak of hostilities around the
mine in 1989 led to the evacuation of hundreds of personnel and a sudden
large boost to Takū's population as perhaps as many as two hundred expatri-
ates fled to the security, if not the material comforts, of home. This population peak gradually dropped away through the 1990s as individuals again
secured employment elsewhere and took their families with them (table 4).
In effect, there are at present two Takū populations, resident and expatriate,
totaling perhaps as many as nine hundred persons. Although its geographical footprint is small, Takū's social community is spread widely throughout
Papua New Guinea.

History Prior to European Intrusion

Much of the information comprising the island's history derives from incidents recalled in stories told by now-deceased family members one or two

Table 4. Takū Population Counts, 1884–1980

Year	Population	Source
1884	64	Churchill 1909, 88
1885	about 50	Parkinson 1911, 517
1896	20	Parkinson 1911, 517
Early 1900s	12 "pureblooded" Takū	Friederici 1912, 299
1922	79	Chinnery quoted in Macintosh 1958, 213
1928	110	Chinnery quoted in Macintosh 1958, 213
1937	161	Leabeater 1954
1950	74	Boag and Curtis 1959, 21
1952	294	Boag and Curtis 1959, 21
1953	305	Boag and Curtis 1959, 21
1954	374	Commonwealth of Australia [1958]
1955	321	Boag and Curtis 1959, 21
1956	338	Boag and Curtis 1959, 21
1957	356	Boag and Curtis 1959, 21
1961	385	Bladen 1961, 79
1968	750	*PIM* 1968, 85
1980s	600	Moir 1989, 43

PHOTO 3. The seventeen persons comprising the entire population of Takū in the late nineteenth century. *(Photographer unknown, possibly Richard Parkinson)*

generations distant to present-day residents. There is no designated historian for the island and no sense of a single history except in the most general sense. Instead, the compilation of details from more than thirty individuals produces an incomplete account that lacks any overall sense of continuity and is sometimes outright contradictory. Adults routinely defer to a clan elder—either their own or that of another clan—for accounts of historical events, since the clan affiliation of named individuals is frequently a significant factor in historical episodes. There is a general belief that the five clan elders command privileged access to information from their respective predecessors, thus ensuring, to a degree, continuity of ritual and historical knowledge. It is apparent, however, that some individuals' personal knowledge of specific cultural elements is superior to that of their elders. Nūnua Posangat and his wife Tūhea are commonly deferred to on matters of song and dance: Nūnua is not genealogically positioned to be a performance specialist *(purotu),* but his knowledge is greater than that of any other resident. For her part, Tūhea's knowledge of poetry, songs, and dances of most forms is unrivalled. Despite her advanced age, she continues to participate in even the more vigorous dances when so moved. By contrast, it is also privately held that the ritual knowledge of one recently appointed elder is deficient in certain areas; not having been adequately groomed by his predecessor, he must rely on others to provide, for example, information on his own clan's mythical canoe.

The loss of such information—whether attributable to the nineteenth-century epidemic, the importation of foreign labor, or the forced move from Takū to Kapeiatu Island with the subsequent loss of community-wide rituals—cannot be corrected, and today the sense of rupture is marked in discussions of the near and distant past.

Mythology

Each of the five clans on Takū has its own colonization myth. Four of the clans claim to have been the first to arrive at the island at a time when there was no atoll as such, merely a shoal that gradually rose as the colonizers heaped up coral pieces. The fifth clan acknowledges that its founding ancestors arrived after those of the other four. Because of the rival claims to first colonization, arrival myths are not freely discussed between people of different clans; such information is normally confined to and discussed among members of the same clan. Sorting out the relative merits of the rival myths themselves is beyond the scope of this present work and is accordingly not attempted here.[3] Still, the myths have elements in common: for example, the assertion that a canoe-load of spirits *(aitu)* arriving from the east *(sopokana)* were ancestors to the first human ancestors of present-day Takū; these spirits lived, and indeed, continue to live, on Takū Island at the locations of their former spirit houses *(hare aitu).* Table 5 presents a list of these founding spirit ancestors.

One spirit, Oroatu, operates outside clan affiliations; his behavior is asso-

Table 5. Founding Ancestors of the Clans

Clan	Founding Ancestors
Hare Ata	Tehuiārau, Nāhui Hakamaru
Hare Mania	[Hui] Tuila, Hūtumua, Takū, Kautoa, Pontanaroa, Orua
Hare Māsani	Tākao
Hare Nāoro	Tehui Latuma
Hare Ania	Nāhui Peilau, Nāhui Telanihakamaru, Tavakelani, Vaesaesae

ciated with all that present-day Takū consider antisocial, reprehensible, or forbidden: "He is a braggart, a thief, a murderer, and a cannibal" (Moir 1989, 71). With the exception of Oroatu, the founding *aitu* are today invoked by clan elders in a variety of ritual contexts associated with canoe launching, fishing, healing, and avoiding attack by predator fish, as well as funerary and commemorative rites. By contrast and in recognition of his notoriety and unpredictability, Oroatu's name is spoken only quietly and with some apprehension.

When the island had been built up from the bones of the ocean, the spirit ancestors set off in search of food supplies with which to stock their new home, traveling to Auri (now identified as Buka Island) for bananas, crabs, turtles, coconuts, taro, sugarcane, and other unspecified plants. Some clan accounts record their canoe returning with women, whom the resident *aitu* married. In all the accounts I obtained during fieldwork, it is unclear just when the first humans were born to spirit parents.

Archaeological Evidence

No archaeological studies have been undertaken on Takū, and the community is united in its view that no excavations should be permitted for fear of supernatural retribution. Limiting the research in her doctoral thesis to non-excavated materials, Moir used the examples of the back-strap loom, village layout and place-names, grave goods, and turtle-bone axes to argue the close similarities in material culture and society among the northwest Polynesian outliers, of which Takū is one (1989, 59–74). She did not venture to offer a broader opinion on the residents' origins.

Relying on information from research on Ontong Java in the 1920s, Hogbin made the bold statement that "traditions independently preserved in all the atolls state that Ontong Java was the home of the ancestors of the inhabitants of all the rest [of the northern outliers]" (1941, 99), a suggestion that may deserve serious consideration, should future linguistic research confirm a pre-European link between these outliers and Tuvalu, which lies between them and Polynesia itself. Most recently, Kirch and Green have suggested a date at least 2,000 years BP for the colonization of central East Polynesia and the outliers, based on archaeological evidence (2001, 292, n 7).

Linguistic Evidence

Few linguistic studies include material from Takū, presumably for lack of published reference material.[4] Irwin Howard positions Takū within a proto-Ellicean subgroup of Samoic outlier languages (1981), a position repeated by Kirch and Green (2001, 61) and Marck (2000, 129–130), who locate Takū in a newly created Ellicean group, where it is classified as an Ellicean outlier together with the languages of Kapingamarangi, Nanumea, Nukuoro, Nukuria, Luangiua, Sikaiana, Tuvalu, and Vaitupu. Marck is at pains to point out, however, that the technical definition of an Ellicean outlier is tenuous, relying on extremely limited evidence, and future research may require modification of this position.

Origin Attributions

Pūtahu Tekapu, the elder of Hare Nāoro clan and the island's oldest man during my fieldwork period, commented to me that he understood the complexion of the original inhabitants had been darker than that of the present population, and that the prevalent fair complexion of contemporary Takū Islanders resulted from intermarriage with the light-skinned men who had drifted there, such as Manauī from Nukumanu, Apuku and Takua from Peilau, and Pūtahu from Liuaniua. Parkinson's photograph of the entire population of seventeen in 1896 confirms overall dark skin tones consistent with Pūtahu's comment, but it is not possible to draw firm conclusions from such fragmentary evidence.

Andrew Cheyne's visit to Takū in 1843 provided an early description of the inhabitants, including their perforated ears and slit nostrils, "the latter giving them an unnatural appearance" (Shineberg 1971, 296). Knowledge of these unusual forms of body decoration has now passed from living memory, although ear perforation is recorded from nineteenth-century Anuta, another outlier (Markham 1873, cited in Feinberg 1981, 10).

The precise identity of Takū's colonizers may never be established, but linguistic association based in shared vocabulary or shared constructions within word or sentence structures suggests an immediate origin from one or more outliers to the southeast.

Travel Prior to European Contact

It is part of generalized folklore that earliest ocean voyages exploited the trade winds, which blowing in one direction for six months at a time would have allowed canoes to cover the sometimes great distances between islands. Canoes, it is said, sailed away from Takū one season to eventually reach Peilau, Liuaniua, Taumako, and Tikopia before returning in another. These Polynesian outliers formed *te atu lou,* a chain of islands believed to be linked by both culture and direct contact. Takū is part of this same chain, whose westernmost island is Nukuria.[5]

Takū myth recounts how the founding canoes *Taoa* and *Hakautu* both voyaged to a number of unidentified islands in the southeast to bring back dances for the entertainment of the Ariki. *Taoa*'s voyage to Samoa and return with the *paki* dance is the best-known example, although the *toki* (from Samoa) and *paronu* dances (from Tikopia) were also fetched in this manner. The islands from which *Hakautu* brought back dances are not named, nor do contemporary accounts identify those dances. However, Samoa is given as the location where *Hakautu*, under the command of the legendary captain Vaika, obtained bird and whale bone combs and the ink used for tattooing women.[6]

Oral tradition speaks proudly of the exploits and abilities of the captains of such canoes—men who could slip overboard to determine ocean currents and perceive the direction of nearby land while lying inside a canoe. Invoking the assistance of clan spirits, these captains could transform mountainous seas into flat calms; they could maintain a canoe's position at night by summoning a spirit to grip the anchor lowered in mid-ocean. Such men combined great skill in seamanship with access to supernatural forces, but once the canoes were abandoned in the 1880s due to a lack of sufficient crews (Parkinson 1999), their expertise changed from a matter of practice to the stuff of legend.

Nukuria (Fead Island)

Although Nukuria is the closest inhabited outlier, and of all the islands its language appears to be most similar to Takū's, there is little evidence of substantial pre-European contact between the two.[7] It was not until the purchase of Takū by Emma Forsayth in 1886 that an ongoing social relationship was established.

Nukumanu (Tasman Islands)

Nukumanu Island is Takū's closest neighbor to the east, lying some 315 kilometers away. It is said to have been known and visited in the era before European contact, since genealogies of residents three or four generations ago contain references to individuals drifting from Nukumanu to Takū, and travel myths refer to Nukumanu as a waypoint in early voyaging to the east. In the mid-nineteenth century a Nukumanu man called Manauī drifted to Takū and was adopted into the family of the Ariki, who had no son of his own. Manauī later became the Ariki himself and his photograph was taken by Ernst Sarfert in 1910 (photo 4).[8]

Ongoing contact began in 1959 during the Australian administration of Papua New Guinea. Alarmed at the mounting birth rate and limited garden resources on Takū, an Australian patrol officer initially sent some thirty

PHOTO 4. Ariki Manauī in full ritual regalia *(nā hekau)* in 1910, wearing the *maro pure* ceremonial belt, *papa* pandanus necklet, *sukiporepore* coconut leaf tucked into his waistband, *haukareva* leaf tips tucked into his armband, and *noti* conical headpiece, and carrying an *iri* fan, *epa* woven mat, and *kaha* coconut shell oil container. *(Ernst Sarfert [Thilenius 1931])*

unmarried men to work the copra plantations on Tasman Island (Allen 1958). Later "married couples with a few children" were similarly allowed to migrate (Sebire 1960b). While working on Nukumanu, Takū men learned several types of local dances (particularly the *rue* and *hula*) and songs (particularly *lani* and *oriori*) and continued performing them after returning to Takū. Many remain part of the active repertoire and are performed at parties and commemorative rituals. Most *lani* currently performed on Takū either originated on Nukumanu or use a Nukumanu melodic type. Takū's indigenous *lani* are no longer a functional genre, and only one man remembers and can sing any of the locally composed items, which all date from the early 1900s.

In the 1960s the owners of the Bougainville Shipping Company used mainly Nukumanu and Takū men for crews because of their reputation for hard work; this kept their cultural contact alive. The *Nukutoa, Nukumanu, North Keel,* and *Ivanhoe* traded throughout Papua New Guinea and regularly visited Australia. Several *rue* song poems composed by Takū and Nukumanu men were set to song by Nukumanu composers in this period. These songs continued to be performed on Takū as recently as 1995.

Peilau (Ontong Java)

Contact with Peilau, either direct or via Nukumanu, appears to have been relatively frequent; it was and remains Takū's single most influential source of musical material.[9] In the early nineteenth century, two influential men from Peilau separately drifted to Takū where they were adopted into local families; Apuku arrived in his canoe *Ssakaina* and Takua (together with his wife Tuilani and son Mōmōsiale) in *Temanumanu*. Both men were master fishermen and introduced new fishing techniques that are still used today—*pakū* (for shark) and *hakasoro* (for oil fish). Takua was evidently also a skilled singer and taught the local men sets of songs that are still in the active repertoire. A set of seven *tuki* songs known as *Te Kaumata* (The taro corms), whose narrative content was conveyed to Takū by Takua, relates travel from Peilau to Liuaniua to collect corms after a tidal wave destroyed Peilau's own gardens. Another set of *tuki* songs apparently composed after Takua arrived on Takū relates the extraordinary fishing exploits of the Peilau master fisherman Teara. Almost two centuries later, both sets of songs remain in Takū's active repertoire.

In the late 1800s, according to oral tradition, another canoe from Peilau arrived at Takū, its occupants seeking sanctuary from a raging epidemic of unknown nature. Apparently unaware that the exiles were themselves carrying the disease, residents allowed them to land but soon fell victim to the same illness and died in significant numbers.[10]

Peilau's influence on Takū performing arts continues.[11] Present-day composition of *hula* songs uses language said to imitate that of Peilau, where the genre originated. The poetry is distinctive, appearing to routinely eliminate all /k/ consonants from words having Takū cognates. And the dance style of fast leg movements called *hakasekeseke* is likewise said to be derivative of Peilau performances.

Liuaniua (Ontong Java)

Lying more distant than Peilau but within the same large group of atolls, Liuaniua apparently had little early contact with Takū.[12] Although he cites no specific evidence, Thilenius claims that Takū was an intermediate point in a pre-European trade route between Nukuria in the west and Ndende Island in the Solomons, with Liuaniua a further waypoint (1902, 52). Travel in the direction of Liuaniua is referred to in one Takū song; the antiquity of the persons identified in the poetry suggests that the voyage occurred in the nineteenth century. Twentieth-century arrivals from Liuaniua (for example, the men Haurua and Tevaru) taught locals *rue* dances from their home repertoire. Some of these are still in the active repertoire, and at least one *kkai* fable from Liuaniua is also known on Takū.[13] Several other *rue* owe their present inclusion in the Takū repertoire to a Liuaniua man, Mannī, who stowed away aboard a trading vessel in the early 1900s and settled on the island.[14]

Sikaiana

Sikaiana figures only infrequently in Takū mythology and contemporary accounts.[15] The mythical canoe *Taoa* called in at the island on its return voyage to Takū from Samoa, and it is referred to in a *lū* song commemorating a journey from Takū to Tikopia.[16]

Taumako

The isolated island of Taumako in the eastern Solomon Islands is included in the *atu lou* navigational route evidently used in even more distant voyaging. The island name itself appears in only one song in the recorded collection, as a waypoint in the journey to Tikopia—"A mountain appeared, Taumako's mountain appeared"—but no details are included.

Tikopia

Mythology records that the canoe *Taoa* briefly visited Tikopia en route to Takū from Samoa, where the voyages learned the *paki* dance. While at Tikopia, the crew learned a local dance known now by the descriptive term *hā-Tikopia* (literally, "in Tikopian style"). Little more is known since, for reasons no longer clear, performance of the dance was later forbidden on Takū.[17]

On the basis of oral tradition, early travel from Takū to Tikopia was undertaken to collect supplies of prepared turmeric; the practice apparently continued until Takū residents obtained their own supplies of the living plant. Turmeric was used on Takū to decorate the human body for a variety of formal occasions: Takū Islanders poured it liberally over a corpse as it lay at the entrance to the cemetery; spirit mediums were painted with it when the village gathered on the *marae* arena after a *tānaki* ritual; brides were decorated with it before their first night with their new husbands, and it was used at a *hakamārama te tinae* ritual, when a mother emerged after five days' confinement inside her clan elder's house at the birth of her first or second child. The pigment is currently applied only to corpses and brides. The stature of ascribed references to Tikopia appears to parallel those to Samoa.

Uvea

Contemporary site nomenclature and recorded oral tradition suggest that a group of people from "Uvea" arrived before contact with Europeans. On the south side of Nukutoa are a series of low mounds known as *nā kava nā Uvea* (the Uveans' graves). Present opinion holds that the Uvea people (referred to as *nā mauvea*) were spirits of short stature that dwelt on the island when it was originally raised from the sea; they were later slain by Aserutahelo, resident deity of Nukutoa. Their bodies were not placed in a grave; earth was simply heaped up over them, hence the present-day mounds.

Samoa

It is sometimes difficult to assess information ascribed to "Samoa" because the name is currently used on Takū as a fallback term for the otherwise unknown country of origin of several introduced songs and canoe voyages. Still contemporary Takū oral tradition includes several pieces of fragmentary information suggesting the possibility of early contact with Samoa, for example:

• the island names Savaiki and Ttuila (cognate with Savai'i and Tutuila, respectively) occurring in accounts of mythological travel;
• an account of tattooing combs brought from Samoa by the mythical canoe captain Vaika, son of Maile;
• a *rue* danced song, whose poetry transliterates that of a Samoan *mā'ulu'ulu* danced song I myself recorded in Samoa in the 1960s;
• several *toha* and *hula* songs whose poetry appears to be in Samoan;
• fictional stories *(kkai)* about the characters Matilahoahoa and Mataikuru that parallel Samoan fables about Matilafoafoa and Gatalaiuluē (Moyle 1981, 196–206), and whose associated songs are transliterations of the Samoan forms;
• an unequivocal identification of Samoa as the source of Takū's *paki* dance.[18]

One cannot hope to assemble a history of contact from such fragments and, with the exception of the origin myth for the *paki* dance, there is little clear evidence of direct contact. By contrast, there is certainly clear evidence that

Polynesian canoes sailed well into the chain of outlier islands: Thilenius cited the arrival of canoes at Liuaniua from "Tokelau" and Tonga (1902, 70); Woodford recorded stories of the arrival of a Samoan and two Tongan canoes also at Liuaniua sometime prior to the Europeans (1916, 42); Hogbin noted the arrival of one Takū canoe during his residence of 1927–1928 on Peilau and Liuaniua (1941, 99); and Thilenius also records contact between Samoa and both Nukuria and Nukumanu (1902, 70). By contrast, and with the exception of one colonization myth, local traditions identify Takū itself as the point of origin of voyages between the two locations.[19] Parkinson's comment, made in 1885, that "Samoan is immediately and without great difficulty understood on the [outlier] islands" (1999, 229) was possibly accurate in a general sense at that time since, although the Samoan language is not cognate with Takū, many individual words are identical or similar, and from personal experience I can confirm that the gist of an utterance in Samoan can be gleaned by Takū residents. However, this is not to support Parkinson's contention, which presumed culture contact between the two regions.

The Significance of Earliest Island Contacts

The frequency of references in oral tradition to Takū's long-established contacts with islands to its east suggests that early voyages were intentional, planned, and purposeful, that destinations were predetermined, and that sailing routes and seasons were already known (see table 6).[20] Thilenius's references to a "trade route" incorporating Nukuria, Takū, Nukumanu, and Liuaniua and extending into the Solomons are given some credence by references in Takū's oral history to the *atu rou*, the chain of named islands through which early island navigators made their way to and from Polynesia proper but details of which are now unavailable. The accounts also imply that Takū's sailors relied on the seaworthiness of their canoes and the accuracy of their navigational methods, and that they were hospitably received on reaching their destinations. Of course we should infer nothing from the absence of oral traditions relating to unsuccessful voyages and hostile receptions. Takū's oldest resident recalls people of her parents' generation still undertaking ocean voyages, but now the practice resides only in stories, fragments of specialized terminology, and isolated pieces of information known to older members of the community. Old men occasionally carve for sale off-island miniature versions of *vaka henua*, canoes that became obsolete before they themselves were born. By contrast, younger men continue to carve canoes that are immediately put to use inside and outside the encircling reef and provide the means of supplying the island's principal food source. Life on Takū remains inextricably bound to the sea.

The above discussions are, of course, predicated on two assumptions: that Takū accounts of the distant past can be contextualized to establish their antiquity, and that such accounts do indeed originate from Takū itself. How-

Table 6. A Summary of Culture Contact

Island	Mythological Era	Before European Contact	17th Century	18th Century	19th Century	20th Century
Nukuria	Founding ancestor deposited there by canoe first visiting Takū				Tekapu migrates, bringing *sore* songs	Kautao migrates, bringing *tuki* songs; Graham Carson employs men as copra laborers; many sets of *tuki* songs introduced
Nukumanu		Waypoint to/from Tikopia			Several drift arrivals, including Manaui, who teaches new fishing technique	Men work on copra plantations; *hula* introduced; many *lani* and *rue* brought to Takū; Takū women are tattooed there; contemporary compositions imitate Nukumanu language
Peilau	Founding ancestor deposited there; departure point for one canoe's discovery of Takū	Waypoint to/from Tikopia			Apuku, Takua arrive, introduce new fishing techniques and sets of *tuki* songs	Manni arrives as stowaway, teaches *tuki* songs; contemporary compositions imitate Peilau language; toddy-gathering technique introduced
Liuaniua	Ancestral canoe visits	Waypoint to/from Tikopia			Drift canoes bring epidemic which decimates population; drift arrival of Putahu	Haurua, Tevapukua bring *rue* dances
Sikaiana	Ancestral canoe visits	Waypoint to/from Tikopia				
Tikopia	Residence of several founding ancestors; ancestral canoe visits to obtain a dance; source of tattooing combs, food	Source of turmeric				
Samoa	Widely suggested as land of origin					
Europeans			Dutch ships sight and name the island	British captain renames island	American crew kills local men; Captain Nauer's crew steal deities; island bought by Emma Forsayth, population moved to Kapeiatu Island	Population moves to Nukutoa Island; residents regain ownership of island; Ariki's death in Kieta affects ritual life

ever, from the mid-1800s, the outliers situated in the Solomons and Papua New Guinea became linked through the activities of European vessels in search of whales, bêche-de-mer, copra, and labor. Recruitment of islander crews followed, with subsequent rapid expansion of personal knowledge of other atolls. This was certainly facilitated by the degree of mutual intelligibility between languages, giving rise in turn to the possibility that stories of the outside world in accounts of canoe voyaging were colored by recently gained knowledge. As things stand, this possibility would be not only difficult to confirm but also virtually impossible to refute. The nineteenth-century decimation of Takū's population and simultaneous loss of knowledgeable senior residents and oceangoing canoe crews, together with the arrival of a substantial body of imported knowledge through the personnel recruited by Emma Forsayth, problematize the present identification of Takū's oral tradition as "local," even though Takū's residents have incorporated these accounts into their understanding of the lives of their forebears. This problem is compounded by the verifiable accounts of migration to Takū from other outliers within the historical period. In this present work, I offer no solutions to these difficulties of interpretation but merely identify some of the complexities and summarize contemporary views.

History of Contact with Europeans

The Arrival of European Vessels

Early contact with European vessels appears to have been infrequent, and contemporary accounts tend to focus on the environmental damage wrought by the visitors. The best-known story is commemorated in a *tuki* song danced at most formal parties by either men or women. Ariki Avo provided the following account of the original incident.

> This is a story about the vessel that came to the place offshore from Nukurekia. That's how that song was composed: it was brought by spirits. The vessel came and anchored at Nukurēkia's beach, and the crew rowed ashore. They rowed in and went on shore. The people who were already there were Kaitū, Mōmōua, Taura, and Hakahenua. They climbed coconut trees and sold dry coconuts to the vessel, to the crew. They sold them for tobacco, food, and everything. At that time, Hakaepārua was not with them, since he had stayed on Takū and came along later by himself. He was angry with his wife, and so he left in a huff. When he arrived, the ship's boat had already returned to the vessel, then came back to shore and the other four came with their goods. And Hakaepārua came along with them. When he came down to the beach, he had his sword with shark teeth embedded and struck a blow to the neck of one crew member. His crewmate grabbed a machete and struck off Hakaepārua's head. The other four—Taura, Hakahenua, Kaitū, and Mōmōua— fled, running along the reef toward the breakers.

Kaitū and Mōmōua followed along the inner edge of the reef. Mōmōua told Kaitū to return to Nukurekia and bring him some coconut leaves, so Kaitū ran back to the point of Nukurekia and got those leaves, brought them to Mōmōua, who made himself a death necklace. Then Mōmōua told Kaitū to run off to Takū and care for their children, but to leave him behind. If he died, it would be all right because he was old. Hakahenua and Taura went behind the breakers and swam toward Takū. Then Kaitū came, and there was a small place at the rear of Nukutapu Island, and laid down in a tidal pool and placed a stone on his stomach.

Mōmōua had already been killed by this time, and the Europeans were now in pursuit of Kaitū. They came and walked all around the place but could not see Kaitū, and when Kaitū saw that they were far away, he stood up and ran toward the breakers. The crew followed him along the reef, and when Kaitū saw them there, he slid down a breaker toward one man, killed him, and retreated. Kaitū then walked with his small shell adze, like a boat-building adze, and returned to the breakers.

The crew grew tired and returned to their vessel. Kaitū swam on beyond the breakers and when darkness fell, he came ashore at the back of the rock formation at Teripunu. From there, he began running along the reef toward Takū, to warn the people that they had been fighting with Europeans. Kaitū did not know the whereabouts of the other two, Hakahenua and Taura, but he believed they had been killed. But those two were in fact also swimming beyond the breakers, and came ashore at the back of Hatutoru.

By then it was dark, and the two of them followed the reef toward Takū and when they reached Takū's point they again swam, following the lagoon because they thought the Europeans had already arrived at Takū. Meanwhile, the people on Takū had armed themselves with spears so that if the Europeans went ashore, they would fight them, and when they saw the two swimming toward them, they were about to spear them. But an old man told them to wait, and call out the names of those who had gone there. And Hakahenua replied that it was he, so the two of them went ashore and told the people that they were not dead. They went home and stayed there until daybreak, at which time the vessel reached their beach.

The boat came there, dropped anchor, and the crew manned a boat and came ashore. They rowed, firing their guns as they did so. The Ariki told his people to go to their houses and stay there. He himself went and saw the boat, and if they killed them, then the whole place would die with him. The Ariki at that time was Tepaia. As the Ariki came to the beach, every animal from the bush followed him—crabs, coconut crabs, birds—they all followed behind the Ariki. The Europeans kept firing but the Ariki was not hit because he was blowing fire ash from the sacred house toward them.

The boat came ashore, and the Ariki tried to get on board, but it reversed away. The crew members were afraid and returned to their vessel. The Ariki also went back. The Ariki wanted to go on board to sink the vessel. The Ariki had supernatural powers.[21]

The song poetry commemorating the events presents a different perspective from that of the spoken account. Founded on conventions of indirect referencing and fragmentary allusion, the poetry relies more on its evocative power than its narrative detail. Adopting the perspective of the Ariki himself, the poem assigns to the singing stabilizer the reference to the subsequent purification of the island, and the sole reference to the disaster. For his part, the Ariki dons his ritual pair of pandanus belts to repulse the invasion. Gazing over the carnage at Nukurekia, he sees the body of Hakaepārua, now in the company of his spirit wife, Telanikivakiva.

[vvoro] Se vaka ni ā?	What did it do?
Se vaka ni aro mai ki taku henua.	It rowed ashore at my island.
[hati] Uāiē, se vaka ni ā?	What did it do?
Se vaka ni aro mai ki Nukurekia.	It rowed ashore at Nukurekia.
[hakamauhua] Nimo ake, takai ake,	I went from there and walked around the land;
e noho ka tohitohia ko taku henua nei.	I stayed while my island was being swept clean.
1. *Uāiē, hakatautau ake i taku ahana,*	Oh, a boat beached in front of my house
nau e noho i taku ahana,	while I was right there.
nau e tara ki te maro pure, nau e huna ki te kie tahi,	I donned my ritual belt and necklet.
2. *Uāiē hakasurasura i ana matahenua,*	Oh, I went to the back of my island
tokatoka iho ki taku henua,	and gazed over my land.
3a. *Uāiē noho iho se tanata i tua tana henua,*	Oh, a man was living at the back there,
e noho iho ma tana āvana;	along with his wife.
3b. *Uāiē, Hakaepārua i tua Te Marumaru,*	Hakaepārua lived at Te Marumaru,
e noho ma Te Lanikivakiva.	along with Te Lanikivakiva.[22]

Of the episodes comprising the story, several match those described by Andrew Cheyne during his visit to the island in 1843 in search of bêche-de-mer (Shineberg 1971) and lend credence to the possibility that the two accounts relate the same series of incidents (see table 7).

For present-day Takū residents, the Ariki's intervention and subsequent departure of the vessel close the episode, but no mention of these events is given by Cheyne, who continued gathering bêche-de-mer for a further fortnight before departing.

Cheyne's was evidently not the first European vessel to visit the island; he himself observed that the residents already possessed metal chisels and tomahawks (Shineberg 1971, 296). Takū tradition also recalls the arrival of another vessel and, in its own way, its impact was as great as that of Cheyne's. The following account, provided by Apava Pūō in 1995, suggests that the boat may have been the first steam-driven vessel seen at Takū. The smoke from the engine was mistakenly believed to result from the deliberate setting alight of the island's spirit figure, taken aboard with firewood.

A vessel appeared, it came on and on and entered the passage at Nukurekia and immediately anchored there at the entrance to the passage. While at anchor at the entrance, the crew went ashore at Nukurekia to collect firewood. The crew were all [from?] "Ponway," and they went ashore together with some Europeans. Having got their firewood, they brought it to the vessel.

When they went ashore, they found Sinateahana there, so they took Sinateahana with them, loaded it on board, and rowed back to their vessel. The Europeans and those Ponway; the Ponway were black people, and they returned to their vessel and put Sinateahana on top. Then they departed. They set fire to Sinateahana on top of their ship, the resident spirit of Nukurekia. The captain and mate wanted to sail away but when they set off, their ship began to list at the far side of the passage. It stayed there, its mast pointing first down then up, listing to the other side. When it steadied itself, they sailed on to the entrance at the back. The waves first lifted the bow up then sank it. The captain sank with his ship, but called out to his crew to get into the lifeboat. The chief officer boarded the lifeboat together with other crew-members. They hoisted sail and set off at the back of the middle reef. They sailed on at the back, then transferred to another two boats. These boats then returned to Nukurekia. The ship itself sank and its cannon fell overboard at the back entrance. The ship sank into a hole, and the Ponway rowed toward Nukurekia. While they stayed there, Takū men came and visited them. The men from Takū gave them food and they stayed there, exchanging stories. Next day, they returned with more food to give to the Ponway, but the Ponway had already departed and nobody was there. They remained there for a while before going fishing, and that is when they noticed this cannon in a place where trevally fish are found.

Quantities of cockroaches and beads also washed up on shore after the incident, and a location on Takū Island was named Tekuro (a type of small

Table 7. Points of Similarity between Accounts 146 Years Apart

The Ariki Avo's Account of 1994	Andrew Cheyne's 1848 Account, as Logged
Vessel arrives at Nukurekia Island	Vessel visits larger islands then moves to Nukurekia Island
Takū man initiates attack on crew, killing one	Residents initiate attack, throwing stones
Crew retaliates, killing Takū man	Sound of gunfire from Nukurekia heard on board the vessel
Crew chase two men back towards Takū Island	Third mate and indentured laborers chase several men
Two men swim back to Takū	Two men seen to leap into the surf and swim out to sea
Vessel anchors off Takū, boats fire on residents	Boats twice sent close to Takū for bêche-de-mer

container) after the quantity of gunpowder apparently also recovered there. A cannon from the ship was later retrieved and mounted in front of Emma Forsayth's manager's house on Kapeiatu Island where it remained for many years.[23]

"Queen" Emma and Her Legacy

On 7 June 1886 "Queen" Emma Forsayth gave Takū's "chief" four axes and ten pounds of tobacco to purchase the entire atoll (Robson 1994, 123) and installed her younger brother, William Coe, as first resident trader there.[24] After William Churchill's 1884 visit (Churchill 1909, 88), Forsayth's brother-in-law, Richard Parkinson, had visited Takū briefly in 1885, noting abandoned oceangoing canoes, vacant house sites on Takū Island, and an overall air of "degeneracy" (Parkinson 1999, 225). Also in 1884 Germany annexed northeastern New Guinea and its adjacent islands and later created "native reserves" of the European-held atolls around Takū (Nukuria, Nukumanu, Carterets, Nissan)—but not Takū itself, for reasons that are unclear. Early in the 1900s laborers were brought from other parts of New Guinea to supplement the local plantation workforce, arriving from Nukuria, Nukumanu, New Britain, New Ireland, Buka, and Manus, as well as Ontong Java, Banaba, and Kiribati (Moir 1989, 119).

With her brother's departure from the atoll, Forsayth transferred title to her female relative Phoebe in 1891 when Phoebe married Joseph Highley (known to Takū residents as Sio). Not long after the birth of their daughter, Frances Emma, Joseph died and was buried on Karuteke Island, where the family had settled to avoid the mosquitoes of the largest island on the atoll, Takū.[25] Phoebe's subsequent marriage to the German doctor Emil Altmann similarly lasted only a few years before this second husband died and was replaced by an Englishman named Calder. Calder is said to have been responsible for importing significant numbers of plantation laborers from elsewhere in New Guinea in the early years of the twentieth century. Their marriages with local residents contributed to the recovery of the population. Calder's building program included wooden longhouses on the beach to accommodate the plantation workers and their families. But not all local residents were willing to abandon their homes on Takū Island and live in Calder's company.

Ariki Manauī resisted Calder's move to relocate the people then living on Takū Island to Kapeiatu.[26] Manauī lived on at the Ariki's traditional house site, Hakātui, as did the other four elders at their respective *hare tapu*—Pure Terupo (Hare Mania clan) at Uea, Rausari (Hare Māsani clan) at Oneai, Pāsia (Hare Ania clan) at Tapueia, and Kateheni (Hare Nāoro clan) at Ketiketi. With Manauī's death, surviving family members moved to the longhouses on Kapeiatu.

The death of Ariki Manauī on Takū Island made continuation of the community's traditional religious life tenuous. Difficulties that had begun more than half a century earlier with the decimation of the population from disease were exacerbated since ritual knowledge, which depended on oral transmission and demonstration for its survival, was with this death threatened further. Although Manauī, who drifted to Takū from Nukumanu as an adult, had not enjoyed the accumulated knowledge derived from a lifetime on the island he was nonetheless the undisputed spiritual leader of the island's population and oversaw ongoing community activities on Takū Island, in both mundane and ritual modes.

The problem of continuity was alluded to by Richard Parkinson after his 1885 visit to Takū. Parkinson met Ariki Manauī and later reported: "The current high priest, a Nukumanu native shipwrecked here, is not totally reliable about the old, original beliefs; in his accounts I have often been able to observe that he has not been able to free himself from the impressions of his youth. . . . To him . . . the old legends about immigration and origin have remained unknown, or if he has heard them they have long since disappeared from his memory" (1999, 226). Still, if anything like present-day restrictions about the details of the Ariki's powers and clan migration mythology applied a century ago, then Manauī's apparent inability to supply such information to Parkinson may well have represented nothing more than a refusal to do so.

With Manauī's passing, the community—then living on Kapeiatu Island— was deprived of the leadership necessary to maintain accuracy of ritual performances at the appropriate locations on Takū. A general fear of calamity resulting from any inaccurate enactment was sufficient reason to discontinue practices relating to the worship of Pūkena and other ancestral deities.

After Calder's death, Phoebe remarried, only to have her fourth husband die a few months later (Moir 1989, 86).[27] She hired a resident manager, the first of several, while she herself divided her time between Takū and her other plantation on Bougainville where her daughter Frances was living with a German husband, Bruno Kroening. Following World War One, however, the British-established Expropriation Board relieved Frances Kroening of her half-share in Takū, selling it in 1926 to a Scot, Jock Goodson (Moir 1989, 87).[28] Goodson's indentured laborers, all local residents, totaled 44 of the total of 110 in 1928, the others having been imported by Calder (Chinnery papers, Chinnery to administrator, 29 Oct 1928, MS 766/5/17). Deteriorating relations between local residents and the Europeans resident on Kapeiatu and also among those same Europeans moved events toward a crisis, and indeed the fate of the atoll and its population was determined in large part by a series of actions initiated during the late 1920s by two men, W E Pearson Chinnery and Goodson himself.

The appointment of Chinnery as government anthropologist to New Guinea on 28 June 1924 and his posting to Rabaul was followed only six weeks later by a first visit to Takū for the purpose of making an ethnological survey and a census (Chinnery papers, MS 766/30/1). Chinnery's diary at this point makes no mention of social problems. Indeed, it was not until his second visit, in March 1925, accompanying the Administrator General Wisdom on an official tour of the territory, that Chinnery recorded his first concerns about the residents' well-being: "The natives have no land or property of their own. All the men & women are indentured to the Expro[priation] Board who own part of the plantation" (Chinnery papers, MS 766/30/1).

Chinnery's next visit was not until October 1928, while serving as acting commissioner for native affairs. By then, Goodson had bought his half-share of Takū Island and established a copra-making business alongside the Highleys and later the Calders. Goodson began writing to Chinnery in March 1928, and the two met several times in Rabaul in June and July on the subject of "land." Clearly concerned for the welfare of the Takū residents, Chinnery visited the island again for three days in October, conveying the administrator's request for an arrangement that would allow the residents more freedom of access to essential food resources. His efforts met with no success.[29] On 29 October, Chinnery formally communicated his findings in a memorandum to the administrator, summarizing events on Takū since the island had been sold to Emma Forsayth. The memorandum, which paints a clear picture of forty years of despair and misery, begins by noting that, on 7 June 1886, the island was "sold . . . by nine of its principal men to Emma Eliza Forsayth for £68 and trade"; those men believed the money and goods represented nothing more than an inducement to allow a trading station to be established on their island. The memorandum continues: "At the present time this community does not own a square inch of land. Its numbers are utterly dependant on the owners for food and shelter, in fact, for everything. An unhappy relationship exists between the owners and unless the Government acts promptly the natives are likely to be driven to some extremity by the force of influences that are in conflict round them."

Chinnery suggested

that the title of the Owners be reviewed at an early date by the Central Court sitting on the spot, on the grounds:

a. Claim by the natives that the Forsayth payments did not constitute a purchase but were merely inducements to give trade.
b. That the transaction that in effect deprived the natives of their land and virtually enslaved them was an immoral one and should never have been entered in the Ground Book (this being supported by the action taken by Governor Hahl in endorsing the Tasman and other titles with a provision that lands essential to the natives must be transferred back to them) long after the original purchases were made.
c. That the transaction is one that cannot be upheld by a British Administration.

Chinnery's recommendations to the administrator were similarly blunt:

1. The island of Takū be acquired for the natives.
2. The Mortlocks laborers at present working with Mr Goodson be repatriated once the land is resumed. (Goodson is agreeable to this.)

3. On the completion of the resumption a system of contract similar to that in Matty and Aua be arranged.
4. *Te ariki* Peo [Apeo] be appointed Luluai [chief] and *Te pure* Marina [Marena] be appointed Tul-tul [secondary chief].
5. A married man and his wife, recommended by Peo be induced to go through a medical training in Kieta and return as male and female medical Tul-tul.
6. Taxation to be imposed on the resumption of the land.

On 15 November the island of Takū, but not the whole atoll, was gazetted as a native reserve. For at least a year before this notice, however, Chinnery had been working on a parallel quest, to allow Takū's residents free access to all of their atoll, and the issue was tested in a defended hearing in the Central Court on 22 May 1930 before Judge Phillips, with whom Chinnery had been in discussion for more than a year. The case itself was limited to the question of whether prescription applied in New Guinea (that is, whether current British law or the previous German law should prevail) and whether long possession of land gave title in the Territory of New Guinea. Although no report of the decisions was forthcoming, the court by order of 22 May 1930, found that the land on Takū was subject to the right of the original residents "to live on and to take and use food and material necessary for their ordinary existence" (Central Court 1973, 657). Chinnery considered the presence at the hearing of representatives from Takū to be sufficiently important to merit sending the official boat, the *Franklin Wisdom,* to the island to collect them. Although neither the court documents nor Chinnery's subsequent correspondence detail the six representatives' extent of involvement, at least one of them, Faite Pūtahu, did give evidence.[30]

The Mediumship of Faite Pūtahu

One of the twentieth century's crucial figures on Takū was Faite Pūtahu. The daughter of a man who drifted to the island from Liuaniua, Faite rose to distinction around 1930 when the local population (as opposed to the laborers imported by Phoebe Calder) moved from Kapeiatu Island to Nukutoa. For the previous forty years, the people, first under the leadership of Ariki Manauī and later directly under Ariki Apeo, had been collectively deprived of access to their food sources and land on Takū Island. In particular, the social privileges and supremacy of the Ariki, Pure, and clan elders were abrogated in favor of a foreign woman who exercised a virtual dictatorship over their lives. A generation of children grew to adulthood, married, and had children of their own while on Kapeiatu without participating in, or even witnessing, the exercise of traditional authority by clan elders through the complexities of religious ritual. Accommodated in longhouses with two couples per room, the former separation of the five clans on Takū Island was discontinued, as were the housing privileges enjoyed by the clan elders. The absence of a *marae* on Kapeiatu further deprived the thirty-odd residents of a spiritual and recreational focus for the very activities that publicly proclaimed both clan distinctiveness and overall cultural unity. By 1930 Calder had succeeded in stripping the people of much of the cultural agency that had bound them together as a functional society.[31]

From accounts of personnel working on Kapeiatu at the time, Goodson's initiative in allowing his workers, all Takū people, to move to Nukutoa was welcomed. Goodson himself predicted a dramatic increase in population with the building of separate houses for each family (Chinnery papers, Goodson to Chinnery, 9 Dec 1929, MS 766/5/18), but before this transpired, a series of religious, social, and health dilemmas had to be resolved. Although clan elder titles had been duly transferred to chosen successors on the deaths of four of the elders who had refused to move from Takū to Kapeiatu (the fifth, Rausarī, was still alive at that time), these new elders were effectively deprived of the means of maintaining their inherited relationship with clan ancestors. Because they lived away from Takū Island, they could not properly practice rituals inside their respective spirit houses and on the *marae*. Since these men could not function as their predecessors had, there was genuine fear that it would be unsafe even to attempt to revive their long-discontinued site-focused religious practices.

To add to the problem, Nukutoa, which had not been permanently occupied before, possessed its own set of resident spirits whose precise powers were unknown and therefore feared. When Goodson started his building program, therefore, he was constantly irked to be told that particular activities and sites were forbidden, as Ariki Apeo and his fellow elders proceeded with caution. The residence of the principal island spirit—Serutahelo, a son of the founding ancestor Pukena—was changed from a point on the northern shoreline to a coconut palm in the Ariki's own yard, paralleling the former proximity on Takū between the Ariki's residence and Pukena's house. And, to the extent that the clan organizations and the *hata* system (see chapter 2) had been in abeyance for two generations, it was not possible simply to establish on Nukutoa a social order identical to the one that had existed on Takū (Chinnery papers, Goodson to Chinnery, 9 Dec 1929, MS 766/5/18).

The death in the 1920s of three senior men, including Ariki Manauī and Pure Terupo, deprived the community of leaders experienced in secular and religious affairs. This, coupled with widespread sickness among the young children fed a climate of anxiety, and it was in the midst of such emotional upheaval that a benign supernatural force revealed itself and rescued the community. The spirit in question identified herself in a series of formal *tānaki* rituals as [Te] Laroteone, spirit-daughter of Ariki Hāriki.[32] Both the father and grandfather of Ariki Apeo, the titleholder on Nukutoa at that time, had been Ariki in the Atui line, but the grandfather's own predecessor, Ariki Hāriki, had been of the Apua line and was indeed the last of that line. Laroteone revealed that she had been conceived after a female spirit had seduced Ariki Hāriki while asleep. The human medium through which these and other revelations occurred was Faite Pūtahu, at that time already a great-grandmother. Faite's grandson, the present elder of Hare Māsani clan, Kikiva Nukuria, takes up the story:

> At that time, people were becoming sick and dying, and the traditions of Takū were abandoned. Elders were dying, they died off in turn, as did young children. Age mates who grew up together died like the elders. The Ariki [Apeo] created the means of rebuilding the island, so nobody else would die and generations would flourish. And that was the Ariki together with the Pure. Then someone was seduced by a spirit from their afterworld, so as to produce a child who came as a medium and restored safety. That applied to every subsequent Ariki; at that time, my grand-mother—Faite—went into trance. She spoke and announced she was Laroteone, someone from the afterworld, a spirit-child of Telauika. While in a state of posses-sion, she gave instructions to build Hare Ata house where the Ariki would live, to build Hare Mania where the Pure would live, and Hare Masani, which is where I—Kikiva—am now living. The Lagoon Clan elder's house was to be called Hare Nāoro, and the northern group's [house] would be called Hare Ania.[33]

In 1930 legal ownership of the atoll was tested in Rabaul's Central Court. The residents were represented by Ariki Apeo, Pure Pūō, Tekapu, Manila, and Faite. Although the magistrate could not reach a decision, ownership was later returned to the local residents and the case itself regarded as a triumph. The event was of sufficient moment to inspire the composition of a set of three *tuki* songs and a further set of *sore* songs. In this poetry, Faite herself is the central character; the songs are phrased from her own perspective, although it is not clear whether she herself composed them. The lyric of one *sore* is given here as an example:

Ē, ko taku henua nei	Oh, my island—
Taku kōti hano ki te hare pepa, se kōti o taku henua nei;	I went to the courthouse in a case about my island;
Ko Teamarua nei taku kōti, hano ki te hare pepa.	Nukutoa, this was my court case, I went to the courthouse.
I hano iho nau ma taku ariki nei, seia iho te lāoi nei;	I went with my Ariki, to seek peace;
E kake iho nau ma Laroteone nei seia iho te lāoi nei.	I went with Laroteone to seek peace.
Eī, tū vasiria nau e te hakamau, pēhea o taratara nei;	I stood there and was asked by the magistrate, "What is your story?"
Kauatu nau ki lono tonu;	I told him accurately;
Eī, tū vasiria nau e siosi nei, pēhea o taratara nei,	I stood there and was asked by the judge, "What is your story?"
Kauatu nau ki lono tonu.	I told him accurately.
Īē, ku tonu iho nau e i te hakamau,	I said the right thing to the magistrate
Hākata nau i te kau hare, no sura koī Malakuna nei;	Going from office to office, until arriving at Malakuna;

Ī ku tonu iho nau mo i siosi,   I said the right thing to the judge,
Hākata nau i te kau hare no noho ko   Going from office to office, until
   Malakuna nei.   arriving at Malakuna.

For her role in prosecuting the atoll's case, Faite received the nickname Loea (Lawyer) and lived the remainder of her life in some esteem for this. Now, more than half a century after her death, Faite's reputation remains high among older residents, who cite her several singular accomplishments—her embodiment of the spirit-child Laroteone, her accomplishments as a prophet until her death, and her identity as the progenitor of several past and present community leaders.[34]

The New Community on Nukutoa

By 1930 Goodson had constructed the beginnings of a separate village on Nukutoa Island, having supervised the building in 1928 of a bungalow for himself (Chinnery papers, Goodson to Chinnery, 9 Dec 1929, MS 766/5/18), and separate houses for each married couple among his forty-four indentured laborers. Most of these employees were Takū, in contrast to Calder's workforce, which consisted principally of imported laborers, most from Buka. The first house on Nukutoa was occupied by Ariki Apeo, and its remnants are incorporated in the present Ariki's dwelling. The building of the Ariki's house was followed by that for Pure Marena and thence the houses of the other elders and their adherents. The separate clan groupings of old were not duplicated, and for a time the population existed as a more or less single sprawling entity, with families initially sharing cooking houses. Because of Nukutoa's relative smallness, it was not possible to duplicate the old spatial separation of the Ariki's house, but an area of some twenty meters around his new house was kept clear, and even today there are no other houses within ten meters of it.

Chinnery's recommendation for a special levy to pay for the return of the land was duly enacted. Through a levy on copra sales imposed over the next several years, the community repaid the £6,000 compensation awarded jointly to Goodson and Calder for the loss of Takū Island, and a further £500 for the repatriation of the remaining islands, except Nukutoa and Pētasi, as determined by the administrator in 1932.[35] The court case stimulated the composition of several songs of the *tuki* and *sore* categories.

Calder was killed in a fishing accident in 1930, and Goodson stayed on only until 1936, when falling copra prices and deteriorating community relations prompted him to depart.[36] He sold his half-share in Nukutoa to Burns Philp and Company, which established a store on the island staffed by a series of Malaysians and one German, Anatole ("Andol") Schültz. Schültz brought the first radio to Takū, and passed on to the residents daily news of the unfolding of World War Two as it was broadcast. Deprived earlier of her half-share in the entire atoll, Frances Kroening inherited Phoebe Calder's half-share in

Nukutoa and Pētasi, but did not activate any possible entitlements. In 1962 a Provisional Order from the Territory Commissioner of Titles formally conferred the right to continue their subsistence economy on Nukutoa and Pētasi on Nukutoa's residents (Chinnery papers, director of Department of Native Affairs to Chinnery, 27 Feb 1962, MS 766/5/19).

World War Two and After

During the period of Australian administration of Papua New Guinea (1921–1975), Takū continued to remain relatively isolated. A 1968 account notes that open access to the atoll was prohibited by the administrator on the grounds that the residents had no immunity to European diseases; all prospective visitors required a medical clearance (*PIM* 1968, 85).[37] For their part, the Takū community had long countered the possibility of introduced disease by having all visitors come ashore in front of the Ariki's house, Hare Ata, where they were ritually cleansed by the Ariki's assistant *(tautua)*, who splashed water over them from his coconut shell container as he invoked the protective presence of clan ancestors. Although this practice has been discontinued for visitors, incurably ill residents sent back from hospital are still met in this manner before being taken inside Hare Ata for the Ariki's protective invocation and then transferred to their homes.

Regular contact with the outside world was limited principally to visits every six months by patrol or district officers (sometimes with an agricultural officer) and annual inspections by health department personnel (Spencer 1967). Reports of the period made by patrol officers frequently refer to dances performed for their entertainment on Takū, and a recurring feature of these reports is the contentment of the population and demonstrated ability to manage their own affairs.[38] Visiting officials came in for attention from Takū's composers, who commented on their various activities in a generally positive, if sometimes humorous, manner. Village hygiene, for example, was stressed during official visits, and the sighting of an approaching government boat sent households into rapid tidying of their properties, as the following *rue* lyric lampoons:

Uhiuhi, uhi ma nā ō tū	Cover it up, that's the way you should do it;
Ē ka uhi te ahana nei ē, tēnā ō uhi	So, cover the front yard, that's how you should cover it.
Uhi te ahana nei e tēnā ō uhi.	Cover the front yard, that's how you should cover it.
Uhiuhi uhi ma nā ō tū	Cover it up, that's how you should do it.
Ka vere te ahana nei e, tēnā ō vere	So, weed your front yard, that's how you should weed it.
Verevere, vere ma nā ō tū.	Keep on weeding; that's how you should do it.
Ka pore te ahana nei, tēnā ō pore	So, shake your front yard, that's how you should shake it.

Pore te ahana nei e, tēnā ō pore	Shake your front yard, that's how you should shake it.
Porepore pore ma nā ō tū.	Keep on shaking; that's how you should do it.

In 1954 Graham Carson, a trader residing on neighboring Nukuria atoll, successfully applied to the district administrator to remove and employ thirty-two men from Takū. They were to work as crew and trochus fishers for his business operations for a period of six months, thus beginning a period of indentured labor that brought Takū and Nukuria people into extended contact.[39] The resultant intermarriages spread knowledge of stories, songs, and dances between the two communities, but in a largely one-way pattern because missionaries disapproved of Nukuria converts participating in any non-Christian cultural activities and actively discouraged performances of Takū material.

Over the years Carson, who was still working his ships until his death in 2004, earned the affection of Takū residents. They honored him with several *toha* danced songs, of which the following Tok Pisin example is typical:

Mi orait yu com Master Graham,	It's all right for you to come, Mr Graham
"I go to you, Mortlock"	[You say] "I'm going to you, Mortlock."
Mifela laikim yu, no ken lusim yu	I like you and don't want to lose you
I do sing to yu happy happy.	So I sing to you in my happiness.

In keeping with its national policy, the Australian administration appointed Takū's two highest-ranking men—Ariki Apeo and Pure Sieki—to the positions of *luluai* and *tultul,* respectively, these equating to the senior and junior government representatives.[40] These positions were annulled after national independence.

Until the 1930s gatherings for social purposes met in individual houses but, shortly after World War Two, the population had grown to a point where it was no longer possible for men and women to meet in a single pair of adjacent houses dedicated to social activities, and the village was divided into a southern and northern section; these were named "America" and "Japan," respectively. This nomenclature continued until 1983 when, it is said, a child's mispronunciation of the mixed-language phrase "style *hoki*" (simply the best) as *"tāloki"* so captured the local imagination that it was adopted as a replacement name for Japan. The southern village division also changed its name to Sialeva at the same time, the word being a Solomon Islands Pijin term meaning "independent." Although the names Tāloki and Sialeva are residential designations, they are also commonly used to refer to the northern and southern ends of the beachfront, and by extension to the pairs of meeting houses standing there. Strictly speaking, the division is confined to the housing area and excludes the area east of the school property. Tāloki and Sialeva represent divisions that have meaning only on formal occasions, for practical purposes (eg, turtle netting and regular work parties attending to village hygiene and safety) and celebrations (dancing and consumption of food and alcohol). There are also critical character ascriptions assigned to these regions: one occasionally hears comments like "Tāloki men are always [+ negative attribute]," or "Sialeva people do not [+ positive attribute]."[41] One such claim of superiority rests on dancing ability. From the perspective of a Tāloki man, the argument runs thus:

Sialeva men know only *rue* dances having few movements, whereas Tāloki knows and performs *rue* having more variety of gestures and is therefore superior, if only in their own eyes. Tāloki occupies this favorable position because of Nūnua's great accumulation of knowledge of both songs and their associated dance movements. In the past Tāloki also was home to knowledgeable composers and teachers such as Puaria Sāre, Tave Atimu, and even the great Sāre Amani himself. . . . Nūnua's acknowledged superiority has allowed him to lead, without challenge, the performance of the *rue Telloi* and *rue Tellahu*, dances whose historical association with the former Sikipura group on Takū Island would, all things being equal, require a Sialeva man to lead. But Willie [Tekapu] was the only performance expert in Sialeva.

From the time the two divisions were set up, each chose a committee to organize large-scale events. By 1999 these committees showed signs of exclusivity on occasions in which the entire adult population would earlier have been involved. A fishing competition announced at a council meeting as applying to the entire community was attended only by men from Tāloki, the location of the sponsor's house; and Tāloki adults showed little desire to attend drinking parties at Sialeva; some even claimed (untruly) that they were unaware of their occurrence.

On two occasions early in 2000 the geographical divisions assumed something of the nature of social distinctions. During a party associated with a *taora* first-born ritual at Sialeva, Ariki Avo stood and announced that, although the entire community had been invited to attend, Tāloki people might feel more comfortable in their own drinking house; he then suggested that they should adjourn there forthwith, which they indeed did. Tāloki was then obliged to supply the tobacco and toddy, which happened to be in short supply, and the partying dried out shortly, provoking the comment *Tāloki sē community* (Tāloki is not [behaving as] a community) from one man disgruntled at the lack of organization. At the same *taora*, Tāloki women were allegedly harassed by drunken Sialeva men simply for being present, despite having been invited to attend.

Reacting in the following week to this act of discourtesy, Tūhea (who lives in Tāloki) announced she would boycott the *hakamaseu* cleansing ritual organized for one of her relatives if it was held at Sialeva. Out of respect for her leadership in the singing and dancing that were part of the ritual, the event was moved to a more neutral location at the rear of the village. The senior Sialeva men explained the change of venue as merely facilitating the attendance of people from the mourning houses nearby. A sense of competition seems to emerge in a decision by one area's committee being immediately imitated by the other, as when Tāloki announced a group netting drive along its foreshore at precisely the same time that Sialeva men gathered at the southern tip of Nukutoa for an identical purpose.

On an individual level, individuals in the two groups frequently indulge in banter:

> During *rue* dancing at parties over an extended period in 1999, Kāua, an excellent though aging dancer, would taunt less competent dancers by calling out to them, "I'll cut your throat" *(tū tō ua)*. He himself resided in Tāloki and aimed his taunt most frequently at men from Sialeva. At a party in 2000, Kāua's former victims turned the tables, throwing his own words back at him whenever he danced a *rue*, a gesture that he accepted in good humor. (Field notes, January 2000)

According to an informal census taken in 1995, the proxemics of residence stood as shown in Table 8, below.

At present, the only visible evidence of this division is the pairs of houses at the northern and southern extremities of the island. Commonly referred to as *nā hare unu* (drinking houses), these buildings are the locations where men informally congregate to talk, snatch daytime naps, and repair fishing equipment; they are also where men assemble formally for large-scale consumption of food and/or toddy. Although both pairs of houses are used informally by men, one house at each location is used by women for formal events. Typically, such events involve group song and dance, and for several hours the air is filled with the jubilant cacophony of simultaneous performances of different items by the segregated groups in houses only a few meters apart.

Partly in response to the imminent overcrowding, partly as a means of encouraging emigration and providing paid employment for the growing number of young men, the administration decided in 1959 to send men from Takū to Teheke Island on neighboring Nukumanu to work copra plantations that Emma Forsayth had established when she bought that atoll some eighty years earlier.[42] In the absence of any commercial boat service, few residents other than those working on Nukumanu had an opportunity to leave the island. About that same time, locals expressed interest in having a school, but this plan was not favored "unless the people are going to be allowed out to work. Education in present circumstances would only breed discontentment" (Allen 1958). Eight years after the Mortlock Community School was

Table 8. Proxemics of Residence in 1995

Type	Tāloki	Sialeva	Total
Adults	123 (41%)	180 (59%)	303
Houses	70 (42%)	95 (58%)	165
Children			132

established in 1960, the education of a whole generation of Takū residents received a boost through the appointment to the staff of Len Murray, an Australian teacher who remained on the island until 1984. It is a measure of Murray's success that many of the students who passed through his hands are now employed in senior positions in the national and local government, as well as the private sector.

Sentimental attraction to the island has remained real and strong, and has been demonstrated in various ways. The men working at Nukumanu's copra plantations and on coastal cargo vessels channeled their emotions and thoughts into creative forms, composing *lani* songs about the difficulty of lengthy separation from Takū's human and natural environment. More recently the large number of expatriate Takū who return each Christmas period for a "holiday" testifies to the need for repeated contact with the artifacts that cumulatively identify them as Takū. This can be seen particularly in the recent tendency to aggregate commemorative rituals for all the year's dead into a single large-scale occasion in December, when expatriate islanders can take leave from jobs and be present.

Takū exposed to European culture away from the island have generally tended to introduce material goods rather than cultural models on their return; they regularly bring back more sophisticated items of audio, cooking, household, or fishing equipment than are available in local trade stores. Only half a dozen houses on Nukutoa are of European design. One was built apparently as a display of wealth, since it remained unoccupied for several years, and the others were made of materials more durable than local wood or leaves. Similarly, expatriate Takū coming home on the December boat from jobs in mainland Papua New Guinea or beyond, display Western clothing styles, sometimes worn only briefly because of their impracticality in a small island environment; these are only rarely copied by permanent residents because of their high cost. The one foreign cultural model Takū have embraced while off the island is Christianity, and some of them consciously and deliberately introduce it on their return.

Political governance of the island is at present in the hands of the community council, comprised of six members elected annually and including the Ariki as representative of the central government, and the Pure representing the village court. Three men appointed justices of the peace act as magistrates in civil matters and are assisted by a clerk. Four people are appointed "police" to restore order in the event of any unlawful disturbances. The council meets at least monthly to determine specific projects for the Tāloki and Sialeva men and women—in four separate groups—as part of "village day" work. On the ringing of a bell on Monday morning, the adult community gathers at the office to hear news of recent formal requests to the council from both residents and outsiders, to voice any criticism of the behavior of particular groups of residents, to report on shipping movements and relevant government announcements, and to announce forthcoming major events. Although announcements are made by a designated council member standing on the office balcony, Ariki Avo frequently gets to his feet to amplify or emphasize particular points. At such meetings, the political image of the Ariki as the single individual to whom the community has delegated ultimate responsibility is maintained, even within the structure of the elected community council.

The course of Takū's experience prior to European contact and history since represents a unique blend of individual and group achievements, chance encounters and planned activities, and a variety of reactions to external presences and organic growth. The unilinear nature of its passage through the past two centuries has resulted in large part from the effectiveness of its leadership, which, until the 1970s, turned on the undisputed primacy of the Ariki, in whom was focused the role of intercessor and protector for the community at large. The late twentieth century has introduced new sets of circumstances: natural forces that may permanently change the structure, or indeed threaten the very existence, of the atoll, and external social agents that have not only the capacity but also the stated goal of changing the community's social structure. The early years of the twenty-first century therefore present the community with momentous decisions that will have enduring ramifications for Takū's future.

Chapter 2
Takū Society as the Locus for Musicking

Singing on Takū occurs not at the level of spectacle or theater for the benefit of an audience, but as an introspective expression of the values and beliefs that allow its residents to function as a community in both domestic and ritual modes. Operating at the levels of family, patriline, and linked kindred, social clustering and the occasions for that clustering are identified, endorsed, and exalted through musicking, and these expressions are further enhanced through dancing. This clustering and its occasions are identified in this chapter.

Takū is a part-foraging, part-farming community, dependent on the reliable availability and abundance of fish and, in a secondary sense, on garden produce.[1] The support capacity of the atoll has never been tested within living memory, nor does oral tradition record the exhaustion of local food resources; reasons other than the density of population are cited for the ongoing process of out-migration that appears to have begun in the 1980s. Any minor variations in the availability of food are accommodated within existing patterns of sharing, sponsorship, and reciprocity. Because of the limited land area, social density remains fairly constant when the community is in secular mode; it changes significantly only on the shift to ritual mode, when all able-bodied individuals are expected to congregate at predetermined locations. On such occasions, social order is maintained by making overt and explicit the structures and relationships that simultaneously unify the community and also define its constituent parts. It is, therefore, in the context of ritual that cultural adaptation helps Takū transcend both the potential and actual limitations of their physical environment. Because the community is small, all the residents are well known to one another, and most are connected by kinship ties. Cutting across these ties, however, are other associations, temporary or permanent, that may not appear in any genealogy but are nonetheless important in daily life.

The largest social unit is the village itself, which is not identified linguistically as a social unit per se or as a collection of houses, but is referred to as *taku henua* (my land) or *te henua tātou* (our land). These terms encompass the entire atoll and the notion of the village as a separate entity having its own name appears foreign. Nukutoa, the name of the island on which the village stands, is used with extreme rarity in a collective sense to refer to the land, houses, and residents. Of the more than one thousand songs I recorded, only three include the word "Nukutoa" in their lyric, and all three are by the same composer. A few locally composed Christian songs use the word in a collective sense, but they appear to represent thinking influenced by Christian teaching and may therefore be counted untypical of local attitudes.

Similarly, only one song poem refers to Takū Island by name, where the community lived until the late 1890s:

| Ā, ko te huriana ko tino henua māoi ē; | Then everyone turned [to watch]; |
| Ā, ko te huriana ko tino Takū māoi ē. | Then all of Takū turned.[2] |

The two-generation nuclear family *(haimātua)* and the patrilineal lineage *(manava)* of two generations older and younger than oneself constitute smaller social units. Each house is normally the home of an individual nuclear family, but lack of space to erect a house of their own may force a newly married couple to live with the bride's family. Close relatives spend much time in one another's company and may work together in food preparation to share cooking facilities. Immediate members of a family sleep in the same house (or outside on very hot nights), although in the past bachelors could sleep in separate houses. The nuclear family is also the principal producer and consumer of food. Husband and wife each own separate gardens on Takū Island, where they work several periods each week. The contents of individual family gardens demonstrate both short- and long-term resource planning: the giant taro planted around the border take at least eight years to mature, in contrast to six months for taro and other crops planted in the central region.

The division of the village into the two sections introduced in chapter 1 does not play a major role in everyday life since members of the same clan or the same family may live in different sections. There are, consequently, no opposing interests across sections in normal circumstances. The sections routinely separate on formal occasions, however, and also when an activity requires large-scale labor. Distinguished by their clothing (Tāloki typically in yellow, Sialeva in red), the sections perform separate sets of dances on the *marae* during *tukumai* commemorative rituals and optionally as part of annual Independence Day celebrations. On such occasions there may be a small degree of rivalry (for example, one group deliberately performing more items than the other despite an earlier agreement to each contribute the same number), but it is always good humored. At the annual school concert they also perform a selection of local dances. Tāloki and Sialeva each possess their own large net, used principally to catch turtles; their men labor with section-mates in this work and share the catch among their families.

Regular parties at Tāloki and Sialeva are expressions of section solidarity, as men (and occasionally women in their own adjacent house) of different clans sit side by side to talk, drink, smoke, sing, and dance (photo 5). This informal, voluntary arrangement arises from practical neighborly reasons, and adults of one section are not generally precluded from attending parties in the other; nor are they criticized if they do.[3] Tāloki and Sialeva are, nonetheless, the focus of residential group social identity, and the special nature of this collectivity, which stands apart from the other aggregating devices of kinship and descent, is permanently visible in the form of their pairs of drinking houses. The boundaries between formal and informal use of these houses is at times blurred, since it is possible to consider the formal singing of *tuki* songs there as an extension of the fishing tales informally recounted whenever men gather to talk into a different communication medium. This extension is both structural and contextual: narratives are processed into poetic format and their subject matter becomes limited to successful expeditions. At planned parties, the separate status of the houses is marked by coconut leaves lashed to the house posts, and those attending the event receive a leaf headband and on occasion partake of a communal meal, special treatment that simultaneously makes them visibly different from the rest of the community and similar to one another.

Takū social structure is believed to persist after death. Accounts of the afterworld in songs received from spirits of the dead frequently refer to clan elders, the person of the Ariki, and even the deities—always in a positive light. The following lines are typical:

PHOTO 5. The adjacent men's and women's houses at Sialeva during a formal party. *(Hamish Macdonald)*

Tau nau ma Fare Mania, ō ki mau ai nau.	I belong with Fare Mania, and remain here.
Ā ku au nau i aku tamana	I have come before my fathers
Noho nau i taku noho nei.	In my former capacity [as clan elder].

One song sent back from the dead indicates that even the institution of marriage continues after death:

Āiē ka noho mai ai ko taku avana;	My spouse was there [in the afterworld];
Āie ku noho mai ai ko Roturotu e.	Roturotu was there.

Decline of the *Hata* System

During the period when Takū Island was continually occupied, local society was divided into the *hata*, of which there were two. Te Morotea incorporated the three northern-based clans: *te Noho i Tua* (oceanside residents), *te Noho i Loto* (interior residents), and *te Noho i Tokorau* (northern residents); and Sikipura encompassed the southern-based clans *te Noho i Saupuku* (southern residents) and *te Noho i Tai* (residents along the lagoon). These divisions appear to have excluded the substantial northeastern area of the island taken up by gardens. The garden area *(mouku)* is itself bounded on the lagoon side by a curved rise of some four meters, said to be the material excavated during the creation of the gardens. Exclusively female *hata* also existed, whose members assembled to perform dances of the *sau, sore,* and *hoe* categories, among others. However, their nomenclature suggests that these groups reflected individual clan affiliations rather than cross-clan amalgamation.

Today's active song repertoire includes occasional poetic references to female *hata*, despite their having been discontinued for over a century. Such songs, however, are not human-composed *(nā mako rā e hatu)* but originate from the spirits of dead residents. Most references to such *hata* are indirect; thus, one particular song is associated with the Ruaiata *hata*, and several *rue* and one complete *sau* dance originated within the Tellahu *hata*.

Male *hata* divided the population principally for group fishing purposes. Morotea and Sikipura each possessed large houses in which their canoes were stored and where members met to repair or construct equipment and to socialize. There is some evidence of exclusive fishing areas, for example, the lagoon location called Tepae is said to have been for Sikipura use only. In contemporary songs, fishing is the principal poetic context for references to *hata*, for example:

Hioi ē te hata nei e ka tō i taku ākau,	The group now goes to my reef,
E roropo i tai te papa,	Assembling at the rock flat on the reef
Ko tū nekeneke ki uta nei.	And slowly drives the fish into the shallows.

(from the *sau Tereimua* dance)

Āiē, tuku kauake taku hata i tai Tepae nei;	My group presents itself seaward of Tepae [fishing ground];
Āiē, tuku kauake Sikipura i tai Tepae nei.	Sikipura presents itself seaward of Tepae.[4]

Poetic references to female *hata* similarly focus on land-based food sources and interpersonal relationships, for example:

A ni tani mai kakau mai aku avana,	My wife swimming there wept,
Manatu ki loto taku hare te henua e apuru i te kai	Thinking about my house and its land's plentiful food;
A ni tani kakau mai e Parekiteika,	Parekiteika swimming there wept,
Manatu ki loto a tana hata Nukutapu e apuru i te uto.	Thinking of her *hata* on Nukutapu [Island] and its plentiful coconuts.

(This comes from the *takitaki* section of the dance celebrating the *Temorotea hata*.)

Ko te hata taku tama ko Tellahu;	My child belongs to Tellahu;
Īē, ko Taputoa nā e,	Behold, Taputoa,
Ko te hata taku tama ko Tellahu.	My child who belongs to Tellahu.

(This comes from the *sau Sione* dance.)

Membership in a *hata* required payment of bride-wealth *(penupenu)* of an appropriate size and value by the woman's family to the man's. Food items and rolls of sennit cord, all available locally and with relative ease, had to be accompanied by one or more shell adzes *(toki, niho)* or porpoise teeth *(karile)* or whale teeth *(niho)*, whose acquisition required considerable effort. Inability to provide the full bride-wealth precluded formal recognition of a couple's union, with drastic consequence on a birth of a child: the newborn baby was taken to Te Kava Tekōpū, a beach site on Takū Island's eastern side, and left to die. This was repeated with each subsequent child until the bride-wealth had been paid.[5] Initiated by Ariki Hakalilo in the distant past, this practice of selective infanticide was discontinued when the atoll was bought by Emma Forsayth and its population moved to Kapeiatu Island and placed under the control of Emma's niece. With dislocation, the *hata* ceased to function as social units. Even with the subsequent move of the population from Kapeiatu to Nukutoa Island in the 1930s and the restored freedom of movement, the *hata* were not revived in their original form or with their earlier social influence.

Payment of the bride-wealth forms the theme of one *lani* song (also see chapter 5 on this genre), composed during the era when the inability to obtain the centerpiece of the presentation was a matter of genuine concern:

E karo ka te hina māua,	People passed by my darling and me,
Ni nonoho i te hare te kata.	While we were inside the house.
Ē taku hina ni mua i anau.	My darling is my first.
Karo ka te hina māua,	People passed by my darling and me,
Ni nonoho te hare te kata.	While we were inside the house.
Ē ku mua nā hai hina mai.	The first to be lovers.
Ē koe ma ki avana koe	You came and we married
Ku seai ō penupenu nei.	But you had no bride-wealth.
Ē tō toki sana ku sē sura.	You didn't provide any adze for your new husband.

It follows logically that an unmarried man or woman was therefore prevented from attaining membership in a *hata,* a predicament that befell the son of Tenehu (the ancestor of the present elder of Hare Ania): he remained unmarried for sheer want of an available woman during a time when the island's population totaled fewer than twenty, and was thereby prevented from participation in *hata* activities.

The *hata*'s poetic association with fishing continued into the twentieth century, long after the institution itself had ceased to exist. As recently as 1995 a newly composed *tuki* song interpreted the unusual arrival of a crocodile in the lagoon as confirmation that the spirit of a local man had safely reached the afterworld, from where both he and his *hata* ancestors watch the animal.

E, ni aroha nau e ki taku soa nei,	Oh, my sympathies go to my wife,
Tokaia iho se ika i taku henua;	Looking at the "fish" at my island;
Ni aroha nau i te atu hata nei	My sympathies go to the *hata*
E tokaia iho se mokotoro i Nukurekia.	As they gaze at the crocodile at Nukurekia Island.

Emotional attachment to one's *hata* is persistent. Some recent songs sent back from the dead identify a *hata,* suggesting that the institution continues in the afterworld, for example:

Ko te hata taku tama ko Tellahu,	My [dead] child belongs to the Tellahu *hata,*
Te haitamana taku hata rā sae mai nei;	Fathers, my *hata* is coming this way;
Īē, ko Taputoa nā ē	It's Taputoa, my child
Ko te hata taku tama ko Tellahu	Who belongs to Tellahu;
Te haitamana taku hata rā sae mai.	Fathers, my *hata* is heading this way.
E uru iho nau ma taku Ariki nei;	I entered together with my Ariki;
E uru iho nau i loto te hata;	I entered the *hata;*
E uru iho nau i loto Tellahu.	I entered Tellahu.
Īē, ko te hata e hora mai ki anau;	The group was expecting me;
Īē, ko Tellahu e hora mai ki anau.	Tellahu was expecting me.

And a *tuki* song composed in 1998 alludes to the Ariki's responsibility for invoking ancestors to assist with the island's spiritual well-being. In the following, he is presented calling on clan members deceased long enough to have been members of a *hata* (Ariki Avo is here identified by his birth name, Sina):

Ki noho te tanata ē i tana hare,	A man sat in his house,
No pena iho ma ko tana riki,	Donning his ritual ornaments,
Hakanohoria ki se haikave;	To invoke his female relative;
Ki noho Sina ē i Hare Ata, kīū,	Sina sat in Hare Ata,
No pena iho ma ko tana riki,	Donning his ritual ornaments,
Hakanohoria ki se Morotea.	To invoke the Morotea group member.

The sole surviving ritual evidence of the *hata* as a social organization is seen on the occasion of a *tukumai* hosted by Hare Mania clan. On such occasions, the elder of Hare Māsani clan (or, more likely, a deputy) is included among the ritual assistants called on to help distribute the pile of taro, on the grounds that this clan elder is the functional successor of the former Saupuku clan elder on Takū Island where the *hata* system had been operational. But this evidence will only be understood by those few persons already familiar with the historical link. By and large, the *hata* as a social organization survives only in memory and is directly referred to only in the poetry of songs apparently composed prior to the dislocation to Kapeiatu in the late nineteenth century.

The Five Clan System

Aserutahelo, the first mortal, had two wives: Teikatākere, whose children founded the Ariki line, and Sānitoa, whose children founded the Pure line. Teikatākere used to sleep pillowed on her husband's right arm, and Sānitoa on his left arm. It was noticed that several of Sānitoa's descendants were mentally disturbed, for which reason the practice of bigamy was thereafter prohibited, on the assumption that such disorders resulted from Aserutahelo's original bigamy. Poroa, brother of Aserutahelo, was the human progenitor of the present Hare Nāoro clan, and similar stories account for the origin of the other clans. By these means, social relations and social distinction were founded. (Field notes, 1997)

The primary kinship unit on Takū is the patrilineal clan, of which there are five, identified at present under the name of the house *(hare)* in which its elder *(mātua)* resides (see table 9, photo 6).

The designation by house name dates back only to the 1930s, when supernatural intervention rescued the community from social disorder and provided a new clan nomenclature. During the earlier era of residence on Takū Island, the clans were termed *noho* (residences), as noted in table 9. At present the clans are routinely identified in terms of either the houses themselves or by the name of their respective elders (for example, *te Hare Avo, te Hare*

Table 9. Takū's Five Clan System, Past and Present

Designation on Takū Island	Designation on Nukutoa	Elder
te Noho i Tua	Hare Ata	Avo Sini
te Noho I Loto	Hare Mania	Kīpū Sieki
te Noho i Saupuku	Hare Māsani	Kikiva Nukeria
te Noho i Tai	Hare Nāoro	Pūtahu Tekapu
te Noho i Tokorau	Hare Ania	Pāsia Piri

Pūtahu). The position of clan head (mātua) is inherited, ideally from father to eldest son, or to a younger brother or adopted son if there is no biological son. However, oral tradition notes more than one instance in which an adopted son nominated by an elder as his successor declined to accept the position, and the refusal was made while the mātua was still alive. Private opinions vary as to the strictness of succession, with some insisting on adherence to "custom," and others identifying the practical need for flexibility in light of the number of men seeking work off the island. There is, however, agreement that all appointees should have a record of maturity and understand the duties of an elder. Although the immediate successors of some clan headships is well known, others have not been formally announced and remain a source of speculation.

Each elder is responsible for the spiritual leadership of his clan. Indeed, his house is known as a "sacred house" (hare tapu) and each doorway is inhabited by a clan spirit (eg, Teporo, Manauī Haite, Pūtahu, Laroteone, Hāriki; see figure 1; photo 7). One of these spirits is invoked at time of sickness while the patient lies in the appropriate doorway, and one particular doorway, known as matakāriki, is the principal focus for the manufacture and application of sacra. It is here that patrilineal deities (nā hhui aitu) are invoked as the elder rubs clansmen's shoulders and places a pandanus necklet and a leaf necklet on each at the start of a tukumai as protection against supernaturally induced sickness.

Until the abandonment of the tānaki song-acquisition ritual, elders also oversaw communication with recently deceased clan members via a medium inside their own houses. The clan elders' houses should be occupied at all times, and if an elder leaves the island, a senior clan member, usually the successor to the title, will move in and reside there until the return of the titleholder "to protect the people."

The Ariki, lying in direct though distant descent from the founding ancestors of the island and thus being the senior direct descendant, is considered to have the best credentials to contact both these and intermediary spirits and to request appropriate assistance from them in time of need. The elder of the Hare Ata clan by virtue of that position also holds the title of Ariki, and as such has overall responsibility for the village's religious life and physical well-being through direct intercession with the island's deities. In this capacity he

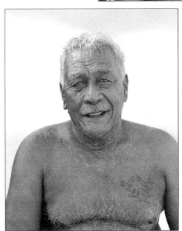

PHOTO 6. The five clan elders in 2000. Top row, from left to right: Pāsia Piri (Hare Ania) and Pūtahu Tekapu (Hare Nāoro); center, Ariki Avo Sini (Hare Ata); bottom row, Pure Kīpū Sieki (Hare Mania) and Kikiva Nukuria (Hare Māsani). *(Hamish Macdonald)*

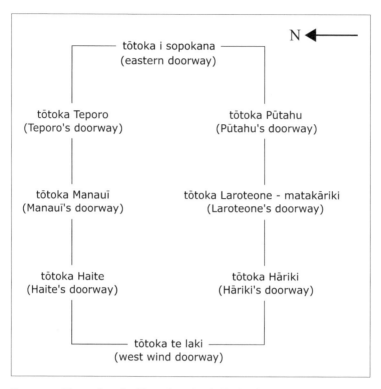

FIGURE 1. Floor plan for Hare Ata, the Ariki Avo's house on Nukutoa

exercises overarching responsibilities for the entire community. It is to the
Ariki's house that any injured person is taken, to lie on the Ariki's sacred mat
in the *matakāriki* doorway for five days in the constant presence of the Ariki
himself, who oversees both traditional and Western medical treatment. It is
the Ariki who formerly led the clan elders' public invocations on the *marae*
to ensure garden growth, adequate rain and sunlight, bountiful fish stocks,
and freedom from illnesses. He also now utters loud invocations as he stands
on the *marae* to ward off heavy rain during dance performances. In these
activities, the Ariki occupies a unique relationship with one of the island's two
principal deities, Pukena.[6]
     In historical times, the Ariki's house adjacent to Sarati on Takū Island
stood some forty meters from *te hare Pukena,* Pukena's house, and it was here
that the community gathered each afternoon for six months to entertain the
deity's wooden image with song and dance. Pukena was ritually bathed with
water from a nearby well, called Vai Orapi. Attached to the end of Pukena's
house stood *te murihata te kata,* the so-called eel's annex, about which little
is now known, other than the ongoing restriction against women approaching the area or sitting with their legs apart, lest they be seduced *(haikavana-*

Photo 7. Sprouting coconuts and tinned food lie outside the *matakāriki* doorway of the Ariki's house as an offering to the house spirits resident there. *(Richard Moyle)*

tia) unknowingly by that deity and bear an uncontrollable spirit child. At the southeastern corner of Sarati lived the deviant founding spirit Oroatu; entry to that site is forbidden, since anything to do with Oroatu continues to carry potentially harmful, if only vaguely expressed, connotations.

As mentioned above, indigenous religion on Takū suffered two heavy blows in less than a century—the removal of the population to Kapeiatu Island under the control of Emma Forsayth's manager and the deforestation of Takū Island itself for plantation purposes. These developments denied the population access to sites and activities of religious significance, and the Ariki's death on Bougainville in 1974 meant immediate and severe trauma to those charged with carrying on the precedent-focused funeral and commemorative rituals. Sarati was abandoned when the population was forced to Kapeiatu in the 1890s, although its border of coral slabs is still visible; a large pile of bleached conch trumpets identifies Oroatu's house site, and a single upright slab remains at the spot where the image of Pukena was erected.

The Ariki's line of descent differs from those of other elders. Until the period of the fifth Ariki before the present titleholder, the position is said to have alternated between members of two lineages within Hare Ata clan known as Atui and Apua.[7] The alternation had its origin in the mythological era and was linked to the need for the deity Pukena, under the supervision of the Ariki, to be brought out from its house on Takū Island and displayed for several months while the population danced before it. On one occasion when the time came for the deity to be taken outside, the Ariki, who was of the Apua lineage, had sailed away on his canoe *Hakautu* in search of food and remained absent. To fulfill the ritual requirements, the Pure asked the head of the Atui lineage to substitute for the Ariki, volunteering to assist him in his duties where appropriate. Thereafter, the position of Ariki alternated between the two lines (figure 2). No specific details survive about the identity of the social units from which these titleholders were drawn, and oral tradition links the discontinuation of the Apua line after Hāriki to the epidemic that decimated the population in the late nineteenth century. One source noted that the head of the non-titleholder line at any given time would act as ritual assistant for the Ariki of the day.

A relic of the alternation process survives in the name and site of the Ariki's house on Takū Island: Hakātui or, more correctly, Haka Atui. No one appears to know of any comparable house-name for the Ariki Apua lineage or of any practice of changing house names to match that of the current Ariki's lineage.

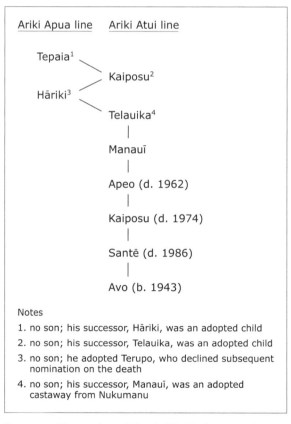

FIGURE 2. Alternation of the Ariki title between the two lines of succession

The elder for Hare Mania clan holds the Pure title, which complements that of the Ariki.[8] Moir notes (1989, 95), "The *pure* is custodian of the land by right of discovery . . . because it was his ancestors who brought other patriline progenitors to the atoll, gave them land, and created a community whose members could marry." (The claim of first right of discovery is, however, challenged by at least one other clan.) The Pure's role in the past appears to have been that of arbiter in civil disputes and allocator of land for house sites on Nukutoa, as well as custodian of the cemetery on Takū Island currently in use.[9]

The positions of Ariki and Pure are further distinguished by being classified as *tuku* (finisher), a designation that Ariki Avo explains:

> That's how we came to this island; we looked after the land and called ourselves chiefs. I am a chief, and Kīpū is one also, and we look after things. If I say that we stop, that's the end of the matter. If the Ariki says something is finished, then it is finished *[e tuku]*. That's why we give ourselves the name *tuku*.

The designation is, however, of recent origin. Elders of the other three clans maintain particular relationships of assistance to the Ariki and the Pure in the enactment of their spiritual and secular responsibilities. The head of Hare Māsani may communicate the directives of the Pure to the community, and the elder of Hare Nāoro then ensures compliance, whereas the elder of Hare Ania acts as ritual assistant to the Ariki (Moir 1989, 95–96). When speaking of the five clans, residents invariably name them in a particular sequence—Hare Ata, Hare Mania, Hare Māsani, Hare Nāoro, and Hare Ania—preserving the sequence of settlement.[10] Seating positions for the five elders on the *marae* are similarly fixed, the heads of Hare Nāoro and Hare Ania are positioned at the right shoulder *(i laro)* of the Ariki, and the heads of Hare Mania and Hare Māsani at his left shoulder *(i aruna)*. These pairs in position are referred to as *nā rua i aitu* (the two spirits).[11]

The persons of the Ariki and Pure embody sanctity *(hākapu)* at all times, and young and old alike take care not to touch or pass close to them, or strike or even jab toward them in jest for fear of supernatural retribution. Such sanctity is intensified and rendered visible on the *marae,* where a combination of protective and invocatory emblems is worn for all to see. These same people's sanctity, however, renders them more vulnerable than other residents to injury or illness caused by malevolent spirits, and accordingly sets of specific prohibitions regarding proximity are observed.

Purotu *(Performance Specialist)*

Anthropologists have long recognized egalitarianism as an important feature of Polynesian atoll communities, although opinions vary as to its cause (eg, Goldman 1970; Kirch 1984; Sahlins 1958). Despite Takū's own egalitarianism, however, nobody is a "100 percent insider in any conceivable context" (Kubik

2000, 12), because of gender-based divisions of labor, age-based hierarchies of secular knowledge, and clan-based apportionments of ritual knowledge. One sphere of activity in which the prominence of an individual is not only tolerated but also expected is the composition of new songs; indeed, formal social recognition of persons so skilled is expressed by a named specialist position, *purotu* (clan performance leader) and by making it a matter of patri-lineal inheritance to ensure its perpetuation within each clan.[12] While the position of clan performance leader was hereditary and all known holders of the position were male, descent was not strictly patrilineal, and the last office holder (Tave Atimu) was the nephew of his predecessor (Sāre Amani).

The duties of the *purotu* were incorporated within those of the *tautua*, the clan ceremonial assistant, so that all *purotu* were *tautua* in their own right. However, their exploits in the context of song and dance creation and per-formance are set off and recalled separately in the memories of old residents. In former times, each clan had its own *purotu* but, apparently through natural attrition and the absence of trained successors, the five had been reduced to two by the 1960s: Sāre Amani (for Hare Ata) and Willie Tekapu (for Hare Mania). A photograph taken on the *marae* in the 1960s (photo 8) shows these two *purotu* seated at the *tuki* slit drum in front of the assembled clan heads.

Willie died around 1975, leaving no successor.[13] Sāre died in 1973 and was succeeded by Tave, who assumed the role of *purotu* for the entire community,

PHOTO 8. The elders and performance specialists on the *marae* in the 1960s. From left to right: Nukuria (elder of Hare Māsani); Pūō (the Pure and elder of Hare Mania); Willie (performance specialist for Hare Mania); Kaiposu (the Ariki and elder of Hare Ata), Sāre (performance specialist for Hare Ata); Pōpī (elder of Hare Nāoro); Tenehu (elder of Hare Ania). *(Photographer unknown)*

leading the performance of existing songs, as well as composing, teaching, and performing new additions to the repertoire. Tave himself continued in this capacity until 1994, when a sudden illness killed him and ended an entire cultural institution on the island: having enjoyed good health prior to 1994, he had not trained a successor.

Some older community members recall the exploits of as many as five past *purotu,* and descendants and family members continue to speak of them in admiration and wonder. The period when Apeo and Marena held power is now considered something of a golden era in Takū's history, and the two specialists of the day, Sāre and Willie, continue to be held in high esteem; Sāre in particular is considered to exemplify the pinnacle of compositional prowess. Sāre and Willie represent the earliest *purotu* whose compositions are still frequently performed and indeed, there appears to be little recollection of the names of their predecessors. Most anecdotes focus on Sāre, whom some men now refer to as the "Tape Recorder" from his apparent ability to sing back a new song after hearing it only once. A prolific composer of *tuki* songs for Hare Ata, Sāre would sing constantly on both land and at sea. One story in particular illustrates his ability and command during performances on the *marae:*

When Sāre began formal mourning in the 1960s on the death of his grandson, local men decided to organize a communal meal to relieve his grief. Shortly before the death, Sāre had taught the men several *tuki*—including two sets known as *te tuki te kaumata* and *te tuki Sikipura*—and the men celebrated these compositions in a novel manner. Assembling on their canoes in the shallows of the lagoon prior to paddling to the fishing grounds, the crews sang the two sets of songs on the water, the sound of their voices spreading throughout the village. On the men's return, the women were instructed by Ariki Kaiposu to gather flowers from Takū Island to make floral garlands. Shortly after midnight, the men went to the mourning house, woke Sāre, and escorted him to the *marae* where the garlanded elders and community were assembled, and the newly learnt *tuki* were given their first formal performance in a lengthy program of songs that lasted until dawn. As soon as the light was sufficient dancing began, and to everyone's astonishment Sāre himself got to his feet, walked to the center of the *marae*, turned to the elders, and began dancing, accompanying himself with a song that had not been heard before on the *marae*. He performed a set of two *tuki* songs called *nā huatana* and established a precedent still unique in the active repertoire: in theory, even today, any individual may simultaneously sing and dance *nā huatana,* although none has dared to try and emulate the feat of the *purotu*. (Nūnua, pers comm 1998)[14]

When Sāre died, several *marae*-based activities once led by him ceased— the informal instructional sessions in which men took turns demonstrating their knowledge of invocations *(kavai)* or their parents' genealogies or practices at which they believed they excelled. The significance of convening such activities on the *marae* was their attraction for the unseen collective presence of the island's spirits, who routinely attended all events over which the Ariki, the Pure, and the elders formally presided (photo 9).

Since the time of Tave's death, Nūnua Posongat has assumed the de facto role of *purotu* but is not formally recognized as such, because he was not trained for the position nor appointed to it by his clan head, Ariki Avo, nor is he a ritual assistant for his clan. More recently, breathing difficulties have prevented Nūnua from leading the singing for more than short periods. Nūnua is frequently joined at the drum by Terupo, but his voice does not carry strongly, either. The widespread view holds that performance standards, particularly the drumming that accompanies several types of dance, have declined since Tave's death. As one man explained, *"Tātou e samu vare saita nei"* (We beat the drum in ignorance now).

When the performance specialist beat the slit drum to accompany a dance on the *marae,* he was called te *murituki*—([the one seated] behind the drum). He could be joined at the drum by a second *purotu* performing complementary beats. At least two beating terms are recalled, although it is unclear whether these referred to the rhythms created or the style of beating or both.

Although the position of *purotu* may seem to be a form of musical specialization, it is rather an extension into the performance repertoire of an

PHOTO 9. Dancers typically stand and face those who are in formal attendance on the *marae:* the Ariki, Pure, and elders, ritual assistants, and mediums. In so doing, the dancers also face the performance specialist who is drumming the accompaniment. This photo was taken sometime before World War Two. *(Photograph courtesy John Sione Konga)*

entire clan of the same kinds of competences that other individuals possess for the output of their own family. And it is important to remember that the *purotu* was a performance specialist in addition to the social requirements and expectations accruing to all adult males. Like the other men in the community, these men constructed, used, and repaired their own canoes and houses; worked in their gardens; participated in group labor activities; and attended to a variety of domestic chores—all without attracting special recognition or recompense. But in performance or ritual these same men exceeded their personal character and assumed an unchallenged leadership role. Deference was universally shown them in such times and food gifts routinely presented in acknowledgment of their leading the community to affirm and celebrate both its existence and the values and practices that have contributed to its ongoing reality.

The *purotu* were socially valued for the role they played in *marae*-based rituals celebrating life's achievements and crises, but now the community must adjust to the absence of this ritual assistant. Performances on the *marae* of the dances once led by the *purotu* occur less frequently than in the past; the de facto office-holders are allowed to beat the drums when such dances are performed and the community accepts the inferior quality of that drumming; and finally, the responsibility for creating new songs, particularly *tuki*, has been spread widely within each clan.

Tautai *(Fishing Leader)*

Each clan has several experienced fishermen called *tautai*, whose main duty is the management of the family tuna-fishing canoe *(vakasī)*—including its construction, preparation, and maintenance, but focusing principally on its activities at sea. Although the term may be used in a general sense to acknowledge a man skilled in sea-related activities, it is also an enduring title applied to specific individuals. While at sea, the *tautai* controls the canoe's technical and religious operations, and he will be personally exalted in *tuki* and *rue* songs if his expeditions are successful, but will also be held accountable if they are not. Indeed, the *tuki sī* express the exaltation *(ahu)* of the *tautai* for his success at catching tuna. In addition to designated titleholders, others are also acknowledged more informally as *tautai* on the strength of their consistent fishing successes. Asimi, for example, is always urged to be the first dancer when a particular *tuki hakasoro* (oil fish-catching song) is sung, in recognition of his de facto *tautai* status and proven success record on the clan canoe.

Within the historical period two men demonstrated such high preeminence at fishing that they were considered *tautai* for their entire clans: Takua (adopted into Hare Ata) and Apuku (adopted into both Hare Māsani and Hare Ania).[15] Both men had drifted from Peilau to Takū, where they introduced superior forms of fishing for the prestige ocean species: shark, tuna, and oil fish.[16] Apuku's dual clan affiliation set a precedent that permits present members of his two clans to share equipment for all three types of sacred fishing and to compose *tuki* songs in praise of the exploits of both their own clan's and the others' named canoes.

Family and Clan

As noted earlier, the smallest social units are the family and extended family. One may call on members of one's extended family and patrilineal descent line to assist with large-scale projects such as house building, the collection of valuables comprising bride-wealth, and feasts associated with funeral and commemorative activities. In the course of the *tukumai* commemorative ritual, individual family members are commonly identified in song poetry. Newly composed *tuki* songs frequently include one or more verses beginning with the set phrase *Ni aroha nau kia* (I grieved for), followed by the name of one (sometimes two) members of the formal mourners who belong to the deceased's family, thus uniting composer, singers, and mourners by their common emotional state.[17]

One's clan affiliation becomes significant on the occasion of marriage. In the past if a man's prospective wife's father or wife's mother belonged to his own clan, marriage was not permitted, but population growth on the island eventually rendered this restriction untenable, and members of the same clan may now marry. One may request a contribution toward the bride-wealth from members of one's clan. Each Takū person belongs to two linked clans *(hare ākina)* and one may talk of the two "sides" *(vasi)* of a clan—the men's/father's and the women's/mother's: the *vasi te tamana* and the *vasi te tinana,* respectively. The clan also may assemble to organize a diversion for a fellow clan member believed to be suffering emotional distress during the months of isolation in the mourning house. This action, worded more precisely as "entertainment" *(hakatatāhaoria),* normally consists of escorting the mourner to one of the smaller islands, most commonly Nukurekia, for a whole day and night of fishing and feasting, coming back to Nukutoa the following morning.[18]

On their return, the men assemble on the *marae* to perform a *sau* dance known as *te sau taupeara* (the young men's dance) to complete the entertainment of the grieving fellow clansman.[19] Another *sau* dance, *te sau Arou,* is considered a companion *(soa)* item and it may be performed after the other. Both dances are associated with the Sikipura *hata* formerly operating on Takū Island, and performance therefore is limited to and for men from the clans devolving from that group, namely Hare Māsani and Hare Nāoro. Hare Nāoro is considered the owner of Nukurekia on the basis of mythological events occurring there, and because the island's resident spirits can assist in alleviating a mourner's grief, it is the key destination for such purposes.[20]

The clan also becomes a visible entity in the days leading up to a *tukumai* ritual, when members organize a procession of principal mourners (the spouse and children of a married person, the parents of an unmarried person) to display to the community at large the fact that they are safe and in good health after their months of sequestration in the mourning houses.[21] Walking in separate groups only minutes apart, the men and women of the deceased's clan proceed silently through the village, following a predetermined route around the outer lines of houses, principal mourners in front. followed by affines, in turn followed by other clan members. Co-membership of this association is invoked at the time of death when, it is said, individuals may discover for the first time that they are distantly related to other individuals as together they provide food or materials for public distribution. The concept of cognatic descent is said to operate between Hare Ata and Hare Ania; they are *nā hare ākina*—linked kindred. This relationship is cited as the reason, for example, why the elder of Hare Ania goes to the Ariki to obtain particular sacra rather than construct them himself. The Hare Ania elder, Pāsia Piri, described to me the mythological basis of this relationship, which centers on the Hare Ania founding canoe being the last to arrive. Pāsia personalizes his account by presenting it in the first person:

> The [Hare Ania] elder remained in that house, and later [the clan] met and decided to shift to another location. That's when I went and took advice from the Ariki.
>
> I asked, "What will happen if we go to another island? What will happen to [our sacred house] Tapueia?"
>
> The Ariki replied, "Tapueia should remain, but I will give you some of my sacred leaves, because when the other canoes arrived, you were the last to come to Takū. That's why I give you part of my garland, so you must follow what I have given to you. If you make sacra, you must come and get their second part from me at the time when you come for your necklet, your armband decoration, and the things you place at your sides."
>
> That's what the Ariki gave to the elder from Tokorau. Tokorau's elder arrived here late, after the other elders had already arrived, and that's how we got our sacra. We went and took advice from the Ariki. From that time onward, my clan gets information from the Ariki because my ancestor was the last [elder] to arrive.[22]

Birth

Until some thirty years ago it was normal practice for any woman pregnant for the first time to give birth inside the house of either the Ariki or Pure assisted by other women of her clan. After the delivery, the woman lay next to a small fire in the house, the warmth aiding a speedy recovery. Five days after the birth, the new mother was formally reintegrated into the community in a ritual called *hakamārama te tinae* (purification of the new mother). The community assembled on the *marae*, the new mother formally decorated with turmeric and seated immediately behind her clan elder (photo 10). A program of women's dances honored the event, although the mother herself normally did not participate.

Photo 10. The last *hakamārama te tinae* ritual on Nukutoa, 1968. A new mother, Putē Lulu, sits on the *marae* wearing her turmeric decorations. *(Len Murray)*

Most women now give birth in the hospital at Buka or Rabaul, but a few decline to leave the island. Although confidence in local midwifery is the reason publicly given, some suspect that, if the child is born deformed or premature, the mother will wish to retain the option of killing it immediately (see Macintosh 1958), a choice unavailable while in hospital. Ideally at the first visible sign of pregnancy but often occurring soon after the birth, the woman's father harvests a small number of swamp taro and presents them to the husband's family, who in turn distribute them to family members and the man's sponsors in a ritual called *te manava e hura* (the swelling of the stomach).

Residence

Each Takū patriline is a unilinear descent group, having a putative common male ancestor; by birthright, all children belong to their father's patriline. Marriage, regulated by clan identity, is normally exogamous; my 1994 census indicates 92 (72 percent) of the 128 existing marriages occurred outside the clan. Among the 36 endogamous marriages recorded, there is wide variation, from 29 (80 percent) within Hare Ata clan to zero in Hare Māsani and Hare Nāoro. (With more than twice as many members as any other clan, Hare Ata has a proportionately smaller pool of potential marriage partners outside its own membership; thus its high incidence of endogamy is not surprising.)

The dividing line separating the Tāloki and Sialeva sections of the village is common knowledge, though conceptual only, and the houses immediately on either side in each row are not distinguished in any way from the others. The results of a survey in 1994 indicate that Sialeva houses and their occupants are more numerous and occupy a greater land area than those of Tāloki (see table 10). However, because Tāloki and Sialeva represent spatial as well as social divisions, such mobility occurs independent of clan affiliation and, with the exception of Hare Mania, members of clans are spread roughly evenly over Tāloki and Sialeva. Relatively few Hare Mania clan members reside in Tāloki, for reasons as yet unclear.

Competitions

As an ideological norm, a man's attractiveness as a prospective husband is enhanced by evidence of industry and competence in activities normally undertaken by men. To this extent, competitions provide a means for non-participants (ie, unmarried women) to assess the measure of such skills. For married men, who presently comprise virtually all the competitors, personal prestige is at stake. Competition and the public display of the results provide an incentive, an added dimension of social pressure, for men to maintain the skills necessary on the domestic level for survival. Fishing contests will produce a winner who will enjoy personal admiration but, despite the emergence of an individual champion, the fruits of the activity are treated as if they resulted

Table 10. Distribution of Residents by Location and Clan

Clan	Tāloki Men	Tāloki Women	Sialeva Men	Sialeva Women	Totals (%)	
Hare Ata	32	41	44	70	187	(47%)
Hare Mania	6	8	18	45	77	(20%)
Hare Māsani	6	7	7	14	34	(9%)
Hare Nāoro	4	4	11	12	31	(8%)
Hare Ania	10	4	14	30	58	(15%)
Totals	58	64	94	171	387	(100%)

PHOTO 11. Egalitarianism in action. Before a fishing competition, all the participants join forces to catch baitfish, which are then divided into piles of equal size for use in the competition. *(Hamish Macdonald)*

from a group activity: women divide the total catch into piles of equal size and, when agreement is reached that equality has been achieved, the competitor's wives each take home one pile.[23] Additionally, at least for any *paretua* competition that uses the baitfish called *te hō*, the total bait catch is divided into equal piles for each participating man to take and use, to ensure equality of material resources before the competition proper starts (photo 11).

Such competitions operate on both an aesthetic and practical level to ensure the maintenance of survival skills, the one to recognize individual achievement and the other to cater for the needs of the community as a whole. Although other forms of competition such as canoe racing provide no comparable material benefits to the community, this sport can be seen as an adjunct to fishing activities. Issues of personal prestige for builder and sailor alike are dominant, and few married women bother to watch the races. Marriage is the principal mode of movement of cultural valuables, the process extending beyond the affines by the *taka* sponsorship system described below.

Death

Although ceremonies surround a variety of events relating to the actions and achievements of individuals and groups, death—by way of both immediate and later formal activities—stimulates the community's most complex sets of rituals. The following is a summary of events.

Day One

On the death of a resident, the body is placed on *takapau* mats in the center of his/her house, lying always with the head to the east. A male family member goes to the clan elder to request a death necklet *(tukutuku manava)* and places it on the corpse so the body will remain still while inside the house. A vigil is then mounted until early the following morning, when *hinaona* (adjacent-generation affines, or parents' affines, in the case of a dead child) prepare a platform on a large canoe and then assist the family to carry the corpse to the canoe and lay it on the platform. In preparation for the journey, the body is put on a *kapāmea* mat and wrapped with ten or more double lengths of new rope.

For the duration of the subsequent funeral events on Takū Island, a designated male affine known as the *sā* officiates but does not participate in any of the physical activities. Before the body is taken to the cemetery (photo 12), the affines and immediate family gather bags of valuables (such as sennit rope, fishing lines, clothing, lengths of cotton cloth) to take to Takū Island. Once the body is on the *kapāmea* mat, it is carried by affines to the beachfront, covered with a *vasa* mat. The canoe with the corpse leads the procession of mourners in their own canoes to Taitekava beachfront on Takū Island, where the body is placed on the ground near the entrance to the cemetery. Turmeric stripes are finger-painted on the forehead, temples, shoulders, and chest of the deceased. One or more whale teeth and floral garlands are placed on its chest and ritual leaves called *nā mānoni* are placed behind the ears. The *sā* sits at the corpse's head. Men and women pack tightly around in segregated groups and sing *llū* from all five clans as the deceased's parents, spouse, and principal *taka* sponsors (or their representatives), together with affines, exchange their bags of valuables. Each bag is opened and its contents counted to ensure equity. (In a similar reversal of normal modes of reciprocal conduct though not immediately apparent, mourners allow their personal gardens to go to waste and dispose of their own personal effects, on the grounds that these had earlier been used by/for the deceased.) The first of several *llū* songs is sung in a process lasting some two hours during which compositions belonging to both the deceased and his/her spouse are performed. After an hour or so of singing, and distribution to all present of laplaps and tobacco, the *mānoni* leaves are removed and the body lifted by young men while a new laplap is fitted and the body ritually washed. The *vasa* shroud mat is spread under the canopy and the body placed on it. More *llū* songs are sung for a further hour before the women sing part of a *sau* song, the change signaling the opportunity for individuals to approach and formally bid farewell *(purepure)* to the deceased by the traditional pressing of noses *(vaisoni)*. Men again lift the body, still on its shroud, and move it a short distance while ten or more short lengths of rope are laid on the ground, then the mat is placed back on them. The *sā* departs in search of suitable material for the death necklet *(henua mate)* while the entire gathering waits quietly. On his return he again sits at the corpse's head and constructs the necklet, removes the one already there and substitutes the new one. As the assembly sits in absolute silence, the clan elder sings the clan's *hakapiri henua* (deck necklet attachment) song. Final tokens are then placed on the corpse's chest by the family, perfume is sprayed or sprinkled on the body, and a liberal quantity of turmeric powder poured on the face to cover the eyes so that the body will not have its sleep disturbed by sunlight while lying in the grave just before the shroud is pulled over the body and the sides and ends of the mat drawn over it and secured by the ropes. Bearers carry the corpse and deposit it at the entrance of the cemetery, where women hurriedly weave a *takapau* mat from green coconut

PHOTO 12. *Te kava i tahā* cemetery on Takū Island. Each grave is bordered with items associated with the deceased. A cassette recorder, outboard fuel tank, frying pan, and kettles are visible among the many ceramic and enamel plates. *(Hamish Macdonald)*

leaves. When the grave is dug and measured for a good fit, the body is placed there, head toward the east, and the earth replaced. After burial, a newly woven *kapāmea* mat is placed on top of the mound of earth, followed by the *takapau,* which is weighted with stones.[24] Then all depart the cemetery. The family spends that night in temporary shelters at the beachfront location Vaihare, a former village site that becomes a functional *marae* during the five-day mortuary period.

Day Two: *Te Aso Nā Lloi* (The Day of the Pile of Giant Taro)
Led by the *sā,* male affines walk to their gardens to gather *lloi* funeral food for all those at Vaihare, including the Ariki, who attends all funerals. As they walk along the beach toward the path leading to the gardens, the *sā* throws down pieces of sacra at specific locations known to be inhabited by spirits, asking them to release their hold on the ropes of the invisible net *(matakupena)* they have erected around the cemetery, and so allow the mourners to step over it in safety and avoid the sickness that would otherwise ensue. Men harvest large quantities of giant taro; formerly one hundred per person, but recently reduced by the Ariki to thirty because the ever-increasing population means fewer gardens per person. The largest contribution (typically more than one hundred) comes from the son-in-law of the deceased (assuming [s]he is old. The Ariki's ritual assistant, now called *rima sava,* organizes the *kanokano* into a pile, the largest on top, and directs the subsequent distribution. Men from the mourning houses distribute the taro, typically ten to the Ariki (the largest of which are given to his assistant), ten to the deceased (uplifted by his/her primary sponsor), one to the *sā* in recognition of his invocations, and the balance divided equally among those people who will camp at Vaihare until day five.

Day Three
Affines spend the day fishing for those at Vaihare.

Day Four: *Te Aso Nā Mminikohu* (The Day for Taro Cakes)
Women from every family in the village harvest taro to make *sōsoro* cakes. Those married to an uncle or son of the deceased have a special responsibility to ensure their own baskets are full to the top with taro, but all those in the deceased's family owning a garden will contribute their own basket. Male affines collect coconuts and stones from the reef flat at the rear of the island for an earth oven. The women scrape the taro, add coconut juice and coconut oil, and then mix all together before wrapping the food in leaves and placing the bundles in the oven overnight.

Day Five: *Te Aso e Huri Takapau* (The Day for Turning Over the Grave Mat)
The *takapau* mat covering the grave is turned over so that the midrib is now uppermost. While the Ariki remains at Vaihare, the entire population goes to

the cemetery and cleans the area, then moves to Vaihare, where the *sā* goes and sits beside the Ariki.

Women open the oven and bring six *sōsoro* cakes to the Ariki. His assistant cuts them into pieces, discarding the crusts at each end before distributing two pieces to each elder, one for the *sā*'s own affines, two to place at the headstone and one each for the shell and coconut water container in honor of the spirits resident in these artifacts. The *sā* gives a female affine an amulet to protect her during the next segment of the rite. He accompanies this woman carrying the conch and water container to the former well at Vaiorapi, where he performs an invocation then draws water to pour over the grave as a libation. (Since the well is now dry, the woman merely fills her shell there from a plastic container.) On an earlier day the man charged with selecting the headstone had already gone to the reef flat behind the island. On day five he waits at the beach at Akare for the *sā* to return from Vaihare and give him a protective amulet before taking the stone and placing it on the grave.

Each day for the next five days, the family returns to Itaimouku, the beachfront location on Takū next to the cemetery, visiting the grave, gardening, and revisiting the grave before returning to their homes at dusk. During this same five-day period, the clan canoe goes out in search of tuna, not so much for its food value as its symbolic significance, since a bountiful catch is a sure sign that the deceased's spirit has safely reached the afterworld of his or her clan. On Nukutoa earlier in the sequence of events, once the corpse had been taken to Takū for burial, the death house's contents were removed, all its doorways were sealed with matting, and the occupants resettled among relatives or at a *pārina* mourning house at the rear of the village. In the normal course of events, the death house remains unoccupied until the first afternoon of the *tukumai* ritual but, on the successful return of the clan tuna canoe during its five-day fishing expedition, the doors are temporarily opened by the principal mourners and the catch is laid outside the seaside end of the house in a public display that proves the deceased's safe arrival in the afterworld. Thereafter it is removed for immediate consumption. This event is occasionally celebrated in new *tuki* songs, as the following two extracts exemplify:

A recently composed *tuki* for the canoe *Ahelo*

Āīē, laka iho taku vaka i tau henua;	My canoe passes by my island;
Te taina tēnei ō ika e tuku i tō hare.	My brother—here are your fish, placed at your house.
Āīē, laka iho soko Helo i Teamarua;	*Ahelo* passes by Nukutoa;
Sēhuri tēnei ō atu e tāraki tō hare.	Sēhuri—here are the tuna that will open your house.

An old composition for the canoe *Marenahau*

Ō ka tuku atu aku ika, e hora i taku hare;	I put my fish there, displayed at my house;
Ka tuku atu aku hailama, tarakina taku hare.	I place there my tuna, thus opening my house.

On return from Vaihare, immediate family members move to the rear of the village and into a house belonging to another family member; this is the *pārina* (the mourning house). The initial phase of mourning takes the form of self-abasement, acknowledging the supremacy of death by a deliberate reversal of normal modes of appearance and conduct—dressing in old clothes, maintaining an unkempt appearance, allowing hair to grow long (and, for men, abstaining from shaving), remaining indoors, and having minimum contact with others. Inside the mourning house female mourners pass the time by weaving mats or plaiting sennit, while men and women may converse and sleep. Several months before the anticipated *tukumai* ritual, these people increasingly occupy their time with composing, teaching, and rehearsing newly composed *tuki* songs in praise of the deceased. An aging person accumulates descendants, and the mourning houses tend to be filled with individuals of grandparental age, as well as younger members of the deceased's nuclear family. This period, lasting several months, is punctuated by periodic assertions of communal inclusiveness, as affines organize mourners to attend *hāunu* parties and there to participate in the drinking and dancing, as well as taking them on the overnight excursions mentioned above to Nukurēkia Island.

If the death occurs off-island, the process of accumulating and disposing of valuables does not occur on Takū Island on day one, but some days or weeks after all the mourners have returned to Nukutoa. Early one morning, members of the *hare ākina* gather outside the house of the deceased (if unmarried or a widow/widower) or the surviving spouse (if married). Inside the house wait representatives of the two lineages comprising the family. Women present large quantities of cotton cloth, and men give pieces of fishing equipment (typically lines and nets); these items are taken into the house and placed on one of two piles, one for the deceased and the other for the survivor; they are later transferred to bags for temporary storage. Women standing in affinal relationship to the deceased (brothers' wives, father's brothers' sons' wives) organize a canoe expedition to the reef to collect clamshells whose contents will be cooked and taken on the following day to the *pārina* for immediate consumption by their relatives there. The people standing in sponsor relationship to the deceased and survivor(s) exchange two bags of clothing and fishing equipment, which are redistributed to the original donors. The deceased's personal property is included in this redistribution. Care is taken to ensure that donors receive something different in either kind or quantity from what they originally provided. The following day, those living in the mourning house will have their hair cropped, eat a meal *(hannai)* of prestige food prepared by the affines, and go to either Tāloki or Sialeva for their *hāunu*, an afternoon of song and dance designed to alleviate their mourning.

The *hāunu* party is organized by the affines, who choose the venue and time, and supply the coconut toddy. Led by their affines, men and women from the mourning houses walk to their respective houses at Tāloki or Sialeva, dressed in new laplaps and daubed with perfume and talcum powder. On arrival they sit silently with heads bowed. Individual affines arrive carrying quantities of laplaps, which they present to the mourners either formally (by asking them to stand and then attaching the garment) or informally (by placing the garment on their lap). Singing begins as the houses fill, and toddy and cigarette sticks are distributed to all present. After some time has elapsed and the singing becomes louder, an organizer will walk along the line of seated mourners, tapping each one on the knee or shoulder to signal that he/she should stand and dance. Although they comply readily, there is usually little initial enthusiasm and they do not join the other dancers in singing as they dance. This attitude invariably changes, however, after the continual consumption of toddy and tobacco, activities in which the mourners are encouraged to indulge. The emphasis is on prolonging the cheering effect for as long as supplies of drink and tobacco last; at one such party in 1998, for example, the men sang a total of fifty-two *tuki* and *lani* songs over five hours while the women in their adjoining house sang and danced thirty *tuki* songs, three complete women's *sau* dances, and a large number of women's *toha* and men's *rue* dances. As much as one hundred liters of toddy, and sometimes more, is consumed on such occasions, occasionally supplemented by bottles of whisky or rum.

In the course of events inside the women's house at a *hāunu,* the deceased's affines are expected to stand and make brief speeches, each one outlining, for example, a piece of significant information (including *kavai* invocations) gained from her father's father. Individuals designated as affines on such an occasion include the wives of the deceased's father, his brothers and sisters, and the deceased's mother and her sisters. In the event of the absence off-island of the mother herself, another may speak on her behalf. At the end of proceedings, the mourners are escorted back to the mourning houses. Men tend to walk back as they arrived—silently and in small groups—whereas women leave as a tight group, singing a *lani* song and led by one of their number beating on a piece of wood or metal, with principal mourners occupying positions in the center of the cluster.

Close family members, whose most senior member is in temporary charge of access to the cemetery itself, make regular visits to the grave, tending its physical condition by weeding or turning over the uppermost mat (see photo 12), or merely sitting beside it in silent contemplation. Such visits progressively decline in frequency from daily to weekly as the distance in time from the death increases and the date of the *tukumai* approaches. Permission from this senior member is necessary for anybody to enter the cemetery area, and such authority remains in force until the occasion of the next death.

For the next several months, participating families ensure that adequate supplies of taro are planted in preparation for the *tukumai.* Responsibility for the timing of this ritual is vested in the most senior member of the deceased's immediate family; although nominally occurring six months after the death— to allow the newly planted taro adequate time to mature—the event may be postponed, for example, to coincide with the commemoration of a fellow clan member or the arrival of expatriate family members wishing to attend.

Either at their own initiative or at the request of others, song composers use this same time to create and organize the rehearsal of one or more *tuki* songs for their first-and-only performance at the *tukumai* (see chapter 4 for details of this creative process).

For close relatives, mourning ends formally only on the removal of the *tau* or *maro*, the piece of cloth family members wear around the neck from the day of the death, and presentation of a quantity of taro to the medium chosen to represent the deceased at the *tukumai*.[25] These acts normally occur several days after the end of the next *tukumai*, that is, after the ritual for the next resident who dies and therefore may occur as much as a year later. Similar food is presented to the medium at that second *tukumai*, the donor typically identifying it as "something for my *maro*." Only after the ritual are the mourners able to leave the mourning houses and resume normal daily activities, having first attended an afternoon of singing and dancing termed *hakamaseu* (disbandment).

The normal timing of the *tukumai* itself may be modified for the benefit of expatriate residents. However, when the *tukumai* starting date is determined, the first visible action occurs in each elder's house, where the *takapau* mat on which each man sleeps is replaced by a newly woven one and the leaf-ends are thrown outside. The mat door covering on the central south-side doorway (*matatkāriki*) of the house (see figure 1), normally kept shut, is opened for an hour or two to reveal the newly woven mat. The public gathering of taro on the second morning of the ritual requires harvest of a significant portion of many garden plots and, to ensure that there are indeed sufficient mature taro for this purpose, hence the six month or more delay after planting, which usually occurs soon after the mourners return from Takū. Each year is commonly punctuated with these commemorative rituals.

In the 1990s as residents left the island in significant numbers initially to work on Bougainville and subsequently shifting to population centers elsewhere in Papua New Guinea, attendance at the *tukumai* of close family members became increasingly constrained by the need to seek leave from paid employment. The logistics of taking leave were complicated by the irregular schedule of boat service to the island, and consequently the community decided the ritual should be postponed to December to coincide with the common period of annual leave. This meant, in effect, that the *tukumai* held at that time commemorated *all* persons dying on or off the island during that year. In the interests of satisfying the technical requirements of the *tukumai* without unnecessary duplication of labor, a clan could hold its ritual jointly with another clan if respective members had died about the same time, while retaining the right to hold the ritual by themselves if they chose to do so. A single ritual could also commemorate more than one deceased person within the same clan, which, again, avoided duplication of labor and materials.

However, by opting to incorporate multiple deaths within a single *tukumai*, the community now places a greater than usual burden of responsibility on its composers, since an unusually large number of new *tuki* songs are required within a period not necessarily longer than that before the ritual for a single person. In 1995 twenty-five new *tuki* were composed for four people; in 1997 the number was seventy-two for thirteen people; and in 1998 forty-five new songs were composed for ten people. The unprecedented mortality rate in 1997 threw virtually the entire adult population into a concentrated period of rehearsals over a two-month period, and much of the village resonated each late afternoon to the low singing of *tuki* as thirteen groups each rehearsed new compositions, most practicing within sight and sound of each other. The spatial arrangement of each group, a core of women ringed by men, was identical to that adopted on the *marae* when the new songs were given their first performance.

A degree of flexibility attends such arrangements. In December 1995, for example, Hare Ata's ritual started four days after the conclusion of Hare Mania's own *tukumai*, whereas in 1997 Hare Ania and Hare Ata held the second day of their *tukumai* jointly for a total of eleven deceased, followed next day by Hare Māsani; the two groups then joining for the period of all-night singing and afternoon dancing. And in November 1998 Hare Ata, Hare Nāoro, and Hare Ania held simultaneous but independent second-day rituals, followed the next morning by that of Hare Māsani. Heavy rain caused the postponement of further activities for forty-eight hours, after which the four clans combined for the all-night singing and set of afternoon dancing sessions.

In the several contexts during the period between death and the end of the mourning—performances of *llū* and *sau* beside the corpse, of *llū* on the *marae*, of a wide variety of dance songs at the *hāunu* parties, and of new and older *tuki* songs and dances during the *tukumai*—song emphasizes ancestral continuities in the face of physical severance. Performances of clan *llū* and the songs of *sau* dances beside the corpse direct attention to ongoing spiritual life after bodily death, reunion with ancestors, and endless freedom to pursue favorite pastimes. For their part, the narratives of successful fishing-related activities embodied in *tuki* songs composed in subsequent months impose sets of positive action statements on the overall negative process of formalized grieving, their cathartic value repeatedly invoked in later months of mourning as the mourners themselves first learn them, then sing them repeatedly. The almost extravagant praise of an individual at death in the poetry of newly composed *tuki* songs when compared with the widely known mediocrity of achievement in life indicates an elevation of status, and certainly nothing negative is invoked in the poetic descriptions of conditions in the afterworld. To the extent that ritual expresses openly things that should never be stated in public, newly composed *tuki* songs, contrary to standards of spoken expression, explicitly and boldly identify by name a recently deceased person and represent the ritual verbalization of corporate grief as they reconstitute personal experiences as public artifacts.

Emergencies

The significance to the whole community of maintaining the integrity of each lineage may be seen in the community's reaction to any act that either disrupts or has the capacity to disrupt that integrity. The social significance of personal injury provides an example. In addition to death, with its attendant five-day ban on gardening and fishing and closure of the *marae* until the nocturnal performance there of *llū* songs, a serious accident, particularly from attack by a predator fish, produces a week-long ban on all fishing and introduces changes to the family's routine. With such serious injuries, adult male members of the victim's lineage gather nightly outside the house where the victim lies for casual low-voiced conversation or merely to show support by their presence. Five dry coconuts are placed outside the house to ward off related injury or sickness to the victim by malevolent spirits. Young women in the family acknowledge the men's presence by serving tea and biscuits at regular intervals. The men's numbers are maintained for the initial five-day period, but taper off thereafter, leaving only the victim's immediate family members. If the injury results from a predator fish attack, the victim is taken immediately to the Ariki's house for treatment and recuperation. On the fifth day of lying on the Ariki's mat in the sacred doorway of Laroteone, all the community's males—from the youngest boy to the oldest man—come to the Ariki's house each carrying a pandanus strip. Either the Ariki himself or senior Hare Ata clan members fashion these into a neckband to guard against any possible repetition of the original attack when the victim leaves the spiritual protection of the Ariki's sleeping mat, in a large-scale dispensation of the Ariki's powers. The house itself is then purified *(hakamārama)* by the provision of green drinking nuts for the appeasement *(hakāitu)* of the spirits resident in its doorways.[26]

A similar concern for the maintenance of family integrity is demonstrated at the ceremonial celebration *(taora)* of the safe return of a first-born child from his or her first period of off-island travel. For this occasion large numbers of giant taro harvested by the father are shared among members of the mother's family.

Concern for potential loss of family integrity is matched by the food-centered celebration at the eventual restoration of such integrity. On the fifth day after a serious injury, the family will assist the victim's father in harvesting ten large giant taro for presentation to their clan elder in gratitude for the victim's safe recovery, and for similar reasons a family will prepare prestige food to welcome home a first-born child after a period of absence. Established treatments for the victims of serious injuries and protective mechanisms for fellow community members allow individual families and the community at large to achieve by these procedures a degree of normality through periods of uncertainty, in the hope that these acts will lead to the reconstitution of the lineage as a fully functional social unit.

Adoption

The practice of adopting infants *(e puru)* is widespread and long established. More than one system coexists. In its most common context, adoption is a means of countering a couple's inability to produce children, on the assump-

tion that the birth parents will eventually produce and retain one or more
other children of their own. Occasionally, however, parents whose own children have married or left home will adopt a child to assist with the kinds
of domestic chores normally allocated to children. In either circumstance,
the practice allows a cultural refinement of normal child-rearing conditions,
whereby more children are able to receive direct parental attention, instruction, and care. Further details are given in Moir (1989, 100–104).

Sponsorship

Even before birth, each resident has two sponsors *(taka),* who may be of either
gender but are not directly related and who are distinguished by the English
terms "Number One" and "Number Two." Although both maintain an ongoing supportive relationship throughout their own lives and that of their charge
(whichever ends first by death), the duties of the primary sponsor are more
extensive and better defined than those of the secondary. The primary sponsor for a first-born child is the father's own primary sponsor, and that of a sec-
ond-born child is the mother's own primary sponsor. Subsequent children are
not automatically sponsored by any particular individual, but their sponsors
are rather determined by parental choice. The choice of secondary sponsor is
less well defined. This role, which is lifelong and carries inbuilt replacement
procedures should a sponsor die, has the effect of increasing the probability
of an individual's healthy childhood by providing him or her access to more
than one source of food. In a small community where the regular supply of
prestige food—fish—may be jeopardized for an extended period by accidental
loss of equipment or even of life, diversification of supply has obvious survival
advantages. For males, sponsorship also improves the chances of being able
to provide satisfactory bride-wealth, spreading the responsibility for the many
hundreds of hours required to produce a large roll of sennit rope as well as
providing the monetary cost of whole bolts of cotton for laplaps. The spreading of a primary sponsor's responsibility over more than one generation thus
sustains family links beyond the lifetime of any single family member and contributes to group solidarity; it also emphasizes the stability of relationships,
whose associated obligations in turn provide for continuity of basic provisions
in the event of a family catastrophe. The existence of a secondary sponsor
appears to function as backup for emergency purposes. Although publicly visible only at crucial moments in the life cycle, sponsorship networks spread an
overarching mantle of support over the entire community.

Interpersonal Relationships

Daily life in both mundane and ritual modes is crisscrossed with a multiplicity of interpersonal relationships that define aggregations (care, loyalty) and
disaggregations (avoidance) within the community.

Ilāmotu (Mother's Brother)

An additional layer of inter-clan material support is provided in the form of the *ilāmotu,* one's "maternal uncle" (MB), particularly for a nephew.[27] The relationship is less visible for a niece and her *ilāmotu,* unless the girl has no father of her own, in which case the uncle will supply her with a significant amount of food and valuables. In the past the girl could theoretically be given a garden plot as her own on reaching adulthood, but the increasing population has forced an end to this demonstration of avuncular support. She does, however, continue to receive specially prepared food and valuables on the occasion of her marriage, and further food gifts of fish and giant taro on the birth of her first child. When dealing with his nephews, the *ilāmotu* tends to give preference to his sister's son over even his own son in matters relating to the distribution of valuables, and he will routinely supply food to his sister's children whenever her husband may be temporarily absent from the island. The intensity of this relationship is well articulated in two lines from a locally composed *hula* song:

| *Te ilāmotu hāsesele;* | My uncle makes a fuss of me; |
| *Lokoī hāsesele lokoī.* | Completely and absolutely spoils me. |

Throughout a boy's years of youth, the *ilāmotu* takes him fishing and to his gardens, not so much to gain extra labor as to teach the associated techniques and skills. And if the boy's mother cannot control her son's unruly behavior, it is the *ilāmotu* who is asked to speak to the lad. The *ilāmotu* also plays a role in his nephew's *tarikai* marriage ceremony, providing fish for the feast. After a nephew's marriage, an *ilāmotu* continues to teach the skills of gardening and fishing, complementing the ongoing teaching of his own father, but the active role of a woman's *ilāmotu* effectively ceases after marriage. Both nieces and nephews will occupy the *pārina* on their *ilāmotu*'s death, and he himself will enter formal mourning on the death of his sister's children.

The *ilāmotu* is a material provider for his sister's children at the time of marriage, a supplier of supplementary food and counseling in time of family need, and a complementary source of instruction on food gathering. The teaching provided during childhood and youth, in particular, ensures continuity of knowledge and skills for survival.

Avoidance

Avoidance relationships take one of two related forms. That of brother-sister is the most common: they may not sit or talk together, touch each other, face each other across a room or house, wear each other's clothes, or enter a house where the other is already sitting. The relationship is characterized as *napa* (embarrassment). Avoidance intensifies after childhood, and is cited as the reason why unmarried men leave their parental home and live in designated single men's houses until marriage. These houses, of which there were formerly five, had individual names. The men did not cook for themselves, relying on their mothers to bring them the best portions of family food each day. The concept of avoidance extends to speech. One does not address one's parent by name, nor one's mother's brother, father's brother, mother's sister, or wife's father, nor does a man address his female affines in the presence of other people. This avoidance is stressed for a man's male relatives, whose attention may appropriately be gained either by direct gaze or by tossing a small stone in front of them but not by calling their name. A man's failure to observe these restrictions specifically for his wife's mother or father is said to indicate lack of respect for his wife. Until the birth of his first child, a man cannot make a direct request to his wife's mother or father, but must ask indirectly via his wife, even for things as small as a cigarette or a fishhook.

There are, however, exceptions to the avoidance of naming and proximity. The ban on uttering the name of the deceased is lifted, in a public context, in song poetry. For the duration of the *tuki* composed in their honor, the dead are named as if they still lived, and they are treated the same as the living in this brief period of egalitarianism intensified by the very frequency with which their names are uttered. Singers standing in an avoidance relationship to such a named person may freely participate in such songs, although close relatives may weep during the rehearsals or at the public performance. On a more formal level, the phenomenon of the *anu haikave*—dancing with one's opposite-sex cousin—is an occasional feature of formal parties at Tāloki or Sialeva. In such circumstances men are not obliged to dance with their real sisters, but rather with their brother's wives, father's sisters, sisters' daughters, or brothers' daughters, all of whom are classified as *haikave*. A woman walks the few meters from the women's communal house into the men's house, takes her chosen man by the hand, leads him to his feet and, still holding him by the hand, takes him into the women's house. Protocol requires submission by all men, even the Ariki. A brief discussion with the man identifies a dance (usually a *rue*) that both he and the *haikave* know, and a separate group of singers begins the song. Other women in the *haikave* relationship get to their feet and join in (photo 13). For their part, men exhibit a wide variety of reactions to the event, from extreme embarrassment and reluctant participation to obvious enthusiasm and skill. Most performances are greeted with shouts of delight from the many women and children crowding in and around the house.

A further exception to the normal avoidance relationship occurs in the *sī haikave* (tuna-fishing with one's opposite-sex cousin/s), a competitive event in which women are included in the personnel but remain seated while the men on board stand and wield their rods for the fish. The same fishing term may also be used to refer to lagoon fishing, specifically for rainbow runners *(kamai)* when the women on board actively participate alongside the men. In either instance, and before the canoe departs, the canoe leader performs what he believes will be the most efficacious ritual to ensure success, but the canoe will be ritually cleansed with seaweed after the event to remove any possible contamination caused by the presence of the woman. This event does not, however, pit individual pairs of cousins against each other as the name might perhaps imply, rather it is between Tāloki and Sialeva, and is based on the aggregate catch of each village section.[28]

Two other forms of name avoidance are practiced. For essentially sentimental reasons several residents are named after older individuals, living or deceased, within the same extended family; one's namesake is termed *hareinoa*. On the death of a *hareinoa,* or indeed of any close relative having the same personal name, an individual immediately and permanently changes his or her name (although immediate family members may privately continue to use the original). Close relatives of the deceased may also choose a new name for the namesake, but restrict its use to themselves.

Name avoidance of a close relative also occurs when that name is also a word or phrase in its own right. For more than twenty years Tommy Atomu has not used the Takū word for fish because this was the name of his brother who died in the 1970s; he substitutes the Tok Pisin word *pis*. In a community heavily dependent on marine resources and therefore frequently using piscine terminology, such a linguistic sacrifice is considerable. The name of the deceased brother of Eros Haramahi was Hareata, also the name of the Ariki's house and clan; both are used frequently in mundane conversation.

PHOTO 13. The *anu haikave* dance in which women force men whom they would normally avoid to dance with them. Temporarily under their control, Ariki Avo dances with his female relatives. *(Richard Moyle)*

Eros now routinely refers to that house by the gloss *te hare lasi* (the large house). And, in a move that was to affect the language of the entire community, the death in 1974 of Mōmoa, brother of Ariki Kaiposu, caused the removal of the word *moa* (chicken) from the vocabulary and the substitution of the term *kuku*.[29]

Shame

The most common phrase parents use to scold a child is *Ē, ku napa ē!* (Hey, for shame!) Shame avoidance is also a social parameter in adult activities, whenever cooperation is temporarily replaced by its antithesis, competition, which always occurs within clearly defined and accepted boundaries of time and place. The public display of personal ability through competitions is shaped by each competition's degree of formal organization. Parents, for example, provide prestige foods—baked vegetables and a choice fish rather than the normal diet of rice and tinned food—for their children at an end-of-year communal meal at the school. And there is no shortage of men to participate in a canoe race or fishing competition. The motivation behind both activities is termed a kind of avoidance—the avoidance of shame. Thus, a man competes at sea *ki sē napa i tana avana* (to avoid being shamed in front of his wife).

Tama Hakasere *(Special Child)*

The *tama hakasere* or *tama sere* (special child) appears to have been an institutionalized position, now obsolete, within the family. This was typically a son who was given special status: he did no work, fishing or gardening, but simply stayed at home, eating and resting.[30] Such people occasionally had songs composed in their honor by spirits and, although the poetry did not include the individual's personal name, the local audience was aware of his identity. The term is no longer used conversationally but occurs occasionally in songs as a poet seeks to artistically elevate the status of a child who has survived his mother's death, eg,

Nau tani atu ki taku taina	I cried to my sister
Ki purutia taku manu ka noho ma koe.	To care for my "bird" as your own;
Nau tani atu ki Huata	I cried to Huata
Ki purutia taku tama sere ka noho ma koe.	To care for my special child as your own.

Indeed, one *tuki* song imagines its composer's post-death status as equivalent to the beloved child of the sea deity Pakeva:

Uāiē, ku noho nau ma tama sere te hare;	I stay at home like a special child;
Uāiē, ku noho nau ma tama sere Pakeva.	I stay at home like Pakeva's special child.

Cooperation and Egalitarianism

In technical terms, Takū's social system represents a compound structure with periodic complex features, individual households catering to their own small-scale subsistence needs but dependent on labor from other households for certain large-scale activities. Family members work their own gardens, where they plant, weed, and harvest taro and giant taro; they travel to the smaller islands to collect firewood, mat and thatch materials, and coral sand for flooring. Individual family members carry out minor maintenance on their houses and canoes, and gather resources such as bêche-de-mer and shark fin purely for sale off-island. By contrast, heavy jobs require mutual dependence among families. Regularly and normally without being asked, men help each other lift canoes on and off their storage blocks at Tāloki and Sialeva, and families cooperate periodically to undertake major house renovations and launch new tuna-fishing canoes.

Of the situations requiring coordinated action, fishing is the most common, since it takes several men to carry the canoe from its storage place to the water, stake out a net and drive the fish into it, or travel to a communal spear-fishing location, as well as returning with the catch and putting up the canoe. Men from more than one canoe typically join forces to deploy large nets: specifically for turtle and mullet, which are difficult to catch unaided, and also for any fish trapped at low tide in the small lagoon near Nukutapu Island and the area between Nukutoa and Nukuāhare islands. Although some men frequently fish alone, and a small sailing canoe is easily handled by one man, men fish most often two or three to a canoe, and those sharing a canoe may not necessarily belonging to the same family. Men who fish together will have established a relationship of good fellowship, a bond described as "those able to share jokes" (tausua).[31]

The men who participate in a fish drive immediately receive an equal share of the catch.[32] Only a very few typically smoke their own surplus in an attempt at storage, and those who do keep the fish only a limited number of days before consuming them. When there is a superabundance of caught fish, everyone is free to take away as much as they want, but the last occurrence of this was sufficiently rare that it became the basis of a tuki song praising the fishing leader. On a smaller scale, when a tuna-fishing canoe first beaches or when the catch is laid out briefly for public display, anyone may theoretically take away as many fish as required for immediate family consumption; but this unspoken offer is only seldom accepted since to do so constitutes an admission of the father's incompetence to adequately provide for his family. The offer preserves the principle of egalitarianism but makes its actual exercise optional.

The highly perishable nature of any fish catch makes any attempt to accumulate surplus food pointless on a long-term basis, and since most individuals own or share a large number of serviceable and fully equipped canoes, status differences based on unequal possession of material goods are minimal. Similarly, the Takū practice of bride-wealth payments ensures the circulation of luxuries among families. Because islanders cannot accumulate surplus foodstuffs and subsequently rely on the continuous availability of fish does not, however, imply a constant threat of imminent starvation. The easily accessible food wealth in the encircling maritime environment represents a storehouse they consider to be of infinite and enduring capacity. Additionally, the recent accumulation of material wealth, for example the stock held in family-owned trade stores, is considered isolating rather than desirable, since it is by sharing what is at hand that the community achieves its equilibrium and maintains its claim in turn to share in others' windfalls.

If weather conditions, bait supply, and other factors permit it, a man will continue fishing until his canoe is full to the point of swamping or until the fish have stopped biting. Although many *tuki* songs speak enthusiastically of canoes returning heavily laden with tuna or other prestige fish, most canoes come back to land because the fish have run out.

The idea of territoriality does not factor in since the islanders recognize a continual abundance of stocks in the waters around them. Fishermen routinely visit a set of predetermined and named locations within the lagoon, trolling in search of baitfish en route to their selected hand-lining spot. From Nukutoa Island, canoes are visible at virtually any point within the lagoon, and the men tend to note the identity of canoes as they depart, the direction they take, and the position where they eventually anchor; this information, depending on the size of the catch, may be recalled for later exploitation. Both the lagoon and the ocean beyond it form a home range whose fishing grounds are equally available to all, but a man will move from his favorite spot to keep its location secret if he sees the approaching canoe of a different family. By contrast, more recent bans on specific types of fishing (eg, on nets, spear guns, and torches between Sauma and Teuasei, and on catching turtles between Sauma and Matākau) appear to be based on a policy of conservation.

Since the creation of the two village sections, locations where large-scale operations such as netting could occur have been delineated separately. The reef channel called Te Ava i Loto is considered the dividing point: Sialeva has access to the reef south of this channel as far as Nukutoa and including the lagoon area off Takū Island, whereas Tāloki has exclusive access to the reef north of this channel and right around to the northern end of Nukutoa and including the lagoon areas of Nukurekia and all the small islands. Individual men may still fish wherever they like.

Equality of opportunity on land derives in part from the lack of specialized technology or utensils used in Takū gardening or building. And at sea the islanders—at least canoe owners—do not universally accept the outboard motor over the paddle and sail as a guarantee of greater success, although the greater ease of travel is undeniable and use of outboard motors is now routine for tuna fishing.

Vegetable foods are regularly and predictably available, but large fish, although high in the optimal ranking of foods, are caught only occasionally. When obtained, however, such catches provide food in greater quantities than a fisherman's own household can immediately consume and are therefore distributed among kin. This means that the successful fisherman's family gains rights to share in the other family's unpredictable abundances in future. Since all people are expected to behave reciprocally *(tokonaki)* toward their kin, any instances of nonsharing are strongly criticized and, according to story, may invoke supernatural retribution. The heavy dependence on fish, not surprisingly, produces a longing for it *(kurumiti)* when an extended period of bad weather confines men to shore.

The apportionment of a catch from group fishing (for example, netting mullet, or a fishing competition) into piles of equal size is based on the idealized equality of participation. In fact, a man's mere presence at a group fishing expedition earns him the right to an equal share of the catch. And on land, attendance at a house building or tuna-canoe launching also qualifies him to receive acknowledgment in food form on a scale equal to that of those contributing labor to the project. For most men, however, attendance means participation, and even the oldest can find themselves a job commensurate with their physical abilities, such as cutting and winding lengths of sennit for thatching or lashing struts. Only the Ariki and Pure refrain from contributing labor anywhere else but on their own properties, although both routinely dignify the occasions with their presence. House building involves much of the community's adult population since the labor needed to complete the task in one day cannot be supplied from within a single family. The guiding operational principle here is again egalitarianism, since the skills for the job are possessed by "all" the men and can therefore be applied to any and all individual instances. Even one's presence constitutes confirmation of social identity and legitimate incorporation into the community.[33]

This same principle does not, however, deny recognition of superiority in particular individual achievements and skills. In fishing generally, and most overtly in fishing competitions, men strive to make the best choice of fishing location and time, equipment, and technique. Likewise, in canoe racing canoe dimensions, choice of crew, and the correct choice of sail for prevailing conditions are recognized factors of considerable significance. In dance, too, the selection of individuals as *tama haimako* line leaders or identification as *tihana* (lithe) is based on the notion of primacy among equals.[34]

In quite another sense, competition has the effect of defining short-term egalitarianism insofar that it demarcates clearly those with whom one is *not* cooperating. Since competition is by definition short-term and limited to specific organized events, and its scale is similarly restricted by predetermined and publicly accepted factors of place and personnel, competitions such as canoe races, fishing, Independence Day sports events, and even the dancing by Tāloki and Sialeva at the school concert and on the *marae*—all cast the key cultural principle of egalitarianism into sharp relief by the presentation of its opposite.[35]

For male or joint competitions, women dress as male police and magistrates and administer short-term control over the competitors, forcing them to be interrogated about their performance, submitting them to the public humiliation of face painting if they fail to achieve the predetermined minimum catch (photo 14) and requiring them to dance even if they are known to be incompetent performers. The overtness and extent of the temporary reversal of gender-based roles ensures general entertainment. Women take responsibility for ensuring equal allocation of the edible proceeds of group activities; they construct the long lines of taro portions at each *tukumai*, routinely sort a large catch into piles of equivalent value (photo 15), and deliver a packet of rice to the house of each man assisting in a house building.[36]

At the weekly drinking parties at Tāloki and Sialeva and at formal gatherings to provide temporary relief to mourners, the principle of egalitarianism is clear. Anyone attending may join in the singing and dancing, and any individual is free to start the singing.[37] All those attending have the option of drinking alcohol from the same cup (although some may bring their own utensil), and normally each man contributes to the supply of toddy. (When women and men gather in adjacent houses, the toddy is first taken to the men's house, then, by general agreement, a quantity of it is conveyed to the women for their consumption.) When singing starts, all those present share

PHOTO 14. A fisherman suffers the humiliation of having his face daubed by women. *(Hamish Macdonald)*

the melody and, when dancing begins, all dance the same actions simultaneously. At Tāloki and Sialeva there is no "head" seat or "lead" position inside
the houses during dancing or singing. Indeed, it is only on the *marae* during
line dances (such as *takere, paki, hoe, sakitao, hula*) that specific individuals
known as *tama haimako* are spatially distinguished during the *taki* portion of
the dance, and even then all dancers continue to perform the same actions
simultaneously.

PHOTO 15. After the judging at a competition, women sort the total
catch into piles of equal size. *(Richard Moyle)*

In a related context, the party that normally follows house building discharges the house owner's obligations to those who provided labor for the construction. Additionally, but less apparent to an outsider, the celebration is a means to other, broader social ends, since it affirms equality by offering all who attend equal access to food, alcohol, and tobacco, and it also affirms the shared social responsibilities of the house owner's lineage members by recruiting them to acquire, prepare, and serve the food. Since affirmation must rest on the preexistence of the values being celebrated, the party demonstrates behavior required by the social principles underpinning island life in general.

The domestic mode of food production is principally directed toward the household's internal requirements, including norms of assistance to parents and affines. Even when the village shifts to ritual behavior at a *tukumai*, with each household contributing a predetermined number of taro to a single large pile, the scale of food gathering for each household again points to the principle of egalitarianism.[38] This occurs through the reallocation of the taro into lots of equal size for removal and consumption by each household. The formation of the big taro pile emphasizes a singleness of focus for the enactment of the ritual, and the subsequent distribution symbolizes the comprehensiveness and equality of the pile's constituent parts (photos 16, 17).

Redistribution, the systematic movement of goods to an administrative center and their reallocation by a central authority, occurs at different levels. The

PHOTO 16. At a *tukumai* for several members of Hare Ata clan, clusters of taro baskets for each of the dead are initially assembled, together with cartons of tinned meat and fish, before being heaped into single piles. *(Richard Moyle)*

wives of individual fishermen or groups of men who have fished together collect the catch and pile it at the beach yard of one of their number before distributing it among themselves, and women of a deceased's clan harvest large
quantities of taro and present them in a single pile in front of their elder's
house before separating them into household lots of equal size. Despite differences in the identity of those responsible for managing these activities, the
principle of equality remains.

The equality of treatment of the dead assumes local residence at the time
of death, a situation somewhat less prevalent now than in the past, since the
seriously sick may go to Buka or Port Moresby for treatment. Most women
choose to give birth at a hospital off-island, and the present number of expatriate residents is probably greater than at any time in the past. The institution of the *tukumai* is, therefore, subject to these new circumstances, and the
response of the community has been to allow off-island dead to be included
in the *tukumai* of a fellow clan member, but not their own separate observances. Neither Papua New Guinea law nor the practicalities of transportation
to the atoll allow the repatriation of a Takū resident's corpse, and the body is
simply buried in the local cemetery.

On Takū Island itself, the same series of rites occurs on the death of any
resident other than a new-born baby or an elder.[39] The family's seclusion
on the island lasts five days after each individual death, and the period of
mourning back on Nukutoa is not shortened or lengthened because of the

PHOTO 17. On obtaining the Ariki's approval, women divide the pile into family lots
of equal size. *(Richard Moyle)*

age, gender, or status of the deceased.[40] The *tukumai* is, thus, an institution for the commemoration of the dead without differentiation on the basis of age, gender, or status.

As an operating principle, egalitarianism appears to offer the greatest survival opportunities to the greatest number of people. In a small society in which the economic contribution of individuals can be crucial to the physical well-being of an entire family, adoption and sponsorship spread responsibility and reduce the potential for economic difficulties at the family level. Group economic activities both apportion equally the fruits of labor to all participants and produce a gender-based dichotomy wherein men are providers and women distributors and processors. In the performing arts, cooperation and egalitarianism are embodied in temporal simultaneity and in the creation of prearranged sets of actions that participants choose to perform together, whether as song or dance. To expand on a suggestion from Shore (1996, 114), song and dance evoke the impulse for creating order and setting boundaries by their predetermined and rehearsed sequences of sounds and movements, while at the same time permitting sufficient individualism in the overall quality of appearance as to evoke audience responses of admiration, excitement, and humor, embodying the human flair for play. Song in turn absorbs the protocols of incorporation in several linked ways: by group singing; by unison singing; by the textual inclusion of named, living individuals; by performing predetermined actions on the *marae* at a set time, in triple-bounded configuration; and by balancing grief for the dead with support for their survivors.

Fishing

The social value of established forms of fishing and a corresponding disdain of certain European methods are demonstrated most clearly during shark fishing. The most elementary time and motion study would confirm that letting large bait down in the main channel will immediately attract sharks, and this could be accomplished most safely from a boat rather than a canoe. But shark catching is not governed by principles of operational efficiency, nor is its purpose simply to provide large quantities of edible fish in a short period of time. Not even the high price fetched in Buka for sales of shark fin, destined for an Asian market, is sufficient incentive to abandon the local method, though it is undeniably more time consuming, more dangerous, and fraught with the possibilities of failure. Shark is a prestige fish not so much because of the superiority of its flesh as a food source as the revered relationship with the supernatural a successful expedition demonstrates. Since the category of prestige fish known collectively as *ikatau* cannot be caught without supernatural support, it is not the success alone but also the method of its attainment that is prized. The means here takes priority over the ends.

A man's achieved status derives from distinction in two activities: canoe building and fishing for prestige fish. For the one, he receives the label *tīhuna* (master builder), and for the other, *tautai* (master fisherman). Both empha-size consistency of performance rather than a single spectacular attainment; *tīhuna* indicates regular success in canoe races or able handling in adverse sea conditions, and *tautai* indicates regular catches of the three prestige fish: tuna, large sharks, and oil fish.[41]

When pursuing prestige fish, the *tautai* does not work by his own talent alone, but recognizes the need for assistance from his ancestors who, although dead, are willing to assist if appropriately invoked. Those invocations in turn have prescribed content and context. For the fisherman, then, life represents a balance of personal skills and endeavor on the one hand, and the assistance of ancestors correctly invoked on the other. As long as the social eminence of the *tīhuna* and *tautai* continue to be celebrated formally in songs extolling their achievements and informally in requests for their advice, and as long as the basis for eminence is not simply the end product but also the means of obtaining it, Takū seem likely to continue their emphasis on verbal and pro-cedural formulas, and the belief system underpinning that locus will endure.

Canoe Construction

The old canoe-building site at Tāloki was abandoned in the 1990s when the need for storage space for completed canoes forced a move to the rear of the island where three or four craft are under construction at any time. At Sialeva the entire headland is occupied by some fifty canoes stored on blocks or under construction, and there appears to be little space for any more. Although the labor of canoe building is the prerogative of younger and mid-dle-aged men, Sialeva is also where older men spend part or all of each day, watching the work, talking, or sleeping. People traveling to or from their gar-dens on Takū Island normally walk through the headland, and this provides additional opportunities for casual social contact.

All the logs made into canoes come to Takū by drifting, reputedly from New Ireland; some arrive complete with root systems intact, but others already sawn and trimmed have presumably fallen from a logging ship. Protocol requires that, when a log is sighted inside the reef, the Ariki must be notified, and it is he who decides its fate, based on who at the time has no canoe of his own and is known to want one. When ownership of the log has been determined, the entire able-bodied adult community is summoned to pull it from the water up onto the flat land to Sialeva. Several ropes are attached and, as the hauling starts, either Ariki Avo or Siwa Kaiposu stands at the rear and strikes the log with the base of a coconut leaf, singing as he does so the *soro rākau* (log-haul-ing song). Ariki Avo's version of the song is as follows:

Tau faka-samoa, tau faka-samoa	Pull like a Samoan, pull like a Samoan
Ka pō, iōiō. Ē!	I strike, thus, hey!
Takū vaka ni tā te motu Savaiki	My canoe was carved on the island of Savaiki

Se uli lalana, se mātamea	Let an *uli* fish or a *mātamea* fish lift it up
Ē tautau pēnā nei ē. Ē!	Let it be as dry wood, hey!
Ē sura mai tana ika, ma se ika,	His fish appeared. What fish?
Ma se ikapō ma te araimea, ma se tusi, ma se lona, ma se kavakava	An *ikapō* and a starfish and a *tusi* and a snapper, and a *kavakava*
Takū vaka ka sē hakarohatia nei ē. Ē!	My canoe is not yet recognized. Hey!
Ko au, ko au, ko au ko Hiuanekeneke.	Come, come, let [the spirit] Hiuanekeneke come.
Ka rō mārama se tai hurahura	Let a rising sea become clear
Ka sasana iho i sana te aumi nei ē. Ē!	Let the sea churn in its wake, hey!
Ma puna ia Tautunu, ma puna ia Kauraro,	Let [the spirits] Tautuna [Tatunu] rise up, let Kauraro rise up,
Ma puna ia Kaumisamisa	So Kaumisamisa can rise up
Ka sasana iho te sopo a te mārama nei ē. Ē!	Let it churn in the rising moon, hey!
Ka sasana iho te hiti a te mārama nei ē. Ē!	Let it churn after the moon rises, hey!
Ko au, ko au, ko au ana numuri, ana numea	I, I, I am its rear end and its front end,
E tātuki ana mata.	Whose face I now strike with a blow.
Ē parapara nei ē. Ē!	[So that the tree's wood] is softened. Hey!
Te ua ni tō anapō ka sē mau.	Last night's rain means that it is not immovable.
Hati mai te pū a Rata	It comes at [the spirit] Rata's trumpet call
Hati mai te pū a Sinata	It comes at [the spirit] Sinata's trumpet call
Nā sorona te vaka e mānuanu i tai.	The canoe leaves a track as it slides in the water.
Hīa oku, hīa oku mauna, pōkia mau.	How many? How many of my mountains are being hauled?
Sikitau ē, nā si ki te ariki	You birds, assemble before the Ariki
Papae lou ake nā	Gather together like that
Tiketike mua, tiketike muri	Swivel the log from the front, swivel it from the rear
Tikoi a tikoi te kainatā mauna, pōkia mau.	You continually hop about but this "food" is hard to eat. It's done!

The *soro* was last performed in 1997, when all men, women, and children pulled up a log at Sialeva, where it was found to be large enough to yield the hulls of two canoes.

Hauhau *(Canoe-lashing Ritual)*

Carving of a new tuna-fishing canoe takes several months of daily labor by the owner and a small group of men from his immediate family. Using part or all of a drifting log for the hull and sometimes also the float, and finding local timbers for the various parts of the outrigger, the builders are frequently joined by one or more old men who, despite their physical infirmity, are happy to maintain a nominal association with this long and honorable tradition by their mere presence in the yard and occasional comments.

Attachment of the outrigger to the hull and the first launch occur on the same day, and the two occasions attract the attendance of most of the men in the community by word of mouth. The more experienced men in the owner's clan attach the central outrigger strut on the hull with the greatest care and often only after long discussions, since the position and angle of this pole will determine the spatial relationship between the float and the hull, a factor crucial to the canoe's overall performance. Attachment of the other parts of the outrigger and the lashing of struts to the float are performed simultaneously by several small groups of men. Men not actively engaged in the work are offered food prepared by the owner's family and then immediately relieve those at work, so that all will have eaten before the canoe is launched. When the outrigger and float have been attached, a dozen or more men carry the canoe to the water, where a senior clan member waits, dressed formally with plaited leaf headband, leaf armbands, and carrying a supply of sacred (kaisuru) leaves. As the other men stand silently on the beach watching, the senior man walks around the floating canoe, rubbing the blessed leaves along the hull and also at specific locations on the canoe before attaching them to parts of the outrigger. As he performs these actions, he constantly utters invocations to attract the benign attention of clan and ancestor spirits and so ensure the canoe's success and safety. The entire process is called hau.[42] On each of the following five days, the new canoe will go out in search of prestige fish, preferably tuna.

The average working life of canoes is less than five years, given the effects of untreated timber and sea worm, as well as damage caused during adverse weather conditions. Unlike the smaller craft, however, tuna-fishing canoes are not cut up for firewood because of their close association with a deceased relative—the corpse transported to Takū Island on the family canoe. Instead, when their condition deteriorates, they may be fashioned into bed frames on Takū or simply leaned against a house until rotten.

Associated Rituals

Although the return of a tuna canoe from ocean fishing normally attracts little attention from those who see it approaching with its crew sitting motionless and silent, two circumstances will generate instant and widespread interest along the foreshore. If, instead of facing the bow, the crew faces slightly toward the outrigger, this position is understood to signal an outstanding catch. A more common means of signaling unusual success readily gains the attention of many people because it is audible. The term hakaiō (literally, "to shout Hiō hē") denotes the call made by the crew of a successful canoe as they enter the lagoon from the ocean fishing grounds. As they make their way back to Nukutoa, the crew sings their clan's tuna-fishing *tuki* songs, and the sound carries far ahead of them, eventually to those on shore.[43] This singing is itself referred to in several *tuki* songs, for example:

Te haikave noho	My female cousins sit
hakarono ki te hakaiō taku vaka nā e;	listening to the call from my canoe;
Manila ma Tekaso noho	Manila and Tekaso sit
hakarono ki te hakaiō Kisokau nā	listening to the call from *Kisokau.*

The sung announcement of fishing success is not confined to *tuki* songs or to tuna, but may be used for any catch of unusual size.

Although outstanding fishing success, especially for prestige fish, is typically attributed to correct adherence to protocols involving contact with the supernatural world, a far wider array of data may be invoked in cases of fishing failure, eg, the incompatible personalities of the fishermen, any preexisting unresolved domestic problems of one or more of the crew, ignorance or incorrect use of sacra and breach of protocol. In other words, potentially infinite justifications exist for fishing failure, without recourse to an outright admission of technical inadequacy, procedural ignorance, or failure of the deities to respond.

In all other forms of fishing and for all other non-prestige types of fish caught, the responsibilities of men cease when the canoe reaches land, since it is the duty of women to carry the catch ashore and there to divide it into piles of equivalent value before taking it away to their respective houses for preparation and cooking. The polarity of male:female :: sea:shore :: raw:cooked :: acquisition:distribution/processing is particularly clear in this context (see also Feinberg 1988b).

Canoe Racing

Canoe races *(tuata)* are regularly held in the lagoon during the season of the southeast trade wind *(anāke);* this allows the craft to sail either a return course to a named location in the southwest (eg, Tepae), or a one-way race in strong wind to a marked location to the southwest, or a two- or three-point course in clockwise movement around the lagoon. The tacking capabilities of the canoes are such that they cannot maneuver properly during the northwest trade winds *(laki),* effectively limiting the races to the mid-year period. Each race is sponsored, typically by one or two men who buy the materials that will constitute the prize pool, and this considerable financial outlay is balanced by the privilege of choosing the date and time of the start, and the route to be sailed. In normal circumstances, a casual comment of intention made during a party or informal gathering is sufficient to generate the rumor of an impending competition and send men checking their canoes and sails. At least one day's notice is given, based on considerations of tide times and weather conditions. All participating canoes are beached side by side at Sia-leva awaiting the sponsor's announcement of the course and his call for the race to start. The sponsor himself participates but ensures that the rest of the fleet has a head start of half a minute or more before setting sail himself, to avoid any possible criticism of unfairness (photo 18). Although races involving the large tuna canoes continued until the 1980s, only three of these had a set of sails in 1994, and by 1998 this number had dropped to one. All races now involve only the smaller craft, of which approximately twenty-five possess sails. During my three-month period of fieldwork in 1994, four races were held, involving 18, 22, 26, and 23 canoes, respectively; more than twenty races were reportedly held during 1998.

One measure of the significance of fishing-related activities in Takū culture is the frequent use of the poetic phrase *taku vaka* (my canoe) in the active song repertoire. It occurs 848 times in the recorded sample, over five times more often than the second most common phrase—*taku tama* (my child). The conceptual importance of the canoe in a generic sense, as opposed to a particular canoe, comes through in the inclusion of a canoe name in fewer than 50 percent of instances. Whether composed by men or women or the spirits of men or women, song poetry is infused with images of canoes in use for travel or, more frequently, as the key instrument of sea-based sustenance. To that extent, in both everyday life on the atoll and the idealized world depicted in song poetry, the canoe stands as a pervasive and enduring emblem of physical and cultural survival.

PHOTO 18. The start of a canoe race heading toward the southwest sector of the lagoon. *(Richard Moyle)*

Games and the Community School

The establishment of the Mortlock Community School in 1960 would affect the lives of both children and adults on the island in a variety of ways. For adults, the daily absence of young family members normally assigned duties of baby-sitting, gathering and carrying back small bundles of foods or light building materials from Takū and the other islands, or canoe maneuvering while the men drift-fished on the open ocean, placed additional responsibilities on older children and on adults themselves. School fees and uniforms represented a new drain on family cash resources where adults either produced saleable goods from the island itself (copra, shark fin, bêche-de-mer) or worked at paid jobs elsewhere in the country. For the children themselves, school introduced the novelties of formal learning and enforced discipline by nonfamily members, of the acquisition of a foreign language, and exposure to nonindigenous subjects and modes of expression.

Included in the curriculum, apparently since the school's early days, European games are now identified as the cause of the decline in popularity of most local games. (One notable exception is *sino*, walking on one's hands, which continues to be popular among boys and younger girls and is featured as a competitive adult activity in Independence Day festivities.) Many of the traditional Takū games incorporate sung or rhythmically recited lines that precede or accompany group or individual actions, and such was their apparent popularity one or two generations ago that adults can recite texts they may not have sung for more than half a century. Although these pastimes are not part of the adult community's repertoire of performed items, I include a summary in chapter 5 for purposes of comprehensiveness.

The school curriculum does provide for the teaching of "culture," and apart from the annual outing to the wildlife sanctuary at Nukurekia (normally out of bounds to visitors), academic (school) and cultural (community) activities remain quite separate. This separation is bridged temporally at the annual end-of-year concert, an all-day large-scale event, at least by local standards. Adult participation in this event operates at three levels. One element—the midday communal meal (commonly known as the "big lunch") eaten on the school grounds by children and their parents—is a competition in all but name. As soon as the concert date is announced, mothers descend on the island's stores and queue up to make bulk purchases of packaged sweets and the more expensive tinned foods, to demonstrate their strength of affection for their children. Parents harvest taro and giant taro from their gardens to make *tarotā* or other formal dishes that serve as the main element of the meal; one or more of the family chickens are slaughtered and prepared. Fathers fish outside the reef on the night before the concert, hoping for an impressively large single fish or a large quantity of smaller ones to supplement the feast. In addition to providing food for this meal, adults constitute the audience for the entire concert and even perform selected numbers.

The concert typically includes a mixture of traditional and European music. In recent years, church groups have begun performing synchronized motions to commercial cassettes of American religious songs, but these performances have been greeted with silent bewilderment by the audience. Both Adventist and United church members also enter choirs singing a bracket of songs in English.[44] Because most teachers are nonlocal, the "traditional" concert items are taught by parents in evening sessions spread over two or more weeks.

The 1999 concert was preceded by an award ceremony at which the United Church performed a series of dances to recorded gospel music, to the annoyance of Ariki Avo, who briefly stopped proceedings with shouts of frustration at being the Ariki but unable to control the Christian content of the school event, content that he neither appreciated nor wanted. Somewhat apprehensively, the award ceremony continued without further incident. The six-hour concert itself contained some thirty-two performances, mostly *rue, toha,* and *hula* dances, many of Nukumanu origin. Several of the groups had been taught by individual men or women, and these same individuals provided the singing and drumming for the dances. As in past years, the dances attracting the loudest and longest audience applause were *rue* whose dancers displayed the vigorous and lithe qualities conveyed in the term *tīhana.* Church groups again participated in the concert introducing an innovation in the form of *hula* dances with Christian poetic content, such as the following:

Nukutoa e, nā uata i te Bible ē.	Nukutoa—it's the work of the Bible.
Aloha īē, nā uata i te Atua.	It saddens me, working for God.
Tū hoi pēlā, noho nau no manatu ē	That's my position, I keep thinking about it—
Nā uata i te Bible ē.	It's the work of the Bible.
Moe nau i te pō, nau sē lavā i te moe ē	I wanted to sleep at night but I couldn't
Nā uata i te Atua ē.	Working for God.

By the 2001 concert, both churches had expanded the customized dances their adherents performed to include boys' *rue.* The language is said to be that of Nukumanu; the following is typical:

Ō mai, ō mai te henua ē;	Come on, come on, people;
Ō mai, ō mai Nukutoa ē.	Come on, come on, Nukutoa.
Senisi senisi senisi nā ola ē;	Change, change, change their lives;
Senisi senisi senisi nā ola ē.	Change, change, change their lives.
Hātina hātina hātina mātou ē;	We'll pressure, pressure, pressure;
Hātina hātina hātina mātou ē;	We'll pressure, pressure, pressure;
Hāvela hāvela hāvela nā lotu ē;	To make the churches come faster, faster, faster;
Hāvela hāvela hāvela Rima Zone ē.	To make the "Rima Zone" churches come faster, faster, faster.

By the end of 2001 the Ariki's position had also moderated somewhat. In a recorded interview Avo noted:

> These days—with religion and traditions—I think they're all acceptable. But what I don't want is for Christianity to come and cause the traditions to die. I know that one part of traditions is good, and can act, for example, to cure sickness, and to cure people. In the old days, we had no doctors—all we had were our traditions—and they have lasted until today. At present, the churches come to me, and I tell them that Christianity and tradition must be able to coexist. It's all up to me. If you want to come to this island, then you can certainly come. You can come and set yourself up, but you must get my permission first. If I approve, then you can set yourself up, but if not, then you'll have to leave. As for these churches, if I see that they're having a bad effect, I'll destroy their buildings. And I am able to destroy them all because this is my island.

At present, then, in the Ariki's opinion, his own personal authority remains unchanged by the presence and activities of the churches, who simply represent another social unit within the community, and therefore are susceptible to the traditional forms of control he exercises by virtue of being the Ariki. Although they have to date confined their influence to their own adherents, the churches remain dedicated to another form of authority, and the social and political relationship between the churches and the Ariki continues to develop.

The school's daily routine begins with the singing of the national anthem followed by the North Solomons Provincial anthem, both in English. And on at least one occasion in the 1990s, a teacher composed a song to mark a special event—the arrival of Michael Ogio, government minister for the atolls on a familiarization tour of the region. The school's song, sung to the melody of the well-known Fijian song "Isa Lei," ran as follows:

Nukutoa tau henua tauareka	Nukutoa, my beautiful home,
Tū sokoia i loto te moana.	Stands alone in the ocean.
Nau aroha nā sopo atu a te lā	I love it when the sun rises
Vāruna nā nui Nukutoa.	Above Nukutoa's coconut palms.
Nau aroha tau henua Nukutoa;	I love my home Nukutoa;
Nau ku hano no noho i lā henua	I go and stay on the islands
Nā kaute nā manoni tau henua.	Among my island's fragrant hibiscus.
Nukutoa tau henua tauareka.	Nukutoa, my beautiful home.

Of interest was the decision to use language said to be imitating that of Nukumanu, as if it were a contemporary *lani* or *hula* composition. Additionally it is interesting that the song poetry was not translated for Mr Ogio, and one can only assume that he was favorably impressed with the act of performance if not its poetic content.

The *Marae*

Although now abandoned for more than a century, some features of the ritual arena on Takū Island remain visible. It is some 50 meters long and 20 meters wide, bordered by thin coral slabs about 30 centimeters high. One larger slab stands where, according to oral tradition, the image of Pukena was erected (photo 19). The houses of the Ariki and Pure appear to have bordered the area, which carried the name Sarati.

PHOTO 19. Coral slabs forming part of the *marae* structure at Sarati, abandoned for more than a century. *(Hamish Macdonald)*

The first assembly area on Nukutoa lay at its southern end, next to a European-operated trade store, but its use appears to have been limited to Christmas parties, partly because of the relatively small number of residents. The present *marae* is an unbounded area of coral sand, which in secular life forms part of the wide road separating the second and third rows of houses and runs from one end of the island to the other. The *marae* is visually indistinguishable from this road, but lies immediately adjacent to the Ariki's house, Hare Ata. It has no specific name and is normally referred to simply as *marae*, or sometimes *te marae* Avo (Avo's *marae*) after the name of the present Ariki, or *te marae nā mātua* (the elders' *marae*), since assembly there requires the presence of all five clan heads. Use of this *marae* is said to date to the 1930s when the first rows of houses were built in accordance with Jock Goodson's directions. But even after Goodson's departure locals did not reorganize the housing arrangement and the *marae* remained in its original location.

Although the *marae* is the venue for all community-wide rituals, and although those rituals are believed to be attended also by a host of invisible spirits, the arena itself carries no intrinsic sanctity of a permanent nature. Most of the time the space is used by women to sun-dry pandanus leaves or coconut fiber, and children routinely incorporate the area into their play activities. By day and night, community members freely walk across its length and breadth. Even on the occasion of rituals, the transition from secular to sacred space is seamless, determined more by the positioning of bodies than physical boundaries, as those attending carry chairs or stools and initially place them next to other family members in one or more rows around the perimeter. The elders, spirit mediums, and ritual assistants are visually distinguished, by both their regalia and predetermined positions at the northern end of the *marae;* all other adults dress in normal attire (photo 20). Children do not attend the all-night singing and dancing of the *tukumai,* but may sit on the ground during daytime dancing if they are interested in the proceedings; many choose not to attend. However, the timing and nature of events occurring on the *marae* are strictly controlled. It is the Ariki's prerogative to approve the start of an event by a spoken affirmation to an assistant and to end it with the command *Tuku ē* (let it finish).

The presence of the Ariki as prerequisite to formal assembly on the *marae* is given audible form by the requirement that the area be "opened" by singing (see photo 20), specifically by singing a song associated with the Ariki's clan, Hare Ata. Afternoon dance performances as part of the *tukumai* complex constitute an exception to this general rule; on those occasions, the clan identity of the person whose death is being commemorated becomes preeminent, and dances belonging to that clan are performed.

The present *marae* is not a purpose-built structure or space attracting permanent formalities or behavioral restrictions, but an area of land that gains significance through alteration of its mode of use from secular to sacred. This alteration is achieved by the presence of members of the island's spirit community, invisible in themselves but tangible in the emblems worn by the five clan elders. The time frame when the *marae* functions as a ritual arena is determined by the arrival and departure of the Ariki. The precise spot where the Ariki places his chair may vary over a one-meter radius, as may the positions of singers seated around the periphery depending, for example, on the location of a shady spot or a large puddle. However, the sequence of elders seated in an east-west line is always the same, as is the location of mediums in the same line as the elders, with ritual assistants leading the singing from a line in front of the elders, and older women singers to the west of those assistants. Relative space is more precisely defined than absolute space, a principle exemplified musically in the form of unison singing.

The *marae* itself has its own resident spirits who, though unnamed, unnumbered, and unseen, require physical sustenance. Consequently, on the first evening of a *tukumai* ritual, the ritual assistant places a whole taro and a tin of meat or fish on the ground before the line of elders as a food offering to the *marae* spirits to ensure good weather for the duration of the rite. The clan performance expert *(purotu)* enjoyed the prerogative of taking this offering and consuming it in the immediately vicinity of the *marae* but, in the present absence of any *purotu*, Terupo Sāre usually performs this action on the grounds that the privilege once belonged to his *purotu* father Sāre, and so has devolved to him even though he is not the clan performance expert.

Events occurring on the *marae* are sacred in the sense that they are attended

PHOTO 20. The *marae* in the blazing afternoon sun on the third day of a *tukumai* ritual. Seated behind the drum in the front row are the *tautua* ritual assistants. Behind them sits Ariki Avo (soon to be flanked by his fellow clan elders), and behind him in turn sit the mediums in full regalia. Only when all these personnel are present can the women's dancing start. *(Richard Moyle)*

by such resident spirits. Unseen in whatever form they assume in their normal places of residence, certain of the spirits are materialized in the emblems worn on the shoulders of clan elders and drummer(s) and in the Ariki's *noti* topknot, which embodies his personal deity, Pukena. More explicitly in the past than the present, one function of dancing on the *marae* is to entertain local spirits in hopes of ensuring continued protection from illness and disaster and continued assistance with successful gardening. Supernatural pleasure at the dancing depends not only on the error-free standard of performance but also on the appropriateness of the structure of the dance itself, particularly for dances of the *sau* category. In the following account, Sione Pilike noted Pukena's critical appraisal of the number of sections in each *sau* performed, the aesthetic benefit of the slower *hakatū* sections of the dance, and the adverse results of a performance of insufficient length:

> You are required by Pukena to count [the sections], because Pukena will count the songs you take to the *marae* and, to be complete, there must be five [of each]. In that manner you will be allowed to go and perform at the *marae*, and if there are more than five, then it will be all right. The *hakatū* section inserted in your performance will make it even better; Pukena won't become angry. But if anything is insufficient, Pukena will be angry at that thing that the people have taken in jest to the *marae*. That's what happened with the song for Nukeria's *hakatū*—for Kikiva's father—it was simply abandoned because they couldn't fit it into an existing dance song.

When the Ariki dons his regalia and walks the few steps from his house to take his seat in the center of the arena's northern end, this act initiates formal activity on the *marae*. He sits there alone until the other *mātua* arrive to take their predetermined places on either side of him. At present, all events on the *marae* are associated with song and dance performance. More experienced singers sit in front of the elders, clustered on both sides of the island's sole drum. Their contribution as de facto *purotu* is intended to benefit the dancers, although other singers sitting behind them may find it hard to hear them. Non-participants sit behind the row of elders. If the event includes female dances such as *sau*, *manakoho*, or *sore*, senior women who provide the singing sit in a tight group before the elder for Hare Ania. And if one or more mediums are present, these sit in full regalia in a single line on either side of the line of elders. The *marae* is used on several occasions central to the community as a whole.

Tukumai *(Commemorative Ritual Complex)*

The five-day *tukumai* makes extended use of the *marae*, with an all-night performance of both newly composed and established *tuki* songs and dances followed by a program of prepared performance of introduced dances that in turn lead into a further series of foreign dances. During the latter the deceased's family members give away valuables to relieve their grief.[45] On the afternoon of the third and fourth days the community again gathers on the *marae,* where women perform dances long established in the community's repertoire and are believed to have been taught by the spirits of dead residents. Men may also perform the *takere* dance and/or a series of *rue* dances. The *tukumai* concludes with a further nocturnal performance of the newly composed *tuki.*

Llū *(Voyaging Songs)*

A short time after the chief mourners have returned to Nukutoa from their seclusion at Vaihare, on a night when the possibility of rain appears unlikely, the community gathers on the *marae* to perform its entire repertoire of *llū* songs.[46] These clan-owned songs recount specific events in the island's earliest days, with a primary poetic focus on the ocean voyaging that appears to have characterized that era. These are the same songs performed on Takū Island by the immediate family as the entire community gathered about the corpse prior to burial. Death has the effect of "closing" the *marae,* but this performance of *lū* is said to reopen the area and "free" *(e tana)* each individual song for future performance on the occasion of the next clan death, thus ending the brief ban imposed with their performance beside the corpse.[47] Clan by clan, in a process known as *hakatū llū,* groups of adults sing all the *llū* they can recall, their singing boosted by participation by anybody else familiar with the material. The singing continues for some hours, and is concluded with a predetermined item of a different category such as a particular *tuki.* The song known as *te tuki i Nukurēkia* is commonly sung for such a purpose.

National Independence

As part of National Independence observances, the central government annually provides money via the provincial governments to assist communities in celebrating the emancipation from foreign governance. Takū receives an amount varying from K300–1000, which the council allocates to the purchase of party food or for equal distribution to Tāloki and Sialeva in recognition of their participation in several hours of special events. Such events may include an adult sport competition (running races, spear throwing, volleyball, and handstanding) followed by a program of dances performed on the *marae,* normally including *rue* and *hula* and possibly the *takere* and an ancient dance, for men and women, respectively. The *marae* dancing is timed around midday, to allow maximum daylight time for the drinking parties that follow and may last the entire night.

Sponsored Dancing

One feature of Takū culture is the private sponsorship of community activities such as canoe races *(tuata),* fishing competitions *(taki, paretua)* or competitive gathering of other marine life, and dancing. Prizes are offered, and a single payment of valuables (eg, cloth, tinned food, fishing equipment) is awarded to the best dance group. A performance of the *paki* dance in 1994, the first in many years, occurred at such a sponsored event.

Hakamārama te Tinae *(Purification of the New Mother)*

Until the mid-twentieth century, celebration of the birth of a woman's first or second child followed five days of seclusion in her clan elder's house. Her face decorated with turmeric patterns, she presented her child to the community at a day of dancing attended by "all" adults (see photo 10). The elder and his wife decorated themselves, and the mother and child sat in a position of prominence close to that of the five elders. Items performed on this occasion were glossed as *anu hakamau* (serious dances) and focused on those of the *sau* and *hoe* genres because their poetry refers directly to the activities of specific spirits. The event socially identified the infant in direct, though distant, line of descent from the ancestors named in the ancient songs. With communal assent, the event might be followed in the evening by a performance of *llū* songs that, similarly, restated clan identity and the significance of maintaining contact with the ancestors. Through this remembrance of links to the past, the celebration of present life was invested with additional significance.

Celebration of Convalescence

Dancing on the *marae* also follows the first signs of recovery for a resident undergoing treatment for serious illness or injury. For five days such a patient lies inside his/her clan elder's house, where a particular type of mat called *te uta* is spread as bedding. During this period, the clan elder remains in constant attendance and senior clan members gather for several hours each night outside the house in a supportive vigil. If the patient's condition has resulted from an accident, a five-day fishing ban is immediately instituted, and if attack by a predator fish is the cause, all the island's males receive protective ornaments and charms from the Ariki and a team of assistants inside Hare Ata. If, after five days of treatment, the patient shows signs of recovery, the community formally celebrates with dancing on the *marae* in the presence of the convalescent.

Sauatari

Fishing competitions for men include the *paretua*, the *taki haikave*, and the *sauatari*. The *sauatari* is described this way: only we men go for the fishing, leaving the women behind. The women remain and when the men come back, they thread their fish on a line ready for the women's arrival. When all the fish are threaded, we count them to determine who is the winner. When we determine the winner, all the canoes come ashore at the beach in front of a place something like Hare Ata's beachfront—that's where we go for our dancing. The women call out the name of the winner's wife, as the men wait by their canoes for the women to arrive. As we stand beside our canoes and when your wife comes to the canoe, she's not allowed to look at you, or turn around and look at anyone inside the canoe. The wife simply comes toward the canoe with head bowed, and picks up the rope end tied to the fish, lifting it up. When she lifts up the rope of fish, if it's not heavy, she will carry it by herself, but if she can't lift it up, she'll look at her husband and the two of them will lift all the fish together and carry them ashore. They go with the fish to the *marae,* where the women ask them what type of dance they want to dance, and they will sing for them. All the couples take a turn: after number two's turn, then comes number three. After these have danced, all the other men and women join in. The other couples also bring their fish up, and we come to the dancing arena, and that's why it's called the *sauatari* [literally, "lifted up by the thread"]. (Nūnua Posongat, 1999)

Marae formality governs not just the nature and timing of the activities there but also the manner in which those activities start and end. *Marae* events are currently occasions for the "entire" community, and although the small number of resident Christians boycott the *tukumai* on the grounds that it is pagan, they continue to attend the Independence Day dancing. Common to all occasions when the *marae* is used is the presence of the Ariki and the four other elders—or their proxies—for the duration of the performance, the positioning of a line of singers (with instruments if appropriate) in front of these five men, and the Ariki's brief final words announcing the closure of the *marae.* Additionally, the identity of the first and last performed items is predetermined and sanctioned by long practice. At present, the first song at a *tukumai* is a composition by Tarasomo commonly referred to as *te tuki kapi* (the restrictions song) and the final item at each of the subsequent afternoon periods of dancing must be one normally accompanied by the drum, such as a *manakoho* or *sore.*

The link between artistic performance and the supernatural is made explicit in formal singing and dancing on the *marae;* both the activity and the location attract the attention and unseen presence of the island's spirit population. Responsibility for the human direction and control over the spirit presence resides principally with the five elders whose own presence, either in person or via a deputy in the case of illness or off-island absence, is absolutely indispensable for any gathering on the *marae.* Although outwardly conspicuous by their non-participation in *marae* activities, the elders as embodiments of their respective clan ancestors are seen to guarantee the ongoing health and survival of the community at large. Although dances to entertain Pukena on the ancient *marae* at Sarati have been discontinued for over a century, people still recognize the importance of maintaining a symbiotic relationship with the island's deities. In their separate contexts, food gifts offered during the *tukumai,* a portion of the catch of *hō* fish set aside, and the depositing of emblems at specific locations on both land and sea all cater to the spirits' own survival and recognition of their presence and status. Through communal belief that the spirits share in the attributes and tastes of the atoll's human residents, *marae* performances, whether song or dance, address other spirit needs by providing them entertainment.

Formality prescribes both persona and place: beginning with the Ariki, the five elders are seated at the northern end of the *marae*. The Ariki not only opens and closes the *marae*, he also confirms major divisions on the first all-night session of the *tukumai*, acting on information received from the singers and announcing the transition from sung *tuki* to danced items as well as the arrival of dawn and the subsequent performance of sets of local and imported dances. It is the indisputable centrality of the Ariki in *marae* activities generally that prompts the common description of the area as *te marae te Ariki* (the Ariki's *marae*).

Formality of another kind is imposed in the actual performances of song and dance. The single most extensive period of performance, occurring on the first night of the *tukumai*, is divided into sections determined by musical and kinetic content: the entire repertoire of newly composed *tuki* intended for singing alone is followed around midnight by the parallel repertoire of newly composed *tuki* intended for dancing; these are followed at dawn by a period of introduced dances, after which a selection of *toha, hula,* and *rue* dances completes the event. At the three subsequent afternoons of dancing, the concluding item is required by convention to be of a type normally accompanied by the community's sole drum; only after this piece can the Ariki stand and declare the day's activities finished. During all performances on the *marae*, adults not singing or dancing are required to remain quietly in their places. Dances whose vigorous actions typically elicit an audience response of shouts of delight—men's *rue* and women's *toha*—may provide contrasting material to the more restrained *tuki* and stately *sau* and *manakoho* dances, but it is these slower dances that will start and end a program on the *marae*.

Economy

Takū exists on a subsistence basis. Limited by the natural environment to two major food sources, the garden and the sea, Takū's residents have achieved continuity of supply through a degree of diversification in both regions. More so in the past than at present, gardeners chose to grow breadfruit, bananas, and yams, as well as the staples of taro and giant taro. Marine exploitation techniques have remained relatively stable since they already represent a multiplicity of options. They continue to include surface-fishing and ground-fishing; fishing the lagoon, reef, and ocean; harvesting day-feeding and night-feeding fish; using single catch methods (hooking) and multiple catch methods (netting), and consuming alike fish, shellfish, and sea worm.

Residents remain small-scale intensive agriculturalists, their ancestors having modified the landscape to produce a fertile basin on Takū Island's northeastern end, subdivided and demarcated by raised paths and borders. The need for intensive exploitation of family plots, however, does not arise from any desire to produce surplus food, rather it is a function of the small size of the plots, which are routinely worked year-round. Domestic food production, principally directed toward the household's internal requirements, also accommodates normal forms of assistance to parents and affines. Even when the village shifts to ritual behavior at a *tukumai* and each household contributes a predetermined number of taro, the scale of food gathering per household remains at a level that will be consumed by its own members in a few days.

Self-sufficiency in food production is maintained by according primacy to fish—the potentially less reliable but immediately more abundant resource. Vegetables—the more reliable but less abundant source—are reserved for nonroutine occasions. Production risks associated with gardening are in turn minimized by producing crops such as giant taro that may be harvested reliably over many years. Largely with the aid of remittances from family members holding jobs elsewhere in the country, and to a lesser extent from local income deriving from the sale of shark fin, bêche-de-mer, and copra, the basic diet is supplemented by rice and tinned meat and fish bought from the several family-owned trade stores as a relish *(kkī)* for meals. Locally the only wage labor available is that of the government employees: council members (at least two of whom operate the radiotelephone), school teachers, and the medical assistant.

Food—its collection, display, distribution, and consumption—defines temporary and complementary social groups as providers or consumers, and the act of public food consumption represents not only an achievement marker and a group identifier but also, incorporating the primary expression of life-giving force (Goldman 1970, 499), the principal symbol of social unity. Let us review the key examples in Takū experience:

(a) The annual school concert is an occasion for parents to demonstrate love for their children through the conspicuous consumption of costly, nonstandard Western foods at a mass meal on the school grounds. On the school principal's announcement of the concert date, mothers mob the trade stores for special foods, and entire stocks are sold within a few hours.

(b) Large-scale production and consumption of food signals the stages of death and commemorative rituals:
  • harvest of *kanokano* and presentation via/to the Ariki at Vaihare marks the first day of funerary rites on Takū Island;
  • cutting the hair of both male and female mourners on return from the five days on Takū Island precedes a communal meal *(hānnai)* held for them and their supporting families before they all walk to Tāloki or Sialeva for their party *(hāunu);*
  • the second morning of the *tukumai,* the mass harvest of taro, chickens,

and tinned food and the taro's display *(kaina)* is followed by distribution to families for immediate consumption;
- the *hakamaseu* meal at either Tāloki or Sialeva signals the end of *tukumai*
  formalities and frees mourners in the *pārina* to return to their homes.

(c) A rice-based meal with a relish of *kumu* leaves and tinned fish is normally
provided by the hosts to those contributing labor at the construction or
major repair of a house, and at the completion and launching of a new
vakasī.

(d) The ceremonial celebration *(taora)* of the safe return of a first-born child
from his/her first off-island travel highlights the social value attached by
a family to its individual members; for similar reasons, a homecoming
family member is given a meal of prestige food on arrival.

(e) The harvest of ten *kanokano,* presented to the clan elder by the father of
a sick or injured person after the prescribed five days inside the elder's
house. This signals the passing of crisis and the advent of recuperation.

(f) Among performers in the *anu haikave* (dance with one's opposite-sex
cousins) until recently each man so identified had to take at least fifty
lagoon fish or at least twenty if fishing on the ocean. On returning he
would summon the women who had danced with him, and they would
mix the fish with giant taro to make the baked dish called *sōsoro,* which
they would all then eat. This practice is not followed now. A similar meal
was prepared and consumed by the participants following other forms of
nonstandard dancing.

(g) The *kaukau* presentation of quantities of raw giant taro or cooked taro
to formal mourners followed their escorted circuit *(areha)* of the village
area.

(h) The *manava e hura* (swelling of the stomach) presentation of giant taro
by a pregnant woman's father to her husband's family is said to publicly
announce and celebrate her fecundity.

Local spirits are believed to need the sustenance of physical food, and
these needs are observed in ritual presentations for them to eat and drink.
Formal presentation of prestige foods such as giant taro acknowledges the
assistance of house-dwelling deities in affecting a person's recovery from illness or injury. Food is similarly key in the rite of house purification that follows treatment of an accident victim at the Ariki's house and the drinking
nuts offered in such cases are consumed by the Ariki and his men on behalf
of the house deities. And on the first morning of a *tukumai,* the spirits in the
house of the affected clan elder receive offerings of taro and tinned food that
are laid out beside each of the eight doorways. Similar offerings are sent to
the houses of the other elders at this time.

As in life, individuals provide food for other family members; so too in
death, a family will seek to ensure that the bodily needs of a recently deceased
member are met. Some days after the *tukumai* ritual is finished, families of
each deceased person send food (several cartons of tinned meat and fish,

cooked chicken, fish, and taro) to their dead relative via their own medium. The medium (plus the husband, if the deceased was a female) dresses in a new costume for the occasion and is presented with all the food in the house for immediate consumption (at least in part). The inevitable excess is then distributed among other family members.

The overall pattern of the Takū economy is not adversely affected by fishing competitions despite the different sizes of individual catches. Food caught in this manner is made available to all participants, regardless of the size, or even the success, of their individual catch. The equal distribution of the aggregate fruits of such competitions ensures that the needs of the community are not jeopardized by any display of individual achievement. Temporary individual prestige complements, but does not compromise, long-term collective equality. In similar manner, the hundreds of taro forming the *kaina* pile at the *tukumai* ritual, the score of giant taro presented at a *taora* ritual or after recovery from a potentially fatal injury, the presentation of a large turtle to the island's resident spirits, and the orderly laying out of prestige fish are all occasions when a brief suspension of egalitarianism is offered for direct scrutiny by the community. By their passivity, community members signal acceptance of the temporary aberration, and by this controlled means, the value of egalitarianism is highlighted and enhanced.

Summary

Nukutoa represents a clan-based community who periodically assemble as a single unit functioning through local organization rather than kinship. In the secular realm, the weekly village meetings constitute one such unit, and the *tukumai* represents a religious counterpart. On the *marae* the clan-based structure of society is displayed in the seated and separate presence in a single line of the five elders. The ritual authority of the elders as a group is exercised through the timing of activities, which may not start until all five are present and seated, and the ranking of the clans is indicated by the predetermined position of each elder vis-à-vis the Ariki. The spiritual authority of these men is proclaimed by their formal dress, whose emblems both advertise the presence of clan spirits and offer general protection against other potentially malevolent spirits. The secular authority of each elder, limited to minor matters within their respective clans, is complemented by the Ariki's spiritual leadership and the Pure's overall governance of issues pertaining to the land and its inhabitants' physical well-being.

Although sedentary by virtue of the extreme limitations of habitable land on the atoll, adults are highly mobile on the reef, within the lagoon, and on adjacent ocean regions in search of food. The primary dependency on fish resources is reflected in the parallel numerical primacy of *tuki* songs within the active performance repertoire. These songs praise the achievements of individual master-fishermen or the skills of specific canoe-builders, and

reinforce their primacy within the repetoire by enjoying right of first performance in gatherings of the entire assembled community on the *marae*.
It is hard to overemphasize the importance of fishing, since both ecologi-
cally and symbolically, it is central to life on Takū. Fishermen, in their reliance on ancestral assistance, which in turn requires their knowledge of the
appropriate protocols and invocations, continue to imbue the act of fishing
with religious significance; indeed, the most common reason advanced for
the return of an empty canoe from the ocean is some breach of established
practice rather than any ecological cause. Through group song the results
of successful connections to ancestral assistance are publicly praised; the evidence of the product is considered to validate the process. Disposal of the
fruits of fishing demonstrates the broad principle of egalitarianism. The community strikes a balance between recognition of individual distinction and
corporate survival needs, the one focusing on fishing's various processes and
necessary skills and the other on its products and on the responsibilities associated with each fisherman's membership within their clearly defined social
units. Indeed, wherever the principle of egalitarianism is applied to material
goods, its leveling function foregrounds social goals as well as purely economic objectives.

In a community founded on such balances—between long-term cooperation and short-term competition, between human endeavor and supernatural
intervention, between the practice of small-scale initiative but submission to
the broad authority of the Ariki and Pure—and operating within a gender-
based division of labor, Takū residents have achieved an enduring formula
for self-sufficiency in economic, social, artistic, and religious activities, accom-
modating new relationships through birth, adoption, and marriage, and
coping with the severance of relationships through death. These balances
are relational, such that the recent shift toward imported foods and Western
material goods and a determined effort by a minority toward an imported
rival religious system have produced organizational changes that seem close
to taking structural effect on the society as a whole.

Chapter 3
Religious Contexts of Music

Information on Takū's religious practices survives in both historical descriptions and contemporary usage.[1] As in the past, much of daily life today is imbued with the supernatural, and this mirrors and confirms to a degree the egalitarian nature of social relations on the atoll. The two activities that occupy the greatest amount of time—the survival pursuits of gardening and fishing—also attract the greatest attention from *aitu* and *tipuna* spirits, whose representatives are believed to be equally accessible to each adult and may be invoked for personal assistance.

The structure of Takū's religious system has parallels in its social and political systems. The most prominent role in ritual is filled by clan elders, particularly the Ariki, and it is they who recite appropriate formulae to the island's spirits to ensure the community's ongoing health and welfare. It is also they who invoke their clan spirits' protection against misfortune on land and sea for the benefit of clan members. Wearing clan deity emblems on their arms and heads, and with additional sacra prepared by a fellow clansman, they provide protection and bring significance to activities on the *marae* by their mere presence. And it is they who are the repositories of clan mythology and ritual knowledge.[2]

Present-day residents believe that their mythological ancestors were anthropomorphic, citing isolated pieces of evidence to support this view. Ariki Avo once told me that he thought, but could not personally verify, that his clan deity Pukena has human form, and there is wide belief that the sea spirit Pakeva has human form and is female. Mythology tells of the founding ancestors undertaking essentially human activities, such as constructing houses, sailing, fishing, and marrying; and in *kkai* fables not only are local spirits visible and in human form, they are also physically attractive and capable of producing human children. As noted earlier, rituals occurring on the *marae* recognize and meet the physical appetites of resident spirits by an offering of taro, and food is similarly placed at each of the six doorways of an officiating elder's house during the *tukumai* ritual. Spirits similarly share the human ability to be shocked by culturally insensitive language. They are also capable of aesthetic enjoyment and so congregate on the *marae* to be entertained by the song and dance; in recognition of their unseen presence the five clan elders

111

don protective emblems while presiding over such events. The physical form of specific spirits, notably those pieces stolen in the nineteenth century and now in the Leipzig Museum, shows them to be clearly anthropomorphic. But this evidence, however cumulatively persuasive, is of less interest to Takū residents than the positive and practical effects of their successful invocation in the business of life and death.[3]

Religious Practice on Nukutoa

Present beliefs do not constitute a complete charter for action, since it is generally accepted that changes to the islanders' lifestyle imposed in the past century, both from outside (eg, theft of images, enforced removal from Takū, the off-island death of the Ariki) and within (eg, death by epidemic of many knowledgeable individuals, lack of adequate training by certain clan elders of their successors) have resulted in the discontinuation of significant elements of pre-European religious practice and belief. There is much that cannot now be explained—such as the meaning of certain religious terminology, details of specific practices, the significance of particular sites and differences between categories of deity or spirit—but the time distance between "the old days" *(te sāita i mua)* and now, and the ongoing and demonstrably successful religious activities currently practiced appear to compensate for any sense of loss or degradation.

The Ariki continues to exercise overall responsibility for the community's religious life, but several factors have reshaped the nature of that responsibility. The removal of the community to Kapeiatu Island, leaving only the five elders on Takū, severed the Ariki's link with the people whose welfare he oversaw; the appointment of a man living on Kapeiatu as eventual successor to the Ariki broke the close connection with Pukena's house and embodiment in a wooden image. It seems likely that the entertainment of Pukena in front of the Ariki's house waned or died at that time, and the theft of Sinateahana and two other images dealt a further blow to religious activities. The discontinuation of the *tānaki* ritual would be one of the more serious of these.

The *tānaki* was a ritual spread over ten days and occurring at a variable point after a local death, but normally between three and six months so to allow a large quantity of taro to mature. The immediate family of the deceased, together with close clan members, went to their elder's house and stayed within for five days and nights, fed by other family members. During this period the appointed medium became entranced *(llea)* and conveyed information from the deceased's spirit, most commonly in the form of a danced song, singing the poetry for those inside the house to learn. The medium sat with eyes open but unfocused, and able to hear and respond to questions. It appears that the performance of a song was not entirely spontaneous, the medium announcing one or more days beforehand that such a song was going to be brought. In response, individual family members prepared to concentrate on specific sections of the song (eg, the refrain, the first verse, the second verse) and to memorize these immediately, since the medium would give only one performance and would have forgotten all details on returning to normal consciousness after the event. Dances communicated in this manner included those of the *manakoho, sore, uī, sau, manu,* and *ororua* categories (refer to table 3). For the remainder of the initial five-day period, the family spent much of their time learning the newly received dance. During the second five-day period, the family continued to spend their nights in the elder's house but emerged during the day onto the *marae* to perform the new dance for the first time in public, together with other *sau, manakoho, sore,* and *uī* dances from their existing repertoire.

Danced songs were not the sole material the entranced medium conveyed at a *tānaki.* Indeed, the present clan nomenclature and much ritual precedent were established in the 1930s at a series of *tānaki* at which the ancestral spirit Laroteone spoke through Faite Pūtahu. These revelations occurred with such frequency they became widely known about, and accounts speak merely of Laroteone doing this and saying that without mention of the person of the medium, Faite.[4] As Nūnua Posongat recalled from the days of his youth:

> When there was to be a *tānaki,* Laroteone [as embodied by Faite] would go and sit in the doorway where it was being held. She also provided them with sacra. Every *tānaki* from this island was prepared by Laroteone. They weren't arranged by the house owners: it was Laroteone who gave them the sacra so the *tānaki* could proceed. Nowadays the *tānaki* doesn't exist, and it appears that those old customs are dead. Nowadays all those things are gone. The reef passages are almost blocked now that these things are already forgotten. All was forgotten when they failed to observe Laroteone's instructions. Laroteone had told them to adhere to the island's [ways].

These received dances were given formal performances, undertaken in the presence of the Ariki, Pure, and other elders, and began with the new dance on day one. The activities on days two to five included giving away valuables such as quantities of oil fish, fishing net, shark-catching rope or sennit cord; they occurred during the performance of clan dances, either locally composed or introduced. If the goods consisted of a quantity of giant taro too bulky to carry easily, the donor carried only a single taro leaf that would later be redeemed for the goods themselves. Led by the medium, a clan member carried the goods in the hand or on the shoulder, according to their size and weight, walking around or through the lines of standing dancers until a member of the audience removed them, at which point the small procession returned to its point of origin at the head of the *marae,* behind the row of seated elders.

The death of Ariki Apeo in 1962 set in motion what some people consider to be a sequence of related events culminating in an unprecedented calamity. Earlier, while the Ariki was away at Nukuria, the resident medical orderly suggested to Apeo's eldest son, Sini (Ahelo), who was acting for his father, that Nukutoa's appearance would be improved by reducing the number of coconut palms. Sini ordered that all the palms on the island be chopped down, in defiance of a traditional felling limit of one tree per man per day. When he became ill and died soon after, residents suspected a causal connection. Further evidence of this link was demonstrated when Sini emerged momentarily from a deathbed coma to recognize his father on his return from Nukuria, which was interpreted as acknowledgment of the son's wrongdoing.

The heir apparent having predeceased his father, succession subsequently passed to Apeo's second son, Kaiposu. In 1974 Ariki Kaiposu was admitted to Kieta Hospital on Bougainville Island with asthma-like breathing difficulties. While there, he was visited by his brother Mōmoa, who had unknowingly contracted an infectious disease en route to the hospital. Mōmoa infected Kaiposu, and the two died within a week of each other, plunging the atoll into unprecedented grief and confusion. There was no corpse to take to Takū for preparation and burial, no grave to prepare and purify, no covering mats to turn over, no successor to receive the titleholder's spiritual power—in short, no physical focus for communal grief. Additionally, and of even greater significance, no tuna-fishing expedition was launched to bring back evidence of the spirit's safe arrival in the afterworld, and therefore Takū was bereft of any spiritual focus for communal hope. Ariki Kaiposu was buried at Kieta, and only a one-day *tukumai* was held for him on Takū Island; no *tānaki* followed.

The spirits of residents buried in the cemetery on Takū Island go to the appropriate clan afterworld, where they enjoy eternal contentment and confirm their happy state in one or more danced songs they compose and send back to their family via a medium. But the spirit of a person buried outside the cemetery is forever denied access to this afterworld and becomes potentially dangerous as it roams about in search of what it cannot find. Of the funerary practices ceasing in 1974, the *tānaki* had probably the greatest social and religious impact. The temporal positioning of the *tānaki* some months after a death assumed the prior completion of other rites appropriate to a deceased clan head. These rites in turn presume the presence of a corpse. Ariki Kaiposu's death and burial at Kieta meant that this requirement could not be met, which in turn made the normal mortuary practices impossible to carry out. Of these practices, the *tānaki* lasted the longest period of time and was the most delicate, since to establish contact with the deceased's spirit meant encountering the unknown and potentially dangerous world of *telā vasi*, the afterworld. Those people who, in normal circumstances, might reasonably have been expected to oversee a *tānaki* were fearful to do so in those abnormal and unprecedented circumstances. Indeed, none of the mortuary rituals was performed, so widespread was the confusion and concern.

This situation became even more complicated when, several months later, a woman died on the island. The mortuary preparations were thrown into confusion when it was realized that there was no genuine Hare Ata clan head to whom the traditional taro offering could be made at Vaihare beach on the day after the burial. The normal presentation did not proceed, and the Pure, Pūō, was called in to substitute. This event brought home to the community the somewhat precarious state of their precedent-based ritual life, which assumed presences rather than absences, knowledge rather than ignorance, and confidence rather than confusion.[5] Avo Sini, the Ariki-designate, had declined to return to the island from his job as engineer on a government patrol boat, and all of the resident Hare Ata men of appropriate seniority declined to be appointed clan head. Finally, Sante, a man who had been adopted into the Ariki's family, offered himself as interim Ariki, and moved into Hare Ata, where he lived for twelve years until his death. By agreeing to act in a caretaker capacity, he accepted that his successor would be Avo, and this indeed transpired, Avo having retired from his patrol boat job and returned to the island.

Several changes to the structure of the *tukumai* occurred in the next quarter century, apparently as a result of the initiative of specific individuals. In the mid-1970s several relatives of a young woman who had recently died were working on Bougainville and they sent back to the atoll large quantities of food for consumption as part of the funerary rites. The sheer quantity of food made it necessary to spread distribution and consumption over several days, and thus was born the present five-day *tukumai* structure. In the early 1990s, for the *tukumai* of an influential senior woman, the second-night singing was extended from midnight to dawn and followed by the performance of foreign dances and gift-giving. Shortly thereafter, at the *tukumai* of another senior woman, tinned food was substituted for live chickens as a supplement to the large quantities of taro, and copious quantities of alcohol were imported for general consumption during the first-night activities. The public abandonment of valuables by the deceased's family was discontinued in 1998 and, in 1999, at Ariki Avo's instigation, more than one hundred live chickens were again added to the common pile of taro but this time together with tinned food. At that same *tukumai,* local and visiting Christians performed what they termed a "spiritual dance" apparently learned at Rabaul; this marked the first formal appearance of Christian converts at an event hitherto boycotted as "pagan."

The presence of one or more mediums and the unpredictability of their behavior, specifically in terms of physical actions and the content of verbal utterances, are key elements in the *tukumai,* and this unpredictability contrasts sharply with the surety of the ritual's overall structure. Through their manifested links to the dead, the mediums ensure that no two *tukumai* will be identical. First-hand accounts of medium experiences are rare, and few mediums claim to remember details of their actions and words after the trance has broken (a notable exception being Sione Pilike, whose story is given in chapter 4); indeed, most say that they have no recollection at all on return to normal consciousness. To some extent, however, the medium's actions are scripted, since most enter the state of altered consciousness only inside their clan elder's house or later, formally seated on the *marae.* The deceased's family members summoned to sit with them are people conveniently on the island at that time; the contact made through the medium on this occasion is initiated by the specific family member being commemorated rather than another who died earlier, and further spontaneous contact with the dead is not considered likely after the *tukumai* has formally ended.[6]

On the afternoon of the second day, following the distribution of the large mound of taro and tinned food, the death house is opened and cleaned, and mats spread to allow clan members to sit. New mats are spread for the medium, who sits in full costume with close family members on either side. During the next few hours as clan songs are sung by the assembled men and women, and as women stand to perform dance items from their own repertoire of *sau*, the medium may periodically and spontaneously break into speech with information from the deceased, an event that instantly silences all activities in the house and brings children running to view the spectacle from the doorways. The continuity of the afternoon's activities is assisted by generous distributions of cigarettes and alcohol.

As a series of related events, the *tukumai* reinforces the powers of the Ariki and clan elders, provides moral sanctions for the conduct of key individuals, and translates shared grief into a substratum of common values and corporate loss into a social bond of common purpose. It is also in the context of the *tukumai* that one of the two categories of ritual assistant plays his most prominent role.

Tautua *(Ritual Assistant)*

Each clan has a male ritual assistant *(tautua* or *tauru)* whose principal duties relate to the *tukumai* ritual, where he functions as the executive officer, and—until recently—beat the drum during formal entertainment on the *marae* (photo 21; see also photo 25 in chapter 4). This patrilineal appointment is nominally for life, although one may be replaced while alive if obviously senile. Selection of individuals to be ritual assistants is based on clan affiliation. Two clans, Hare Māsani and Hare Nāoro, use the same invocations and techniques for making sacra, and so they supply an assistant for each other's *tukumai;* together they constitute *nā rua i aitu* (the few spirits).

At a *tukumai,* the assistant wears the same ritual ornaments as his clan elder but, for the duration of the ritual, actually outranks the elder. This is because he plays the intermediary between the human and spirit realms as he presents the food offering to the house spirits, while the elder merely sits and presides inside his house. In recognition of this temporary elevation, the assistant is entitled to receive a greater share of the valuables (taro and tinned food) than his clan elder. In the course of his duties at a *tukumai,* the assistant of the host clan distributes sacra to senior women as protection against malevolent spirits lurking unseen and also distributes quantities of food. It is he who places taro and tinned food outside the sacred doorway of the elder's house (photo 21), carries other food offerings to the principal mourner inside the house, and selects taro from the large pile outside and (in his additional capacity as a *tauru;* see below) carries them to the houses of the other elders. He later divides between himself and his own elder the food set out for his clan's house spirits.

Because events on the *marae* are attractive to spirits and some of those spirits are known to be dangerous, the assistant's duties render him potentially vulnerable to supernatural harm. On such occasions it is the presence of the elder that affords additional protection and so, as Ariki Avo commented to me, *"E noho te mātua te marae ki sao te tautua"* (The elder is present on the *marae* so the assistant will be safe).[7]

The *tautua* also assists at times of illness in a clan. When a sick person brought to his or her clan elder's house has lain for five days in the sacred middle doorway *(uta)* on the southern side where the clan elder alone may safely lie in normal circumstances, the assistant receives a *hau* protective headband from his elder before collecting coconuts and husking them on a stick outside the *uta* for, without the headband, he would be killed immediately by the resident spirit for having trespassed in that sacred area. The coconuts are deposited inside the house as refreshment for the spirits, but more in the manner of a gesture than an offering, since they are privately removed within a day or two and consumed by the *tautua.* The *tautua*'s relationship with his elder's house is focused on events occurring in that location, whereas

PHOTO 21. A *tautua* assembles the taro and tinned meat for placement at each of the doorways of the Ariki's house as an offering to the house spirits resident there. *(Richard Moyle)*

attention to the house itself is the responsibility of the second class of ritual assistant, the *tauru*.

Tauru *(Ritual Assistant)*

For all *tukumai*, the duties of *tautua* and *tauru* are identical, but the responsibility for providing these ritual assistants is not shared equally among all clans; it is limited to the three participating clans of the mythological *hakautana* covenant, now represented by Hare Ata, Hare Mania, and Hare Māsani. Senior men recalled to me that office holders were dominated numerically by members of the Ariki's clan, Hare Ata, which exclusively supplied *tauru* for *tukumai* hosted by Hare Nāoro and Hare Ania as well as for Hare Ata itself. Formerly, the *tautua* and *tauru* together distributed taro from the communal pile at a *tukumai*, but this task is now handled by a *tautua*.

The duties of a *tauru* are linked conceptually to one clan elder and associated materially with that elder's house, the *hare tapu*. By tradition the duty of building and maintenance resides with the *tauru* assigned to a house, although nowadays even the elder himself can occasionally be seen directing children or family members to replace thatch panels. At present the duties of *tauru* appointed to Hare Mania and Hare Ania are limited to uplifting selected taro from the communal pile and presenting them to the spirits resident in all five elders' houses. Those appointed to the other three elders' houses merely maintain or repair or rebuild them.[8] The *tauru* also organize the *taora* pregnancy celebration for the daughter of an elder.

The word *tauru* itself refers to the top leaves of a plant or tree, in distinction to the Ariki's clan, Hare Ata, which is conceived as the trunk; this provides the rationale for Hare Ata sending its "plant top" (that is, a *tauru*) to work at the *tukumai* held in Hare Ania. The duties of the *tauru* have lessened over the lifetime of present titleholders, and some younger men hold the view that the name refers simply to the ritual assistants of Hare Nāoro and Hare Ania clans, that *tauru* is a substitute name for *tautua*. The *tauru* appointed to Hare Ania clan are referred to collectively as *nā mata vela,* apparently in recognition of specific duties now discontinued and forgotten, whereas those attached to Hare Nāoro are called *nā purotu nā tahito* (performance experts who are the foundation [of the elder's house]), and it is they who lead songs and dances on the *marae* for their clan's *tukumai*.

Categories of Spirits

Specific categories of spirits are identified on Takū, although there is not the sense of comprehensive ranking found in Polynesian cosmologies elsewhere.[9] In most instances, identification occurs in the course of an invocation, and in the use of their personal names rather than categories. One location of both attributes and an information source enduring beyond the invocation act itself is song poetry. As a general rule, the events described in poetry are believed to reflect reality, but a degree of historical manipulation and truth-stretching is acknowledged and privately criticized. Matters in fishing-related poetry such as the size of a catch, the personnel in the canoe, and the succession of specific events are always subject to scrutiny against the yardstick of communal memory, but matters of the spirit world remain immune from detailed evaluation because of the intimacy of the relationship between a person and his or her ancestors, and between people and their personal spirits. Individuals may privately harbor suspicions that a new *tuki* song whose poetry purports to present the perspective of a dead relative is in fact a fabrication designed to endorse decisions made or activities already undertaken within the family. Still no public criticism is likely to be voiced because of uncertainty about the full details. Song poetry brought from the dead via a spirit medium frequently contains references unintelligible, except perhaps to immediate family members, and the semantic opacity of such compositions appears to be generally accepted.

Of the several categories of song believed to have been sent by the spirit of a community member, the few *sore* songs in the local repertoire contain the most transparent accounts of life in the afterworld. The following example was received from Faite, the woman who had been active in the 1930 Rabaul court case to secure the return of island ownership to the community:

Ae taka rā te matani, taka ifo ki te tokorau.	The wind shifts, it shifts to the north.
Nimosia nau ana matani kavea ki hano ki aruna;	I turn in the wind; I am taken up;
Kavea ki sura ki te lani ē.	Taken to appear in the heavens.
Ko nau ko Tenimomatani ē,	I am Tenimomatani,
Utania ki te vaka te Ariki.	Loaded on to the Ariki's canoe [ready for burial].
Ka tukua iho ki tino henua;	Then set down on the mainland;
Ka tukua iho ki te Ariki.	Then set down before the Ariki.
Ē tū atu nau ki aku tamana, eia;	Now I stand before my father;
Ē tū atu nau ki Telauvika	Now I stand before Telauvika
Hakatonu mai e ki anau ki tau nau ma Hare Ata;	Who confirms my eligibility in my clan;
O ki mau ai nau.	I'll be safe there.

This *sore* contains comforting information for the bereaved: Faite has reached the afterworld and been deposited not on some barren, insignificant place there but on the mainland of Takū; she is in the exalted company of the Ariki himself and the familiar presence of her father; she is there, not with any sense of shame or inferiority, but assured of her proper place. Faite's enduring social status is thus assured.

Atua

The term *atua*, referring to a category of spirit, is no longer in active conversational use but is recognized as an indigenous term by older residents; it appears in a few song compositions.[10] Whatever specific connotations the term may once have had, present references in the poetry of *tuki* songs appear identical to those for other spirits such as *aitu* and *tipuna:* they all are invoked to ensure success in fishing or provide comfort in times of personal distress.

Aitu Nnui

There are two broad groups of spirits known as *aitu,* each member of which is distinguished by personal name. The first type, *nā aitu nnui* (the great spirits) were either already in residence when the original colonists arrived or were brought along by the colonists. The following list of spirits is not meant to be exhaustive, since clan association could not be confirmed in all cases for which information was collected.

Clan	Aitu Nnui
Hare Ata	Nā Hhui Ārau, Nā Hhui Lahakamaru
Hare Mania	Te Hui Ttuila (Nā Hhui Tūmoa), Hūtumua
Hare Māsani	Tākao
Hare Nāoro	Tehuila, Latumau
Hare Ania	Nā Hhui Peilau, Nā Hhui Te Lani Hakamaru

These spirits now reside in their respective spirit house sites on Takū Island—at Hakātui, Uvea, Oneai, Ketiketi, and Tapueia, respectively.[11] Complementing these ancestors is the clan-independent deity Oroatu, of whom Moir notes, "This Takuu deity figures in each of the five origin myths; he plays a different role in the founding of each patriline, but in most cases he exemplifies behavior that by Takuu standards is reprehensible, or tapu, or both" (1989, 71–72). Clan colonization myths include names of the children of the *aitu nnui;* these were *aitu* in their own right. Although it is sometimes possible to see the shadows *(inaina)* of these spirits, their bodies remain invisible and they tend to remain beyond human contact.[12]

The second broad group of spirits, *nā aitu nā tama mmate* (spirits of dead [ancestors]), are always invisible but may maintain contact with the living through a medium. The contact may be formalized, predictable, and considered positive—for instance, in the *tukumai* and former *tānaki* rituals—or informal, unpredictable, and either positive or negative. Contact of this latter type may induce vomiting, loss of speech, or other temporary dysfunction; it may also shed light on the cause of illness in a deceased's family member. The connection with the supernatural world is such that one does not simply make contact with a particular deity: one invokes the deity in the hope that contact will result.

The great spirits achieved their status because of the scope of their powers, which is related in accounts of their activities in the prehuman era. They live on, invisible, at particular locations on one of the islands but know what is happening everywhere. I once overheard one elderly woman comment to another, *"Pukena te aitu hakalilika"* (Pukena [one such deity] is such a fearful deity), her voice kept to a low whisper. These spirits may safely be invoked only by clan elders, whose ancestors they are believed to represent. It is only the Ariki, for example, who may stand on the *marae* in the course of the *tānaki* ritual and invoke his clan deity Pukena to come and render assistance in time of disaster. Such public invocations are known as *taku* or *larokina,* and their performance is limited to the five elders who, in accordance with the formal sequence of clan ranking, stand and shout out the ritual formulae to their respective clan spirits in a style called "singing" *(huahua)* but which lies somewhere between song and speech.[13]

These utterances are designed to ensure the continuation of plentiful land and sea food. One of Ariki Avo's *taku,* given here in translation only to preserve the privacy of the original content, typifies the contents, which invoke the spirits of immediate past elders, former Ariki, and founding ancestors:

And now once again, the elders of [my spirit] Telani Hakamaru,[a]
All of you, heed the final dancing in honor of [my spirit] Tehui Ārau,[b]
Who gather the sacra from the sacred door of the Ariki's house, Hare Mouna
To ensure there are no disasters while handling the sacred coconut at the end
of the *marae.*

Pay attention, my associates, you—the presence of Kīpū[c] and the presence
of Sieki;[d]
Pay attention, all of you, and listen to what has been presented to Tehui Ārau
as he sits in the sacred doorway of the Ariki's house, Hare Mouna;
To ensure there are no disasters while handling the sacred coconut at the end
of the *marae.*

Heed my companions, oh presence of Kikiva[e] and the presence of Nukuria;[f]
All of you, heed the final dancing in honor of Tehui Ārau;
And the gathering of sacra from the sacred door of the Ariki's house, Hare
Mouna;
To ensure there are no disasters while handling the sacred coconut at the end
of the *marae.*

Heed me, oh presence of Apeo,[g] and spread the rising sun's rays;
Let the white clouds drift toward the setting sun, and scatter them over Nukutoa;

---

a. The Ariki's personal ancestral spirit
b. An alternative name for the Ariki's personal ancestral spirit
c. The present Pure
d. The father and predecessor of the present Pure
e. The present elder of Hare Māsani clan
f. The father and predecessor of the present elder of Hare Māsani clan
g. Former Ariki, the paternal grandfather of the present Ariki, Avo

Let the pale coconut leaves spread at the tops of the trees;
And heed my women, oh presence of Te Laroteone.[h]

All of you, heed the point in the flippers,[i]
And so raise up the head and right flipper of the sacred turtle.
And so make welcome all that is on the long reef and the fishing grounds.
Heed my women, you, the presence of Maria,[j] and turn your attention to those
    things;
You who care for our gardens—kill the insects eating taro leaves and hanging on
    taro leaves, to allow them to grow upward.
All of you, heed and listen to what has been presented to Tehui Ārau as he sits in
    the sacred doorway of the Ariki's house, Hare Mouna.

Heed my elders.
All of you, heed and listen to what has been presented in the sacred doorway of
    the Ariki's house, Hare Mouna;
To ensure there are no disasters while handling the sacred coconut at the end of
    the *marae*.

Although present residents are unable to identify many of the individual
spirits named in this *taku* and can only surmise the significance of other references, it is evident that it represents a list of the topics over which the Ariki
of the day was held responsible and believed capable of controlling through
direct intercession with the appropriate spirits—clement weather, garden
fecundity, community health, and a bountiful ocean. In both this *taku* and
others of Ariki Avo, these domestic-focused powers are complemented by references within each section to the sacredness and potency of specific locations (the central southern doorway of the Ariki's house) and actions (the
handling of a sacred coconut, the emptying of the contents of ritual containers), to give an overall picture of religion's key place in both the community's
mundane and ritual life.

As a generic category, *taku* currently occupy a unique position in the
island's repertoire because they exist but cannot be performed unless the
tānaki rite is reconstituted in the active ritual repertoire. While in this period
of limbo, clan elders cannot fully exercise religious leadership and the community is in turn denied a significant part of its supernatural protection.

Aitu

As well as constituting a generic term for supernatural beings, the word *aitu*
also connotes a category of such beings. Where such beings are anonymous

---

h. A *masalai* spirit child believed responsible for the salvation of the present community on
Nukutoa; see pp. 39–40
i. Certain parts of a turtle ritually butchered are reserved for the Ariki and Pure; correct
observance of protocol ensures continuation of bountiful numbers of this prized food source.
j. A woman, allegedly Samoan, brought to Takū by Emma Forsayth but later repatriated to
Samoa.

they are held in some fear because, lacking a name, they cannot be precisely identified in any protective invocation. As one man commented to me, "*Aitu* are killers." Inexplicable illness is frequently attributed to the malevolent work of these beings. Unnamed *aitu* are believed to be attracted to a clan elder's house during the second morning of the *tukumai* ritual, and formal steps must be taken to protect clan men from the potential danger that their presence invokes. The elder makes *mminilua* pandanus leaf neckbands for his assistants, projecting his family ancestors' power into each neckband with an incantation as he attaches it. The assistants in turn repeat the process for all the fellow clansmen gathered inside the elder's house so that, as one man put it, "*e ppui tō haitino nā māhana*" (your body is protected against the dead).

Aitu, whether named or not, are able to make contact with humans in an intimate manner. In both the precontact and historical eras, individual men have reported identical symptoms: an inexplicable and insatiable desire to return to a particular location, such as a place in their own garden. Unknown, a female *aitu* had taken up residence there, and she would eventually succeed in seducing the man completely without his knowledge in an act called *haikavanatia*. The product of such a union was one or more spirit children, who would attempt to get their father to join them in the afterworld by appearing to him in dreams and calling to him. The appearance of unknown children in this manner allowed the man to infer the existence of the female spirit and provided an explanation for his earlier attraction to her place of residence. No recent occurrences of this phenomenon have been reported. Likewise, an annex to Pukena's house on Takū Island *(te murihata te kata)* said to have accommodated a supernatural eel has been banned to women lest they be seduced by the creature and unknowingly bear spirit children.

The greatest concentration of individually named *aitu* is associated with fishing. Although they are known collectively as the children of the sea deity Pakeva (see below) they are invoked individually by name and as personal ancestors. While on the water a man invokes his ancestors to neutralize any invisible negative substances on the body of the first fish caught that might prevent him from catching another like it. Similarly, catching an *ikatau* prestige fish is fraught with danger that requires the shielding invocation of ancestors because its body contains an *aitu* of unknown identity; when bringing such a fish onshore, the men recite further protective invocations and apply turmeric to its body to protect their canoe from being dogged by bad luck in the future.

Pakeva

Takū's spirits are geographically anchored, with varying degrees of specificity. Operating with the broadest spatial scope Pakeva, deity of the sea, is active in all aspects and manifestations of the human-fish relationship. In addition to providing tangible evidence of a spirit's safe arrival in the afterworld, Pakeva acts as guardian of conservation and protocol, inflicting sickness on anyone fishing in restricted areas and injury on those who fail to observe other protocols. A man will directly invoke his own dead father or grandfather for fishing success but will also request their intercession with the sea deity to send up large numbers of fish.[14]

Pakeva alone among Takū's ancestral spirits has a named place of residence, the *hare ika* (literally, "fish house"), a nonspecific location in the ocean that is also the preferred residence of souls of the dead. From there Pakeva can command a school of tuna to rise and meet a fishing canoe in the five-day period shortly after a local death, this being the cue that the spirit of their clan member has safely arrived in the afterworld. The fishing canoe would be the same one that bore the corpse from Nukutoa to Takū Island, thus completing the ritual cycle: transport of the dead followed by living proof of the spirit's safe conduct. There are, additionally, other sea-dwelling spirits known collectively as *lau tanata Pakeva* (Pakeva's men), and it is specifically they who carry out Pakeva's command to bring forth fish to meet a canoe.

These same minor spirits are routinely invoked by men fishing for prestige fish *(ikatau)*; they are requested to intercede with Pakeva so the trip may produce a bountiful catch. In an identical manner, a man may call out the name of his dead father or grandfather, asking that he in turn ask Pakeva to send up plenty of fish. In certain ritual formulae, Pakeva may also be directly invoked before or during fishing, as men seek help in their quest for success. Although the form of most spirits is unknown, since they are invisible, Pakeva is able to become visible at will, and is said to have a human female body but the tail of a fish.[15]

As with all spirits, Pakeva is capable of action in response to any abuse of resources. Failure to observe proper fishing procedures is commonly advanced as the reason why a particular fisherman met with an accident or fell sick: angered by some act of desecration, Pakeva had caused the accident or sickness as retribution.

Tipua

Tipua are locally resident unnamed spirits known more for their mischief-making than useful contributions or potential threats to daily life. Children in charge of younger siblings frequently tease them by suddenly exclaiming, "It's a *tipua*! A *tipua* is coming!" which sends them scuttling to the safety of their guardian's arms. Even adults are reluctant to walk at night through particular areas behind the housing area, for fear that these beings will trip them or otherwise frighten them. And both children and adults may wake in the night to see the shape of an abnormally tall person scrunching the sandy paths as it walks past their house: this is a *tipua*. There appears to be no means of establishing contact with *tipua*, nor indeed any inclination to do so.

The occasional references to *tipua* in fables suggest their powers may be more dangerous, and one story in particular details the deadly capabilities of such beings, who disemboweled a sleeping old woman and ate her intestines before positioning the body as if it were resting, even arranging the lips in a smile for the grandchildren to discover the next day (Moyle 2003, 138–141). Such stories doubtless contribute to the fear of such beings. Overall, however, *tipua* are regarded as more mischievous than terrifying.

Masalai

Nā masalai are demigods, offspring resulting from the seduction of a human by a spirit of the opposite sex and are distinguished from other kinds of supernatural beings by their ability to change physical appearance.[16] The seduction occurs without the knowledge of the human partner, who innocently and repeatedly spends time sleeping at a specific location, not realizing it is the residence of a spirit. Accounts tell of both men and women being exploited in this manner, although discussion is confined to private occasions for fear of inadvertently summoning back the unwanted spirits.

Taku residents widely believe that the *masalai* Laroteone single-handedly saved the entire island from social chaos by many acts of intervention and by speaking through Faite at the 1930 court case won back ownership of the island for its original residents.

Hatuvave is another *masalai* of note. He is the mythological trickster who used multiple changes of form to bring fire to the island from the heavens and to gain access to the powers of the founding ancestor spirits then sailing away to the end of the world and disappearing.

Masaurani

The *masaurani* (also known as *nā mauvea*) are dwarf-sized beings who were the first non-spirit inhabitants of the atoll. Although invisible, the *masaurani* leave small footprints and crawling marks in the sand on Nukurekia and Nukutapu islands.

Masaurani appear to enjoy a benign relationship with living humans and with human spirits after death; in both circumstances they act in something of a guardian role. These protective beings are accessible even when Takū residents are away from the atoll. When Rabaul's volcanoes erupted in 1994, for example, Tautea Willie happened to be in that town and was forced to flee. He composed a *tuki* song that included a verse acknowledging the protective role of his personal *masaurani*. Tautea died soon after his return to Takū two months later, and this *tuki* was first performed at his *tukumai* in 1995. Other song poetry identifying this type of being depicts them in a similarly positive light.

Present-day references to the *masaurani* are few. A mound on the southern side of Nukutoa is said to be the site of a mass grave of them, and the existence of a *sau* dance called *te masaurani* further suggests their mortality, since "*sau*" denotes the spirit of a deceased person.

Tipuna

Consistent with the notion that humans have both a body *(haitino)* and some kind of vital spirit *(manu* or *mouri)* is the belief in ancestral spirits, who are held to retain an active interest, and even membership, in human society. Like living persons, the ancestors *(tipuna)* are capable of being either benevolent or malevolent, according to the circumstances in which they are invoked. And, on the evidence of song poetry believed to have originated in the afterworld, the *tipuna* retain essentially human characteristics—they experience emotions and above all a desire to dance. The word also refers to one's grandparents, and in that sense, one's living *tipuna* include all those from whom one stands in line of direct descent and who are two or more generations senior to oneself. One's deceased *tipuna* include persons of these same generations as well as same-sex siblings of one's parents and grandparents and even more distant generations within the patriline; these constitute the body of people whose spirits may be invoked in time of need. Such invocations may be either private, as when uttered at sea by a fisherman, or public, as when incorporated into song poetry and sung on the *marae* in the course of the *tukumai* ritual.[17] The sole human provision for the ancestors appears to be confined to *marae*-based entertainment in the form of song and dance, a practice existing in a more amplified manner on Takū Island until the 1880s.

After the death of one's *tipuna,* their spirits are individually contactable by means of invocations that summon one or more of them by name, either to assist in a particular activity such as fishing, or to extend in a more generalized manner their protective influence against illness or other forms of physical harm. In the former context, the benefactor is the individual man making the invocation, whereas in the latter, the invoker seeks protection on behalf of individual fellow clan members. The more significant the occasion, the more *tipuna* are invoked. When men assemble inside an elder's house on the first day of a *tukumai,* for example, the elder and assistants invoke their respective *tipuna* while applying spirit-infused oil to the shoulders of fellow clansmen, that is, to men who also claim such people as ancestors.

The general view is that, during a *tukumai,* contact with the dead is spontaneous and unpredictable; if several mediums are present together inside an elder's house, there is no way of knowing in advance which, if any, will be contacted by the relative for whom the ritual is being enacted. However, a number of consistencies emerge from comparison of various occurrences of the ritual that suggest the timing and content of the contact fits cultural expectations: the timing of the period of contact coincides with the installation of the medium inside the elder's house or the clan gathering later that same day; the spirit communicates through the medium preselected by the family; the duration of contact coincides with the period when the pile of taro is being assembled or divided up on the first morning of activities; family members summoned by the deceased via the medium are those present on the island at that time.

In a small, confined society containing three or more living generations in several families, where the patrilineal descent of clan elders is a matter of common knowledge, and where issues of inheritance based on primogeniture affect each family, the descent-based nature of ancestor worship mirrors existing social practices and values and uniquely links time past, present, and future in a meaningful continuum.

Mouri

After death the ghost *(manu* or *mouri)* of the deceased—whether adult or child—leaves the corpse and travels to the afterworld (Teone) of its own clan, where it takes up eternal residence in the company of fellow clan members (the "ancestors") who have predeceased him or her.[18] While living in Teone, the *mouri* undertake no work, but spend all their time decorating themselves for singing and dancing—the ultimate in desirable activities.

Sau

In one set of circumstances the spirits of the dead make their presence known to the living as an omen of impending death by means of song or, to be more specific, by audible singing. Between and around Takū's islands lie tidal flats that are the visible locus for the clan afterworlds lying invisible beneath them. The spirits in each of these locations belong to the category known as *nā sau*.[19] These spirits, on learning that one of their human number is mortally ill or injured, will go and remove that person's spirit in its still-living body and take it temporarily to the afterworld, where it will be made to dance in that liminal state, in a kind of prelude to the eternal dancing that characterizes life after death. The faint sounds heard at night by passing fishermen are those of the *sau* as they sing for this dancing, and some men claim to have also heard the distant sound of drumming as the resident spirits provided instrumental accompaniment. This phenomenon is the subject of a men's *rue* dance in which the composer dreamed that he had died and his corpse placed on a canoe for transportation to Takū Island, only to be taken briefly to the afterworld for a period of dancing:

Utania nau ē i te vaka te aitu;	I was placed on the canoe by the spirit;
Kavea nau ē i te vaka Tenonoa.	I was sent on the canoe *Tenonoa.*
Te tamana sē kite nau ku kake te vaka	But my father didn't see that I was on the canoe
Te tipuna sē kite nau ku anu te mako.	And my grandfather didn't see that I was dancing to the song.

The clan identity of other danced songs sent from the afterworld may only be inferred from the individual proper names contained in their poetry.

Tāura Aitu

The term *tāura aitu* (spirit medium) is referred to in one account of the origin of a *lū* song. In the account, this medium could see the spirits of dead island-ers invisible to all others and learn directly from them details of the song relating their death. Although this *lū* song is owned by one of Takū's clans, the *tāura aitu* in the story was resident on Nukumanu, and there appears to be no local equivalent office or term.

The Supernatural World in Song Poetry

Typically, poetic references to supernatural beings adopt a two-stage refer-encing practice of preceding personal names in the second part of a verse with a generic reference in the first part. In this manner, *tipua, tipuna, aitu, atua,* and *masaurani* spirits are identified both by category and individually.

Atua

In a *tuki* he composed for a young relative who died in 1997, Nūnua Posongat describes his invocation to an unnamed *atua* before the poetry shifts to the perspective of the young man himself:

Taku mokopuna	Here is my grandchild
Nau ku noho ka tanitani nau ki taku atua nei.	I sit here, crying to my god.
Ko soko Rehu.	Here is Rehu, all alone.

Pukena

Three songs in the recorded collection include references to the Ariki's per-sonal spirit, Pukena, and in each instance the identification and presence of this powerful spirit adds significance and authority to the occasion. One *hakatū* section of the ancient *sau Tellara* dance is typical, placing Pukena in an afterworld so welcoming and attractive that even the spirit residents are moved to praise it:

Ao īē tukua te tai Teone	The sea calms in the afterworld
Ko nā aitu e ahu i te tai nei.	Even the spirits boast of this afterworld.
Ao īē vaea te tai Teone, uhua te tai Teone.	The afterworld is divided by the sea's backwash.
Aē ko te aitu ku toki ki loto Teone nei;	A spirit stands inside the afterworld;
Ko nā aitu e ahu i te henua nei.	Even the spirits boast of this afterworld.
Ā ko Pukena ku toki ki loto Teone nei.	Pukena himself stands inside the afterworld.

| *Ā ni uru atu nau ki te tautua nei;* | I came inside because of the attendant; |
| *Ā ni miomio nau i tuahenua nei.* | I created ripples at the rear of the island. |

In each of the three songs, the spirit is essentially passive, imparting significance by its very presence.

Aitu

Although it is normal poetic practice for generic references (spirits, humans, canoes, fish, locations) in one half verse to be identified specifically in the second half verse either by named category or personal name, the recorded collection includes a few instances in which a spirit remains undifferentiated and is referred to simply as *aitu*. In such circumstances, the normal performance procedure is followed: the half verse is repeated. Takū residents cannot suggest any possible reasons for this phenomenon. The following are typical:

An old *rue* danced song:

| *Tani taku varo i taku atua,* | I cried out my plea to my deity, |
| *Taku vaka ku nā tasi ma te tai.* | When my canoe was laden to the gunwales. |

A *lū* song:

| *Ā ki no huri taku tani ē ki aku tama;* | I direct my crying on behalf of my children; |
| *Ā ki no huri taku tani ki aitu e aku tama.* | I direct my crying to the spirits on behalf of my children. |

A *manakoho* danced song:

| *O āiē ni tataka nā itu i Teone lā,* | The spirits from the afterworld roamed about, |
| *Noho mai koe, noho tū nau tini taku hina ē.* | You were there as I stayed, calling to my lover. |

Other poetry may refer without comment to *aitu* resident on specific islands or attending specific events, as in the following lines from two *sau* danced songs:

Ā ni tū te aitu ki tuahenua nei	The spirit was at the back of the island
Ā ni tū ko Tavake lā ni ki tua Nukutapu	Tavake was there, at the back of Nukutapu.
Ā te aitu ka tū i loto te sau.	The spirit stands among the dancers.

Despite the absence of explicit explanations or details within the poetry itself in such instances, attention to the spirits' continued existence and presence, always in an essentially positive context, reinforces the popular view that *aitu* are "everywhere" and therefore relevant to a wide variety of activities.

Public acknowledgment of supernatural assistance in fishing is proclaimed in songs, particularly *tuki*, performed on the *marae* most often as part of a *tuku-mai* ritual. Trends of categorization and conceptualization may be observed:

(a) Fish, particularly the prestige fish, are caught with the assistance of personal *aitu* correctly invoked:

Āīē, te aitu ro ni kake ki aku vaka;	Āīē, the spirit boarded my canoes;
Āīē, Kirihotu ro ni kake ki aku vaka.	Āīē, Kirihotu boarded my canoes.
Ē oriori iho e Urimoana, taku rima	Urimoana himself jigs below as my own
e oriori.	arm jigs.

(b) The practice of ritually cleaning a prestige fish on shore, normally done by a clan elder, may have its significance elevated when performed by an *aitu:*

Te aitu huia nā ika;	The spirit ritually cleans the catch;
Kāmuti huia nā parumea.	Kāmuti himself cleans the *parumea* fish.

(c) Successful contact with one's personal spirit is established only if the spirit accepts as valid the identity of the invoking person; recognition of the invoker is essential:

Te aitu nau e mātino,	The spirit recognizes me,
Nahuiteika nau e mātino.	Nahuiteika recognizes me.

Pakeva

Several song poems refer to Pakeva, in each case using false causal reasoning (that is, after the fact therefore because of the fact). These texts exalt the favored relationship that has produced an outstanding catch of fish. A representative sample is given below. Three *tuki* in the recorded collection contain lines referring directly to this deity in ways that illustrate the essentially productive relationship with her enjoyed by fishermen. One, a *tuki hakasoro* exalting *Haivelo* canoe's ability to catch oil fish, attributes the canoe's success to a doubly intimate bond with the sea deity:

O, ka mua iho ki uta tamana nau ki	I'm the first ashore, Pakeva is my father,
Pakeva,	
Taona iho ki te hoe, e tinana nau ki	Sheltered with a paddle; Pakeva is my
Pakeva.	mother.

A shark-catching *tuki* for *Ahou* canoe details a similarly favorable relationship:

Hohora te vusi ni lono i Pakeva,	While I was spreading out things in the garden, Pakeva heard,
Ni sura mai ko Pakeva,	Pakeva appeared,
Ni kata mai ko Pakeva,	Pakeva laughed,
Ni tani ni napa i Pakeva.	Pakeva wept from embarrassment.

A passage noted earlier, an ancient *tuki naperu* whose specific references are no longer understood, claims incorporation into the deity's own family as the basis for one master fisherman's success:

Uāiē, ku noho nau ma tama sere te hare;	I stay at home like a special child;
Uāiē, ku noho nau ma tama sere Pakeva.	I stay at home like Pakeva's special child.

Poetic mention of Pakeva's place of residence, the *hare ika* (fish house), is sufficient allusion for the audience to recognize the identity of this spirit, for example:

E se tanata e hano ma tana kave nā e	A man went with his sister
e uruhia ko te hareika, nā ē;	and entered the house of fish;
Ie, Tāsani e hano ma Pātoko nā e	Tāsani went with Pātoko
e uruhia ko te hareika, nā ē.	and entered the house of fish.

Sinateahana

Unlike other spirits whose gender is unknown, Sinateahana's femininity is established in one verse of the song for the *sau Tellara,* a women's dance genre whose poetry focuses on the activities of ancestral women:

Ā ko te hahine nei ki hakapotopoto;	The woman crouches while dancing;
Te hahine nā ē, anu torotoro i te sau nei.	The woman dances as if crawling during the *sau* dance.
Ā ko Sinateahana ki hakapotopoto;	Sinateahana crouches while dancing;
Te hahine nā ē, anu torotoro i te sau nei.	The woman dances as if crawling during the *sau* dance.

Tipua

Just as in daily life, where the activities of *tipua* spirits are unpredictable, so too in songs sent from the afterworld, the poetic references to this category of spirit stand apart in one significant respect: they include no invocations for assistance, as the following extracts from two *sau* danced songs illustrate:

Ē ko taku sau hakamau ki ana tipua;	My own spirit is firmly established with its own *tipua;*
Ē ni hakamau atu ki Kaetēlātana.	It is firmly established with Kaetēlātana.
Ā, ko aku vaka rua ka sori ki te matani,	My canoe faces into the wind,
Noho ake ko tipua a se tai.	And there stands the *tipua* of the sea.

Masalai

Although no song in the recorded collection contains the personal name of this type of spirit, one danced song of the *manakoho* category includes the name of a spirit, Kerilaro, believed to be a *masalai:*

Noho nau ki aruna taku One,	I get to my feet in my afterworld,
Nitia nau te Taiteone;	I am struck by the sea there;
Noho Kerilaro te Taiteone,	Kerilaro lives in my afterworld's sea,
Nitia nau te Taiteone.	I am struck by the sea in my afterworld.

Masaurani

The opening of an old shark-catching *tuki* song for the canoe *Sakaina* reports the supportive presence on board of not one but two types of spirit, a *tipua* and a *masaurani:*

Te kanahau te tipua e mauvi taku vaka;	The *tipua*'s rope is fastened securely to my canoe;
Te matua karoro te masaurani e hau i Sakaina.	The *masaurani*'s rolled fiber is also fastened securely to *Sakaina*.

As noted earlier, on the occasion of the eruptions at Rabaul in 1994, Tautea composed a *tuki* relating his terror and subsequent invocation to his protective spirits:

Īē ko te hatiana te mouna	At the shattering of the mountain
E ko tere ko nau nā e i aku rimarima;	I ran away as fast as I could;
Ko tere ko nau nā e i aku morimori e tani ko nau	I ran away, but I was too slow, so I cried
Ki taku masaurani, ki Auri Matua nā Huitepapailaro.	To my spirits Auri Matua, and all the Huitepapailaro.

Tipuna

Since ancestors are invoked in time of need, most commonly during fishing, it comes as no surprise that their assistance, and particularly the successful outcome of an invocation, is praised in song, as the following shark-fishing *tuki* illustrates:

Ko Pakeva, taku rono tākoto i tua;	Pakeva, news about me was heard over the ocean;
E lono i taku tipuna nei;	I was instructed by my ancestor;
Ko Pātē, taku ata tākoto i tua,	Pātē, my technique stays on the ocean,
E lono eia Terupo nei.	I learnt it from Terupo.

Ancestors are routinely invoked in newly composed *tuki* songs intended for performance on the *marae*. In 1995 Tarasomo composed one such on the occasion of his wife Teume's death, a song notable for its several detailed references to his ancestors:

Ē taku ssomo nā e tuku i taku tipuna,	My garden's growth has been entrusted to my ancestor;
Nā uru nā ki loto te vusi, tani taku aroha.	I enter the garden, crying my grief.
Īē ko taku ssomo nā e tuki e ki Apeo.	My garden's growth has been placed in the hands of Apeo.
Uru nau ki loto te vusi, ni aroha nau ki Teume.	I enter the garden, thinking about Teume.
Īē ko taku tama manatu anau te uru a Tai Mouku;	My child, I think of the vegetation at Tai Mouku;
Īē Sina manatua nau nā huata o Hare Ata.	Sina thinks about Hare Ata's [plentiful] harvest.
Īē e ko aku tamana nau ssare atu ki te vusi;	Oh, my fathers, I'm going there, to the garden;
Īē Pōpī ma Sieki nau ssare atu ki te vusi.	Pōpī and Sieki, I'm going there, to the garden.
Īē ko taku tamana nā e taka ma nau.	My father and I go around together.
Īē ko Temurilaki e tukua mai taku sao.	Temurilaki provides me with a season.
Īē ko taku tipuna e tukua mai te kaukareva;	My grandfather requests food from me;
Īē ko Timu e tukua mai te kaukareva.	Atimu requests food from me.

Similarly, in a 1997 composition apparently sent back from the afterworld by Pātoko, who had died in that year, she reports the comforting information that she is safely accommodated with her ancestors:

Taka iho ō i nau;	I wandered around;
Ni taka iho i vaetelani ni.	I wandered around up in the sky.
Uāiē, te tamana nau e noho ma taku tipuna;	Father, I am with my grandparents;
Uāiē, ko Sioneatua e taka iho ma Pātoko.	Sioneatua is with Pātoko.

Manu / Mouri

The activities of one's own spirit after death are detailed in several categories of song poetry, although the specific terms *manu* or *mouri* appear only rarely; the words are more commonly associated with spoken comment and description. One particularly clear example comes from a set of *sore* dances sent back from Arehu, one of which is given here.

Ē ko taku manu ni au i vaetelani,	Oh, my spirit arrived from the horizon,
Fakamoe ki aruna taku hare, ōīē tū īō;	And settled on top of my house, *ōīē tū īō;*
Ē ko taku manu ni au i vaetelani,	Oh, my spirit arrived from the horizon,

Fakamoe ki aruna Hare Ata ō Rehu,
  ōīē tū īō.
Ā ni fakarere taku manu ki aruna,
Fakamoe ki loto marae, ōīē tū īō;
Ā ni fakarere taku manu ki aruna,
Fakamoe ki loto marae Arehu, ōīē tū īō.

E tū atu nau ki aku tipuna, hē ia?

E tū atu nau ki taku tipuna,
Fakatonu mai e ki anau.
E tū atu nau ki Temarena, hē ia?
E tū atu nau ki Temarena,
Fakatonu mai e ki anau.

And settled on top of Arehu's own
  house—Hare Ata.
My spirit is flown on high,
Then settled on the *marae, ōīē tū īō;*
My spirit is flown on high,
Then settled on Arehu's own *marae,*
  ōīē tū īō.

I stand before my ancestors, but where
  am I?

I stand before my ancestors,
And they give me guidance.
I stand before Temarena, but where am I?
I stand before Temarena,
And he gives me guidance.

Sau

The *sau* spirits lend their designation to the most common type of dances performed on ritual occasions, dances themselves called *sau. Sau* songs of the deceased's clan sung as the corpse lies by the beach on Takū Island accompany the deceased's *sau* spirit as it joins other clan *sau* in the afterworld. For the same reason, *llū* (voyaging) songs of the deceased's clan are also sung at that time. The autobiographical poetry of each danced song of the *sau* category contains multiple references to the deceased's *sau* as it resides in the afterworld and participates with the spirits of fellow clan members in a variety of activities, but most especially dancing. Only *sau* danced songs identify the category of spirit; the following is typical:

Iē ko nau ku hano rō, tū ki te sau nei

Ioīē ko Tau ku hano rō, tū ki te sau nei.

Ē ko taku sau nei e hakatū ki hea?
Ko nau ku hano rō, tū ki te sau nei.

Ā ki hakatū ki taku marae tapu;
Ā ki hakatū ki taku ahana tapu.
Ā ki hakariro ko nau ia Tau ē;
Ā ki hakariro ko Tau ki Ahotu,
Ko Tau ku hano rō, tū ki te sau nei.

I go and stand there, where the *[sau]*
  spirit is
Tau goes and stands there, where the
  spirit is.
Where shall I put my own spirit?
I go and stand there, where the *[sau]*
  spirit is.
I put it there on my sacred arena;
I put it there on my sacred yard.
Then I disappear from Tau;
Then Tau disappears from Ahotu,
Because Tau is going to where the *[sau]*
  spirit is.

The *sau* spirits from Hare Ata clan insert a poetic marker in the songs they compose and later send back to the human community via medium, by including the name of the site called Tematarupe in one or more lines of the poetry. The *sau* spirit of Ariki Manauī sent back a *manakoho* danced song in the early 1900s in this manner, confirming his arrival and residence in Hare Ata's clan afterworld:

Īē, ko tuku he mako ki taku one, hiō hiē.	I deposited a song in my afterworld, *hiō hiē.*
Ūāē, moe nau ki loto taku hare, tere iho te vaka ki anau;	I lay dead in my house, and a canoe came for me;
Ko tuku he mako ki taku one, e hiō hiē.	I deposited a song in my afterworld, *hiō hiē.*
Ūāē, moe te Ariki ki loto Hakātui ko tere iho Hakautamanu.	The Ariki lay dead at Hakātui, and *Hakautamanu* came for me.
Ūāē, tuku nau ki aruna taku one, ni tokia nā matani Teone;	I placed it on top of the afterworld, while searching for the wind at the afterworld;
Ūāē, tū Hakanake ki tua Tematarupe, ni tokia nau nā matani Teone.	Hakanake stood by Tematarupe, while searching for the wind at the afterworld.
Ūāē, noho nau ki aruna taku one, ni taia nau te tai Teone;	I stayed above the afterworld, splashed by the water at the afterworld;
Ūāē, noho Kerilono ki tua Tematarupe, ni taia nau te tai hutohuto.	Kerilono stayed behind Tematarupe, and I was splashed by the rising waves.
Ūāē, tere mai te tai a taku one, tere iho ki tua mātou;	Here comes the sea at my afterworld, rising behind us;
Ūāē, nimonimo te tai a taku one, tere iho ki tua Tehakamaru.	The sea swirls around in my afterworld, rising behind Tehakamaru.

Takū appears to be an exception to the general rule in Polynesia (Handy 1927, 74), in that details of life in the afterworld are indeed known. They are conveyed in the contents of danced song poetry sent back to the living, though interpreted through the filter of poetic convention and referencing.

Summary

Religious beliefs constitute mechanisms for conceptually reducing in the variety of domestic activities elements of the unknown, the unpredictable, the unchangeable, and the undesirable by invocation of a class of nonhuman beings held to possess the ability to accomplish such ends. Much of daily life on Takū is imbued with the supernatural, to a degree mirroring and confirming the nature of social relations on the atoll. The two activities that occupy the greatest amount of time—the survival pursuits of gardening and fishing— attract the greatest attention of *aitu* and *tipuna* spirits, to whom each adult is believed to have access and to whom each may address requests for personal assistance.[20]

In traditional Takū religious ideology, links between the Ariki, clan spirits, and the phenomena of wind, rain, and sunshine, meant the Ariki can control the elements to a point by direction of his own and the spirits' energy. It sometimes happens, however, that crops fail, fishing is unsuccessful, and the weather turns bad despite the Ariki's best efforts, and on such occasions, he is expected to provide an explanation. These explanations present an inference from the capabilities generally ascribed to spiritual powers rather than any specific intention attributed to the spirits. Accordingly, disaster may be attributed to the inadequacy of humans acting in situations directly or indirectly involving the spirit realm, either in ignorance or disregard of restrictions, or through incorrect adherence to ritual procedure.

Takū's religious ritual imposes the familiar on the unfamiliar—the Ariki controlling natural elements through invocations, the practiced healer exerting authority over the unknown by manipulative intervention, the renowned fisherman summoning the unseen with incantations—making sense of what the senses collectively cannot comprehend. Takū's religion thus has an explanatory function, answering "why" questions, when unusual or unexpected events directly involving humans are believed to have a cause that may be determined by the application of false causal reasoning. Events of social significance are linked causally and retrospectively to other events of significance:

> Why did the rain fail to stop when Ariki Avo uttered his invocation on the *marae* in 1995 during a *tukumai?* Because a visitor had traveled to Nukurekia Island without Avo's prior approval, and so angered the *aitu* resident there.

> Why was a particular person attacked by a predator fish or injured on land? Because he or she had disregarded a ban relating to a specific location or activity and thereby angered the spirits.

> Why do the crops of one man grow faster and larger than anyone else's? Because he alone knows the appropriate ritual formulae to utter to local spirits while in his garden.

Through tales of the simple conveying of food samples and founding crews and passengers from other islands, mythology accounts for the presence on the atoll of crops, animals, spirits, and humans without providing answers to questions such as the creation of the world and the origin of humans generally.

Religious belief on Takū assumes an explanatory and visible dimension, however, when the continuity of manageable existence is disrupted. As a reaction to the ultimate severance—death—religion offers the hope for continuity first through the tangible results of successful tuna fishing and later through the intangible evidence of songs sent from the afterworld. As a human initiative also, acts arising from religious belief attempt to extend personal abilities and enhance individual skills at imposing some order on aspects of the universe otherwise beyond control. At times of social crisis, for example, Takū's religion provides an effective counter to anxiety, uncertainty, and perceived loss of control over natural forces. A society heavily dependent on the sea for economic survival focuses many of its rituals on the security of its canoes and the safety of their occupants; recitation of ritual formulae on land and sea secures supernatural assistance to create positive outcomes and avert negative possibilities.

Death forces the living to confront the realities of both the loss of physical contact and the maintenance of spiritual contact. A death makes the spirits particularly active on land and sea, requiring both placation and intercession. The grieving family seeks a sign that the soul has arrived safely in the after-world, and this sign is sought in terms of the atoll's principal resource, fish. Pakeva, the resident sea deity, sends such a sign to the canoe in the form of a whole school of tuna.

Although personal sanctity resides in the clan elders, that of the Ariki exceeds all others as an adjunct of his responsibility for the spiritual well-being and protection of the entire community. Active only in religious ritual until the end of the nineteenth century, living alone and communicating directly with his ancestors and personal spirits rather than with his people, each new Ariki assumed a combination of far-reaching powers and complex responsi-bilities that required the abandonment of normal domestic life and relation-ships. As his time became more occupied with religious matters, his person assumed something of the unworldly quality of the beings he invoked and thus it became sacred. In a parallel development, spirit became interwoven with "earth body,"[21] in the person of the *masalai* Laroteone, who spoke and oper-ated through the medium Faite. So closely identified are spirit and medium in this case that contemporary accounts omit references to the human woman herself and speak of Laroteone as an entity both audible and visible.

Takū's religion supports with both sanctions and attractions the society's basic institutions and values. Religious belief penetrates a great many activi-ties on land and sea, particularly the successful completion of long or difficult operations, for example, completion of a new tuna-fishing canoe or shark-noosing rope, purification of an elder's house after a patient's convalescence, purification of a new mother, catching a large turtle or a prestige fish, creat-ing rain in time of drought, dragging ashore a large drift log, as well as the complex rituals of death and mourning. Failure to heed the protocols associ-ated with such events, either through ignorance or defiance, is believed to be punished by the spirits through illness, injury, or death.

Takū belief in many spirits who assist and protect individual clans and who may be invoked individually and by name suggests a religious system that has a fragmenting, rather than integrating, function within Takū society as a whole. To some extent this function was in the past balanced by the overarching influence of broadly accessible spirits such as Pākeva.

Religious beliefs validate and reinforce social relations. Through shared beliefs and communal rituals, through the knowledge that the mythical spirit ancestors brought to Takū the edible and otherwise useful flora for the perpetual benefit of their human descendants, and through the continuation after death of the social organization existing in life, it imposes a sense of the familiar on the unfamiliar. When appropriately contacted, appeased, and entertained, the spirits can be prevailed on to assist with common goals of economic security and general health and well-being. Takū's system of mediumship, which constitutes the sole form of verbal communication from spirits to humans, is founded in the belief that the spirits of dead relatives use mediums to voice their wishes, comments, and explanations, and also convey their original musical compositions. Such songs, their poetic allusions sometimes masked by semantic opacity, focus on the continuation in another realm of personal and communal values held dear during life. They publicly proclaim through subsequent performance that death is a changer of the mode of existence rather than a form of ultimate and permanent destruction.

Takū's religion was and is the distinct domain of men.[22] Although women take an active role in food-related rituals of the *tukumai* and lead singing groups on the first night and subsequent afternoons' dance performances on the *marae,* and although women may even act as mediums for the deceased, in all these activities they act under the instructions of a clan elder, who is always a man. Some women do know incantations and may demonstrate this during the *tuki heiva,* when women individually demonstrate their understanding of religious matters. These recitations occur typically during a *hāunu* party organized for principal mourners by their affines. Additionally, in a family whose first male child happens to be considerably younger than his sister(s), the eldest daughter will hold in custody the ritual information given from the father until the son is old enough to be entrusted with it. Women's construction of *kaisuru* sacra appears limited to that used for the treatment of skin ailments, such as an unburst boil.

Only two of the present clan elders have ever used their clan invocations on the *marae;* the last occasion was prior to the death in 1974 of Ariki Kaiposu, and the ritual formulae have remained dormant for some thirty years. The other three elders have learned the formulae from their predecessors but have not used them, since they assumed their positions after 1974. For both groups of elders, the future holds no immediate prospects of any performance occasion, and thus they are in an unusual situation of being the custodians of a body of ritual information that they may never put to its intended use. These men represent the first generation of religious leaders to have the means, but not the opportunity, of publicly invoking clan spirits for the material and bodily benefit of their clan. Older residents are adamant that, despite changes to the island's religious life over the past one hundred years, the power of the founding spirits is both enduring and undiminished. As Nūnua Posongat once remarked, *"E sē lavā te oti, te power rā e moe"* (It is incapable of finishing; their power still exists). But the growing numbers of Christians are determined to prove this assertion false.

The Ariki's inherited authority to voice a decisive view on virtually every matter affecting the community, and his ability to invoke the atoll's most potent spirits for the continuation or restoration of physical well-being and social order has created in his institutionalized person what Lieber calls the "tangible manifestation of the community's integrity" (1994, 11). From this, it follows logically that any perceived weakening of the Ariki's authority or effectiveness will impact negatively on communal integrity, so the most likely context for such a situation appears to be the rise to dominance of a rival religion.

Takū traditional practice made few allowances for group activities for the young, who were left largely to their own resources until puberty. Christian churches have exploited the absence of existing structures to introduce their own programs, backed up by the machinery and resources of international organizations, which, in a sense, they represent. Off-island training, admission to church-owned schools, eligibility for scholarships, promotional literature and the visual attraction of uniforms and proliferation of executive titles all combine to offer to Takū's children powerful persuasions against which traditional values and practices can offer little defense. Evangelical Christianity seems to provide the young a degree of compensation for their subordinate social position by offering individual recognition and a well-defined infrastructure through which they may proceed up formalized ranks to realize a balance of responsibility and authority unparalleled in secular community life. Similar attractions appeal to some of the adult female population, particularly those whose husbands are absent for long periods, for example, crewing on the *Sankamap*. For men, however, Christianity is considered more a threat to their own authority, both within the family and clan. While friction erupts only infrequently and on an individual basis, the growing influence of the church in Takū seems to have it poised to assume more assertive forms of social presence.

Chapter 4
Processes of Takū Music

Composition

Human Creation

Human composition is an active and conscious process. Either spontaneously or on the request of another resident, a composer (the numbers of males and females are approximately equal) starts by *mānatu tonu* (focusing) on a given theme, from which first the poetry and then the melody are developed. In theory, anyone is free to go to a recognized composer and suggest a particular idea, poetic phrase, or theme for a new composition. The following account, by Nūnua Posangat in 1994, is typical:

> Sieki [the former Pure] asked me to compose a *tuki* for [the canoe] *Hauvaka*. I sat down and started to think, recalling the recent tuna-fishing contest on the island that was won by *Hauvaka*, having caught the most tuna. And that was when I composed this *tuki* for *Hauvaka*:

Penapena taku vaka haite aku tama.	I built my canoe to test my children.
Ka penapena Hauvaka ni aro iho mo ki tua.	I built *Hauvaka* and paddled it toward the ocean.
Ō ka te tausua te henua hurihuri taku vaka;	During the contest, my canoe used a variety of methods;
Ō ka te taki atu Nukutoa hakapiri Hauvaka.	During Nukutoa's tuna contest, I rested the canoe on a coral head [for ritual purposes].
Ō ka te ika ni a te moana, ni huri mai ki te vaka.	A pelagic fish turned toward the canoe.
Ō ka te atu roto te moana, ni huri mai ki Hauvaka;	A mid-size tuna turned from the ocean toward *Hauvaka;*
Ō ka se lono ni ā se tanata, e lono tonu i tana tamana;	Someone had got advice, hearing it straight from his father;
Ō ka se lono ni ā Kīpū, e lono tonu i Sieki.	Kīpū had got advice, hearing it straight from Sieki.

The introduction of the *hula* to Takū in the recent past opened a new range of creative possibilities to the island's composers. The *hula* is typically danced by unmarried women to the accompaniment of one or more guitars. Its most prominent composer, Mary Tāmaki, explained:

As I heard the story, this is how the *hula* was introduced to our island. It was brought here by a man called Kameru and his group. When Kameru was here, I was still at school. He came and sang his *hula* and that's how I came to know them. He came and taught the young people how to perform them. When the *hula* was introduced here, only the young people used to dance it.

When the dance was introduced here, we women composed some to praise those two men who went to Moresby, the ones Dr McCarthy took—Kaiposu [the Ariki] and Huarani.[1] . . . I knew what a *hula* was like, so I thought about composing one myself. At that same time, we were building a copra drier and as we were working together, I was thinking about the composition thus, the way we women were acting, and similarly for the men. So I composed that *hula,* starting "Women and men, the moon is rising." I composed that song in the early morning, when the women left us and returned to their houses. We stayed at the "fire house"; that's when I composed it, but not everybody knew that we had spent the night there at the drier. Our fragrance spread over the entire island during our performance, and I composed about that too. At moonrise, I was thinking about my song. I finished my *hula* then, then gave thought to setting the actions, so I started the song and then set the actions:

Hahine ma nā tanata te malama lā u sopo,	You women and men—the moon has risen,
Koe ē tali ia te manoni u tele vave hale,	As you wait, the fragrance spreads over the houses,
aloha iē nau tali atu ē.	I feel sad as I wait.
Pena tō hale, pena tilotilo ē.	Prepare your house, prepare the young leaves.
Mmata mai ōtou nā hai America,	You Americans can look at it,
Conclusion mātou nei say goodbye, hāoti ē.	But we conclude by saying goodbye, and finishing.

Among song types generally, lesser composers aid both their own work and that of the singers by deliberating modeling *(tautari)* their melodies on an existing stereotype, of which several are in use, particularly among *tuki* songs. In preparation for a *tukumai,* three to five new *tuki* are composed for each resident who has died over the previous six to twelve months. The music of more than 80 percent of such *tuki* composed between 1997 and 1999 was identified as using existing melodic patterns, the reduced original material easing the learning process, in line with established practice:

Newly composed *tuki* merely imitate the old songs. When you compose a *tuki,* you must imitate the old ones, you can't compose your own songs differently. You compose by imitating the old *tuki*, the melody of an old song. (Nūnua, pers comm, Dec 2000)

The general belief that individual song categories have distinctive melodies is matched by a general expectation that the musical style of newly composed songs should continue these established patterns. As Nūnua once put it, if a new composition uses the melody of a *tuki*, then it is a *tuki*. However, not all residents accept melody modeling. During the months of rehearsal prior to the 1997 *tukumai* for thirteen people, one man was reportedly furious with his female cousin for using the melody of a *tuki* composed many years ago for his grandfather, and substituting present-day proper names for the original ones. When confronted, the cousin replied that she was a maternal grandchild of that same man and therefore was as entitled as the complainant to use the material. Men privately siding with her suggested she and her group sing it repeatedly at future practices and loudly on the *marae* at its formal performance, to emphasize her point and humiliate her critic.

It also happens that plans to introduce material composed off-island may be thwarted. In the early 1990s, for example, a resident traveled to Nukuria and requested from composers there a set of *tuki* to celebrate his own status as an accomplished fisherman. These were duly delivered some time later on audiocassette, but the object of their poetic praise died soon after, and so the songs were to be learned by his family and clan for performance at his *tukumai*. As late as three months after this group started their rehearsals, using the recordings, the singers were still having difficulty, unfamiliar with the language of the poetry. Takū residents are, however, eclectic performers, and dance programs on the second morning of the *tukumai* routinely include more foreign than local material. Indeed, one resident cynically characterized Takū people as "rubbish collectors" because of their apparent inability to compose sufficient new material to meet all local performance needs.

New *tuki* are composed for the *tukumai* of both adults and children, and those who died locally and off-island, but there appears to be no direct link between one's personal reputation while alive and the number of *tuki* composed for one's mortuary rites. One male teenager who had suffered severe mental retardation since childhood was ignored by virtually all adults and teased by children; he spent most days simply watching the domestic activities going on around him. But with his death in 1997, five *tuki* were composed and sung at his *tukumai*, a figure surpassing that composed for some of the adults jointly honored at the same ritual, and the song poetry attributed to him a variety of positive (but demonstrably untrue) attributes: that he raised a prolific garden and participated skillfully in tuna fishing. Islanders routinely compose new *tuki* for dead children, but not necessarily in the same numbers as for an adult.

There is a general expectation among Takū's residents that the poetic content of a new song, which is basically descriptive in style, be "factual" *(tonu)*. But not all new compositions meet this expectation. Particularly in *tuki*, the poetry may speak of actions that are verifiably false, generating criticism, if privately voiced. Such songs are characterized as *hatu hakallelesi* (deceitfully composed), or *ahuvare* (arrogant), or *ahu matani* (empty praise). One man explained the community's public tolerance as follows: "If lies occur in a song, we know it but, out of respect for the composer's ancestors, we say nothing—even though in our hearts we know it is untrue. We will still appear happy." Despite the risk of criticism, the dividing line between justifiable praise for a successful master fisherman and the extravagant claims of a lesser fisherman may be breached in the interests of adherence to the poetic convention so that the composer and thereby the singers may boast of the exploits of their clan's master fisherman. Several men privately voiced dissatisfaction with specific new *tuki* on their first performance at a *tukumai;* they claimed the size of a tuna catch included fish they themselves had caught, but in another canoe. Others noted the unlikelihood of catching more than thirty tuna by one canoe, using the old trolling method; this threw into doubt poetic claims of significantly greater catches. "They're singing nonsense!" *(E hua matani koi)*. But on such occasions, men—perhaps predictably—will claim accuracy of reporting in their own *tuki*.

In a departure from normal preparation for the *tukumai* in the following year, Tarasomo composed a *tuki* for his dead wife, Teume. Although this was not in itself a novelty, the poetic content of the song became the subject of widespread, though discreet, criticism, even among members of his own rehearsal group. Departing from the normal textual practice of praising the past exploits of the clan fisherman, this *tuki* lamented the composer's personal loss and sang publicly of emotional states considered more appropriate to be spoken privately:

Ō te kauaso ma te kaupō taku manatu atu ē.	By day and by night I ponder [my loss].
Na tiputipu te henua ē, ni tuku ki taku manava nei.	The events occurring on the island are kept in my heart.
Aku mokopuna nei huro tatani mai ē;	My grandchildren run to me, crying;
Kiliala ni tere tatani mai.	Kiliala ran to me, crying.
Takū soa e nā taratara tāua nei, tuku kina manava ē.	My lover, the things we used to talk about are kept in my heart.
Takū soa ē nā taratara tāua nei, tuku kina aroha ē.	My lover, the things we used to talk about form part of my grief.
Aku tama nei huro tatani mai ē.	My children run to me, crying.

I attended several gatherings in which this song was rehearsed, the singers' surprise at its poetry evident in the widespread eye contact made among group members as Tarasomo first sang through his composition, their glances registering concern. Their initial surprise over, however, the group devoted their attention to the task of learning, which was duly accomplished without incident, despite private expressions of unease. In this instance, public sym-

pathy for the widower's grief did not entirely obviate the general desire that
its expression be channeled through established and essentially retrospective
themes. Such was the strength of his emotion that the composer could still be
heard singing this song by himself in his yard a year after the *tukumai,* as his
sorrow continued unabated.

The establishment of an island judicial system for dealing with minor incidents places institutionalized constraints on, among other things, verbal criticism of fellow-residents. Composers routinely exploit poetry's allusive powers
and singing's appealing delivery as a way to exercise a highly effective right of
reply. I give here two examples that I myself observed.

Following a verbal exchange with his neighbor while under the effects of
toddy, a man was taken to court in 1994. In a state of exasperation after the
court appearance, he composed a *hula* and taught it to his children. The
neighbor was highly indignant about the song, but was powerless to take
action about it.

Nā tama te hare hotahi hataoto hoi pehē.	Unthinking, the people of that house went ahead with it.
Kōtia nau ē, hāloha so nau ē.	I was taken to court, I felt ashamed.
Nā tama te ma hotahi, hataoto hoi pē.	Those same people with whom we regularly share food went ahead with it.
Tō koti nā nau sē iloa, heveni la hoi e iloa	I knew nothing about your complaint, heaven alone knows what it was about.
Na lou tō baepol, nā Satani lā hoi e aka.	There are laws in your bible [which you broke], but it's Satan who is now laughing.
Na loto nā nā ni loto hoi te aleve.	You acted on something that happened as a result of the toddy.
Tiputipu outou nā hāloha tama ē.	Your attitude brought shame on somebody.

In 1992 while on Nukumanu, a Takū man was sentenced to one week's
labor after an apparent misunderstanding concerning a local woman's nubil-
ity, her parents having promised her to another man. He was sentenced on
a Friday and started clearing undergrowth beneath coconut trees on the following Monday. Two years later, while working at a formal drinking party at
Sialeva as a nondrinking barman, he startled the other men by breaking into
song—he was not noted for his singing ability or enthusiasm, and it is normal
practice for older men to begin singing at such events. When it was apparent
that his song—a *lani*—was new and related his experience on Nukumanu,
the entire gathering fell silent and heard him out. On completion there were
general comments of approval, and he was asked to repeat the song. As he
did so, a few singers started to join in the refrain—*Hē u hāloha so nau ē* (I'm so
sad)—leaning forward as they concentrated on his words.

Tau tamana ē, koe e noho ia e nau ponotia i te hale courti?	Father, how can you just sit there while I'm here in jail?
Hē u hāloha so nau ē.	I'm so sad.
Tau tinana ē, koe e noho ia e nau ponotia i te hale kōti?	Mother, how can you just sit there while I'm here in jail?
Special Monday nei tū mai nau vālalo nā niu saele velevele nā veve hoi.	On that special Monday there I was, under the coconut palms clearing away the weeds.
1992 nei nau ka mea pēhea ē?	It's 1992, what am I to do?
Tau tipuna ē, oe e noho ia e nau ponotia i te hale kōti?	Grandfather, how can you just sit there while I'm here in jail?
1992 nei u hāloha tama e nau ka mea pēhea ē?	It's 1992, somebody is sad; what am I to do?

Spirit Composition

Parallel to human composition, until the Ariki's unexpected death on Bougainville in 1974, ran the phenomenon of a medium "bringing" *(tō mai)* complete danced songs from a recently deceased resident at the *tānaki* ritual. Such songs were not considered "composed" *(hatuhatu)* but existing "from antiquity" *(i mua)*. Several features of the act of "bringing" were noteworthy:

1. Because the medium normally had no later recollection of events occurring while in a state of trance *(llea)*, a new song was uttered only once and therefore the family had only one opportunity to memorize the material.
2. Only the song was conveyed via the medium; the dance gestures *(āuna)* were added later by consensus and always in accordance with the poetic references, insofar as these might be understood.
3. Neither the singers nor the eventual audience had an opportunity to ask for an explanation of the poetic references. Typically, the poetry of *sau* and *manakoho* songs, for example, contained references to specified movements (eg, "turning," "sliding") whose significance is unknown to present performers.

Until the dissolution of the *tānaki* ritual in 1974, songs received from the spirits of the dead included several categories of women's dances: *sau, manakoho, uī,* and *sore.* The *uī* and *sore* dances have a unified structure, whereas the *sau* and *manakoho* dances in the active repertoire consist of two to five pairs of alternately slow and faster sections called *hakatū* and *takitaki,* respectively; they are sung with a break of only a few seconds, or even none at all. Two such pairs appear to constitute a minimum acceptable composition, and indeed two specimens containing a single pair although duly conveyed by a medium were not subsequently taken to the *marae* for performance. In such cases, attempts may be made to graft the newer composition onto an existing song, as Sione Pilike explained:

> If somebody had died and brought and introduced his *manakoho,* but it had only one *hakatū,* then we'd search for a place to fit it in. So we'd take it and insert it in an existing *sau,* so there would be enough for it to be a dance. One *hakatū* by itself isn't enough to be danced, so the *hakatū* brought by the dead person has to be fitted into an existing *sau.* That's what happened for the *sau* for Kikiva's father: it had a single *hakatū,* one *hakatū,* and *takitaki.* But they couldn't fit it in anywhere, so it was abandoned, just left like that. There was no clan *sau* that they could fit it into. If there had been somebody related to them, someone from Hare Mania, then they should have fitted it into the *sau Marena* or the *sau Sione.* They could have inserted it so that it could have been danced because, on the *marae,* it's not possible to have just a single section—that's the custom from earliest times. You're not allowed to go and dance a single section. You have to dance all five [pairs of *hakatū* and *takitaki*].
>
> You are required by [the founding spirit] Pukena to count [the sections], because Pukena will count the songs you take to the *marae* and, to be complete, there must be five [of each]. In that manner you'll be allowed to go and perform at the *marae,* and if there are more than five, then it'll be all right. The *hakatū* inserted inside your performance will make it even better; Pukena won't become angry. But if it's insufficient, Pukena will be angry at what the people have taken in jest to the *marae.* That's what happened with the song for Nukeria's *hakatū*—Kikiva's father—it was simply left there because they couldn't fit it into anything.
>
> The *sau* dance is something very important, a part of our tradition, bigger than the *manakoho.* The *manakoho* is less important; the spirits for all our clans came with our *manakoho* [but not any *sau*]. But as for the *sau,* they're very important; when you communicate your *sau* [ie, after you have died], you have to do it according to custom. Only then can you come and dance [on the *marae*], because of Pukena's presence. That's what happened with the *sau* for Kikiva's father; it consisted of no more than a single *hakatū* section.

Individuals selected by the deceased's family to act as mediums at a *tukumai* maintain a close relationship with that family after the ritual has concluded and may, for example, be requested periodically to identify the reason for a member's illness or accident, or to forecast deaths in the near future. On such occasions, the medium enters the state of altered consciousness and voices the response. Few people who have acted as mediums ever recall those events in detail, but there appears to be one—Sione Pilike—who remembers the details of bringing a *sau* danced song from a spirit of the dead.[2] The following is Sione's account of the origin of the *sau Marena:*

> When that particular person passed away, we went and buried him; we stayed on at the cemetery and buried him. His name was Marena, and we went and buried him in the cemetery. People were staying at Vaihare, then I returned here to Nukutoa.

While I slept that night, I had a dream about him, a dream about that person. I saw him flying inside a meteorite, in a meteorite shower he flew toward me from above. I didn't know who the person was, that one flying to me and coming right up to me. I immediately lost consciousness. I went numb and I was afraid of him.

After I regained consciousness that night, I went and bathed in the sea and my body returned to normal. Then I sat there. On the second night with those people at Vaihare, I dreamt about him. Again he flew to me in a meteorite shower. He flew over and came to me, and again I lost consciousness, my body suddenly felt bad, and I was afraid of him. Then I awoke and went to bathe. That was on the second night.

On the third night, I thought that he wouldn't come, that he wouldn't come in the meteorite, that thing that had flown in the middle of the night. But he flew up and struck my body and I became unconscious until that thing left my body, then I went and bathed.

On each of the five nights when the people were at Vaihare, the same thing happened. He didn't come in the form of a person, but as burning flames. That was on the fifth day that the people were at Vaihare, and I returned to Nukutoa. That afternoon we were sitting there, and at nightfall I found that I couldn't walk outside, I was so frightened. And when night fell, I was unable to go down to the sea off Hare Ata. When people asked me what was happening, I said it was nothing, then hid, afraid of his presence. I sat listening to the people: they had heard that the [official clan] medium wanted to come, but I just remained inside Hare Ata. They brought the medium who was about to come but hadn't. [But nothing happened.] On the seventh night they again brought the medium who was going to come but hadn't. [Again, nothing happened.] So then he was replaced and I was summoned, and I went and stood in front of them at that house and the person—Marena—came to me. I lost consciousness, and it was as if I had been struck by a gust of wind.

Then I spoke, but not knowing what my words were. I sat and spoke to his brother Pūō in the morning when the *tānaki* was to take place. Pūō said to me, "Are you sure about the *tānaki?*"

"Yes."

"What are we going to sing?"

"Some *sau*. Tonight, I'm going to sleep, so will you come and collect me at daybreak?"

"Yes, we'll get you from the house, so go and sleep there."

"And who's the person who will know how to sing the things that will come from this house?"

"Willie."

Willie was instructed to come at daybreak. I spoke like that, without knowing, because the words were those of the spirit.

Then, when we were finished, we all went to the house, and Marena took me there. I went to sleep that night, and right at midnight I suddenly saw him. He took me to a place called Tai Vokosea. He had me stand there, and I saw a fire flying from Vaihare. The meteorite flew over and reached me. Then I realized I was not standing at Tai Vokosea, but at the cemetery beach. Then that person flew up and struck me, and I lost consciousness. When I recovered, I found myself sleeping at the cemetery beach, and he was standing on top of a coconut palm above me. And there was his death belt that he was wearing.

I asked him, "What am I doing here?"

"I brought you."

"Why?"

"I want you as a spokesman. I want to use you because of my father, Terupo, who asked me to use a fellow clansman. I am not to use someone from my mother's clan, but from his clan."

Then, two nights later, I was asleep and again he flew to me and struck me so that I fell unconscious, and it was then that I knew that the thing was a *sau*. That had been the first section of the *sau Marena*, and then I arose, awake in the middle of the night. I wanted to sing that *sau*, but I also wanted to sleep. Since it was about 3 a.m. I went back to sleep, and then I knew that the *takitaki* was being sung to me.

I slept then started singing that *sau* on the morning that Willie came, straightaway singing the *sau* to him. He didn't come using his mouth and the words: he came and stood there, so I didn't see his mouth singing: the body of the thing that appeared in my heart was simply there like that. Then came a period during which I knew the *sau* was no more, and I awoke. That was the tenth night, and I simply held on to that *sau* so I could sing it to Willie.

I returned home that day and slept, and again he flew to me and sang that *sau*. Then, around 2 p.m. that afternoon, I went and slept. Then four [pairs of song sections] were complete. Pūō told me on the tenth day that we were to end the *tānaki*. So we left it there and sang just those four things. But then the two of us talked together and I came back to my house, I was unable to sleep because the *sau* was still coming in my stomach. I called Willie to come, and the two of us sang that thing, the sixth part. Again I called to Willie that there were two more things left, to make ten sections: five *takitaki* and five *hakatū*. And so, the next morning when Willie came, I told him that it was finished, that all that was left was the incantation *tuki*, that [the *sau*] was finished, and that nothing remained in my stomach.

Then I slept inside the house, and on that day I didn't dream; I fell into a deep sleep. That was the eleventh day, and we held the *tānaki* and on that night, the people sang inside that house. And that was the *sau Marena*.

Significantly, Sione himself did not actively "learn" the *sau* from Marena, but was simply the receptacle and then the conduit through which the material was communicated to the waiting family at the *tānaki*. Marena's spirit supplied the material to and through Sione in individual sections, quantities small enough to be memorized at a single hearing. However, because a new dance section was provided each day, the learning process would necessarily have been both intense and prolonged.

In theory, any adult may be contacted by the spirit of a recently dead fellow clan member and told to be the medium for transmission of a new danced song. Nūnua, however, considers himself an exception because his long-deceased namesake is actively preventing him from becoming a medium:

> I was given the name Fakatūtūfenua; that's my birth name, Akae Fakatūtūfenua. I haven't yet been a medium, nobody has come because my namesake doesn't want anyone to come through me. My namesake has prevented it. If someone were to come through me, my name would be discarded and I would be named after the one using me as a medium [only for the duration of the *tānaki*]. But my namesake, Fakatūtūfenua, has prevented that from happening to me. The dead can't come through me because that one is preventing it. The one I'm named after was [the Ariki] Apeo's son; after his death his name was given to me. Three days after his death, my mother gave birth to me.

Through the public performance of danced songs received from the dead, the community as a whole gains access to a deeper comprehension and acceptance of death and the afterworld as the poetry externalizes and objectifies otherwise inchoate or inarticulate experiences. At each *tukumai* the newly composed *tuki* include a few whose poetry fits the model of those brought from the dead, but that are privately believed to have been composed by a living resident in that style. In other words, the historical accuracy of poetic narrative cannot be deduced from an examination of the lyrics of a new *tuki*, but any doubts about authenticity tend to be maintained privately. The following is an example of this sort of circumstance. Teonetua and Teume were among the several women who died in 1997 and, in the *tuki* song subsequently received by women in Teume's husband's family, the husband (Tarasomo) was reminded—ostensibly by Teume herself—to keep to himself certain information relating to the neighboring atoll of Nukuria, whence her grandfather emigrated many years earlier. Teume's father, Pāsia, was similarly reminded of the five-day tuna-fishing period following the death, during which the spirits of the two women sent up a large quantity of tuna from the depths as a signal they had safely reached the afterworld. Both women expressed grief at their separation from their respective children.

Neva te vaka te hānau.	The children's canoe is always there.
Takoto i taku manava nei.	Residing always in my heart.
Te vaka Teonetua ma Teume.	The canoe belonging to Teonetua and Teume is always there.
Nā manu ni ō iho i vaetelani, hakatūria se matakupena;	Their spirits come down from the horizon, and give us the fruits of the net;
Kōrua ni tara ō iho i Nukeria, hakatūria se matakupena.	"You came as gulls from Nukuria, giving us the fruits of the net."
Takū soa nā taratara te henua nei, tuku ko koe ki tō manava ē;	"My friend, the news from this island must remain in your heart" [said Teume];

Tarasomo nā taratara Nukutoa nei tuku ko koe ki tō manava ē.	"Tarasomo, the news from Nukutoa must remain in your heart" [she said].
Te tamana te sao ni tukua mai;	"Father, a period of time was set aside [for tuna fishing]";
Pāsia te sao ni tukua mai.	"Pāsia, a period was set aside."
Ni aroha nau ē ki aku tama;	I grieve for my children;
Ni aroha nau ki Sione ma Atimu.	I grieve for Sione and Atimu.

Local skepticism emerged also in 1994 when a young mother died in childbirth at Buka hospital and her surviving infant daughter was subsequently given to the mother's sister to raise, despite some opposition from other family members. The adopting family sang a *tuki* at the mother's *tukumai* whose poetry confirmed that she herself had requested that her sister raise the child. Private criticism circulated that the song had merely been "designed to appear as if it had come from the other side, from the spirits" *(e mē pē se tuki e au i telā vasi, nā aitu):*

E tū nau ka tani i taku aroha i tamana ma taku tinana;	I stood crying from grief for my father and mother;
Nau e tataka i vae te lani;	I roamed around the sky;
E tatani ai nau ma taku aroha i taku henua, tuku e.	Crying at grief for my island, that's all.
E tū Mōmia ka tani i taku aroha i Manauī ma Tolo.	Mōmia stood crying from grief for Manauī and Tolo.
Nau tō iho te haitinana	I was brought here by the mother and son
Ki kite ai ko taku tipuna e nonoho i tana henua;	For my grandfather to see while he was on his island;
Nau tō iho Kalevao ma Tautea	I was brought here by Kalevao and Tautea
Ki kite ai Pūtahu e nonoho i tana henua.	For Pūtahu to see while he was on his island.
Nau tani atu ki taku taina	I cried to my sister
Ki purutia taku manu ka noho ma koe;	To care for my small daughter as your own;
Nau tani atu ki Huata	I cried to Huata
Ki purutia taku tama sere ka noho ma koe.	To care for my dear child as your own.

In addition to the poetic style criterion for evaluating the claimed source of a contemporary composition, its subject matter is also critical. Anything genuinely sent from an *aitu* is believed to relate exclusively to spirit matters, such as accounts of life in the afterworld and journeys of the spirit itself, and not events in the world of humans. There is additionally a general expectation that the poetry of danced songs received from the ancestors will be less readily understood, not so much because of specialized vocabulary as indistinct or ambiguous referents, although it is believed that such references are understood by immediate family members. Extracts from three such songs will serve as examples:

The *sau Moehiti*:

Ē ni tū taku tao i loto te ava;	My spear is lodged at the channel;
Ē ni tū taku maro i loto te ava.	My loincloth is at the channel.

Here, although reef channels are known to be the residence of spirits, the significance of the spear and loincloth is quite unknown.

The *sau Mausaurani*:

Te Masaurani e ara i te moana, ko ia e
     ara i te moana;
	The Masaurani awoke in the ocean, she
	     woke in the ocean;

Taku raki mua ki tauhia mai ki mau.	Hold fast the northwest wind for me.

Penapena mai taku raki ki saunene ki
     mārama;
	I create a wind for myself to blow but
	     still remain clear;

Te lākau te laki nā e hakamataku e au ma
     nau.
	The log drifting in the wind is great,
	     and accompanies me.

Although spirits are believed to be able to create wind either for their own purposes or to aid fishers in distress, but the specific referents in this song are not understood.

The *sau Tellara*:

Ā ko te hahine nei ki hakapotopoto,	Decorate the woman because of her womanhood,
Te hahine nā ē, anu torotoro i te sau nei;	Dancing in a crawl through the crowd;
Ā ko Sinateahana ki hakapotopoto,	Sinateahana dances while crouching because of her womanhood,
Te hahine nā ē, anu torotoro i te sau nei.	Crawling through the dance.

Ēiē ko te hau ō Sina e tū piri ki loto te
     ahana.
	Sina's garland is suspended inside her
	     yard.

Ā ni vurusia ki tana tuahenua,	Turn it around to dance at the rear of the island,
Ki anuanu te tuahenua,	To keep dancing at the rear of the island,
Sina ko tū e, tū ki loto te ahana.	Sina stands there, inside her yard.

Here, dancing is believed to be a favorite activity of the human spirit after death, but present-day Takū say they cannot understand more than the literal meanings of these lines.

The *tānaki* ritual, until its cessation in 1974, established and formalized the occasion during which the spirit of the dead taught a new *sau* dance to surviving clan members; it also confirmed to a significantly large number of people both the identity of the communicating spirit and the details of the song poetry. No *sau* were introduced after 1974, and only *tuki* songs are now believed to be brought from the dead. However, no such body of people now gathers and witnesses the communication of a *tuki* song from a deceased family member and, indeed, the apparent absence in the active or remembered repertoires of such *tuki* more than a few years old suggests that the phenomenon itself may be relatively new. Dances kept in the active repertoire over many generations reiterate clan identity—and, specifically highlight women's role in the maintenance of that identity; they also reinforce relationships with named ancestors, whereas newly received dances foreground the reduction of communal grief and anxiety at a time when memory of the death remains clear and the loss keenly felt.

Tuki Poetry

The maritime world of Takū *tuki* poetry, with its paddled tuna-canoes, water-darkening flocks of sea birds, and unfailingly bountiful ocean, belongs not to the present but to an era that effectively closed in the 1970s when foreign elements were introduced to the material culture in the form of outboard motors and imported fishing equipment, and when a gradual decline in ocean fish numbers first became apparent.[3] Through the ritual of singing these songs, participants revisit that era, but always selectively since the poetry details only its positive qualities. It is, as Small notes (1998, 119), a kind of theme park constructed from episodes in the lives of *tuki* creators whose details may in fact never have existed beyond the hopes of those whose names are identified. Since the songs more importantly perpetuate an ideology rather than present an impartial register of agreed fact, their poetic history may be changed by a sympathetic party if the act will contribute to a fuller presentation of that ideology; this will be considered in detail below. Additionally, not all poetry is considered of equal quality, and each year's group of new *tuki* songs invariably includes compositions that attract criticism for their poetry, focusing on either what is present but deficient or what is absent but considered necessary, or both. These attributes can be categorized.

Deficiencies of Poetic Structure

The two-part nature of individual poetic verses, in which the second part makes explicit what is stated only in general terms in the first, assumes the factual accuracy of the general–explicit match. However, in the first verse of the following *tuki,* the individuals identified by name in the second part do not fall within the relationship specified in the first part. That is, Tenehu (a man) and Maria do not stand in a mother-child relationship And, for a *tuki* honoring a man known for his fishing prowess, the total absence of fishing references also drew criticism.

Ē ko te kipu ni hau mai, nā ē,	The south wind blows strong,
Ni tuku iho ko taku tamana ma te lāoi, nā ē,	Going to my father during the peaceful time,
Nau e noho ē i taku hare nei.	While I remain here at home.
Ē, ni aroha nau ki te haitinana nā ē;	I grieved for the mother and child;
Ē ni aroha Tenehu ki Maria, nā ē.	I grieved for Tenehu and Maria.
Ē ko te kipu ni hau mai nā ē,	The south wind blows strong,
Ni tuku iho Tenehu ma te lāoi nā ē,	Going to Tenehu during the peaceful time,
Nau e noho ē i taku hare nei.	While I remain here at home.
Ē ni aroha nau e ki taku tama, nā ē;	I grieved for my child;
Ē ni aroha ko Terupo ki Telauika, nā ē.	Terupo grieved for [her adopted son] Telauika.

Demonstrable Errors of Fact

Although not commonly occurring in the lyrics of new songs, incidents of manipulated history are immediately recognizable to both singers and audience alike, for example:

- an elderly man no longer capable of strenuous tasks is depicted as standing in a tuna-fishing canoe and hauling in the weighty catch;
- a man who has opened a death house is incorrectly named;
- the poetry suggests that a particular tuna-fishing expedition was successful, when in reality it returned empty-handed;
- a flock of tuna-following birds is said to gather inside the channel, even though such birds always congregate in the open ocean;
- a catch of five hundred fish is proclaimed without mention that this figure includes fish other than tuna

It is in *tuki* poetry that the ongoing relationship between the spirit of a deceased resident and surviving family members is made explicit. The following paired verses are typical in this respect:

A man calls on his dead child to attach an *ikatau* (prestige fish) to his hook:

Uāiē, ki nohoria iho ko se tukuna	While at the fishing spot
Ni kārana nau ma ki taku tama	I called to my [dead] child
Hakapiri ake ko he ika tau ē.	To attach a prestige fish [to my hook].
Uāiē, ki nohoria iho ko se tukuna,	While at the fishing spot,
Ni kārana nau ma ki Temarena	I called to Temarena
Hakapiri ake ko he parumea ē.	To attach a *parumea* fish [to my hook].

The deceased person's spirit arranges for a school of tuna to appear and be caught:

Ko he tanata ni karana ki tana tama,	A man called out to his son,
Tēnei tāua aso e tukua mai te tinana,	"This is our day, arranged by my aunt;

He lākau tana ika e neva i te moana, iē	That log is surrounded by her milling fish on the ocean."
Ko Kaitū ni karana ki Mōmoa,	Kaitū called out to Mōmoa,
Tēnei tāua aso e tukua mai Tekataha i te lākau,	"This is our day, arranged by Tekataha;
Tana atu e neva i te moana, iē.	That log is surrounded by her milling tuna on the ocean."

A welcome sight to greet fishermen as they enter the ocean is a floating log, where tuna are known to congregate in large numbers and can be easily caught. The appearance of such a log is not sheer coincidence but rather the result of spirit activity: it has been sent there by either the deceased's own spirit or that of an ancestor in a gesture of spiritual support for the survivors:

Ko te haitama nā tahurima te lākau, nā ē;	The tuna accompanied the [drifting] log;
Ko Sieki ma Kaumania tū i te lākau nā ē.	[The ancestors] Sieki and Kaumania were on the log.

In a parallel manner, once a man has invoked an ancestor to assist with tuna fishing, that spirit will effectively take command of the expedition, causing the tuna to rise from the ocean depths and approach the canoe and causing the canoe itself to undertake the correct maneuvers:

Ko Temaehe huri ake ki te kapakau a Sieki nā ē;	Temaehe turns at the hand of [the ancestor] Sieki;
Ki maru ake te manu a taku vaka i te hakahua rā, tuku ē.	To make a flock approach my canoe through the ocean swell.

The size and close-knit nature of the community obviates the need for song poetry to name a deceased person in a newly composed *tuki* song for nonfamily members at the *tukumai* to correctly identify him or her; the routine inclusion of the names of living family members and ancestors is sufficient identification in itself. Other individuals identified by name in *tuki* poetry may include those who performed a special role during the burial ritual, such as placing sacra on the corpse's ears *(manoni)*, or the *henua mate* necklet around the neck. In the same manner, naming the family canoe is sufficient to identify its deceased owner. Cumulatively and by association, naming these kinds of people and property provides a linguistic trail back to the deceased.

Criticism of Contemporary *Tuki*

The late Nūnua, composer of many songs and the de facto performance specialist for the entire community, was highly critical of composers who produced what he called "short" *tuki*, merely assembling phrases or entire verses from existing compositions. How many *tuki*, he once asked rhetorically by way

of example, started thus: *Aro iho taku vaka, aro iho mo ki tua* (My canoe paddles out, paddles out into the ocean) or *Sepu iho taku vaka* (I alight from my
canoe) or *Se tanata ma tana vaka* (There was a man who had a canoe)? Nūnua
interpreted this lack of originality as indicating an inability to think creatively.
On another occasion he also criticized recent compositions as sounding like
mere speech (by which he meant long periods of level melodic movement),
whereas a clear distinction in sound between singing and speaking was highly
desirable. This view was echoed by Tekaso Laroteone in unshakeable logic: "If
you compose words in the same style as speech, then you are only speaking,
not singing." This comment referred specifically to grammatical changes that
appear in poetry, the most frequent of which is the insertion of /a/ or /o/ as
a genitive article (eg, *te ika o te moana*) for purposes of increasing the number
of syllables in a line to complete a predetermined rhythmic figure.

Two opposing influences operate in the period following a death when
composers are at work. Traditionalists both inside and outside the deceased's
family may express disappointment bordering on disgust at the high incidence of poetic (and to a lesser extent, musical) redundancy. As one man put
it, "They're not singing right, so I simply don't want to participate." For similar
reasons in 1998, Nūnua was reluctant to provide any new *tuki* for the *tukumai*
of his fellow-clansman Puāria. The active repertoire, so he told me, already
contained many *tuki* referring to Puāria's canoe, so it would be a simple matter for anybody (by which he meant anybody *else*) to substitute contemporary
proper names and avoid the effort of creating and learning a completely new
piece. This, in fact, was what happened. A parallel situation holds for *tuki*
melodies, which partake heavily of stock phrases. Statistics on *tuki* composed
for *tukumai* in 1995, 1997, and 1998, for instance, indicate that more than 80
percent of the melodies were based on existing compositions. People recognize that the large numbers of new *tuki* required for *tukumai* commemorating
several deaths in the same clan place a heavy creative responsibility on family members. Established composers may provide as many as four (or even
more) new items but any additional songs must be sought elsewhere. Lesser
composers and family members reluctantly accepting requests for several
tuki acknowledge the reduced effort required to produce a song based on an
assemblage of stereotyped poetic and melodic phrases, a view endorsed, predictably, by singers at the many rehearsals. Takū is grappling with the cultural
economics of an ideology that encourages and praises freedom of expression
while preserving social harmony (McClary 1987, 41).

The creation of a new *tuki* that satisfies musical, linguistic, and aesthetic
standards can therefore be reduced to a balance between boredom (excessive
repetition) and destabilization (excessive innovation), the one maintaining
interest, the other maintaining overall performance unity and unison. We
may safely assume that poets and composers do not intentionally set out to
create either of these two extremes. Most contemporary *tuki* represent single-
use commodities that are sung once in public and then discarded; they do
not normally reemerge at parties, although a small number may be heard

at a party where the poetic focus for at least part of the event is narrowed to songs closely associated with, or composed about, the person for whom the principal mourners grieve. It is thus theoretically possible to deduce a formula for minimum originality—ensuring instant oblivion after the initial performance:

melodic content:	a copy of an existing melody or having extended level movement
rhythmic content:	most notes having the same duration, clapped accompaniment
poetic content:	conventional structure, stock phrases.

Cultural artifacts are classified as "old" and "new," but these are not necessarily mutually exclusive categories, since the one may be the foundation for the other as is the case with newly composed *tuki* whose melodies are those of older *tuki*. Old and new occupy discrete cognitive fields that have both areas of exclusivity and shared elements.[4]

Although a composer receives no direct social or material recognition from fellow residents, the performance of a local composition engenders a degree of satisfaction. One's personal identity is stamped on a group activity, and to that extent, exerts a form of temporary social control over one mode of group expression. Composition also offers an opportunity for personal aggrandizement following an event of social significance, especially an unusual or spectacular fishing catch,[5] as well as enduring and positive personal reputation beyond one's own lifetime. And despite the absence of opportunities for and social recognition of skills of oratory, song phrases have an evocative quality unrivalled in social discourse to which both men and women respond with spontaneous emotion, especially while dancing. These responses range widely, from weeping to shouted delight, and they in turn feed back into matters of personal identification and reputation. Ultimately, however, broad approval provides the basis for enduring distinction.

Tuki *Poetry from Dreams*

Takū pay particular attention to dreams, both to the subject-matter recalled on awakening and to anything spoken while asleep and presumed by hearers to have originated in a dream on the subject of the utterance. The significance of these phenomena lies in the belief that, while asleep, one's mind is receptive to contact from the supernatural world. A wide range of activities and time frames may be presented when dreamers subsequently recount their dreams; identifiable personnel—particularly if they are dead—are particularly important because such people are believed to be attempting to contact the sleeper to communicate specific information. Song poetry is the most common type of message.

The varying creative abilities of Takū's composers are thus matched by a range of culturally acceptable human processes of song composition that expresses a continuum of poetic and musical originality. The poles of this continuum are susceptible to criticism: an assembly of stock phrases and melodies from existing songs is considered inferior, although it will not normally be rejected outright by the rehearsal group; still, a completely novel approach will also earn disfavor. In either case, expectations of originality within an established framework will not have been realized. Repetition holds little aesthetic appeal, and individual songs, even those regarded highly, are not sung more than once at any party; this habit is intrinsically related to a positive attitude toward new compositions. For parallel reasons, replication is viewed with disdain as indicating an absence of creativity and originality. Still, the presence in the active repertoire of large numbers of songs based on melodic stereotypes suggests that originality in the music is considered less significant than the criticism of better composers might suggest. Even the structures of songs from the dead conform in general terms to the expectations of the living. The two components—poetry and melody—combined reinforce the notion that Takū singing is an effective, memorable, and aesthetically satisfying vehicle for the group communication of the uttered word.

Performance

> I sit with Tūhea, our heads bowed over a sheet of paper—hers peering with polite bewilderment at its dots and lines, mine struggling in the dim light to read my musical notation of a song that she herself led in a recorded performance the previous year. As I start singing the refrain, her initial astonishment is replaced by instinctive participation in the artistically familiar, and she joins in, immediately drowning my voice as she continues to bend over the notation. Then, sitting back and looking around to catch the eyes of the others present—as singers do when their excitement is aroused—she starts to move her arms in the associated dance actions, her face a portrait of wrinkled delight. (Field notes, Oct 1998)

The ability to participate in the expressive arts is assumed for all but the youngest children and the senile. Entire classes of schoolchildren routinely perform *toha* and *rue* dances as part of the annual concert, supplying both voice and motion, and the lips of even the oldest residents who attend formal dance gatherings can be seen to move during singing. Occasionally the elderly surprise their younger companions by getting to their feet and joining in. General musical competence is an assumed attribute of adulthood, and willing participation in musical performance is one of many social responsibilities that one accepts as an adult. Only the recluse Apava rarely attends social gatherings and, when he does so, he usually sits and does not join in the singing; but it is well known that even he can be persuaded to stand and dance two or three specific *tuki* that praise his own fishing ability.[6]

"Musical communities tend towards uniformity when musicians share

a common competence that includes most aspects of musical knowledge"
(Brinner 1995, 81). The occasions on Takū for informal performance of
music are many, principally when small groups of men (and, less frequently,
women) gather to drink toddy, as they routinely do several times each week.
Formal performance occasions, by contrast, involve large numbers of participants: either the inhabitants of Tāloki or Sialeva or the entire adult community meeting on the *marae,* and it is at such large-scale gatherings that uniformity of musical competence is plainly revealed. The general expectation that
"everyone" will participate, by singing as a minimal level of contribution and
also by dancing, is largely borne out. Even those who have been escorted from
the mourning houses and initially sit silently with heads bowed are eventually
induced to stand and dance, solemn-faced and silent at first but progressively
thawing in the general air of excitement and the effects of toddy to become
vigorous and audible participants.[7] Musical competence is not constrained by
social distinctions between singer and non-singer, dancer and non-dancer,
composer and non-composer: it appears that song's social functions are too
vital to the community's interests to entrust to only a few individuals. Just as
in the recent past when any adult could be a medium for the transmission
of a danced song from the dead, so too today the creation of new *tuki* for a
forthcoming *tukumai* is not left to the designated few. On the contrary, any
family member may contribute a new song, first to a core group within the
mourning house and later to others in the patriline over a period of several
weeks. Similarly, songs of the *hula, lani,* and *toha* categories may be composed
at any time in response to specific events on or off the island.

On the level of individual emotional response, performances of *lani* songs
convey intensity and delight; pairs of singers lean forward and fix one another
with a steady gaze if seated on opposite sides of a house or incline their heads
toward each other if seated side by side. By contrast, dancers tend not to seek
eye contact (photo 22); only if a dancer is unsure of the sequence of movements does he show any interest in the actions of other dancers. Indeed, the
highly desired state of *tihana,* when a dancer's body is totally focused on the
dance, arises from an intense mental concentration that eliminates all else
from the mind. At the opposite end of desirability in performance, substantial
errors in singing or dancing attract immediate attention and occasionally spoken rebuke; but both dancers and singers commonly make excited comments
about their performance after an item has concluded, and the excitement
often stimulates dancers in particular to stand and participate in an unbroken
series of pieces.

A few people can articulate their understanding beyond what is "good" or
"correct," for example, by using the phrase *e pū tana reo* (its melody resonates)
when singers are in tight unison in pitch and rhythm. *Pū* is also the name
for the conch shell, thus suggesting an alternative translation of the phrase:
"the melody is like the conch," in the sense of producing a clear carrying
tone (cf Averill 1999). Achieving this aesthetic imperative may induce the
singers' desire to stand and dance, a euphoric state given physiological form

by the erection of body hair. "My hair was standing up" *(Taku huru ni masike)* is a comment occasionally heard as a particularly energetic dancer takes his or her seat. The statement "We're all aroused!" *(Nā huru tātou e masike)* may likewise follow a well-performed *rue*. Interaction of a different type occurs in the performance of *lani* songs, because they alone in the repertoire have two voiced parts. Each singer possesses a passive knowledge of several aspects of the other part so that their singing is complementary, but neither will cross from one part into the other.

The distinction between producer and consumer of artistic enterprise is blurred, most evidently during dancing. Virtually all those who are not dancing are singing, the only exceptions being principal mourners (who sit silently with heads bowed much of the time) and pairs of people in private conversation, for musicking is a time for social contact as well as artistic expression. At the same time, not all those present maintain a single status—dancer, singer, spectator—for the duration of each song. Singers as a group commonly take twenty seconds or more to get to their feet and dance in all but the formal presentations on the *marae*, and older dancers who tire easily may regain their seats before an item has finished; those seated around the dancing area may alternate between singing and conversing, and some may perform arm actions while seated and singing (photo 23). Dancers and singers do not stand in a producers-to-consumers relation, since the hair-raising plateau of emotional stimulation can be achieved by both groups.

PHOTO 22. Each oblivious to the presence of singers and other dancers, Nake Tepaia, Tekaso Laroteone, and Supia Kīpū perform a *tuki* at Tāloki. *(Hamish Macdonald)*

PHOTO 23. Even for those who are seated, the act of singing generates a desire for physical movement. *(Richard Moyle)*

PHOTO 24. Ausi and Eping, winners of a *paretua* fishing competition in 1998, celebrate their victory in a *toha* dance. *(Hamish Macdonald)*

Dance may elevate an individual for displaying *tīhana,* a litheness expressed through the entire body. Faster dances provide greater opportunities for this display while maintaining the principle of egalitarianism, since the dancers must work within a prescribed sequence of movements at a speed determined by the accompanying song and always in unison with other dancers. In formal performances on the *marae,* more experienced dancers normally occupy front positions, but occasionally in *rue* dances, an individual may leap into the front row as the dancers begin to move forward, in an act of blatant self-promotion.[8] Front-row dancers are also aurally distinguished by tending to sing as they dance, while those behind them, if they sing at all, may be inaudible to an audience. Such silence seems intentional, since it is by the synchrony of all dancers' movements that prior knowledge of the successive lines of poetry is demonstrated. A few female dances of the *uī* and *sore* categories position one individual in front of the group of dancers. This individual is not a solo dancer in the sense that her actions differ from those of the group behind her; rather her brief visual prominence constitutes a statement of two superior qualifications: her genealogical links with the deceased persons from whom the dances were communicated, and her seniority and performance knowledge. Similar circumstances prevail in the choice of the two women who lead the column of dancers circling the *marae* in a *manakoho* dance.

On the *marae* singers sit in tight groups. On the first night of a *tukumai,* each rehearsal group *(akona)* sits in concentric circles and sings its newly composed *tuki huahua* (non-danced *tuki* songs) according to a sequence determined by the groups' leaders. Several such sequences have been used in recent years. One plan calls for each group to sing one song before another group—any other group—starts a *tuki* from its own repertoire, this hit-and-miss procedure continuing for several hours. Another arrangement has the groups follow a predetermined and publicly announced sequence; they perform either one song or a predetermined number (say, three to five) before yielding to the next group. This process continues until all groups have exhausted their stock of new items, at which point they begin to perform the songs composed for dancing.[9] Before these start, however, virtually the entire body of adults present shifts to a new configuration, as all the singers now move to the *marae*'s perimeter, facing inward. When the newly composed danced songs begin, supporting clan members spontaneously get to their feet and dance; men flank the women on the outside, and sometimes those dancing outnumber the singers remaining on their stools and chairs. The new *tuki* dances are followed by a period of two to four hours during which old *tuki* are danced, drawing heavily on compositions by two of the last performance specialists, Sāre and Willie. As the numbers of dancers swell for these performances, the dances expand to circles around the *marae,* and even the spirit mediums may be stimulated to join.[10] On the afternoons of the third and fourth day of the *tukumai,* formal dancing again takes place on the *marae;* this time women singers sit in a group to the west of the seated row of elders, senior women in front, and all face the dancers.[11]

Off-*marae* dancing is required of all adult community members—whether one is accomplished or not—in men's fishing competitions *(taki)*, and it may also be offered as a privilege to the winners of the *paretua* competition for married couples. In both contexts, the expected performances consist of a single well-known *rue* or *toha* dance chosen by the dancer(s) (photo 24). On such occasions, neither the quality of dancing nor the social status of the dancers identifies the activity as noteworthy; rather it is the short-term exclusivity of the participants as they are celebrated for their moment of success—that is, the absence of egalitarianism—associated with the criterion for participation.

Cueing

The rectangular outline of plank seating at both Tāloki and Sialeva allows uninterrupted lines of sight for any singer who leans forward to confirm a visual or aural signal from another singer, or alternatively, to give such a cue to other singers. The meaning of such signals is determined by convention and is part of a common communication repertoire. Song performance typically entails giving and receiving cues, physical acts "specifically produced for the purpose of initiating an interaction—that is, bringing about a change in the performance of others in the ensemble—that would not occur otherwise" (Brinner 1995, 183). Eye contact is one means of transmitting information, and pairs of singers may establish such contact across a gap of several meters, either to assist a less knowledgeable singer or to proclaim a personal association with the sentiment of the song poetry. The more common medium for cueing, however, is audible—most often in the form of calls from a senior singer:

1. *Tāumi:* A call typically given during the refrain of a *tuki* to repeat the last verse already sung rather than move to the next verse.
2. *Hati tasi* (single refrain): Also given during a *tuki*'s refrain, this call requests the singing group to move straight to the next verse, rather than repeat the last verse already sung. The call may alternatively be called *tautasi*. This sequence of singing represents the norm, and the cue tends to be given following earlier confusion among singers; thus it is essentially restorative.
3. *Pēsia* ("leave it"): During the last verse or refrain of a *lū* song, a call of *Pēsia!* signals the imminent end of the song. But, when given during the refrain of a *tuki*, this call signals the imminent move to a new verse rather than the repetition of material already sung; in this context, singers acknowledge their understanding by singing the vocable *āē* at the end of that refrain.
4. *Ku sopo* ("move on"): During performance of a *sau* danced song, this call confirms the end of one section (eg, the *hakatū*) and the imminent start of another section (eg, the *takitaki*).

On a larger scale, the performance of one well-known item, such as the *tuki i Nukurekia* signals the end of an extended performance on the *marae,* whether for singing *llū* songs following a death or at the end of an all-night session of singing and dancing *tuki* during a *tukumai.*

In each of the above contexts both the signal and its timing determine the development of the performance. Fellow singers know the structural location (ie, the end of a refrain or verse) when the option to give a signal may be exercised, but they will not, in normal circumstances, know in advance whether this will in fact be exercised. By calling out a signal as other singers are in the final syllables of a verse or refrain, a "leader" ensures continuity in the flow of sound. The authority of the caller, whose status is determined by association with the song, ensures general compliance.[12]

A number of conventions attend the performance of any group song. At points of structural intersection as one named section ends and the next begins, the possibility of an individual singer making a melodic or textual error is greatest because a composer may exercise a degree of flexibility in the sequence of the sections. For example, in departures from the established norm, some songs may not repeat the opening section or may have changes to the wording or frequency of the stabilizer or refrain sections.[13] A singer who is not alert may easily spoil a performance by innocently but confidently voicing the wrong material. Similarly, the many contemporary compositions built on existing melodic frameworks necessarily cut and paste to accommodate new material within the old forms. Spoken cues such as those listed above cover most situations, but melodic shape provides an additional cue. For example, after the first half verse of a *tuki* song, a stabilizer ends with a rising pitch but, when repeated after the second half verse, the pitch of the stabilizer remains level; these differences identify to less experienced singers the poetic material that is to follow.

Vocables

Insofar as vocables are distinct formulaic utterances quite different from normal speech and are thereby immediately apparent to other participants (ie, they are not fully integrated in a linguistic sense), they too represent a form of cueing. And although cueing itself is not an integral part of a melodic line, it is considered integral to successful performance, since experienced singers signal whether the next material to be sung consists of the refrain or the next verse by means of vocables annexed to verses. Vocables are thus a kind of additional performance aid to the precise calls listed above.

It is common in songs of the *sau, tuki,* and *lū* categories for verse sections to end with vocables. For *sau* and *tuki,* the range of possibilities includes *āē, īē, ēāē, ēīē, ē, ho hiē,* and *nā e,* and for *llū,* the range includes *mao heiē, hiē oiē, e aoku ē, ū lō tuku ē,* and *tuku ōiē.* Most singers say that these vocables, which are sung by all participants, exist "to finish the verse" *(ki hakaoti te puku),* but a few people believe they provide a brief period of respite during which singers can think ahead and confirm just what material follows.

Learning

In line with their explicit principle of egalitarianism, Takū say that there are performance initiators but no leaders as such; in most observed instances this is indeed the case, certainly for individual songs and dances that have been in the repertoire long enough for most people in attendance to be familiar with both the song and the associated motions. However, Takū attending formal and informal performance events do not share the same level of experience with each item sung or danced; for the young in particular these events entail a learning component, whose total duration is in inverse proportion to the frequency of their exposure to a particular song or dance. Likewise, with *marae* performances of *sau* and other women's dances brought back from the dead, in which the spatial and conceptual separation of performer and audience is highlighted, the infinite nuances in relationship between these two groups are shaped by the closeness of association between them, that is, familiarity and interest.

Both men and women dance for virtually the whole of their walking lives, although the types of dance they perform vary according to age. Girls are taught *toha* and *hula* at the local school but their education in local dances ceases when they are at high school off-island, and only the young women who do not receive secondary education maintain the unbroken line of reception and performance. Older women continue to perform *toha* at the school concert, where the spontaneous audience laughter each year at the incongruity of large bodies attempting fast actions suggests a deliberate foregrounding of humor in such performances. And when older women participate in both *toha* and *hula* dances on the *marae* as part of the *tukumai*, they tend to do so merely to provide a sufficiently large performing group, staying in the rear rows, uncostumed, while younger women dance in costume to the front. When a woman marries, she is theoretically eligible to participate in the parties at Tāloki and Sialeva, which provide a semi-formal introduction to *tuki* dances and others categorized as *hakamau* (important); most of these are *sau*. The practical demands of caring for a very young family normally prevent women from attending parties until at least their mid-twenties, and their incorporation is gradual, progressing from attendant, silent then singing, to participant in a rear row. When one considers that, with the exception of the *tuki i Nukurekia* and one other song sung at virtually every party,[14] a novice may wait several weeks or even months before a particular item is repeated so she may advance her familiarity with its music and movements; it is clear that participation requires commitment to what amounts to an extended apprenticeship period. A similar process occurs for young men, who routinely learn and perform *rue* dances as boys at the community school but must wait until marriage before regularly attending parties. At the parties they tend to sit outside the houses in a separate group, talking and drinking but also listening, watching, and learning. For them also, the parties are occasions to begin learning the older, renowned *tuki* composed by Sāre and Willie that now form the backbone of any extended period of song and dance.

For the infrequent performances on the *marae* of the two *takere* dances, it is normal for one or two rehearsals to be called at Sialeva where, under the tutelage of Āpē, the dance's present owner, and Kikiva, whose clan traditionally supplies one *tama haimako* line leader, men of all ages refresh their memories on melody and movements. On the *marae* itself the experienced men occupy the front formations and display their abilities to all assembled there, and the younger men are positioned at the back where they remain virtually unseen.

Newly composed *tuki* songs are intended to be learned and sung by all the adults closely related to a deceased relative, but unfamiliarity with the occasion and company tend to limit the overt participation of younger men and women, who typically sit unobtrusively in rear positions and may, in the case of men, show little or no interest in the rehearsals but spend much of the time smoking or quietly conversing. Although these same people are present at the nocturnal first public performance on the *marae,* any limitations in their singing are so quiet as to be inaudible, and they tend not to join the subsequent period of *tuki* dancing.

Song Accompaniment

Instruments are used in an integrated role only. With the exception of the few *sau* and *manakoho* dances using the slit drum, the interactive system by which performers coordinate their sounds and movements is body percussion, of which there are two types, *poko* and *ppā*. *Poko* is the term for handclapping, which is a form of accompaniment in songs for *sau* dances (with or without the drum) but more frequently occurring in *tuki*, both sung and danced. Such pieces are classified as *tuki poko* (clapped songs). Clapped accompaniment for *sau* songs takes the rhythmic form of either a pulse or as a hemiola, at the rate 2:3 against the melody, as shown in example 1:

Example 1. Hemiola handclapping (an excerpt from the *sau Tereimua*).

By contrast, clapping for *tuki* songs maintains a pulse throughout the song, although this rate may halve during the first ten to twenty seconds as singers settle in. In all instances, the hands are cupped to clap.

Nā tuki ppā (slapped tuki songs)

Within the repertoire of *tuki* songs one group is distinguished not only by their relative slowness, means of accompaniment, and melodic outlines, but also by the presence of meter. These *tuki* are referred to as *tuki ppā* (slapped songs).[15] In *tuki poko* songs, all singers who clap do so in a unison pulse, but in *tuki ppā* songs, slappers fall into one of two categories: those who slap once per metric unit and those who slap several times, usually varying their rhythmic pattern in the course of the song. Such layering of accompaniment is complementary rather than conflicting, and a single primary meter is maintained. Since the concept of meter implies a first beat, the evidence for such a phenomenon in *tuki ppā* must now be examined. The rate of slapping in quintuple meter is based on the melodic note of shortest duration, and the identity of a first beat can be deduced from the coincidence of four elements:

- the moment of striking a single hand on the thigh while singing, when beating once per bar;
- the inclusion of this "beat" in each "bar" in whatever multiple slapping pattern singers choose to use (and which may vary in other ways from bar to bar).
- the moment when a dancer's foot contacts the ground at the *end* of a lateral movement (whereas the moment of the *start* of this movement may vary among dancers according to age, body weight and experience).
- the first syllable of a word in the song poetry.

No other regularly recurring point in time contains similar coincidences, which suggests a conceptual prominence not incompatible with that of the start of a metric unit; in the transcriptions, bar-lines have been placed accordingly.

Not all singers confine their percussive accompaniment to regular slapping of one thigh. Older male singers tend to use both hands and create multiple beats within each metric unit. In this work I have notated *tuki ppā* in 5/4 meter; according to this meter, the accompaniment appears thus:

This pattern may be varied periodically by the addition or removal of one or more slaps. Most men seem to insert variation spontaneously into their performance, but Nūnua has formalized his by alternating between one bar each of what he terms "fast" and "slow" slapping; the former are represented in the notation above, and the latter involves strikes on beats 1 and 5 only. By contrast, when women perform these same songs, their accompaniment is confined to single strikes on the first beat of a bar.

The Tuki Drum

The island's principal traditional musical instrument other than body percussion is a single wooden slit drum.[16] The present large drum on Takū is in the

style of the New Guinea *garamut* (McLean 1994, 52), complete with long pro-
trusion at one end, and it is indeed referred to by that Tok Pisin name *(karamutu)*. The instrument is of acknowledged foreign origin, having been carved
on Bougainville in the 1980s. Earlier versions of the community's slit drum
were smaller and carried the name *tuki;* each was the property of the Ariki
and was stored in or beside his house. They were beaten with two hardwood
sticks *(kaisamu)* solely to accompany dancing on the *marae*. Photos 25a, b, and
c show two *tuki* and the present *karamutu*. No detailed information survives
about drumming practices on Takū Island before the mass move to Kapeiatu
at the end of the nineteenth century.

During their enforced residence on Kapeiatu Island, particularly under
the management of Phoebe Calder, Takū could not sustain their cultural
activities. But when Jock Goodson moved to Nukutoa in 1928, taking his
indentured laborers with him and settling them into individual family houses,
domestic life was restored to something like former levels of freedom, and
this included the resumption of dancing. Although the precise date when
the present *marae* became active is not known, evidence suggests a time no
later than the 1940s. Community identification of individuals in photo 25a
(showing the earliest drum) has established this as the first such instrument
on Nukutoa.

Drumming is generally slow and not of virtuoso quality, although the old
specialists Sāre and Willie are frequently cited as having been more accomplished than present practitioners. Two styles of playing are identified by
name: *samu ffuti* (pulling stroke)—each arm in turn moves out from the body
to strike the drum then lifts and pulls back toward the body ready for the next
stroke, the arms moving in a series of vertical circles; and *samu ka oro* (rubbing
stroke)—after striking, the drumstick is held in contact and rubbed over the
instrument's upper surface to produce a damper effect.

The only other manufactured instrument is a long length of stout bamboo
with a slit cut between each pair of nodes. Also called *tuki,* this instrument is
laid on the ground and struck with single sticks in a fast unison pulse by several people as accompaniment to the men's *rue* and the women's *toha* dances.
By convention, the final dance performed on the *marae* before the Ariki formally closes it is one accompanied by a drum. If the drum in use on a given
day is the wooden *tuki,* the dance is likely to be a *manakoho* and, if the bamboo
tuki is used, the dance will be either a *rue* or *toha*.

The Individual as Performer

One element of social maturity is assumed proficiency in dancing, an ability
occasionally put to the test in a deliberate departure from the twin norms
of group dancing and egalitarianism. One such occasion occurs as a con-
comitant of fishing competitions where men (together with their wives if the
competition is for married couples), regardless of the size of their catch, must
stand and dance a *rue* or *toha* while a group of women sing and beat lengths

PHOTO 25. The island's sole drum (a) three men beat to accompany dancing, circa 1940 *(courtesy John Sione Konga);* (b) two men beat during the dancing associated with the ritual of purification of a new mother, who is seated beside the further drummer, circa 1970 *(Len Murray);* (c: facing page) the *garamutu* drum currently in use for dances on the *marae. (Hamish Macdonald)*

of bamboo, and other women and most of the island's children look on. The spontaneous hilarity that greets any error or incompetence arises from the perceived mismatch between physical and social maturity. While the preparation of the alcohol and tobacco that accompany performances obviously requires planning, much that occurs at participatory level is in fact less spontaneous than it appears. Songs, with or without dances, follow no predetermined sequence, and the identity of those who start the singing or stand to dance may appear to vary widely as hour follows hour, but deeper and more subtle influences and expectations actually shape the development of the event. On occasions that foreground the social identity of principal participants rather than their skill, the performance functions more as a visible artistic means to a cultural end. Most commonly, men or women will foreground themselves or their own clan by initiating songs composed by themselves or fellow clan members. Most of the other adults present routinely join in, but a few—typically members of another clan—may choose to converse or simply sit during the singing before initiating a clan song of their own.

The dancing style of the village recluse, Apava, for *tuki* songs deserves specific mention for two reasons. Among the men it is distinctive: his face is kept completely blank and he avoids eye contact by having his head down; he does not lift his feet and indeed moves them only occasionally—his style approaches that of women dancers. It is said that Apava's son Tefatu deliberately models his own dancing on that of his father: typically his face also is blank, his eyes open but unfocused, and he uses less leg movement than other

men. Despite the smallness of the population base and emphasis on uniformity of sight and sound in dance performance, micro-variants such as these (and perhaps others of a more subtle nature) not only exist but also are being perpetuated alongside mainstream styles, with the knowledge and tolerance of the majority.

In the course of twelve months' fieldwork, I recorded more than a thousand songs. Of these, some 332 are *tuki* composed for specific *tukumai* between 1994 and 2000 and not sung again, but virtually all of the others remain in the active repertoire. When the prospect of performing a particular song no longer excites the interest and imagination of the people assembled to sing, that song has effectively dropped out of the active repertoire. I use "prospect" advisedly, since songs are started by one person beginning the *vvoro* section, and there seems no good reason why one should start a song one considers unworthy or uninteresting. At group gatherings, and particularly at a *tukumai*, singers respond promptly—within a second or two—to join the one who initiates the singing, in a sonic display of unity and empathy with the composer. It is immediately apparent that such a huge repertoire of songs can best be retained when the songs' organizing principles at both the compositional and performance levels minimize the necessity to learn all the details of each song. By dint of their repetitiveness, the singing stabilizer and refrain contribute to the poetic elements of such a principle, as do the binary structure of individual verses, the heavy use of melodic stereotypes and cueing devices, isorhythm, standard themes and sequences of topics, and dance movements regulated in their form and timing by such sequences.

The dancing preferences of the present generation of Takū's teenagers cause some concern among older residents. As Nūnua complained to me in 2000, "They don't dance in synchrony, and the music isn't sung—it's played from a machine." Takū's danced songs assume that all dancers will perform the same gestures at the same time, both the movements and their timing determined by the sung poetic references. The logical links binding singing and dance are philosophically inseparable: the presentation of either alone does not qualify it to assume the meaning that accrues to the simultaneous presence of both. The object of Nūnua's complaint represents a frontal attack on Takū's central performance principles. By definition, dance represents song in a visual mode, and singing is a specialized form of linguistic behavior by people present with the dancers, and of course people may change from one activity to the other in the course of a single song. Technologically and conceptually, then, dancing to song not produced live by fellow islanders is totally foreign.

Musical performance at the drinking houses presents clearly and unambiguously a certain set of relationships in which the autonomy of the group is exercised over the individual. Active participation by all is expected regardless of age or experience or status, distinctions between dancer, singer, and spectator become blurred, and anyone attending has the theoretical right to begin a new song or to be first to stand and dance. And because people attending parties at Sialeva or Tāloki go voluntarily and—to judge by the generally high-spirited nature of such events—appear to be enjoying themselves, we may reasonably adopt Small's suggestion that in these secular circumstances such relationships represent some kind of ideal in the minds of the participants (1998, 43). By contrast, musical performance on the *marae* presents with equal clarity a complementary set of relationships, in which the clan elders, and in particular the Ariki, exhibit visual distinction, passive attendance, and spatial separation to match their ritual responsibilities and social superiority. Their exercise of authority over the timing, content, and duration of the event, in which relatively small groups of dancers and singers perform items belonging to clan repertoires rather than those universally known, creates temporary but discrete separations of performers and audience.[17] The attendance of virtually all adults at such gatherings is again voluntary but occurs with an awareness and acceptance of their formality and with serious determination rather than the expectation of enjoyment. Interpersonal relationships on the *marae* mirror what might be termed idealized relationships of the society at large.

It is not only the distinction between dancers, singers, and listeners that blurs, as individuals move between two or more of these categories during performance (Small 1998, 115). Composers and performers also become one, as the "official" composer's work is "reworked" in performance by the singers who make subtle variations to the material as originally taught. The impetus for continuing the performance to its end is thus diffuse, a responsibility shared by all contributing to it and thereby lending it the authority of corporate approval.

Dancers wear costumes when they wish to foreground the social unit they represent over their individual identities. This situation is most evident at the school concert, where thirty or more items are booked in advance and announced by group, most of which have formed for that occasion only and will not appear in subsequent concerts. Costumes are worn on the *marae* when the division between performers and audience is clear, for instance, for performances of the mostly foreign dances on the second morning of the *tukumai* and subsequent afternoon exhibitions. All such occasions follow formal rehearsals, some emphasizing their separateness by being held away from public gaze or at night, or both. Costumed and non-costumed performances occupy opposite poles in the continuum of spontaneity. Even when a costumed group performs locally composed material well known to the community at large, the separateness of the dancing group and its distinct composition are held inviolate; should any audience members spontaneously leap up to join in, they are immediately reprimanded and if necessary (as may happen if they are drunk) be escorted away by a senior clan member. These values are reversed for performances at the drinking houses, where spontaneity is indeed the basis of most dancing, and the individual identities of those who dance or sing or merely sit is likely to change with each item.

Formality constrains behavior by temporarily redefining relationships as either inclusive or exclusive of particular modes of action, in a deliberate departure from the egalitarianism whose boundaries of time and place, sound, as well as appearance and action, are precisely defined and of limited duration. Normal forms of social authority are not jeopardized by the brief appearance of abnormal groupings that may assemble for the primary purpose of providing entertainment—often singing in words unintelligible to most and thus shifting attention from sound to sight, to the novelty of costumes and actions rather than the communication of a shared language. Of course, this is not to suggest that all forms of formality imply mere entertainment. The rituals on which community existence itself is believed to depend in part—those invoking spiritual assistance to control what cannot be controlled by human means alone—are intensely serious.

Informal gatherings at Tāloki and Sialeva represent undifferentiated collectivities wherein only the Ariki achieves distinction if he is present, not by dint of any deference or preferential treatment extended to him but by the ban on dancing associated with his position. In this respect, and apparently only in this respect, the Ariki cannot identify with the common man. At a *tukumai* in 1994 and while very drunk, Ariki Avo rose from his chair on the *marae* and walked toward a group of men dancing an item he knew, but an immediate chorus of shouts, "Don't dance, chief!" and "Avo, you mustn't dance!" persuaded him to return to his seat. At parties Avo can be seen and heard singing for hours on end, and from a seated position he may even mirror a set of arm movements that standing dancers are using only a meter or two away. Still, he is not permitted to stand and perform those same gestures as a dancer per se. The act of dancing, it seems, is such a clear, profound, and powerful marker of shared social identity by individuals of essentially identical status as to exclude, by definition, participation by an Ariki.[18] Only in the context of an *anu haikave* (dancing with one's opposite-sex cousins) is the reversal of social authority so complete that even the Ariki is not exempt.

Tuki dancing provides a brief opportunity in a ritual and public context for individuals to celebrate their own separate identity. Often singing as they dance, men and women proclaim by words and reinforce with gestures their personal identification with the poetry and so affirm the religious belief underpinning much of its content. As individual members of a particular nuclear family or patriline, they affirm the validity of certain activities that proclaim these relationships. By working together, by expressing delight at a large catch of prestige fish, by their identification as grieving survivors, connections within and among families are made and relationships formally noted.

Summary

Performance focuses on engagement, engagement of linguistic elements through singing and of the kinetic elements through dancing. Running parallel to physical involvement is an engagement of mind amounting to empathy, as seen in a dancer's absorbed unawareness of the presence of others or a prolonged expression of pleasure when singing of a fishing triumph. And what might be termed an engagement of the heart is apparent when performance stimulates poignant recollection of a loved one to the point of inducing tears and a temporary inability to continue active participation. This same set of responses in humans is also believed to hold for spirits, and thus performance constitutes a form of group communication with the supernatural. It was by dancing that the islanders entertained Pukena at the *marae* on Takū Island and it is through their singing and dancing that Pukena and other spirits maintain their benevolence as they invisibly attend all performances on the *marae* on Nukutoa. Until the cessation of the *tānaki* ritual in 1974 performance also communicated in the reverse direction, with the dead providing the artistic vehicle by which the living celebrated their religious belief. In all these ways, performance generates a holistic engagement of a person's faculties and epitomizes both individual and social identity.

Chapter 5
The Nature of Takū Song

In earlier sections of this book I have favored the term "singing" over "song" to emphasize the social significance of the activity over the artifact, but this is not to suggest that local residents speak only in general terms about the elements that constitute a song or that there exist no aesthetic preferences. And although performances are not normally intended for any audience beyond themselves, this does not mean that the creation, rehearsal, and performance of songs is treated casually or in any way limited to events of little significance or confined to purposes of entertainment. Specific concepts and preferences do indeed pertain "to the song itself" *(te tino te mako)*. The term *pese* refers in an undifferentiated manner to anything that is sung; its verb form is *haipese* (to sing), but neither is in common use. The generic term for song is now *mako,* and the repertoire is divided initially into songs that are sung *(nā mako e hua)* and songs that are danced *(nā mako e anu).* On all occasions, the dancers themselves usually sing, an act that on a conceptual level allows individual identification with the poetic content and on a kinetic level aids synchrony of movement among all dancers. As one person put it, "If you can't sing, you can't dance." Having discussed the processes of composition and performance in the previous chapter, I turn now to the contents of the artifact, to matters of pronunciation, poetry, and music structure.

Poetic Pronunciation

Differences have been noted between spoken and sung forms of pronunciation in the languages of several Polynesia outliers. Reported observations from Anuta (Feinberg pers comm), Kapingamarangi and Sikaiana (cited without reference in Love 1998a, 327), Bellona (Rossen 1987, 1, 312–313), and Tikopia (McLean 1990, 119–120; Firth 1990, 40) identify the change in both medial and terminal vowels, but offer no explanation for the change. On Takū, composers and singers insist that this same phenomenon represents a poetic convention whose occurrence and extent are determined at the discretion of the composer. In most cases, all /a/ vowels in a single word convert together, so that *vaka* (canoe) becomes *voko; ava* (channel) becomes *ovo;* and *tamana* (father) becomes *tomono.* Exceptions do occur, however, for example, *tokitaki* for *takitaki* (lead); *ākou* for *ākau* (reef); *tanoto* for *tanata* (man); and several verbs beginning with the causative prefix *haka-* (which retains its /a/). Only rarely does a word with its vowel(s) changed coincide with an existing word and so create the confusion for listeners. The refrain of the *tuki i Nuku-rekia* ends with the line *noho ka tohitohia ko taku henua nei,* in which the word *tohitohia* may be translated in its sung form as "shattered" ("I remain while my island is shattered") or as a sung form of *tahitahia* (swept) ("I remain while my island continues to be swept away").

At one level, these pronunciation changes recognize that a song would not "sound right" if spoken pronunciation were retained. Singers are well aware of the pronunciation changes, but few appear to have given thought to the matter and to hold an opinion as to its purpose. Several informants explained the phenomenon similarly, that is, in terms of "making the singing correct" *(ki tonu i te hua),* or "making the singing good" *(ki taukareka i te hua).* Nūnua Posongat offered a reflective explanation, using as an example the word *ava* (channel):

> [It is done] so that the pronunciation is correct, so that the things sung are correct. The correct way of speaking is to say *"ava."* But if we want to compose, we look for the correct pronunciation so that the singing is right. And we can then ensure that the singing is not bad—so that it doesn't sound simply like sung speech—and the singing will then be correct, the sound will be correct. If a word doesn't sound right, we make a small change, "half"-saying it so that the pronunciation is correct, and so we can then sing it.

Men and women alike express a preference for sung poetry to sound "heavy" *(mmaha)* so that it is more audible to dancers (particularly when combined with vocal pulsations) and so facilitates their moving in unison. Retaining the /a/ vowels creates a "light" *(mamahua)* sound and increases the ease of rapid pronunciation, a phenomenon not favored in local compositions, whereas a change to /o/ vowels adds weight to the words and facilitates the extended *(huti)* vowels that characterize much Takū song poetry.

It is normally the composer's prerogative to determine the extent and position of all vowel changes in his or her own compositions, hence the variation in pronunciation of the same individual words across the community's overall repertoire. At rehearsals singers appear less tolerant of textual than pitch variation, and a frown from one singer is usually sufficient to identify a fault in another, although verbal criticism may be resorted to in extreme cases.

Two types of exception occur. Proper names—those of people, places, and canoes—are routinely sung in their spoken form. There is, additionally, a discrete vocabulary—of small size but indefinite because there is not universal agreement about certain of its contents—that, likewise, retains the spoken pronunciation. These words have no "heavy" sung form: words such as *moana* (ocean), *atu* (bonito), *hailama* (tuna), and *ika* (fish) belong to this group.

And in a related pattern, relatively few vowel changes occur in the opening lines or refrain of a song, because of the preference that these lines have a "light" sound compared to the other song sections.

The Takū repertoire shows less evidence of a composer's desire or intention to conceal meaning behind indirect references than is reported elsewhere in Polynesia.[1] One important exception, however, is the song poetry created by the spirit of a dead Takū person and communicated to the community via a medium. The poetry of dance songs of *sau, manakoho, uī,* and *sore* categories contains many phrases whose meaning may be ambiguous or unclear to all but immediate family members, but such songs seem no more difficult to learn and the popularity of these dances is not adversely affected.

Large-scale language change occurs routinely in the poetry for *hula* songs, of both foreign and local composition, and to a lesser extent for *rue* and *toha* danced songs. The changes, identical for all three dance forms, are said to be a deliberate attempt to change the language from Takū to what poets understand (mistakenly, in fact) to be Peilau. They consist of:

(a) omitting one syllable: *(hahine —> hine)*
(b) omitting the consonant /k/: *(taku —> tau, ku —> u, lakepa —> laepa, koe —> oe).*

In the case of *hula* songs, the changes arise from a desire to preserve the foreign identity of the song category itself; *rue* and *toha* songs containing such language are also usually of foreign composition. The attractiveness of these songs, and especially the danced songs, rests in the wide desire for novelty across all the expressive arts.

Song Poetry

Takū society does not recognize the poet as a distinct category of artist. Until the recent past, the creation of poetry for singing was but part of the job of the clan performance specialist, and although a few individuals may now create new *tuki* poems for performance at a *tukumai,* any new song sung for that occasion is likely to have its words and music created by a single person. Regardless of its origin, however, the quality of a song's poetry will inspire the audience's initial emotional reaction and its enduring evaluation of the work. The overall significance of musicking lies in both the process (that is, the singing) and the vehicle of that process (the poetry). Song poetry gives verbal expression to the principles that legitimize and sustain social relationships, that underpin mundane activities and define idealized lifestyles, and that, taken as a whole, unite the island's residents into a functional community.

The large recorded sample allows some generalizations. Song poetry avoids reference to the negative, in particular to the limitations and potential hazards of atoll life, real and recognized though they are. (Despite first impressions, even songs of ridicule can be considered positive insofar as they use humorous contrast to emphasize essentially affirmative values.) Poetry focuses on the kinds of skills and positive achievements necessary to counter threats to social order and the society itself, for example:

Threat	Poetic Theme
garden failure or famine	success of crops
failure at fishing	successful fishing
inadequacy of fish stocks	a bountiful supply of fish
ineffectual water craft	skillful canoe building
personal loss at death	perpetual union with ancestors after death

Compositions from the dead add another dimension of social stability particularly consoling to the survivors because such songs are linked to the individual identity of a person close to them. Like the statements of positive achievement found in *tuki* songs, songs from the dead make no direct reference to the soul's potential problems; these are identified only by reverse implication:

Adverse Condition	Thematic Countermeasure
loneliness	the company of members of parental generation
leaderlessness	the company of the Ariki or elder or primary *aitu*
lack of social structure	maintenance of elder's position after death
insecurity/social disincorporation	legitimate incorporation within the appropriate afterworld

On an atoll of small land area and a densely packed resident population, there are few occasions when an individual is apart from others for any length of time, and the notion of loneliness, of the unfulfilled desire for familiar company, is somewhat foreign. Indeed, there is no single word describing such a mental state.[2] The theme of loneliness emerges, however, in *hula* and *lani* songs composed by expatriate male Takū living or working abroad, mostly during the 1960s and 1970s, while in the copra plantations on Nukumanu or on vessels traveling national or international commercial routes.[3] Some of these songs tell of loneliness shared by those left behind. Although composed off-island, they have remained in Takū's active repertoire for the past thirty years and are routinely sung at both men's formal and informal parties.

> *Te vā e lasi hoī, e ki hiti ai hoi nau*   The ship is so big, and I want to go on it,
>   *taka nau,*
> *E taka hāloha taka nau e ki te mate.* But I will stay here grieving, having signed
>   away my life.

In contrast to *tuki* poetry, in which individuals are presented as expressing loneliness for their island home, *hula* and *lani* typically portray the singer as longing for a lover, as the following two show:

Kia ō moe la moe laoi mai tō hale,	While you lie comfortably in your bed,
Tele nau ma te laki hāeo.	I am running before the dangerous westerly wind.
Usu tau vā no haele	My boat was about to leave
Tū tani mai, tū aloha mai ana	You stood there weeping, standing in grief at
noho hāloha ē.	the dreaded departure.

Social structure of a sort is implied by the presence of the spirits of those who were human community leaders (eg, the Ariki, clan elders) in the afterworld, with their status continuing after death. By such means, song poetry presents the community with images of what it can achieve if traditional values and practices are honored in life, and what happens to individuals in the afterworld after death. Just as each new arrival on Takū—whether by birth, adoption, or marriage—is incorporated as a legitimate member of the community, so too in death the process of inclusion within the clan afterworld ensures the continuation of the sense of "community" and of social cohesion. The differences in lifestyle between the living and dead are minimized, at least on the evidence of descriptions sent back as song poetry. For all the consolation it affords and despite detailed discussion of its contents, such poetry retains a degree of semantic opacity, which on the one hand marks its nonhuman origin and on the other hand supports multiple interpretations, allowing individuals to believe what they want to believe, as well as preserving an element of mystery. Only retrospectively, in a sense, is the boundary between life and death bridged when the soul reports back through a medium several days or weeks after the burial.

Song poetry deals with a number of broad themes, some of which have already been noted. The most common poetic focus relates to the procurement of the most important food source—fish—and individual songs may refer to two or more of the associated activities: preparation of the equipment and canoe, travel to the fishing ground, invocation of ancestral assistance, catching the fish, triumphal return to shore, public display of the catch, and hints of social elevation arising from public praise of successful fishermen.[4]

One index of the strength of personal relationships occurs in song poetry, particularly *tuki*, expressing the loss of a loved one. Typically, the poetic voice uses the first person singular: "my sympathy goes to" one or more people standing in a specific relationship to the deceased; this reference is amplified in the following half verse by inclusion of personal name(s). A survey of some three hundred *tuki* texts reveals certain trends (table 11).

The comparatively large number of references in *tuki* to children reflects more than recognition of the loss of a parent figure; they frequently acknowledge and bewail the absence of a functioning family unit caused by residence off-island: "my children living far away" *(aku tama e nnoho mmao)*. The spread of relationship terms in the recorded sample as a whole reveals several poetic emphases, including adoption of the personal perspective and acknowledgment of individual value through identification by name. Individual residents' social value is also acknowledged in *tuki* poetry as key family members are named and their relationship to the deceased stated. The spiritual value of the deceased is recognized by accounts of their safe arrival in the afterworld.

At times of emotional intensity song poetry containing themes of great emotional resonance is created for public performance—crafting a fast and seaworthy canoe, successfully fishing for prestige fish, mastering adverse weather conditions, invoking ancestors, demonstrating the well-being of the deceased's spirit, emotional support for surviving family members—and all these figure prominently in *tuki* songs composed for a *tukumai*. Human ancestors are invoked for different reasons: to give reassurance that the world they knew, the values they espoused, and the skills they demonstrated are all capable of duplication in a modern setting. Spirit ancestors are summoned to demonstrate a continuation of their powers as celebrated in myth and oral tradition (including song) in circumstances beyond human control. In both contexts, links to the past evoke evidence of continuity and stability as the basis for assurance—or at least hope—for the present and future. Ritual thus conflates multiple dimensions of time, projecting the past onto the present for the benefit of the future.

During the performance of song, with or without dance, experience is inten-

Table 11. An Index of Relationship Terms Appearing in *Tuki* Poetry

Relationship	*Tuki* Using the Term	Occurences in All Recorded Songs
taku kave (my sister)	5	30
aku kave (my sisters)	2	16
taku taina (my brother/sister)	1	39
taku hina (my sweetheart)	1	14
taku soa (my special friend)	4	57
taku tamana (my father)	1	141
aku tamana (my fathers)	—	53
aku tinana (my mothers)	1	21
aku mokopuna (my grandchildren)	2	16
aku tipuna (my grandparents)	1	46
taku tama (my child)	5	119
aku tama (my children)	49	101
hai taina (pair of same-sex sibs)	1	4
hai tipuna (grandparent and grandchild pair)	1	12
hai tinana (mother and child pair)	4	7
te hānau (the brothers)	3	21
mātou hānau (we brothers)	1	1
nau (myself)	1	197
taku henua (my home)	4	95

sified and the passing of time is measured in terms of the rhythmic structure of the song itself. Emotional involvement is frequently evident: an old woman breaks into tears at mention in song poetry of her long-dead husband's name, a man calls out *E tonu!* (That's right!) in support of a song verse reporting the successful invocation of a family spirit in a fishing expedition, and two men on opposite sides of a house lean forward and sing a *lani* with eyes locked as each proclaims personal identification with the poetry (see photo 26). The emotional involvement of dancers has some of the external aspects of trance. Spatially separated from the singers but relying on them for the supply of sonic stimulus, dancers, particularly more skilled ones, are also psychically separated and appear unmindful of their physical circumstances. Eyes unfocused and oblivious to the sounds of the singers and the sight of fellow dancers, they avoid any eye contact as they sing and dance but also manage to avoid physical contact with other dancers or stumbling over the containers of toddy clustered on the ground as they act out the "I" actions in the poetry.

In common with other Polynesian languages, Takū includes both inclusive and exclusive forms of its first-person dual and plural pronouns—"we" and "us." In this respect, the act of singing may proclaim a conceptual position either within or outside the group assembled at the time when the song is

PHOTO 26. Watched by an appreciative audience, Thomas Puāria and Seuaka Pātē lock eyes to sing a *lani* during a party. *(Hamish Macdonald)*

sung. *Lani* and *hula* songs frequently use *mātou* (we [plural, exclusive]) to highlight the psychic as well as physical separation of gangs of laborers working off-island from those who stayed behind; by this same means the poetry of *sau* and other dance songs brought from the dead adds a linguistic level of separation between the human and spiritual worlds. In the entrance songs that each section performs while proceeding onto the arena for costumed dancing, Tāloki and Sialeva not only proclaim their separateness but indeed boast of their corporate individuality:

Tā mai, tā mai, tā mai nā rue, nā anu atu.	Sing, sing those *rue* to us as we dance forward.
Anu atu, anu atu, mātou e tapolo.	Dance, dance, we're doubling [the speed].
Tapolo, tapolo Tāloki e hāvela.	Double it, double it: Tāloki is hot.
Hāvela, hāvela, hāoti ē.	Keep it hot until the end.
E nau he tama e uru he tama te soa nei.	I am the one, the one at my [drinking] place.
E mata mai, e kila mai mātou.	We look, we gaze at it.
E nau he tama, e nau he tama Sialeva.	I am the one, I am the Sialeva man.

By contrast, *tuki* songs have personalized poetry; indeed, in my recorded collection of 332 *tuki* performed between 1994 and 2000, the word "we" appears only twice, but "I" occurs in virtually all such songs.

Poetic Devices

Poets achieve their aims through forms of language that differ from those of normal speech, principally by using patterns of themes and linguistic devices. In contrast to the more overt forms of reference that may be immediately apparent even to a cultural outsider, symbolism represents a discrete type of verbal communication, comprehensible in direct proportion to one's depth of cultural knowledge. Takū's reef channels, for instance, figure more frequently in song poetry than any other locations on the atoll, and it is apparent that their cultural significance goes well beyond their physical dimensions. While canoes commonly cross the reef at high tide to reduce travel time to the ocean fishing grounds, this practice goes unacknowledged in poetry, in which "all" canoes are said to use one of the three channels.

Clearly, the channels provide access to and from ocean fishing grounds, but equally clearly they demarcate two worlds. They are a focal passage from the known to the unknown, from sheltered lagoon to open ocean, from secure incorporation in a group to solitary exposure to potential danger, and from the company and residence of humans to the home of Pakeva and her spirit children. Song poetry referring to the channels invariably does so at the outset, establishing a narrative setting which, through long familiarity, the audience knows will invoke positive attributes of skill, strength, and bravery. It is only for ocean fishing that group protocols of preparation are enacted, summoning supernatural presences, and it is only while on the ocean that fishermen invoke ancestral help; any song poetry failing to acknowledge such links is criticized as inferior. By way of corollary, the principal demarcation of worlds focuses on control: land and lagoon are under the disposition of humans, whereas the world beyond the reef is under the direction of the spirit realm. Human control is restricted to the visible and finite, but much of the world beyond the channel is invisible and infinite. The notion of the ocean as the residence of spirits, a region where religious practice necessarily coexists with fishing practice to achieve the desired end, is consistent with the notion that the point of entry to this world itself is revered; indeed, several songs designate this interface "the sacred channel" *(te ava tapu).* Takū fishermen achieve enduring fame by demonstrating consistently successful management of activities in both realms.

More than other song categories, *tuki* poetry, which normally foregrounds the twin themes of grief and supernatural encounters in the context of fishing, routinely introduces the symbol of the channel in its opening line, thereby preparing the audience for the unexpected and the unusual that may follow in succeeding lines.

Singing is the principal medium for incorporating foreign words and phrases, much more so than spoken language. The repertoires of *lani, hula,* and *rue* include individual pieces composed on other outliers and learned and brought to Takū by returning plantation workers or crews of coastal vessels. These genres also include many specimens composed on Takū by local residents having—or at least claiming—competence in the languages of Nukumanu, Peilau, or Liuaniua. The performer's intention is identical in each instance: the display of artifacts prized for their difference. Homophones such as *Ingilesi* (English), *kiloki* (clock), *masini* (machine), *puringi* (bearing), *samarini* (submarine), and *seini* (chain) are typical. It seems unlikely, however, that the inclusion of foreign words is symptomatic of a broader attitudinal change toward local egalitarianism. Rather, as in competitions, this phenomenon points to a prevalent cultural attribute by the temporary and controlled display of its opposite characteristic; this display of difference in a context whose occasion, duration, and personnel are clearly delineated is yet another means of reinforcing the overarching social value of egalitarianism.[5] It is no coincidence that the song genres in which such linguistic adoptions appear entered the repertoire in living memory and as a result of circumstances atypical and even unprecedented since contact with Europeans first occurred—namely, the large-scale and extended removal of adults to work off-island either as coastal vessel crews or plantation laborers. During the years of their overseas sojourns, these people encountered a variety of domestic and work-related experiences unknown on Takū itself.

The large number of songs recorded allows a further generalization about poetic style. Singing about a past event in fact brings that event into the present, and performance generates a whole spectrum of emotional responses among singers, from muffled weeping to shouts of delight, responses that sometimes parallel those of the original event and may be detailed in the poetry itself. Some song poetry uses the past tense, some uses the present, and still other songs contain a mix of both. But none, not one song out of a thousand recorded, refers to the future. For reasons we can only guess at, singing is a means of celebrating what was and is, but whatever *will* be is evidently not in the poet's repertoire of topics; it remains an area of vernacular silence.

Song Structure

An outline of typical song structure and terminology appears in the preface (table 1). In some songs, the content of the opener *(vvoro)* is identical to that of the refrain *(hati)* or the singing stabilizer *(hakamauhua)*. There is, however, an explicit aesthetic preference for each verse to have a bipartite structure. The notion is encapsulated in the phrase *nā soa puku* (companion verse), the use of the plural form *(nā)* denoting a plurality of components within the verse unit. Nūnua, one of the few Takū able to verbalize an analysis of song structure, explained, "The first part of the verse hasn't yet specified the subject matter" *(Te puku rā i mua seki ttapa te mē e ttapa ai)*. It is normal practice to repeat the refrain before proceeding to the next verse, a procedure known as *tautau tikirua* (singing in sequence, [the refrain sung] twice [after] each [verse]). The structure described in table 1 is not followed with absolute fidelity but, in instances where a verse is not split into two, it is commonly sung twice (followed by the singing stabilizer and refrain) before moving to the next verse, thus maintaining in performance if not in poetry the essential bipartite structure of the verse.[6] A parallel situation occurs with the *vvoro*, which is normally repeated, the start of the repeat typically beginning with *ka* (and) or *ni* (tense marker). The pervasiveness of this practice is such that exceptions in which the *vvoro* are repeated exactly may not be sung correctly by all singers.[7]

Song poetry is but one form of verbal expression and, although idiosyncratic in some respects, it does not operate independent of other modes of expression. On the contrary, certain structural conventions seem to apply to the linguistic content of song, fictional narrative, and normal speech. In spoken fables *(kkai)*, a sentence typically presents two or more pieces of information, the last of which is repeated as the first datum in the next sentence; the last datum in that next sentence in turn is repeated as the first datum in the following sentence. Not all sentences are linked in this manner, and some stories may contain only a few such instances, but this pattern seems to operate as a general rule; examples taken from three stories appear in table 12.

Table 12. The Interlocking Structure of Narrative Sentences

1	2a	2b	3
(a)			
Apuna ma te Ariki	*e mē lāua tama ko Sina.*	*E mē lāua tama ko Sina rā,*	*rā ku nnoho i lātou hare.*
Apuna and the Ariki	had a child, Sina.	They had a child, Sina,	and they all lived together.
(b)			
Ānei Sina rā ku hano	*ku hano no utu nā vai.*	*Hano no utu nā vai rā,*	*ko te vai sisikitau.*
Then Sina came,	she came to draw water.	She came to draw water	at the bird's drinking place.
(c)			
Tēnā rā na ku ō	*ki hano Asifo no kake.*	*Asifo ku kake ā nei,*	*tēnā nā huihui rupe rā ku llē mai.*
The pair left,	and Asifo climbed a tree.	While he was up the tree,	pigeons approached.

This usage parallels a common conversational procedure wherein a reference unidentified in the first utterance is identified, on prompting by a second party, in the second; such conversations may be structured in two ways:

(a) "I saw someone fishing last night."
    "Who?"
    "It was Y."

(b) "Who was that woman I saw in the gardens?"
    "It was X's sister."
    "Do you mean Y?"
    "No, the younger sister."
    "Was it Z?"
    "Yes."

Song poetry also is essentially narrative in content and favors an interlocking framework paralleling that of spoken narrative with its immediate repetition of material presented earlier before advancing to new material. Singing, an essentially group activity, requires a formalized framework known to all singers if vocal unison is to be maintained. The "one step back and two steps forward" structure of the spoken narrative outlined above is duplicated within named sections of songs and formalized so that the "one step back" uses the same linguistic material on each occasion. The *hakamauhua* (singing stabilizer) performs a stabilizing role insofar as it functions as a reference point for the listeners, a sort of two-directional aural marker, pointing backward in time to identify the end of each verse section, and forward to identify the new poetic material that follows. This same marker aids the singers themselves, in the sense that they benefit from having signals for moving en masse from one verse section to the next, with eye contact between more and less confident singers frequently confirming what point in the song has been reached. The refrain functions identically between whole verses.

With only a few exceptions, Takū melodies are syllabic, and the melodies of a great many songs, particularly *tuki,* consist in large part of the serial repetition of a single rhythmic figure, of which the most common is

To maintain such a rhythm, it is sometimes necessary to change the poetic text. An additional syllable may be generated by the insertion of the genitive particle /o/ (of) to change, for example, the spoken form *te ika te moana* (a pelagic fish) into the poetic form *te ika o te moana* (a fish of the ocean). The insertion of the definite article /ko/ into the spoken form *ka tohitohia taku henua nei* (my island was shattered) results in the poetic form *ka tohitohia ko taku henua nei,* which carries the same meaning. On other occasions, it may be necessary to reduce the number of syllables in a poetic line, and this is achieved either by elision, a device most commonly applied to personal names whose first syllable is a vowel, for example, Akae, Ahou, Ahelo, or by the elimination of that first syllable in all instances where the name is used.

All these modes of discourse are characterized by a linguistic progression from the known to the unknown. The interface is bridged, as it were, by holding on to the one while reaching out to the other in a procedure that resonates with a clearly defined social system and a precedent-based religious system, as well as responding to new circumstances by the application of existing practices.

Tuki Song Poetry as Historical Artifact

That the focus of song poetry is essentially retrospective, depicting the recent or distant past rather than offering any action plan for the future, raises an important issue. One assumption about oral tradition in the Pacific in general, and particularly with respect to song poetry, is its accuracy of detail and accuracy of transmission. Underlying this judgment both in academic discourse and to a lesser degree in legal proceedings is the assumption that musical and textual redundancies in Polynesian song contribute to the historical accuracy of their textual contents.

Ruth Finnegan's introduction to the 1990 "South Pacific Oral Traditions" issue of *Oral Tradition* refers to scope for individuality within collective traditions, "interesting variants" of themes, layers of meaning, complex metaphors, witty wordplay, and subtle and reflective comment (1990, 177–178), but among the papers in that issue only one touches on the boundaries of fact and fiction, and the criticism that follows departures from established story lines (Huntsman 1990, 284). In similar fashion, several papers in the 1992 issue of *Pacific Studies* devoted to "The Arts and Politics" refer to the relationship between performances of song and dance and matters of legitimacy, assertions of identity, tradition, and ethnicity in ways that reinforce—by implication or more directly—not just claims of accurate transmission but also accuracy of depiction, give or take an occasional poetic embellishment. Thomas makes the point that "songs [from West Futuna] probably do not set out to document historical events simply by retelling a sequence of acts . . . but would encapsulate some of the main experiences and values, which therefore remain a watermark in people's emotional recollection" (1992, 229); this advances—correctly, I believe—the possibility of selectivity and a hierarchy of significance and/or veracity in poetic contents. But even Thomas's material is claimed to "reliably communicate the essence of past events" (1992, 236). By default in most instances, recent writings on oral tradition ascribe to song poetry generally such reliability. Among studies of deceit (eg, Besnier 1994; Mitchell and Thompson 1986; Baily 1991; Biebuyck-Goetz 1977; Gilsenan 1976; Goldman 1995), however, song poetry is rarely mentioned. And among studies specifically examining Polynesian song texts (eg, Burrows 1963; Thomas, Tuia, and Huntsman 1990, 41; Hoëm, Hovdhaugen, and Vonen 1992, 9; Mahina 1993; Orbell 1991; Pond 1980, 1982, 1983; Pukui and Korn 1973), veracity of reportage is taken for granted. By contrast, Takū poets may deliberately choose to include in a nonhumorous song category material widely known in the community to be false, whether this is done by linguistic sleight of hand or misleading suggestions or direct statements of nonfact. Ironically, the function of such songs may be identical to those emphasizing quite the opposite characteristics, namely the portrayal of an idealized society.

The largest category of Takū song is the *tuki* and the normal occasion for its first public performance is the *tukumai*. Individual *tuki* are additionally categorized on the basis of their performance mode; they are called either *tuki hua* (sung *tuki*) or *tuki anu* (danced *tuki*). There appears to be no formal occasion after the *tukumai* for subsequent performances of *tuki hua*, but *tuki anu* are routinely incorporated into both formal and informal men's gatherings and parties. Danced *tuki*, even those composed *by* a woman *for* a dead woman, focus on the island's chief source of food—the sea—and on the category of people normally responsible for harvesting it—men. Each newly composed *tuki* at a *tukumai* belongs to one of the *hānota* (fishing) or *hua* (sung) categories. Table 13 shows the numbers of such new compositions between 1995 and 1998.

The central social importance of fishing is reflected in the first group of *tuki* sung on the first night of the *tukumai*, which relate to the three sacred forms, and also to canoe building. It is worth restating that the explicit function of the *tuki* genre—to exalt the fishing leader *(kii ahu te tautai)*—remains unaffected by the gender of the deceased person. In fishing-related *tuki* most, if not all, lines are devoted to descriptions of travel to the fishing grounds, of the fishing itself, of the triumphant return to land, and the display of the catch. By contrast, *tuki hua* (songs intended purely for singing) directly focus on the sense of grief, loss, and other circumstances related to the death, for instance, the arrival of a chartered helicopter bringing mourners, adoption preferences for

Table 13. Statistics for Newly Composed *Tuki* of Named Categories over a
        Four-year Period

Category	1995	1997	1998
tuki hakasoro (oil fish catching)	2	1	5
tuki sī (tuna fishing)	29	39	57
tuki pakū (shark fishing)	—	6	—
tuki tihuna (canoe building)	3	3	5
tuki hua (*tuki* for singing)	8	12	4
Totals	42	61	71

a newborn orphan, calls for family members to stay close to each other, and
expressions of concern for family members unable to be present.

As mentioned earlier, the deceased's family camps at Vaihare on Takū
Island for five days after a death, then organizes a feast. The next five days
is the designated time for the family's canoe to set out in search of tuna.
According to Takū ideology, the canoe, under the command of a recognized
master fisherman, will be successful. In reality, one or more of these three
elements—the five-day period, the presence of a fishing leader, and the expedition's success—may not work out but will be falsified in the subsequent *tuki*.
Some examples:

1. The five-day fishing period. Recent instances have occurred of a canoe
   going out for six—not five—consecutive days because of lack of early fishing success.
2. The presence of a recognized fishing leader. Each tuna canoe is under
   the command of a fishing leader. Each clan has its own designated fishing leader who has specific duties during fishing-related rituals on both
   land and sea. For the purposes of the five-day expedition after a death,
   the family canoe will normally be under the control of one such man.
   However, when no experienced clan member happens to be resident on
   the island at the time of a death, another male family member substitutes
   and, for the purposes of the expedition *and* of the *tuki* songs composed
   in honor of the expedition, that person is accorded honorary leader status. Normally, this is no problem, but one of the 1995 expeditions fell to
   the command of a man known to be an inept and routinely unsuccessful
   fisherman because no one else in the family was resident at the time. But,
   with the poetic equivalent of a straight face, this man was accorded *tautai*
   master fisherman status in the *tuki* and duly praised for the success and
   size of his catch.
3. Accounts of failure—the canoe returns empty in full view of the village and
   the men who always wade out to meet a tuna canoe. Even if a canoe does
   not meet with success during the designated period, a *tuki* will nonetheless
   be composed, with the appropriate family references included; however,

the fishing expedition referred to in the song poetry will be an earlier—
successful—one.

The songs, then, recount successes in a perhaps predictably selective process that takes no account of failures, small catches, or the rates of success.
The disappointment, embarrassment, and even private ridicule that normally
follows the return of an unsuccessful fishing trip is suspended at this time
in recognition of the greater need to properly carry out the *tukumai*. This
is commonly termed *ki pesi te aroha* (to remove worry). Once the purpose of
the *tukumai* is achieved, then communal peace of mind, the dignity of the
deceased, the self-esteem of the canoe crew, and the interests of social conformity are all satisfied.

The *tuki* texts are regarded as incorporating evidence of direct communication from the deceased, as clan statements of traditionally correct practices
(especially those relating to tuna fishing), and as statements of extended family unity in which historical facts are molded to a conventional framework that
depicts both fishing success and family unity. In other words, the *matakāina*,
the basic family unit, is presented as complete and functioning. Alternatively,
the texts may be viewed as part historical fact, part favorable interpretation of
post-death fishing events, and part statements of family identity.

So all is not what it seems on the surface. At one level, the *tuki* are historical markers created at a verifiable time and with a specific performance
event in mind. They speak of real people, genuine relationships, and actual
events. And as the new tuna-fishing songs are incorporated into the repertoire, these essentially positive elements tend to be foregrounded. But these
same *tuki* also perpetuate an ideology based in the concept of "tradition"—
life on the island two generations ago when the *sī* tuna-fishing technique was
introduced, when all Takū people lived on the island, when all canoes were
paddle-powered, and when all men were skilled fishermen, masters of both
the sacred and technical elements of tuna fishing. A one-dimensional examination of *tuki* songs, based solely on their poetry and assuming the veracity
of the references, would likely produce a set of false conclusions because not
all the poetry is intended as unembellished history. In its praise of the master
fisherman, the rule of custom bends the rule of fact, such that *tuki* are socially
positioned between reality and ideology, and partake of both. By agreeing to
compose, rehearse, and perform *tuki* of this style for the past forty years—and
perhaps longer—Takū's residents have in effect chosen to freeze time, to
place individuals and circumstances in stasis.

Death wears the cloak of the master fisherman and speaks with a voice
that is both positive and familiar, so the living can take comfort from the
deceased. The dead for whom the *tuki* are composed become incorporated
into the poetry, not as they are fondly remembered, but as they are in death:
members of *telā vasi* (that other side) in the spirit world. The living are incorporated into an idealized scenario, often using stereotyped phrases and situ-

ations, in which named family members either participate in the fishing, or express delight on seeing the size of the catch. Had these people not acted this way in reality, the discrepancy is deemed less important than adhering to the conventional account. There is comfort gained rather than concern at the public display of such reconstructions.

As Takū is confronted by assertive Christian churches on both traditional religious belief and secular authority, as well as by encroaching foreign ideas, technologies, and values, particularly among externally educated youth, *tuki* offer a kind of stability. They provide community members an opportunity to imagine an idealized lifestyle and immerse themselves temporarily in that lifestyle by participating in a form of poetics emphasizing the first-person perspective. By the circumstances of their composition, rehearsal, and performance, and through the subject matter of their poetry, locally composed *tuki* function as the prime unifying feature in *tukumai*. There are, to be sure, other related events involving groups of people, but not in such active roles. No matter how great the personal or corporate grief following a local death, the past cannot be restored. Even if it could, it would not necessarily be that depicted in the *tuki*, for the circumstances of *tuki* creation and performance reflect and sustain a comforting ideology and provide a formalized expression of family wishes.

Categories of Song

Llū

In common with the oral traditions of other Polynesian islands, Takū accounts of the era before European contact include both local events and travels to other islands. Unlike neighboring outliers, however, Takū accounts exist within a category of song called *lū*, which residents believe is exclusive to their atoll.[8] With two exceptions, discussed below, popular opinion positions the *lū* within the precontact era, and each song is considered the property of one individual clan. Each clan groups most of its own *llū* into named sets and controls the right to begin performance. Individual *lū* relate oceangoing travel to Nukumanu, Luaniua, Peilau, Taumako, and Tikopia; one named set focuses on ocean travel to collect turmeric, and another set recounts voyaging from Nukumanu to Peilau to collect coconut seedlings following a tidal wave. Other named groups of these songs have been discontinued within living memory; they are described, using the language of euphemism, as currently lying "shaded" inside clan elders' houses.

The *llū* are unique in oral tradition because Takū's first specimens are popularly dated to the mythological past when the island had not yet appeared above the ocean. At least three such songs survive in the local repertoire and are believed to be the very ones referred to in mythology, on the basis of their

poetic content. While sailing on the ocean's vastness, the mythical brothers Telaki and Teanāke came across the sound of singing. As Parasei Pūō's
account relates the episode:

> They heard people singing from the horizon's clouds, singing *llū*. From the hori-
> zon's clouds they sang their *llū*, and those singers were Tepure Rōroa and Tepure
> Tauria, Teara Kamia and Teara Saerea, Telaumiomio and Telaumisamisa, and
> Pure Horau and Tenanumea. The brothers listened to the people singing then
> brought all those people's *llū* with them and sailed off with them while the singers
> themselves stayed back there, at the horizon's clouds.

Example 2 presents the start of the song relating to the mythological women
Hunaki and Kimotia, whom the brothers encountered in their travels.[9]

EXAMPLE 2. The opening of the *lū Ssaka Teahua,* as sung by Nake Tepaia.

E āē ma te ava aku ē, āē iē,	My reef passages, āē iē,
E ā he ma taku tanata, iē.	Oh, my manhood.
Eāē iē, ā ka ni ava aku ē.	Oh, my reef passages.
Ka ni moeketia ē he ā?	Why do you sleep there?
Āē ma te ava aku ē ā [etc]	Oh, my reef passages [etc]

In a similar vein to the maritime myth of Telaki and Teanāke, other individual *llū* from the mythological past may be described as *te lū te moana* (a
song of the ocean) or *i loto te moana* (from inside the ocean), in distinction

to other songs composed in both the pre- and postcontact eras, which are *llū hatu* ([human-]composed songs). The following is a typical example of a *lū* from the not-too-distant past, as performed by Possiri Pōpī (example 3).

Ā tū ē te laki hau akoe.	The west wind blows hard.
Ko taku vaka nei.	Here is my canoe.
Ā vausia taku laki ē.	Give me a west wind,
Ia usu ē i ē.	*Ia usu ē i ē.*
Hau nau ki aruna ē.	So I can go up [ie, to Tikopia].
Ā ni tokia ko tuahenua; ā moea ko Sikeiana ē.	I arrived at the rear of the island; it was Sikeiana.
Ā ni tokia tuamarama ē; ā moea ko Sikeiana ē.	I arrived at Tuamarama; it was Sikeiana.
Ā terekia tua te ākau nei ē; ā terekia tua o tono ē.	I traversed the reef, I traversed the mangroves.
Ā terekia tua te henua ē; ā terekia tua Sāpai ē.	I traversed the island, I traversed Sāpai.
Ā sura te mouna te henua e, a tuku ki te atu hanohano ē,	The island's mountain appeared, then passed by in favor of the onward waypoints,
Ā sura te mouna Taumako e, a tuku ki te atu hanohano ē,	Taumako's mountain appeared, then passed by in favor of the onward waypoints,
Ā rono te Ariki te henua e, ko te rena ni taria ma nei.	The Ariki received the news that the turmeric had been collected.
Ā rono te Ariki Tikopia e, a ko te hati nā ni saria mai ē.	Tikopia's Ariki received the news that the turmeric had been collected.
Ā moe Tupa ma ki Tikopia e, usu e iē.	Tupa was [the Ariki] on Tikopia, *usu e iē.*

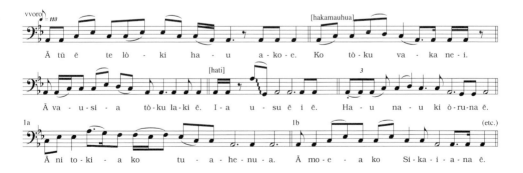

EXAMPLE 3. The start of the *lū Tearaua,* from the set known as *Matāvaka Kaitū,* as sung by Possiri Pōpī.

Unlike other named categories of songs, which may be sung on a variety of occasions and at a variety of locations, performances of *llū* are circumscribed in both of these counts. As noted earlier, one or more of these songs are sung as clan members strip and decorate the body of a fellow clan member soon after taking it to Takū Island for burial; the songs sung are always those of the deceased's clan. Some days after the mourners return from Vaihare, what is believed to represent the community's entire repertoire of *llū* is sung, clan by clan, on the *marae* in a marathon nocturnal performance. Death has the effect of immediately closing the *marae* for all ritual activities, and only by singing *llū* can it be reopened. Judging by the age of those observed singing *llū* on the *marae,* it is not until middle age that an adult can expect to participate; doubtless, the relatively infrequent performance of these songs and limitation of performers to the same clan will slow the rate at which a singer will become proficient at them.

Llū are not private in the sense that they may not be sung in the presence of nonclan members, but ownership issues are more closely defined than for other categories of song. They may be sung in public only by clan members, and nonclan members who happen to know them may sing them only in the company of clan members. Ownership can, however, be transferred away from normal patrilineal descent if, for example, a man demonstrates an enduring interest in learning the *llū* of another clan, and sits continually with an older man of that clan until he learns them, after which the older man may tell the pupil he can now look after the songs as his own. It is common knowledge that Nake Tepaia and Tommy Atomu learned several *llū* in this manner from the performance specialists Willie and Sāre, respectively, when the old men felt unable to entrust them to younger men of their own clans. Older men are now said to be motivated by the desire to ensure perpetuation of the part of their clan's intellectual property for which they have personal responsibility. But not all attempts to learn *llū* are welcomed: it is known, for example, that a man (still resident) unintentionally used the wrong pronoun when asking a *purotu* to teach him—saying *se lū tātou* (one of our songs) instead of *se lū kōtou* (one of your songs)—whereupon the old man bluntly refused to proceed. On the *marae* groups of people sit in clusters by clan to sing their *llū,* but when it comes to songs belonging to Hare Mania clan, Nake sings by himself the two he learned from Willie, a practice that has continued for many years.

Most *llū* relate to the ocean, either to travel generally or to specific incidents of which the most common are moments of danger or disaster. In the years before his death in 1995, one of Hare Ata's most knowledgeable representatives, Nes Mōmoa, recorded the following example, known as "the song of the dimensions" (example 4):[10]

> This *lū* is about a sailing canoe going from place to place; its name was *Hakautu.* The captain's job was to run the canoe, and he was respected as a captain. When the canoe was ready, it left and she sailed on and on. One man became ill and, before dying in mid-ocean, begged the captain to return his body to Takū, but Takū was

far away and he died. After he died, they buried him at sea. When discarding his body in the ocean, they attached sacra. Only the body was abandoned in mid-ocean; his spirit returned to Takū, even though it seemed that the spirit was reluctant to return, it seemed to want to get back on board and stay there. There is a type of [black volcanic] stone like this [he demonstrates], a stone belonging to the Ariki, and if you died at sea, you would still be able to return to Takū. Your body would be at sea but your spirit would return to Takū. At the time of travels to Samoa, you would die like that at sea. That's how the song was composed; it was composed for that man who died. You would return even though the canoe continued on, visiting all those islands. After visiting all those islands, the canoe returned to Takū, whereupon people asked for the body of that man, requesting his corpse. They were told he had died at sea, but that his spirit had returned to Takū, dragged back by some supernatural power. That power was the same size as that black stone. This man gave his name to the stone, which is now called Pukuhatu—a fragment of stone. The stone's name was Pukuhatu. In extended form, it is known as Pukumoremore Tehuiārau, that's the name of that fragment, that stone.

EXAMPLE 4. The start of the *lū Makovā*, as sung by Nes Mōmoa.

Iaiē, ko te makavā,	Oh, the [canoe's] dimensions,
Ē ka te a ku ma ōūōā ko āiēiē.	[meaning unknown]
Ā ni tō mai ē ka te horau i ē Nanoki.	The voyage arrived at Nānoki.
Ā te Ariki ē ka te kiato ku hahahati;	The Ariki was there when the outrigger shattered;

Ā Sikitonu ē ka te kiato ku hati.	Sikitonu was there when the outrigger shattered.
Ā te Ariki ē ka te kiato ku hahahati;	The Ariki was there when the starboard platform shattered;
Ā Sikitonu ē ka te kiato ku hati.	Sikitonu was there when the starboard platform shattered.
Ā ni tukua nau ki te sau nā Ariki.	I was then placed on the ocean together with the spirits of the Ariki.

For reasons not clear to singers, relatively few specimens of recently composed *llū* are contained in the active repertoire, and those whose composer is known are less than two generations old. By way of example, in the 1950s, the performance specialist Willie was one of the crew on a commercial coastal vessel searching for *trochus* shell in the region of Peilau when the boat was struck by high winds and forced to turn back, which the crew interpreted as supernatural punishment for the removal of the shells. Willie later composed a *lū* about the event, naming it *te manava Pukena* (Pukena's lineage):

Ai ko te manava, te manava ē ka hō ka rerere, ē ki tokorau ē;	A group of people is about to head north;
Ē ka hakarerere, ē ki tokorau, ēiē.	About to head north, *ēiē.*
O āi ko te manava o Pukena ē	It is Pukena's group
Ē ka hakarerere ki tokorau ēiē.	About to head north, *ēiē.*
O āi oi ko ta tau tere ko he tanata ko tau tere ki tua, oke.	When I go, there will be a man there when I go to the back of the island.
O āi oi ko tau tere ko Telavena, ko tau tere ki tua, oke.	When I go, Telavena will be there, moving to the rear.
O āi oi ki nā tiripā i te hau ē, ka tautari ōi ka nau ē.	[meaning unknown]
Āi oi ki no tipa i te hau ē, ka tautari oi ka nau ēiē.	Veering off toward the hibiscus, and I followed.
Īāi e takoto atu kia i te loi, mata o te kō, ēiē.	It's there, at the ritual food heap, facing the husking place.
Āē ko rue i loto Oahoe ko ssē ke ki he tana manu ē;	It shakes inside Oahoe as it searches for his spirit.
Āē ko rue i loto ko he tonu nā mata ko ssē kē ki he tanamanu, ēiē.	[meaning unknown]

Despite its semantic opacity, this *lū* is regarded as a legitimate item within the repertoire, but the same cannot—at least at present—be said of another specimen composed in 1997 by Teinoa Tenehu. Described by fellow singers in such terms as "deceitfully composed," "pure vanity," and "idle boasting," this composition has attracted more criticism than any other single item. Teinoa's solo singing of it on the *marae* in 1997 was interpreted as evidence of lack of clan support, as was his subsequent act of giving the song to Hare Nāoro, which is not his own clan. Unlike other *llū*, any performance of Teinoa's composition may legitimately be stopped since it is "not a real *lū*." The topic outlined in the song's poetry may seem innocuous—the use of compost to stimulate garden growth—but at the center of the disapproval is the view that Teinoa should not be singing about planting techniques he himself had not already understood and could not demonstrate since, if the normally secret techniques had indeed been revealed to him, then he should either have kept them to himself or shown through demonstration of the results that he had mastered them. Entitled *nā verevere Tekaso* (Tekaso's planting techniques), the composition is as follows (example 5):

Ā ni taratara ē te ko taku tamana nei *I te aka ē e ora nei.*	My father spoke about the living root.
Ā ni taratara ē ē ko Tenehu nei, i te aka *ē e ora nei.*	Tenehu spoke about the living root.
He ēi ē.	*He ēi ē.*
Ā ko taku tamana nei i te pela e vai nei.	My father told me his planting technique.
Ā ko Tenehu nei i te pela e vai nei.	Tenehu spoke of his planting technique.

Ā ni tukua taku vao nei, ni ahani ē ki
  aku rima nei.
	I added in my compost, opening it up
	  with my hands.

Ā ni tū te kopana nei, ni huri ki aku
  rima nei.
	I added in giant taro stems, turning
	  them over with my hands.

Ā ni tūtia nau ē ē ko te hā poto nei, i aru
  nau ki aku matani nei;
	I cut a short branch, then counted how
	  many winds [would elapse before
	  more composting];

Ā ni tūtia nau ē ē ko te hā poto nei, i aru
  nau e toru aku matani nei.
	I cut a short branch, then calculated my
	  winds as being three [before
	  harvesting].

Ā ni lono nau ē i taku tipuna nei;	I listened to my ancestor;
Ā ni lono hoki ē ē i Piri nei.	I simply heeded Piri.
Ā se hakaohooho hoki ē ko Tekaso nei.	That was Tekaso's special method.

The poetry of *lū* songs consists of paired verses in which general references in the first verse are replaced by more specific material in the second, and includes opening phrases, a singing stabilizer, and refrain; structurally, this arrangement is identical to most *tuki* songs, as discussed above. Musically also, much of the melodic structure parallels that of *tuki*, presenting different shaped phrases for each line in the paired verses. Despite these structural similarities, however, the sound of a *lū* performance is quite unlike anything else in the repertoire. When performed by a group of singers, the absence of any means of accompaniment or a clear pulse, a slow tempo and notes having a wider variety of durational values than other genres combine to produce an imprecise unison. Additionally, the presence of such typical features as a falling glissando, vocal accentuation within the refrain, and rests within verses are clear identifiers of this genre. The vocables at the end of each verse are

EXAMPLE 5. *Te lū nā verevere Tekaso*, as sung by Teinoa Tenehu.

called the *taki* (lead), because they "lead" singers into the next verse, rather than repeating the present verse, and are usually sung by one singer only (the "leader"). Such nomenclature is unique to this song category.

It is evident that *llū* occupy a special position in Takū's performance repertoire. Sung in association with funerary rituals, first beside the corpse and later on the *marae*, they unite surviving relatives in both a shared activity and a common heritage. The songs' performance association with death is intertwined with that of the ancestors. Indeed, insofar as those ancestors are believed to be present on the *marae* during performance, attracted by the sound of singing, the *llū* achieve social restoration in a broad sense, reinstating the functional link between the two worlds as the human visible repeatedly proclaims to the spiritual invisible acknowledgment of their genealogical oneness.[11]

Lani

Huli tāua tuahenua;	We came around the rear of the island;
He limu nau penapena ē.	I prepared the ritual rubbing material.
Huli ma he tua Sauma.	We came around the rear of Sauma.
Te aho mua e tolu nā rau;	On the first day, three hundred were caught;
Te aho lua he mataono.	And a further sixty on the second day.
Tau mē nei hulihuli lua,	My invocations can be used in two ways,
Tau limu nei huli nā ia, huli nā hahine.	They work for rubbing material and also on women.

Lani are topical songs typically sung by a pair of men at parties; although women are free to sing these songs, they do so only infrequently. Many of the *lani* in the active repertoire are in the Nukumanu language and were brought to Takū by men who learned the songs while working on the copra plantations at Nukumanu in the 1950s and 1960s. Takū men crewing coastal vessels composed others and, predictably, these focus primarily on nautical matters. Locally composed *lani* have maintained the musical style of the originally imported items, and some even continue to be composed in the Nukumanu language.[12] Typical subject matter includes shipboard life and fishing for *ruvettus* or tuna. *Lani* consist of personal statements of achievement, either real or fantasized, and are possibly the closest poets come to a form of solo expression, both literally and figuratively. For this reason, at a large party more than one *lani* might be performed simultaneously by pairs of singers seated in different parts of the drinking house.[13]

The musical style of the *lani* is easily distinguished by its two voiced parts—a melody and a drone, each sung by one man. Men who take particular pleasure in performing *lani* may choose to form a singing duo, routinely sitting next to each other at either Tāloki or Sialeva; Eric Pūtahu and Teinoa Tenehu are such a pair (photo 27). Although designated as a category of song, *lani* performances are usually accompanied by spontaneous and unsynchronized arm movements similar to those of *tuki* dances.

Contemporary *lani* are performed in two basic styles: with the drone in the upper or lower parts. Songs having a lower drone are sung slowly and without any discernible meter or pulse, each line is separated by a rest of several seconds to allow the singers to draw breath. Typically the drone part begins each poetic line, the higher singer starting several syllables later with an upward leap of a fifth from the drone pitch itself. Each line of the upper melodic part consists of two arched phrases, the first longer than the second, starting

PHOTO 27. A regular singing pair, Eric Pūtahu and Teinoa Tenehu sit together to perform a *lani*. (*Hamish Macdonald*)

and ending on the drone pitch. The final one or two syllables of each poetic line may be inaudible, or may be sung by only one of the two singers, since this is the moment when a breath is taken for the following line. Unlike the drone part, whose rhythm for each line is unchanged if that line is repeated, the melodic part normally varies, both from one line to the next and also on the repetition of any line. These variations result from melismatic changes, which singers say are spontaneous and, for that reason, it is rare to hear more than one singer performing this line, even when the song is well known by all. If other singers want to join in, they tend to do so on the drone part. A *lani* composed by Eric Pūtahu is typical in all these regards (example 6).

Te vā te haitaina ē, ko ai e tele te vaka māua?	There were two brothers on the ship, but which one ran our ship?
Matoko te haitaina ē, Pāsia e tele te vaka māua.	There were two brothers on the Matoko, and Pāsia ran the ship.
Te ina hea nau sepu ai ē ko ai ē?	Where will you leave the ship?
Ē ko ai ē tele te vaka mā[ua]?	And who runs our ship?
Tai Buini nau teletele ē, Pāsia e tele te vaka mā[ua];	I'll leave at Buin, and Pāsia runs our ship;
Tai Honiala nau tele ē, Pāsia e tele te vaka māua.	I'll leave at Honiara, and Pāsia runs our ship.[14]

EXAMPLE 6. A *lani* composed by Eric Pūtahu.

Lani having the drone in the higher part structure the melody in groups of five "beats"; this pattern, clearest in the lower part, usually consists of the sequence

for the duration of the song. The upper part is not a true drone, in the sense that it uses more than one pitch, but most of the time it maintains level movement on the pitch of each phrase final. Example 7 presents a typical *lani* in this style.

Tū i te papaliki ma nau;   I stand on the bridge, I the captain;
Lolosi te vaka ma nau.   I look after the ship.

EXAMPLE 7. A further *lani* of local composition.

Te taina mmata mai, e iloa oe ma nau;	My brother looks at me, he knows it all;
Temanoni mmata mai, e iloa oe ma nau.	Temanoni looks at me, he knows it all.
Tū i te haleliki ma nau;	I stand on the bridge, I the captain;
Au ae teletele te teke ma nau.	My legs ran along the deck.
I au soa tēnei te course ma nau;	My friends, here is the course;
Nā Moroloko e kosi midishipi ma nau.	The course is to the Mortlocks, so, "midships."

There exist also a few indigenous *lani,* said to have been composed in the nineteenth century, that remained in the active repertoire until the 1970s. At the time of my fieldwork, only Apava Pūō recalled them clearly enough to sing, although Samuel Elbert had recorded several during his visit to Takū in 1962. They differ in musical style from more recent compositions by having a single voice part, more in the style of a *tuki,* and their poetry speaks of romantic love with a unique explicitness. The following example (example 8) is typical; it was composed by Tehatu, father of the island's oldest resident (Karaoi).

Aō tū takai ko te roto taku hina.	I stood there, furious with my beloved.
Ma taku hina ka roto ake,	My darling became enraged,
Tū takai ko te loto taku hina.	I stood there, furious with my beloved.
Ma taku hina ka roto ake.	My darling became enraged.
Ka hano taku hina ka tiake nau, hietū.	My darling went and abandoned me, *hietū.*
Ā ō ka uru tāua ki tō hare nei,	We went inside your house,
Tāua tokatoka ki te taenamu nei.	And looked at the mosquito net there.
Tāua saesae ki te suhana nei.	We broke in through the wall.
Ā ō ka hakatipe atu nau ki ō vae nei;	I reclined there on your legs;
Ka moe atu nau ki ō vae nei.	I slept there on your legs.

Contemporary *lani* are typically sung at parties at Tāloki and Sialeva some hours after the singing of *tuki* has started, at a period when not all the men present are continuing to sing, some because of tiredness, others because of the effects of the toddy. One man will start a *lani,* singing either the upper or lower voice part, and will be joined by one or more others at separate locations within the house. Alternatively, two or more men may deliberately sit together as a group and begin singing even before the other men have stopped their *tuki.*

Like *hula* songs, *lani* poetry provides an opportunity for public fantasizing and emotional release. It also has a particular appeal to more outgoing individuals who, according to their peers, like to "display their voices," and to that extent the songs provide a counter to the anonymity of the individual singer that characterizes Takū's group songs. However, the allocation of *lani* songs to the later stages of a party, that is, after the singing of *tuki,* when partygoers are beginning to talk rather than sing continuously, suggests that their social significance is considered lower than those other categories.

EXAMPLE 8. An old *lani*, as sung by Apava Pūō.

Shaming Songs

The performance of sexually explicit songs designed to shock or shame members of the opposite sex is reported from a few Polynesian outliers—Tikopia (Firth 1990, 205–233) and Peilau (Hogbin 1941, 39–41), and Takū men confirm a related practice on Nukumanu, although it is now restricted to Christmas Day. Evidence of this practice on Takū survives in a set of songs recorded in 1963 by Samuel Elbert, where the singing is preceded by a spoken announcement by the performance specialist Sāre, who assigns no genre name to these items.[15] They are identified as "humorous" *(tausua)*, and Sāre adds that he had learned them from his grandfather, Terupo. From this information it seems reasonable to believe that Terupo had been living on Takū Island at a time when such songs were still being sung. The period when such songs were routinely performed, however, lies beyond the lifetime of any current resident, and during my fieldwork only a few older men recalled hearing that they had once existed. Unlike songs with similar content on other outliers, where performance is reportedly informal and intended for a local audience, the performance occasion of these old songs on Takū is recalled to be an essentially sacred moment, intended for nonhuman ears.[16]

The occasion when a newly carved image of Pukena would be carried from its construction site to the god's house adjacent to the *marae* at Sarati was hazardous because of the presence of potentially malevolent *tipua* spirits resident throughout the island. If such spirits chose to inhabit the log from which the image was created, Pukena's benign powers would be weakened or even destroyed, and chaos would result. Therefore, songs with shocking lyrics were sung to distract any lurking *tipua* while the image was in transit.[17] On the evidence of the few specimens still extant, the poetry of such songs, whose performance was the prerogative of the Ariki via his *pūrotu* specialist, focused on sexually explicit matters, as shown in examples 9 and 10:

Ko hine tākoto,   The woman lies there,
Mata konia mai ku ssono.   Copulating incessantly and stinking.

EXAMPLE 9. A shaming song, as sung by Sāre in 1963.

Nā rauhine sakesake mai, sakesake mai,   The group of women keep lifting their skirts and lifting them again,
Īe a hakatū tō ure tanata koī,   While you merely stand there with penis erect,
Tere te vai i tō muri.   And sperm flowing out from your anus.

EXAMPLE 10. Another shaming song, as sung by Sāre in 1963.

Children's Game Songs

As noted earlier, there is a widely held view that indigenous games declined as a result of the introduction of European games by the island's first Australian schoolteacher, Len Murray. Certainly during the fieldwork period I only rarely observed or heard children playing games their parents said they had enjoyed as children, preferring instead a variety of British games taught by their teachers. From 1994 to 2000 only one indigenous game enjoyed a revival of sorts, albeit in changed form. For the 1999 school concert, Kāua Sāre choreographed a set of actions for the old game song *Tomilomi ai nei* and taught it to a group of boys. Few young adults in the audience that day seemed to realize the origin of the words, and I did not observe children playing the game itself in the weeks following the concert.

With the exception of walking on one's hands *(sino)*, indigenous games have passed out of the active repertoire of pastimes, and most of the information I gathered came from adults; it is included here for the sake of comprehensiveness. Most of the games exist as single specimens of their kind and are referred to by the first line of the associated text. Those known as *ttau, ssopo, sivi, tori,* exist in sets, each having a unique text; these are referred to collectively with the plural definite article *nā—nā ttau, nā ssopo, nā sivi, nā tori.*

Nā Ttau (Counting Games)

These are typically played in the sand by day or on moonlit nights, marking the numerals either on the fingers or by poking into the sand. The counting, from one to ten, parallels the division of each text into ten rhythmic groups of equal duration (examples 11 and 12); the game's object is the error-free rendition of the text. Numeral names themselves may be incorporated into

EXAMPLE 11. A *ttau* song.

EXAMPLE 12. A further *ttau* song.

the text in either full or partial form, that is, *rua* (two), *toru* (three), *hati* (*hā*, four), *anoi* (*ono*, six), *tahito* or *hitu* (*hitu*, seven), *vaū* (*varu*, eight).

Other texts (such as example 13) consist of a string of apparent nonsense syllables:

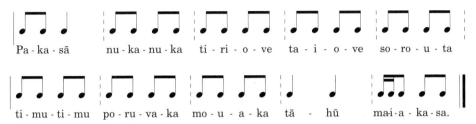

Pa - ka - sā   nu - ka - nu - ka   ti - ri - o - ve   ta - i - o - ve   so - ro - u - ta

ti - mu - ti - mu   po - ru - va - ka   mo - u - a - ka   tā - hū   mai - a - ka - sa.

EXAMPLE 13. A *ttau* song.

Kinikini Lōatā (Biting Ant)

Children sit in an inward-facing circle and make a vertical pile of their flattened hands, each pinching the one below it and reciting; the poetry translates simply as "The ant keeps biting, on top and underneath; pass it up." The bottom hand then moves to become the new top hand and the recitation is repeated ad nauseam (example 14).

Ki - ni - ki - ni lō - a - tā,   I a - ru - na i a - la - ro. Tu - ku a - ke.

EXAMPLE 14. The song for the game *kinikini lōatā*.

Te Unamea Mmea (The Red Turtle)

Turtles brought to shore are frequently kept for one or more days before butchering; upturned onto their shells, the animals are unable to right themselves and escape. Children sit around an upturned turtle and tap its underside (example 15), identifying in turn the names of the various colors in its skin, for example, *mmea* (red) or *uri* (black):

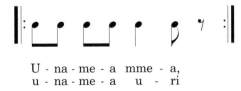

U - na - me - a mme - a,
u - na - me - a   u - ri

EXAMPLE 15. The song for the game *te unamea mmea*.

Teputepu Te Lau Rau

Children seated in a circle each have a shell, and one shell is visually different from the others—this is the "spirit" (*aitu*). During the recitation (example

16), the shells are passed around the circle and the child holding the *aitu* when the counting sequence reaches ten is disqualified. The elimination process continues until a single child remains and is declared the winner.

Te - pu - te - pu   te   la - u   ra - u.   Pa - re - a   ma - i   se   a - i - tu.   Nū - hē   nū - hē

ta - si   ē.   nū - hē ma   ru - a   ē,   nū - hē ma   to - ru   ē...   nū - hē ma   si - na - hu - ru.

EXAMPLE 16. The song for the game *teputepu te lau rau*.

Ssopo

The game procedure for *sivi* and *ssopo* appears to be identical, although the former was played by boys and the latter by girls. Adults report that, in the past, each child recited the text, poking a finger in the sand in time to the words to produce an outward spiral of holes, then immediately repeated the text, this time obliterating each hole in time to the words so that the completion of the text coincided with the obliteration of the final hole as proof of having uttered all the lines. Children today appear to have abandoned the spiral shape in favor of a triangle, the intention being to judge the size and distance between holes so as to close the outline on the utterance of the final line. Central to the performance of either shape is the maintenance of a pulse to accompany the evenly timed proddings in the sand. The game *hakatūtū siko* is said to have an identical procedure; an example appears below.

The textual content of the following *ssopo* (example 17) as performed by Tūhea Nūnua is typical of those in the recorded sample; individual lines form intelligible phrases although the sense flow between successive lines may not always be obvious. On the basis of its subject matter, this particular *ssopo* dates to the period when Takū women routinely had forearms and thighs tattooed in parallel decorated lines. When this practice ceased on Takū, apparently sometime before the mid-1800s (Parkinson 1999, 232), women traveled to Nukumanu for their tattoos. At present, fewer than a dozen resident women are said to have such tattoos, and the practice has now ceased.

Iē ā koe nā ē lani mai	You call me, saying
Ma taku kataha sokotasi nei,	That my bed stands alone,
Mā nau ki napa i akoe.	So I feel ashamed for you.
Se napa fou ia,	What will you do with that shame?
Ka napa koe ki ō taupu mouri,	Shame on your Maori girls,
Na ē piko mai ana kanu.	Her tattoo is not straight.
Ka lli ai tō roto.	And so your anger wells up.
Iē, taku manihi taurekareka nei,	My lips are inviting,
Ki tō ma kōtou ē	To take for all of you
No ffao ki tō manava	And insert in your belly

Ka napa koe ki aitu ssae.	Which would bring you shame for the spirits.
Īē, taku kanutao	My tattoo
Ki mārama ka kavea,	Should be light so as to be transportable,
Ki Sikeiana no tuku ai ki ta na marae,	To Sikaiana for placement on its *marae,*
Ki fakatere taku kanutao,	And so allow my pattern to be displayed,
Ki tinia ki se tua vaka.	And proclaimed on top of a canoe.

EXAMPLE 17. One song for the *ssopo* game.

Sivi

The object of *sivi* is the word-perfect recitation of a long text comprising both real and nonsense words, each syllable of which receives the same duration. The example below provided by Nūnua is performed at the rate of around five syllables per second, pausing only to take breath.

> *Ko sivi e ko sivi tasi vao rā, ni kite sanai lana tauriparipa soana sari paoso ko tuna ko sokoi muri pa nei kauata sa penu sapenu fure repae kamausana. Sere mase sokana varu soro i sokana te hara ku mea i sokana i te uri sauhata nā i ta uini ko se uini sokosoko ie ko sa meti lana te ila me tara ila puna ko are sare sako mana koare sane sapoiri e. Rekireki poki, ē ni pokia surusuru rani surusuru tukituki rio hati suru sapei, hati nā rerei manu. Oiau.*

Tori

Like *nā ssopo*, *nā tori* were girls' games. The principal distinguishing feature of *tori* is the presence of a refrain using the word *tori* after each line; the following two examples are typical (examples 18, 19).

Tori, koī Sove nei, e tori	Sove here
Ki tō vaka moe nei, e tori	Your canoe is here.
Tai te one one nei, e tori	At the sandy beach

No sepu ni apu nei, e tori	He went in search of *apu* shells [for adze blades]
Tūtū kautoki nei, e tori	And cut an adze handle
Nonoa ana pitouka nei, e tori	Then tied it with a cord;
Ē te niapu Sove ku hakatau, e tori.	Sove's adze is now attached [to its handle].

EXAMPLE 18. A *tori* song.

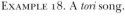

EXAMPLE 19. Another *tori* song, recorded in 1963.

Tori. Taku fanoana atu nei, e tori	When I went there
Kata ki tua anau, e tori	They laughed behind my back
Sē sapaia nau, e tori	And didn't support me.
Taku notoa nei, e tori	When I was taken away
Taku tama taka nei, e tori	My adopted child became
Se soa Te Pure nei, e tori	A companion for the Pure

Ki tari ake nei, e tori	To wait there
Ki te karokaro nei, e tori	For the *karokaro* [meaning unknown]
No tuku atu nei, e tori	Then put it down there
Ni tā e marae nei, e tori	And sing on the *marae*
Ni masike mai nei, e tori	Then arise from there.
Tō avana nei, e tori	Your wife
No tūtū mai, e tori	Standing there
Ē, sē avana i nau, e tori.	Didn't marry me.
Ka vela tō lima,	May you burn your hand,
Ka tini mai tō takū,	Then call for your adze,
Ka fano ma nau.	To be taken away by me.

Hakatūtū Siko

As noted above, this game appears to be identical in structure to *sivi* and *ssopo* but was played by either boys or girls. The text recited contains a combination of real and apparently invented words (example 20); the meaning of most of lines is not known.

EXAMPLE 20. One song for the *hakatūtū siko* game.

There also exist imperfectly in the memories of adults several games long in disuse and now recalled only by the first line of their associated song or recitation. The example of *Tomilomi ai nei* is typical in this respect, although Kāua Sāre revived it at the 1999 school concert, teaching it to a group of boys as a *rue* dance; the sole musician for the dance, he vigorously beat on a large tin while rhythmically reciting the words some twenty to thirty times (example 21).

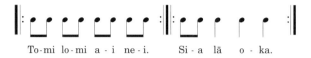

To-mi lo-mi a - i ne - i.   Si - a lā   o - ka.

EXAMPLE 21. The song for the *tomilomi ai nei* game.

Other such games include *i lani tatau, e tasi o pūraeva* (a counting game), *te arere kaepā,* and *tana tekikito.*

Because most of the games detailed above are no longer within the active repertoire of children on the island, and their inclusion in this work arose largely from salvage investigation among adults, it is difficult to draw conclusions about the games' function and significance, although it is apparent that they draw on such skills as manual dexterity and text memorization. It is also apparent that there is attraction in the sheer quantity and variety of foreign games introduced through the school and aided by the high annual turnover of teachers. The evidence of the period of fieldwork suggests that the occasional revival of indigenous games may be insufficient in the long term to retain knowledge of them as games in their own right.

Summary

In hypothetically idealized circumstances there might well be little need for spoken comment about the mechanics of song creation, rehearsal, and performance. However, despite widely shared domestic skills among adults, islanders recognize their differing ability to create new songs. Until the 1990s this recognition was formalized in the institution of the *purotu* creative specialist in each clan and, although compositional responsibilities are now spread more widely among the adult community, the evident superiority of the specialists' abilities continues to be borne out in the ongoing popularity of their songs. I have explored indigenous terminology for the building blocks of song structure and for the superior danced performances of specific individuals, as well as certain widely held views on related matters such as stylistically correct pronunciation and the historical accuracy of poetic narrative.

The poetry and performance of Takū song categories embody relationships: among people coresident on the island, with people living off-island, and with the spirits of former residents. The nature of Takū's religion is such that spirits are capable of being entertained by human singing and dancing on the *marae,* and indeed the spirits routinely attend performances there. Unlike dancing, which requires the presence of singers, singing can proceed on its own, but the impulse for participation is strong, and it is exceptional for people present at a purely singing event not to join in. The additional impulse to physical involvement even in creations called "songs" is evident in the spontaneous arm and torso movements of people singing *lani* and *tuki.* Thus, on one level, singing appears to satisfy a desire for formal linguistic engagement with a topic, at the same time it creates a desire for bodily response, in an orderly and predetermined manner called "dancing," to which our attention will now turn.[18]

Chapter 6
The Nature of Takū Dance

Tātou e anu koi ki nā taratara.
We simply dance to the words.
—Nūnua Posongat 1999

As one of the expressive arts, dancing occupies a unique position. Nūnua's statement here indicates that the nature, duration, and timing of the specific actions of dance are linked in a form of artistic dependency to the singing of the song poetry; dance constitutes an extension into the visual realm of musical elements in the aural realm. There can be no dancing without singing. At first glance it may appear that the verbal terms of aesthetic judgment and the spontaneous emotional responses of an audience are evoked by dance alone, and certainly substandard performers are singled out for immediate ridicule, but such reactions are more an evaluation of the match achieved between sight and sound, an assessment of what Takū identify as dance's function of "imitating" *(tautari)* the song poetry.

On the level of personal involvement, it is probably fair to say that, given the choice, Takū prefer to dance than to sing. At large-scale parties at Tāloki and Sialeva it sometimes happens that more people stand and dance a particularly popular song than remain seated and sing, and even people obliged to sit outside the houses for lack of space inside may rise where they are and join in the movements. Inside the small women's house at Sialeva, dancers are frequently so numerous that their movements are blocked by the crush of bodies, and the outstretched *sava* movement extends past fellow dancers on either side. Any criticism voiced about the cramped conditions is not directed at the dancers—their spontaneous participation is always welcomed—but at the size of the house. The women's house at Tāloki is more spacious (photo 28).

As mentioned previously, dancing also is the medium in which a degree of artistic individuality may be exercised in both formal and informal contexts, sometimes as a test of the performance competence associated with social maturity and sometimes as an opportunity for individuals to depart briefly from the principle of egalitarianism and display superior artistic skills.

Takū attend large-scale parties and participate in the singing largely in response to a social imperative, whereas dancing is more a spontaneous reaction to the singing, particularly when their emotions are primed by the consumption of tobacco and toddy. At formal performances on the *marae,* dance categories are determined by the generic nature of the occasion, and particular dances are chosen on the basis of the specific reason for the gathering. This in turn determines the identity of dancers in terms of clan and family. In such cases social solidarity is foregrounded at the expense of spontaneity and overt emotional involvement. Together, these two qualities support the expression of both social and individual objectives.

As noted earlier, dancing is understood to be an enjoyable activity even for the dead, and indeed the spirits of those mortally ill or having just died are given a foretaste of the delights in store in the afterworld by a brief visit there in which they are welcomed with dances. It is common in song poetry brought from the spirits of the dead for the poet to portray him- or herself as dancing or preparing to dance, or perhaps offering compliments on the dancing of other named individuals. Indeed, dancing is identified more frequently than any other single activity undertaken by the dead, and always it occurs in a positive context. The following references are typical:

the sau Horau (**Horau's** *sau* **dance**)[1]

Ē ni hakauru atu te sau ki taku rō mārama,	I opened my dance with smooth movements,
Mārama ki taku akau.	And it was welcomed by the people.

PHOTO 28. Women joyously hold the *sava* position during a *sau* dance at Tāloki behind a suspended float of toddy. *(Hamish Macdonald)*

te Uī (the Uī)

Ā ki hakanohoria ki se laoniu matani	As we sit on coconut leaves, the wind shifts
Masoro ki se anu tihana.	Toward a superbly performed dance.

te sore Faite (a *sore* dance [sent from the dead] by Faite)

Ē ko aku tamana i tai Teone	My fathers reside in the sea at Teone [2]
Nau e noho i loto Teone	I am living inside Teone
Tū te aitu i loto Teone;	The spirit stands inside Teone;
Tū Pūkena i loto Teone.	Pūkena himself stands inside Teone.
Sopokia mātou te mārama	We are caught out by the rising moon [as we dance]
Ē ni momoe ake tana urutono.	The spirit slept at its own patch of mangroves.

te sau Marena (the *sau* dance sent back by Marena)

Na noho mua e tatari ki anau e	Those already dead await me
Nā ko nau i taku noho mai.	And I am still a member of my clan.
Ni fakatū te sau i roto Teone	There is dancing in the afterworld
Ni fakatū te sau te Tamatārima.	A *sau* dance was rehearsed at Tamatārima Island.

Of the two categories of group songs not danced, the *lū* and the *lani,* only the former is performed with no body movements, whereas the latter, even though designated a "song" *(mako),* is typically accompanied by arm gestures the seated singers make. There is, it appears, something inherent in the act of singing that stimulates the desire for kinetic involvement and, although most movement repertoires are specific to individual categories of dance, they share the regulating mechanism of song poetry in their design and timing.

Tīhana

At a dance rehearsal for the 1998 school concert, a teacher exhorts one child whose movements appear awkward, "Get your body flexible! Be flexible! Can you make yourself flexible?" *(Ki hakatīhana tō haitino! Ki hakatīhana ana kiā koe! Koe ki hakatī-hana kiā koe?)* And then, in exasperation at the whole group of students, "Just look at these people—they're so stiff" *(Mmata nā tama nā sē hakatīhana nā haitino lātou).* (Field notes, 1998)

Tīhana is the term of high compliment that describes the suppleness and whole-body involvement of an accomplished dancer. Until he left the island in 1997 to work on a coastal ship, Pūreva Pāsia was a noted dancer, one whose performance was frequently praised with the term *tīhana.* Among women, Loea Pāsia (no relation) commonly received the same compliment as fellow women-dancers both literally and figuratively looked to her and copied her movements. The parents of both of these people are said to have been noted dancers in their own day, and Loea's accomplishment causes little surprise since her parents are the island's recognized performance experts, Nūnua and Tūhea. It is through performances of such a high standard that even dances long in the repertoire elicit a near-rapturous response from singers and non-performers alike. This is particularly so for men's *rue* dances, whose final movements call for speed and precision, and for *toha* when performed by middle-aged women, whose increased body weight is matched against the fast and light leg movements of the dance. *Tīhana* entails reaching an emotional-somatic state equivalent to experiencing intense empathy with the poetry. As one man worded it, "If a man is pleased with his canoe, then he will achieve *tīhana* when dancing to a song about it."

Nā Āuna (Dance Movements)

Takū distinguish three types of movement in their dances. The first is mimetic, or *e tautari nā tatara te mako* (imitating the song words). Although Takū dance is characterized by a large repertoire of body movements, only a few actions are identified by name because such training as is required proceeds on the basis of example rather than direct instruction. Dancers explain this situation variously as: *nā āuna tātou e taratara* (our movements are descriptive); *nā āuna sē hatu* (the actions are not randomly invented); *e āuna i te hua* (the actions are in accord with the singing); *sē hai āuna ni hatu* (they aren't movements that are merely invented); *tautari nā tātara* ([we] imitate the words); and *e āuna i taratara* (moving according to the words).

Dance actions are linked conceptually to states of mind and physical movements described in song poetry, and they are timed to coincide with the singing of the respective references. Individual lines of poetry are divisible into semantic units, which in turn are expressible in movement sequences. In most instances the verb in a clause within a poetic line identifies the appropriate movement and constitutes the trigger for action. Less experienced dancers waiting until the trigger word is sung before starting the movement may thus find themselves slightly behind other dancers who think ahead to the next poetic segment and who may even start the appropriate action before the trigger word is reached. Table 14 presents examples of dance movements that mime specific real-life actions familiar to most adults and featured frequently in contemporary *tuki*.

The second type of movement consists of actions associated by convention with particular poetic lines of a song, but not intended as mimetic. These actions focus on the person of the poet, as indicated by first-person pronoun and possessive article but presented visually by the dancer. The stomach area *(manava)* being the seat of the emotions, dance movements illustrating "I," "my," or "me" finish by identifying this location. For example the poetic phrase *ni aroha nau ki taku* [relation term] (I grieve for my [relation term]) is presented with the left hand held against chest; the right hand straight

Table 14. Poetic References and Their Associated Movements

Reference	Associated Movement
(a) Actions	
sura (appear, emerge)	one hand (either one), index finger points up, arm straight ahead then moves 90° to one side, other hand may be across chest, also with index finger pointing in same final direction
tere (set off, sail away)	same as for *sura*
huti (pull in a fishing line)	both hands move across the body, fingers closed as if holding a cord
aro (paddle)	paddling action using both arms, one side only, one action only
sau iho (return)	one hand at waist on side, one hand at waist front, both move up and across the body
sepu iho (descend)	same as for *sau iho*
tuku iho (deposit, lay down)	both hands 30 centimeters apart, place "canoe" in front of body at waist level
hora (spread out, display)	both arms at front, together then move apart
toko (pole a canoe)	both arms mime a single poling action
(b) Emotional States	
hiahia (rejoice, be happy)	one or two hand claps with hands at waist level
kata ki taku manava (I inwardly laugh)	one hand stretches out at waist level then returns to the chest

out, palm up, fingers together, then pulled back with palm cupped to finish beside the other hand.

The third type of movement is nonspecific, *nā āuna koi* (mere movements). It sometimes happens in the course of a *tuki* that a dancer is unsure of the correct movements for a particular line of poetry and resorts to what amounts to a holding position, a kinetically neutral stance that is maintained until regained memory allows the performer to continue in synchrony with more experienced dancers. Additionally, poetic references that fall outside the standard movement repertoire generate the same response in both *tuki* and *sau* dances. The position called *sava* is used on such occasions, the term connoting a stance in which the arms are held out horizontal or slightly upward on each side, fingers either open or closed, while the feet continue their side-to-side movements. This arm position is maintained for as long as the accompanying poetic references remain non-specific (or not understood in the case of *sau*), which may be ten seconds or longer in some *sau*, but much shorter in other dances. An alternative form of *sava* consists of stretching only one arm out to the side, while the other is held against the chest.[3] A more overtly neutral stance is a standing position (*ē tū*) with arms by the sides and only the feet maintaining their side-to-side pulse (photo 29).

Most actions are associated with specific genres of dance, and the following is a summary of these.

Sau

Although the poetry and music of the *sau* dances came from spirits of recently dead residents via spirit mediums, the dance actions accompanying them resulted from discussions among family members sequestered inside the elder's house for the five-day period. Since the *tānaki* ceased with the death of Ariki Kaiposu in 1974, no new *sau* have entered the repertoire, and our information on the creation of dance movements must rely on memories more than a quarter century old. One constant in all *sau* in the present repertoire is the movement of the legs, which is largely confined to marking time by an alternating transfer of body weight from one leg to the other; the timing and speed of the movement is regulated by clapping of the singers, thus:

On the quarternotes between these movements the knees slightly flex.

Photo 29. Inside their house at Sialeva, women perform the *sava* movement during a *sau*, their weight momentarily supported on their left legs. Canoe masts and sails lie stored in the rafters above their heads. *(Hamish Macdonald)*

Tūhea Nūnua once observed that *sau* have their own sets of movements that do not parallel the poetry in the way *tuki* dances do; they therefore needed to be learned in rehearsals before public performance. The movements are not composed, she said, but merely "exist" *(tākoto)* in indefinite numbers and descriptions. *Sau* represent the longest dances in the island's repertoire, typically lasting up to twenty minutes, and transmission strategies were needed to bring all the elements of a new dance song up to *marae* performance standards, theoretically, in a few days' time. Chief among these strategies is the exploitation of redundancy:

- The actions of more recent *sau* were modeled in part on those of earlier dances, and the process of assembling a succession of movements for a newly received dance song was simplified somewhat by the adoption of movements to similar elements in both overall structure (the succession of *hakatū* and *takitaki* sections) and individual line references or poetic themes.

- The repertoire of torso and arm movements is smaller for *sau* than for contemporary dances, and this, coupled with holding the *sava* position for ten seconds or longer on several occasions in each section of the dance, effectively reduces the extent of memorization required.

- The basically stationary style of the *sau*, requiring only swaying as the weight is transferred from one leg to the other, further reduces the degree of memorization needed for mastery of these long pieces.[4]

By these means during the period when new *sau* were routinely introduced, it was possible for dancers to quickly acquire an acceptable level of proficiency. But learning procedures have changed somewhat in the period since Ariki Kaiposu's death. On the one hand, the relatively few specimens (fifteen in all) in the active repertoire at that time have in general been maintained (although a few have not been performed in recent years). Gone, however, is the concentrated burst of learning during the *tānaki,* and women now learn through participation, initially standing in the rear row of dancers and imitating the actions of those in front; their relative lack of familiarity is occasionally evident from their slightly late changes from one movement or position to the next, their sporadic sideways glances at other dancers, and their continued silence while the other dancers also sing. The absence of rehearsals and the relative infrequency of performances of complete *sau* combine to prolong the learning process to a period of several years, but there remains an expectation that all younger women attending performance of a *sau* will dance, whereas older women, particularly those rendered infirm by age, contribute by singing from their seated positions in front of the five elders.

The *sau* dances are not only the longest in the repertoire but also the most complex, since their poetry comprises named sections—*hakatū* (foundation) and *takitaki* (processional)—whose melodies and movements are each distinctive.[5] The strategies employed in learning to dance *sau* have also been applied to other categories of dance introduced via spirit mediums, including *manakoho, te Uī,* and *sakitao,* and indeed, several of the movements are shared among these genres.[6]

Tuki

Tuki are unique in the performance repertoire in that some are designated by their composers for dancing *(nā tuki anu)* and others for singing only *(nā tuki hua).* *Tuki* comprise the only danced repertoire that men and women share, though they perform them together only during the *tukumai* ritual.[7] *Tuki* are danced most frequently at Tāloki and Sialeva as part of formal gatherings or—for men—the informal drinking sessions held on weekends; the dances are always performed in the segregated houses on such occasions.

As mentioned above, the identity, sequence, and timing of *tuki* dance actions are determined by poetic references, to the extent that the actions are said to "imitate" *(tautari)* the words. Indeed, by prefacing movement descriptions with the phrase *te āuna* (the dance action [consisting of]), it is possible to compile an inventory of named movements, for example:

te moe (sleeping)	head down, one arm out in front the other out behind
te sau (lifting)	arms held horizontal to each side, hands fisted
te hakatū (erecting)	arms alternately raised horizontal in front of body
te hoki mai (return)	hands beckon toward any other dancer
te saua (carry)	both hands palm up move across body at waist level then lower.
te tokatoka (gazing)	inclining the head first to one side, then the other

Perhaps thirty such actions exist in the *tuki* repertoire, all applying to the upper body since, as with the *sau,* movements of the feet function principally as time markers.

The inventory of *tuki* movements and the timing of their performance are sufficiently well known for dancers familiar with a song to perform without rehearsal or instruction. Indeed, newly composed songs are normally danced in this manner in the context of the *tukumai.* Certain melodies are confined to *tuki hua* (sung songs), while the others may be danced if this was the composer's intention and is announced during rehearsals; the use of any particular melody does not of itself guarantee that dancing will ensue when it is sung. On the first night of a *tukumai,* following the five to six hours of singing newly composed *tuki hua,* the newly composed *tuki anu* are performed for the first time; some of the men and women from the respective rehearsal groups get to their feet and dance and, such is the effectiveness of the referencing system that, by and large, synchrony is achieved (photos 30, 31).

For a *tuki ppā* (slapped song) with relatively slow melodies in quintuple meter, the metric unit coincides with the foot movement pulse. Dancers rise to the balls of the feet in a movement called *toetoe,* starting this action at the moment I have indicated in musical notations as the first beat of a bar and returning the whole of the foot to the ground two beats later. While standing in the risen position, dancers move one leg to the side and follow with the other. Men's movements tend to be faster and larger than those of the women in *tuki* dances; men complete two separate actions in the same time it takes women to perform one. That this is achieved in an orderly and synchronized manner stems from the structure of Takū song poetry. Verses are divided into halves, and each half contains one or two key words, almost all of which are verbs (see table 14 above), and it is these words that the dancers' torso and arms "imitate" *(tautari).* Dancers say that, by thinking ahead as the song is sung, they can execute the appropriate movement by the time a poetic line has finished. In other words, *tuki* dancing can be described as embodying many positions rather than continuous movement. The principal reason women's dance movements change at a slower rate than men's is because women are "imitating" fewer key words per half verse than men, and instead, hold individual positions for long periods, particularly the gesture-neutral *sava* position. The following half verse, from a tuna-catching *tuki,* will serve as illustration.

PHOTO 30. At around midnight, dancers at a *tukumai* perform a newly composed *tuki* for the first time. Despite never having rehearsed the actions, a high degree of synchrony is achieved; the movement depicted here relates to the word *tuku* (put down) in the song. *(Richard Moyle)*

Īē ko nau i tua te ākau nā ē,   I was beyond the top reef,
Se manu ni au i vaetelani no tuku;   And a bird came from the horizon;
Ma rono nei ē.   People talked about it.

Men dancers execute three movements here, each corresponding to a verb:

"I am"   arms out straight in front and lowered, palms up
"came"   one straight arm sweeps across the body, pointing
"talked"   the fingers of both hands briefly touch the chest

Women's actions omit the third of these gestures; they hold the arm longer in the position of the second gesture.

Toha

The *toha* is performed to a short song repeatedly sung slowly as dancers execute relatively slow movements of the upper body while the feet remain stationary. When the singing suddenly increases in tempo, one of two types of

PHOTO 31. Mediums are permitted to dance at night during a *tukumai*. Here, five costumed mediums participate in a *tuki*, their movements representing various stages of a gesture to the word "laid out" in the song. *(Richard Moyle)*

action ensues, depending on the choreographer's wishes. Either the dancers move rapidly forward in shuffles or skips while they continue their upper body movements, finishing directly in front of the seated group of singers and percussion beaters, or they remain where they were but bring their feet into play, balancing on the balls of their feet and pivoting their feet inward and outward continuously in a movement called *firipoi* until the end of the song. Even before dancing starts, the participants in a *toha* are visually distinguished by their tasseled headbands; these tassels disguise each girl's identity as they partially cover the face as the head is kept lowered for the entire dance (photo 32).

Toha dance actions are not said to imitate poetic references on a one-to-one basis, and many of the gestures are short and repeated several times. Dances in this genre brought to Takū from Nukumanu and Peilau continue to outnumber local compositions.

Rue

In its structure, the *rue* is the male equivalent of the *toha,* starting with arm movements only as the dancers stand in one or more lines while the singers go through the short song several times. The process is known variously as *hatusei* or *e mārō te hua* (emphasizing the song) and is not considered dancing. When the dancers signal their readiness with shouts, the singers immediately

PHOTO 32. Girls dance the final, fast movements of a *toha,* their feet using the *firipoi* actions and their faces lowered. *(Richard Moyle)*

increase their tempo and beat their *tuki* drum or ad hoc instrument much more loudly, and at this signal the dancers begin forward movements as their whole bodies—arms, torso, and legs—spring into motion. A notable feature of many *rue* is the choreographed lifting of one leg to the front as the rest of the body continues to move with the dancer rhythmically hopping on the other leg (photo 33); although most dances use this movement in only a limited fashion, one recent composition requires dancers to make sixteen hops with the other leg raised while performing fast arm actions facing first one direction and then the other. In contrast to other categories of dance, the movements of each *rue* are taught because they are not mimetic and cannot be deduced from poetic content alone.

One *rue* is unique in the repertoire of Takū's dances for its incorporation of bodily contact between dancers. Known as the *rue vaisoni* (kissing dance), it is danced by men who form facing pairs. They slap each other's hands and press noses in traditional greeting, then one turns away and stands on one leg with the partner holding his other leg horizontal behind the first dancer adopting a "bird" position with arms outstretched horizontally to each side. On the repeat of the song, their roles are reversed.[8]

Unique Dances

Although Takū's dance repertoire for the most part consists of named categories and multiple specimens within those categories, there exist also stand-alone dances having in common an ascribed nonhuman origin, formal entry

PHOTO 33. The typical leg-lifting action of a *rue* dance. *(Richard Moyle)*

(taki) and exit *(sari)* components, distinctive sequences of movements, performance accessories, and musical style, and well-defined and widely known principles of ownership and performance protocol. These dances are performed only on the *marae* and include the *paki, takere,* and *hoe.* In addition to these identifiers, the trio is also distinctive in that, in one or more sections of the performance, dancers acknowledge the existence of fellow dancers and interact with them, either by forming inward-facing lines and mirroring the actions of the person opposite (as in the *paki* and *hoe*), or forming quartets and rhythmically striking the accessories of other members of those quartets (as in the *takere*). Because all these dances have song poetry whose words are not understood, it is not possible to investigate the nature of any word-movement link and, for their part, the present owners of the dances say they were content to accept without question the performance details as they originally learned them.

Dancing provides the visual vehicle for song poetry, a visible artistic form of egalitarianism by means of synchronized movements while simultaneously allowing for the possibility of aesthetic prominence, a means of social identification in a ritual context and emotional release in informal circumstances. Insofar as all dancing is dependent on singing and it is singers who determine performance details such as tempo and optional repeats of particular poetic sections, one might characterize dancers as agents of singers, while acknowledging that the dynamics of individual performances are susceptible to blurring of identities and to a variety of influences.

Categories of Dance

In presenting the several categories of dance, I have used as a framework the conceptual distinctions Takū themselves make between local dances sent via a medium and glossed as *nā mē nā aitu* (things of the spirit realm) or *nā mē i mua* (things from antiquity), and more recent compositions, glossed as *nā mē e hatu* (composed things). A third category contains items of acknowledged foreign origin that has now been incorporated into the local repertoire; Takū appear not to use any collective term for these items and their appearance together here is merely for referential convenience.

Nā Mē Nā Aitu *(Things of the Spirit Realm)*

Sau

Performers distinguish three types of *sau* dances: women's dances from ancient times *(te saita i mua ilō)* transmitted from specific deceased individuals, women's dances originating within living memory and known to be named after the deceased, and *sau* danced by men.[9] Almost the entire repertoire consists of women's dances brought from the dead, and each of these is associated with the deceased's clan. Two further *sau* of ancient origin and danced

by men are associated with specific clans, although the origin of the association itself is not known. The *sau* dances in the active repertoire consist of
two to five pairs of the alternately slow and faster sections called *hakatū* and
takitaki.

In his later years, Sione Pilike was the only living medium who had brought
a *sau* from the dead during a *tānaki* ritual. His description of transmitting the
sau Marena appears in chapter 4; his account of another dance, the *sau Sione,*
appears below. During the *tānaki* ritual for Sione, the adopted son of the former Pure Marena, Marena once again appeared in a dream to Sione Pilike
and sang him a *sau* for his dead son; Sione Pilike duly sang this *sau* to Willie,
the clan performance specialist, who in turn taught it to other clan members
before its subsequent performance on the *marae*.

Because only the musical elements of the dance are communicated by a
medium, the nature and duration of specific dance movements are determined by the poetic references and consequently they are taught by demonstration or description. The movement repertoire for the *sau* is limited, confined to the arms, which hold series of positions for several seconds. Common
to all *sau* is the *sava* stance (photo 34), in which the arms are held horizontally to each side, and the *toetoe* foot movement, in which body weight is transferred to one foot, which rises onto tiptoe before the weight is transferred to
the other foot and the action repeated; this process continuing throughout

PHOTO 34. The *sava* dance movement during a *sau* performed on the *marae*. In the
foreground where she sits on account of her health, Tūhea Nūnua joins in, and the
other dancers look to her for the correct movements. *(Richard Moyle)*

the dance.[10] Because of the antiquity of many of the *sau* and their poetic references, much of the significance of the poetry is no longer understood, even
though the literal meaning of the lines may be clear.

In *marae* performances of *sau*, men are permitted to sing with women (and
indeed it is included among the ritual duties of a *tautua* assistant), but women
alone provide the singing when at Tāloki or Sialeva during, for example, a
hāunu party or other formal event. By convention, the program of women's
dancing on the *marae* on the third day of the *tukumai* ritual is confined to *sau*.
If the *tukumai* commemorates only one deceased clan member, two or more
complete dances may be performed but, if the ritual is for a number of members of the same clan, only excerpts from several *sau* are danced for reasons
of time, each one associated with a specific person.

Two *sau* in the local repertoire are danced by men, the *sau taupeara* and the
sau Arou. Until the 1960s performance of the *sau taupeara* (literally, "the bachelors' dance") was a normal occurrence following a large-scale fishing expedition; it was, therefore, particularly well suited to the old *hata*-based activities
on Takū Island. Since that time, performance has tended to follow the *areha*,
the period when men take the principal mourner to Nukurekia Island for the
night while they themselves go and fish. Two types of organization have been
used in the last thirty years. In the first, the island's men as a group walked
clockwise around the exposed reef area from Nukutoa to Nukurekia Island
on the far side of the lagoon, a distance of some eight kilometers,[11] while the
women did the same in the opposite direction. After spending the night on
Nukurekia, they returned to Nukutoa. On arrival, they found that the people
who had stayed behind had lined the road leading to the *marae* on both sides
with ropes, from which hung new laplaps for them to wear for the subsequent
marae performance of the *sau taupeara*, which constituted the first item in a
program of dancing.[12]

A newer scheme enlisted all of the island's men in escorting the principal mourner(s) by canoe or boat to Nukurekia. Leaving the grievers and
the elderly on the island, the able-bodied men fish through the afternoon
and night, returning next morning to Nukutoa and a program of dancing
on the *marae*, starting with the *sau taupeara*. In 1996 people speculated that
the dance would be performed on the return of the fleet escorting Apava to
and from Nukurekia following the death of his wife, but on that occasion the
dances were limited to *rue*, and the *areha* tour has not been repeated since.
The accompanying dance (categorized as *te soa sau* [the companion dance])
for the *sau taupeara* on such occasions was another male dance, the *sau Arou*.
Neither dance has been performed for many years, because there are now
few men familiar with the song and dance and apparently insufficient motivation to teach it to others. However, the songs of individual sections continue
to be performed without their associated movements at parties at Tāloki and
Sialeva, but by a minority of the men present.

The *sau taupeara* was owned by the Sikipura group on Takū Island until
the twentieth century and is now considered to belong to Hare Nāoro clan.

Although it is entirely possible that Morotea, the other group, had its own equivalent dances, that knowledge is said to have been lost when the performance specialist Sāre died in 1973. Twentieth-century performances appear to have been done by men alone and were unconnected with the selection of a future wife (hence the "bachelors' dance" title for the genre). Its poetry focuses on fishing.

Performance of a *sau* typically lasts as long as twenty minutes, but memorization of its details is eased by division into units lasting only a few minutes. In terms of organization, a *sau* consists of aggregations of short songs, each distinguished by title and melody, and separated by several seconds while singers regain their breath and dancers return to their seats. Unifying the overall organization is an identical structure for each short song; this structure in turn conforms to the "basic" Takū song arrangement—opening, succession of paired verses, singing stabilizer and refrain. The melody of each *sau* section is unique both within that *sau* and also within the genre as a whole.

Because of its duration, it is not possible to include here a transcription of an entire *sau,* but I present below (example 22) the first three sections from the *sau Tereimua* to illustrate the style. Each section is accompanied by handclapping, usually in a slow pulse, but occasionally in a hemiola rhythmic pattern unique to this category of dance.

Establishment of the hemiola is not immediate. As shown in example 22, singers first clap a pulse, at the rate of a half beat in the transcription, then in the *takitaki* section the pulse is divided into the three-beat pattern that lasts to the end of the section.

Until the discontinuation of the *tānaki* ritual in 1974 the community expected that the clan of each deceased person commemorated in a *tukumai* should be represented in a *sau* performed on the *marae,* although the *Uī* or a *sore* dance was considered an acceptable substitute. But since no new *sau* have been transmitted for over thirty years, the genre's repertoire has become fixed in size. Contemporary performance no longer functions as the celebration of the successful arrival of a human soul in the afterworld; it has become more a confirming statement of clan and family ancestors. Since a *sau* may no longer be danced in its entirety for reasons of time, in 1999 a meeting of senior women decided that only two *hakatū* and two *takitaki* sections from each of three *sau* should be performed as part of *tukumai* activities for several dead residents. The option to shorten the performance further highlights this dance genre's symbolic import over its purely artistic merits—it is valued for reiterating the deceased individual's social identity as a member of a particular clan and strengthening the link with the clan ancestors and spirits.

Performance does not attract the comments of audience approval or the emotional involvement associated with other dance genres; active interest appears to have been replaced by passive respect or tolerance. What was once a category of dance within the living tradition has become reified and preserved; it is retained as part of *tukumai* proceedings because of attachment to convention and the absence of any other dance type categorized as "major"

EXAMPLE 22. The first three sections of the *sau Tereimua*.

(nnui). The repertoire is limited in both performance occasion and the number of specimens. During the fieldwork period, some *sau* were danced less frequently than others and occasionally more than a year elapsed before a repeat performance occurred, making it difficult for less experienced participants to improve their familiarity with a piece, and possibly marking the beginning of a downward spiral toward removal from the active repertoire.

Manakoho

Along with the *sau, sore,* and *manu,* the *manakoho* is a category of women's dance sent from the dead via a clan medium. Very few such dances remain in the active repertoire; performances are infrequent, perhaps only one or two per year, and the numbers have been in decline since the stasis caused by the 1974 discontinuation of the *tānaki* ritual.[13] At that time a dance program on the *marae* customarily consisted of one or more *manakoho* together with *ororua* and *manu* dances, both of which are now discontinued. Whatever the form of the program, the final dance was—and still may be—a *manakoho,* not on account of the significance of its poetry or movements or specific origin or popularity, but because of its accompanying instrument, because by convention a drummed dance closes the program. Due to the supernatural nature of its origin, the poetry of *manakoho* songs tends to be understood in its general referents but less so in its specifics and particular significance.

Although using the same gesture repertoire as *sau* dances, the *manakoho* is visually distinguished by the dancers lining two abreast and slowly executing one clockwise circuit of the *marae* as they dance, the entire maneuver lasting several minutes and timed to coincide with the duration of the song (photo 35; example 23). The obsolete *ororua* and *manu* dances also followed this encircling pattern, and some people believe them to be subsets of *manakoho.* Like some of the very old *tuki* songs, *manakoho* dances either exist singly or form sets danced in sequence. The last such set was conveyed sometime before 1974 by the medium Taura from the spirit of Pōlis, father of Sione Pilike.

Ā ni morano,	It emerges,
Ni morano i tai te one.	it emerges in front of the sandy beach.
Āīē, ō nā kauvaka ni aro mai ē;	Canoes paddle in this direction;
Āīē, ō nā tautua hati aro mai ē.	The leader paddles vigorously.
Āīē, tani taku varo momoe te kauvaka;	He calls out, the sound echoing through the fleet;
Āīē, tokina iho ki tana moea nei.	It was dragged to his sleeping place.
Āīē te aitu noho ma te pure manatu;	The spirit sits there with its net;
Āīē, soko Sina noho ma te pure mana nei.	Sina sits alone with its net.
Āīē, tō hiahia ko te hareika nei;	How happy you are in the afterworld;
Āīē, tō hiahia ko te hare a Pākeva.	How happy you are here in Pākeva's house.[14]

PHOTO 35. *Manakoho* dancers in the last minutes of their circuit of the *marae.* *(Richard Moyle)*

EXAMPLE 23. Part of the song for the *manakoho* dance.

The song itself is strophic in structure, and accommodates differing numbers of syllables in individual half verses by extended or reduced level melodic movement.

Sore

Only a few specimens of the *sore* women's dance survive; like the other types of dance communicated from the dead, no new specimens have entered the repertoire for a quarter of a century.[15] Unlike other "ancient" dances, however, *sore* exist in sets linked by name and poetic content, but which may optionally be performed separately. Performances are rare and are confined to the *marae,* where they are typically danced during the third day of *tuku-mai* proceedings. Because the dancing is accompanied by drumming, it normally occurs last on the program. The dance form is not unique to Takū and indeed at least two specimens were composed on Nukuria and later brought to the island by men immigrating there in the early twentieth century: While on Nukuria, Tekapu, father of Pūtahu E Lasi, had the name Tuiatua, and it is by that name that his *sore* are known now—*nā sore Tuiatua*. His fellow islander, Vakapū, brought a set of his own.

Among *sore* of local origin, only those of the notable medium Faite Pūtahu and Arehu, daughter of Ariki Apeo, are still danced, though a few people know of others now discontinued (for example, Telloa, Maisi)—not from lack of recollection but from fear of retribution because the spirits named in the poetry are still present and still potent. The restriction, however, applies only to the *sore* when danced, so the *sore* of Telloa, for example, may be sung beside a dead member of Hare Nāoro clan as part of the songs sung before burial, an act known as *oriori.* As with other dance types obtained from the dead, the performed actions of the *sore* were the result of consultation and indoor rehearsal among clan members during the *tānaki* ritual.[16]

One account given me by Tepuka, mother of Ariki Avo, of *sore* transmission is noteworthy for its passing reference to one of the attributes of the then Ariki in his capacity as spiritual leader—his ability to contact residents of all the clan afterworlds for the betterment of the community:

Faite lay dying inside Hare Ata [house], then passed away there, after which [Ariki] Apeo performed his rituals, which reached the people in the heavens, and then Faite came, bringing her *sore*. She gave them [via the medium, Emi] first so that Apeo could hear them; then moved on to Sauma, Apeo's [clan's] beach at Sauma, after which they were revealed to us here on earth. Faite's *sore* appeared for Apeo to hear because she had been strengthened by Apeo's actions.

The poetic content of the *sore* matches that of other dances from the dead, providing a first-person perspective of life in the afterworld, sometimes perfectly clear in its language, other times referentially opaque, but always positive in attitude.[17] The music of the *sore* is similar in style to that of other women's dances, notably the *sau* and *manakoho,* having a clear pulse and structural units of verse and refrain. The following, from Faite Pūtahu, is typical, detailing life in the constant company of other women in the familiar setting of an island home rich in fish:

Ē pukepuke ake i larohenua	The ground rises to a mound
Nau e noho i taku hare.	And I live there in my own house.
Ē nohonoho nā hahine taku hare.	Together with other women.
Ē puipui ki tai taku henua.	Netting occurs on my island's beach.
Te matani e ma ite hare Akena.	The wind blows steadily in Akena's house.

Example 24 presents one of Faite's four *sore.*

EXAMPLE 24. The first of Faite's *sore.*

The future of the *sore* appears to be in some doubt, since more specimens exist in recollection than in practice, the prospect of acquiring new specimens is unlikely, performance is infrequent, and relatively few women now dance it.

Nā Mē e Hatu (*Composed Items*)

Hula

The first specimens in the local repertoire of *hula* women's dances appear to have been those learned at Nukumanu by Takū men working in the copra plantation in the 1950s and 1960s; they were subsequently introduced to Takū at the end of these workers' contracts. The men had been told that the genre had been recently introduced to Nukumanu from Peilau. The *hula*'s popularity grew in the 1970s, boosted by the temporary presence on Nukutoa of a Nukumanu man called Kāmeru who taught several Nukumanu specimens of the songs and dances to the unmarried young men and women. Indeed, many present-day *hula* in the Takū repertoire retain a Nukumanu attribution. After Kāmeru's departure, Takū composers turned their attention to the possibility of creating their own *hula*, with evident lasting success.[18]

One of the first local compositions in this style celebrated the medical evacuation of a local man to hospital:

Dear Tauposi, aleha i tēlā vahi;	Dear "Tauposi," you toured all over that place;
Dear Kaiposu, aleha i Pāpua.	Dear Kaiposu, you toured Papua.
O lono lā e hulo i tō henua;	It's said you went to your own country;
O lono lā e hulo i Nukutoa.	It's said you went to Nukutoa.
Saua oe te manu te lāepa;	Borne up in the European's plane;
Saua oe te manu no Navy.	Borne up in the Navy plane.

Other *hula,* composed by Takū men while crewing on coastal boats, feature homesickness, nostalgia, or love lost as their themes, for example:

Tau soa ē, tēhea tō ina e tū ē?	My beloved, where are you?
Nau sesē nau sē ite.	I searched for you but didn't see you.
Darlingi ē, tēhe a tō ina e tū ē?	Darling, where are you?
Oe lā hē? Oe tahao vā hea ē?	Where are you playing around?
Oe lā ihē? Oe muni vā hea ē?	Where are you hiding?

Takū women say there is nothing incongruous in singing *hula* composed by men and having a male perspective, which may discuss specific women or Takū women in general. By contrast, the poetic themes of *hula* composed by women and performed at school concerts or on the *marae* as part of the *tukumai* are confined to domestic matters.

Ideally, a *hula* should be danced by girls or unmarried women (photo 36), and the performances by married women that necessarily feature in National Independence festivities when many of the island's young women are away at school, attract private criticism. It is only during the Christmas period that most resident *taupu* (unmarried women) are on the island, and the frequent timing of the *tukumai* rituals then allows sets of *hula* to be performed formally on the *marae* by these young women. In the years before the crisis on Bougainville, however, *hula* and *rue* also comprised the dance program provided as onshore entertainment for visiting yachts. Like the *rue, hula* are not considered "major dances" *(nā anu hakamau),* a phrase connoting supernatural elements; they function more as entertainment *(tahao).*

The distinct status of *hula* and *lani* poetry and performance is thrown into sharp relief against a background of religious belief. The retrospective basis of ancestor worship paralleled in the backward gaze of the poetry to major received dances—*sau, manakoho, sore, te Uī*—maintains its prominence because of enduring belief in the continued powerful existence of ancestors. The abandonment of the *tānaki* ritual may have ended the formal communication of such dances, but the spirits' initiatives continued, albeit on a

PHOTO 36. Girls dance a *hula* at the school concert, 1999.
(Hamish Macdonald)

small scale. Confining their creative activities to relatively short *tuki* songs, the
dead now communicate only occasionally and always privately with specific
family members. In these *tuki* and in others deliberately and openly composed on request, the poetry represents an essentially historical narrative,
focusing on the recent past and, in particular, on favorable interpretations
of recent events. By modeling the present on precedent-bound procedures
in the recent or distant past, the community draws conviction from the continual and benign nature of its association with the ancestors. However, when
emotions rather than achievements are the focus; when seeking rather than
succeeding is the theme, for what might be rather than what was; and when
personal goals rather than communal benefits move the poet, the thrust of
hula and *lani* compositions expresses something radically different from the
large body of material that is the expressive corpus of communal religious
belief. These are essentially secular songs.

Women use two distinct modes of *hula* performance. When performed
simply as a song—as, for example, to accompany a women's informal group
activity—there may be several seconds of silence or even short conversation

between consecutive poetic lines, or individual lines may be repeated as the performers wish, and there is no accompanying instrument. In 1994, women sang a total of fifty-three *hula* songs in this manner over a three-hour period while they prepared food for a marriage ritual. By contrast, no such discretion is possible when the performance is danced because a continual flow of sound is needed to mesh with movements of predetermined duration. *Hula* performed on the *marae* are a standard item in dancing that concludes the first all-night performance in the *tukumai;* the dances are typically accompanied by a group of male guitarists who also sing the song. Distinct musical styles are associated with each performance mode. When singing unaccompanied among themselves, women spontaneously create two or more voice parts in addition to that carrying the melody, their improvisation facilitated by a relatively small melodic inventory for the song category as a whole and a selection of stereotyped melodic outlines (example 25).

By contrast, when singing to guitars, the normally small group of singers resorts to paralleling the melody in thirds and sixths. For both performance

EXAMPLE 25. A typical *hula* as sung unaccompanied. The text appears on page 233.

modes, however, the music retains its distinctive diatonic contours and triadic harmonies, and for both only the melody part is taught, singers creating the other voice parts as they wish.

Example 26 is the first *hula* composed by Mary Tāmaki (see chapter 4) and one of the first to be composed on the island. The music of more recent specimens has retained much of the style of this song, with repeated melodic outlines and verses of identical duration, as well as reliance on dominant and tonic chords from the guitars.

EXAMPLE 26. A *hula* composed by Mary Tāmaki, in its guitar-accompanied form.

Although the *hula* is danced formally only by women, many specimens are known by men, who may perform them in the course of informal parties. The rhythm of the men's singing style on such occasions is more regular than that of unaccompanied women, with several poetic lines conforming to an eight-beat melodic pattern as example 27 shows:

Tini tō soa, tini tau soa.	Tell me your lover and I'll tell you mine.
Tēnei se manu hāoti hoi, ki oti ma tau manava.	She's absolutely the most beautiful of all.
Tini tō lupe, tini tau rēia.	Tell me your *lupe*, and I'll tell you my *rēia*.
Vaea tāua nā manu te lani,	You and I are separated by the ocean birds,
Ppulu atu oe se tavake toto,	You clutch a red-tailed tropic bird,
Te kumi la e moe tana lima.	With a band on its hand.

Nau hito ahe tala moana e,   I want such a seabird,
Ppulu atu nau se tavake toto,   To take hold of a red-tailed tropic bird,
Te ringi la e moe tana vae.   With a ring on its foot.

EXAMPLE 27. A *hula* as sung by a men's group, Tāloki, 1994.

At parties, *hula* are sung toward the end of the event, after *tuki* (for both men and women), *sau* and *te Uī* (for women only), and their typical performance by a small group rather than by all those attending is indicative of the fragmentation that occurs after several hours of constant singing, dancing, and consumption of toddy.

For the *hula*'s entire history on Takū, comment on topical events has remained its dominant poetic theme, in contrast with other contemporary forms of song poetry; *hula* commonly includes the presentation of direct emotion such as lamentation for love lost, nostalgia, and homesickness. Yet despite the sometimes intimate revelations in both *lani* and *hula* poetry, a degree of modesty remains, since personal names are rarely used and even generic terms for "woman," "unmarried woman," or "lover" are shunned in favor of poetic devices. In men's compositions, birds (particularly the *tavake* tropic bird and *tara* gray-backed tern) or flowers (particularly the *kautei* hibiscus) occur as metaphors for the object of a man's attention. A desirable woman may additionally be compared to a Samoan, a wristwatch, or some other novel or valued item of material property. *Hula* composed by women are confined to topical events, whereas those composed by men additionally speak of romantic love. Precisely because their poetry practices indirect referencing, *hula* have can be an effective tool for social comment and social control. They offer critical opinions sufficiently detailed in their depiction of recent events to be immediately understood by a local audience without the specific identifications that might attract legitimate complaint. A further example in a *lani* appears in chapter 2.

Singing has the capacity to constitute a formal speech event because in song individual persons, living or dead, are normally referred to by their formal names, even though these may not be in common use. By contrast, personal poetic references in *lani* and *hula* songs may use nicknames, suggesting they fill a role more informal than that of other forms of song poetry.

The *hula* dance formation normally consists of one or more straight lines of standing performers across the arena who maintain their line position during the dance. In one variation, known by the English term "come along," performers peel off from their straight lines and form pairs, singing as they walk slowly in a large circle around the arena. In all instances, dancers' heads are angled down, their eyes fixed on the ground in front of them. The movement repertoire is relatively small, and does not "imitate the words" but consists of "simply actions." Indeed, of all of Takū's dances, the *hula* has the least variety and specialization of movements. When men dance, their movements appear to be limited to a slow circular shuffle with arms held loosely in front of the body, which characterizes several *hula,* even when these actions differ from the movements that women normally perform for those same dances.

Within the framework of shared human emotions, the creation and performances of *hula* and *lani* provide a creative outlet for the expression of individual desires and hopes, even though this poetry is delivered in group rather than an individual mode. The adoption of common themes reinforces the shared nature of the whole gamut of emotions experienced by unmarried men and provides a vehicle for fantasy and emotional release. Taken at face value, these experiences apparently linger in the heart, since the most prolific male composers of *hula* have long been married. Additionally, performances of *hula* and *toha* dances represent the only occasions when the community's unmarried women gather to form a discrete and visible social unit.[19]

Toha

The subject matter and language of many *toha* danced songs suggest that this genre was also introduced to Takū from Nukumanu with the return of plantation laborers in the 1950s and 1960s. Although several *toha* songs in the active repertoire are in Nukumanu language, many others are local compositions in the local language. Mannī, a twentieth-century stowaway from Peilau is also credited with introducing *toha* from his own island. The period when *toha* was introduced happened to be one in which Tok Pisin had become the principal communication medium throughout the country and, on Samuel Elbert's 1963 recordings from Takū, men and women introduce their sung items in Tok Pisin (Elbert 1963b). Not surprisingly, several contemporary compositions are either partially or completely in that language.

A few *toha* songs were composed by Takū men crewing vessels of the Bougainville Shipping Company and incorporate words or phrases apparently picked up while the ships were in Australia and at ports around the country. Words in the languages of the Rabaul region and Buka appear, along with "German" phrases said to date back to the pre–World War One period. The subject matter of more recent compositions, in Takū's own language, relates to domestic tasks routinely undertaken by women, such as the collection and cooking of food. *Toha,* typically danced by girls and young women, are a routine component of the annual school concert and of the daybreak dancing that follows the first all-night ritual of the *tukumai.*[20] For the concert performance, younger girls are organized by school class, and older girls join a group representing either Tāloki or Sialeva, their numbers supplemented by married women dancing in one or two rows behind them. On the *marae* the older girls assume an identical formation, but younger children do not participate.

The poetry typically consists of two or three couplets. In the following example, the text is believed to be a corrupted version of another language and is not understood (example 28):

EXAMPLE 28. A *toha.* The meaning of the words is unknown.

> *E toitoi olomē*
> *E toitoi olomē*
> *E lomi le lanai*
> *Pita pita pita*
> *Hina e, hina e, hi hi hi!*

Dancers stand in one or more parallel rows across the arena and, as with all Takū dances, their movements are performed in unison; but in both the dancers' stance and movements, *toha* dancing is distinctive. For the duration of their movement sequences, dancers bow their heads and fix their gaze on the ground before them as they sing. Their faces are further obscured from view by a tasseled headpiece of dyed cotton, which rings the head and hangs over the upper part of the face. A distinctive leg movement called *firipoi,* a further identifier of this dance genre, consists of pivoting on the balls of the feet so that heels are alternately together then apart. Performance incorporates several repetitions of the song by both the dancers and the group of seated women who strike a pulse on a length of stout bamboo using wooden

beaters. Initially the dancers stand still and use only hand and arm movements, after which—and usually cued by a shouted call from one or more of
the singers/dancers—the tempo increases markedly. At this point, one of two
changes in the movements occurs. If the choreography calls for the dancers
to remain in their positions, they will adopt a half-crouching pose as they
perform the more rapid actions, their feet using *firipoi* movements, but if a
"charge" is called for, now is the moment when it starts, the dancers skipping
or fast-shuffling forward, ideally reaching the line of seated singers just as the
song ends.

The following (example 29) is a *toha* as performed at school concerts.

Iesa, Iesa ni, I never worry;   Iesa, Iesa, I never worry;
I dream of you to say Iesa.   I dream of you, just to say [your name]

EXAMPLE 29. A *toha* frequently sung at school concerts.

In recent times a dance known as *salamoni* was introduced from Bougainville, and imitations of this import created by local composers are considered
the functional equivalents of *toha.* Their musical style differs from the *toha,*
however, in that its vocal range extends to an octave, or even more, requiring
women to change from a head register to a chest register as they sing, with
noticeable shifts in volume (example 30):

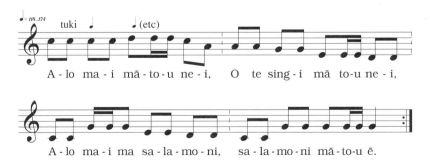

EXAMPLE 30. A *salamoni.*

Alo mai mātou o te singi mātou nei;   We paddle and we sing;
Alo mai ma salamoni, salamoni mātou ē.   We paddle and dance the *salamoni.*

Whether sung in unison or in parts, *toha* show clear evidence of European influence, in both the language of their poetry and the triadic or diatonic shape of their melodies. But such elements are of no particular concern to performers or audience and are considered representative of one period in the island's history.[21]

Rue

The *rue* is a short dance, typically performed by men (although women may dance them on occasion); at least 120 exist in the active repertoire. Because they are of short duration, *rue* are typically performed in sets at formal events on the *marae,* most often using men representing Tāloki or Sialeva, but at informal events, where such dances usually start only after several hours of singing and dancing *tuki,* individuals are free to participate as they wish. It is not unusual for twenty or more *rue* to be performed practically nonstop on such occasions. Like the *toha,* some of the sets are named (eg, *nā rue Tellahu, nā rue Reitama*); such sets are known by the collective term *kaurue.*

Rue are distinguished among men's dances by the sudden increase in tempo from the singers as the dancers explode forward in vigorous action; this follows an initial period of singing through the poetry slowly a few times as the dancers stand in position and limit their movements to arm motions. The musical content of the singing also changes, pitches moving from precise to imprecise and sometimes approximating shouting, and rhythms moving from regular to heavily accentuated, and including syncopated accents. Accentuation is not limited to whole syllables but also occurs on long notes, whose duration is audibly measured by such beats. Both styles are typified in example 31, which illustrates the singing first at the song opening and then at the start of the period of dancing.

Tautau te pō i tai, tautau te pō i tai.   We anchored at the beach at night.
Te pō, te pō, te pō lanā, te pō, te pō, te pō lanā.   Every night, that night.
Ora ē taonā, ora ē taonā.   Put it down then wake it up.
Hē ka miria koe, ka miria koe.   It drills into you.
Heia mai te rā, heia mai te rā, hē.   [meaning unknown]

The distinctive movements associated with the *rue* are described earlier in this chapter. The *rue* is also noteworthy in that some specimens incorporate a dance accessory: a stick or, in one particular case, a paddle.

The stated purpose of the dance is to praise a master fisherman, and each one is typically composed in a first-person perspective in honor of a notable fishing event. The poetry, however, demonstrates a variety of approaches, as illustrated in the following typical examples:

EXAMPLE 31. The typical song for a *rue* dance, from a set called *Tellahu*. The forward movements begin only when the tempo quickens, as shown in the lower notation.

Direct praise:

Tautai lā i heō,	I am a master fisherman, *heō,*
Asimi lā i heō.	[I] Asimi is a master fisherman, *heō.*
Tautai mārama i he tai,	One who is always successful,
Arehu mārama i he tai.	Arehu is always successful.

Allusion:

Tere mai tō vaka i anau sē kata ina;	Your canoe returns, but nobody laughs at me now;
Tere mai ko Teatu a Piri sē kata ina.	Teatu returns, but nobody laughs at me now.
Tau ake i tau henua hakanau nā tanata;	When I beached at the island, men on the shore came and applauded;
Tū Piri i tai te hara hakanau nā hahine.	Under the pandanus tree, Piri was applauded, even by the women.

Technique:

Tātā te hoe.	Carve a paddle.
Llē te hoe tau arohia.	Then let your paddle fly.
Llē te hoe tā tuaina te hoe.	When paddling, I let the paddle fly.

Supernatural intervention:

Huti ai, huti ai taku hanamea, ma rere, ma rere.	I heaved and heaved at my snapper.
Tau hanamea ni au ma nau.	I brought my snapper with me.
Hāpiri mai hare tatara ia te au hanatu.	I put it up inside the house, then talked about how it happened.
Aina e tipua, ha ha	But then a spirit ate it, *ha ha.*
Aina e oti e.	Ate all of it.
A riri akoe, a riri akoe, ia koe, ia koe.	[meaning unknown]

Understatement (on the single-handed catch of a marlin):

Tere mai taku rono,	News of me spread,
Tere mai te rono Arehu.	News of Arehu spread.
Ku sopo i te aumi, huri sara i te murivaka.	It leapt in my wake, turning away from the stern.
Taku aitu ni hano ma nau ku tō i te o rua te laku.	Together, my spirit and I caught it by the bill with a double hook.

Rue are also popular items in the annual school concert, where individual men teach one or more of the dances to a group of four to eight boys in their extended family, then sing the songs and beat on a length of bamboo for the performance. Some men simply teach items in the active repertoire, whereas others, in search of something different, deliberately revive dances which have lain dormant for many years. And there exists at least one *rue* created specifically for the young to perform. When Terupo Sāre was a young man, perhaps as early as the 1950s, he composed a *rue* parodying the movements of a child as it played with a necklace dangling from its neck; the words, which are rhythmically recited rather than sung are simple: "the necklace dangles."

Ki-ki-la-ni ta-u-ta-u.

As noted elsewhere, men occasionally use *rue* on the *marae* as a vehicle for personal advancement (photo 37), both figuratively and literally, jumping forward from a rear row of performers to a position of visual prominence. At parties, by contrast, the smaller number of dancers can usually be accommodated in a single line.

The general popularity of the *rue* is undeniable, as reflected in the size of the repertoire, frequency of performance, opportunity for personal recognition within a group dance context, and spontaneous audience delight. The shortness of performance time and variety of poetic styles give even less accomplished composers a vehicle for emotional and physical release in a manner that, on a larger scale, recognizes and celebrates the community's ongoing dependence on the sea.

PHOTO 37. Kāua Sāre performing a *rue*. *(Hamish Macdonald)*

Tuki

Unlike other named categories, *tuki* span genres of song and dance, differentiating *tuki hua* (sung *tuki*) from *tuki anu* (danced *tuki*). Within the metagenre, several types are distinguished by name, as shown in figure 3, where numerals represent the numbers in the recorded collection.

Most categories are descriptive. *Nā tuki nā horau* relate the mythological voyages of the five clans' founding canoes and their subsequent ocean travels; the repertoire is small and fixed in size. The phrase *nā tuki hānota* (fishing songs) relates to three named fishing methods used on the ocean, as opposed to inside the lagoon, and to the associated practice of canoe building; these categories have associated dances for some, but not all, of their number. *Nā tuki hua* (songs for singing), by contrast, are simply sung without actions.[22]

There exist in the memories of older men a few *tuki* no longer performed frequently. Some were performed at my request, but required rehearsal to

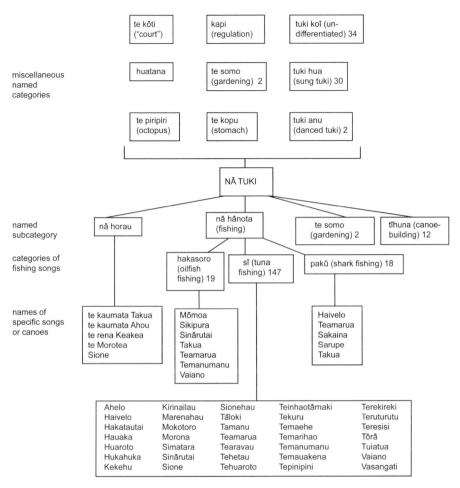

FIGURE 3. Named categories of *tuki*. Where the number of recorded examples is more than one, this figure appears in each box.

ensure accuracy. They include *nā tuki naperu, te huatana,* and *te tuki te kopu.* Their poetic content is only partially understood.

As a result of Nukuria men being brought to Takū as laborers in the 1890s, Takū men working on Nukuria in the 1940s and 1950s, and the steady if not numerically significant tendency toward intermarriage over the twentieth century, a significant number of *tuki* songs from Nukuria (at least fifty) are known on Takū. Most of these receive a first public performance as part of the *tukumai* ritual, when a deceased resident's Nukuria family connections are publicly acknowledged. The imported items differ from local compositions in the language and subject matter of their poetry, and in their presentation as unbroken sets of songs.[23] Where, as a result of prior discussion among the organizers of a *tukumai* for more than one deceased, agreement is reached that each representative group sing a predetermined number of *tuki* before allowing the next group to perform, the performance of *tuki* from Nukuria constitutes an acceptable exception since the practice of singing the *entire* set is followed.[24] All are sung without actions, and the singers command varying levels of understanding of their poetry. Several named types of Nukuria *tuki* may be distinguished (eg, *te tika, te lautono, nā hakavaipuna, te kuana, tīmea*), and their performance typically occupies up to two hours of the first night of the *tukumai*.

Some local *tuki* also form sets whose individual songs are normally performed in sequence. All but one celebrate events believed to have occurred in the period since contact with Europeans:

nā tuki Teara	four songs celebrating episodes in the life of Teara, a master fisherman from Peilau, probably in the nineteenth century
nā tuki te kaumata	five "songs of the nursery" celebrating the efforts of men on Nukumanu to obtain coconut seedlings from Peilau in the nineteenth century
nā tuki te kōti	four "songs about the court case" in 1930 that enabled the return of much of the atoll to local ownership
nā tuki te somo	two songs whose poetry focuses on garden growth aided by supernatural means

There are additionally a few individual *tuki* whose poetic content allows them to stand outside named categories; they include:

te tuki kapi	"the restrictions song" composed by Tarasomo at the request of Ariki Apeo
te tuki te piripiri	"the octopus song" describing the catching method; composer anonymous
te tuki te moto	the "outboard song," composed by Nūnua

These three compositions have drawn a mixed reaction. Tarasomo's composition has achieved a unique status: It is routinely performed to start the singing on the first night of every *tukumai*, a standing widely ascribed to Ariki Apeo's enduring esteem. Apeo, the first Ariki resident on Nukutoa, instituted a series of regulations resulting in the more efficient conservation of both land- and sea-based food resources. The "octopus song," by contrast, is a light-hearted nineteenth-century composition about a man hunting octopus who was seized by his intended prey. Nūnua's *tuki* represents a composition not accepted into the active repertoire because the language of its poetry breeched a convention; although it accurately depicted contemporary fishing techniques, it did not conform to the idealized image of life on the atoll in the pre-motorized era, and its popularity was only short-lived.

Elsewhere I have discussed the poetic conventions associated with *tuki* songs, which focus on an idealized idea of life on the island as it might have been two generations ago. Since *tuki* represent the largest category of performed items on Takū, I provide here a brief summary of their musical styles. The sheer quantity of recorded *tuki* necessitates an overview here, although a more detailed examination is planned for future publications.

Example 32 is a 1997 danced *tuki* composed to commemorate Ansett, the familiar name of a severely handicapped young man who died in that year. The first verse half is sung with hesitation, and the full singing group joins in only at the start of the second half, when the rhythm is stabilized by the addition of handclapping. All verses have paired texts, each pair having close similarity in their number of syllables and rhythms. Variation in the number of syllables between verses is accommodated musically by the presence in the verse outline of three periods of level movement capable of expansion in rhythm and duration to fit the poetry; these positions are identified in the outline below by stemless notes. Significantly, singers made the greatest deviations from unison during these same periods as some of their number initially struggled to identify the melodic and rhythmic framework underpinning the verses (example 33).

EXAMPLE 32. A conventional danced *tuki*.

EXAMPLE 33. A skeletal outline of the melody for example 32.

This melodic type allows the composer a degree of freedom to vary the number of words in each verse; this permits individualized expression while retaining a melodic and rhythmic framework, and thus creates reference points for the singers and facilitates learning and memorization. Vocal pulsations are used through the song at the duration of a quaver, and some vowels are split by staccato enunciation on the first of the two notes; these features are found in several song categories.

Ē ko taku vaka, nau ka tui ma ki tua	It's my canoe, and I paddle to the ocean
E aro ki tana inaho nei, ko taku vaka.	Where his [Ansett's] flock of birds is.
Nau ka tui ma ki tua,	I paddle to the back,
E aro ki tana inaho nei, ko Simata rā.	Going to his school—it's *Simata*.

Uāīē, hano iho he tanata ma tana rimu	A man comes with his seaweed
No terekia i te vasi ama,	Rubbing along the port side,
Ni karana nau te haitamana	As I call to the father and son
Hakamārama iho taku vaka.	To guide the canoe.
Uāīē, hano iho Tehīlau ma te rua rimu	Teheilau comes with his two clumps of seaweed [25]
No tere i tai te vasi ama,	And works along the port side,
Ni karana Kalevao ki Arehu	As Kalevao calls to Arehu
Hakamārama iho Tesimata.	To attract fish to *Simata*.
Uāīē, uru taku vaka i loto te taumanu	My canoe enters the flock of birds
Ni mapuna mai ki taku katea,	And the fish are on my starboard side,
Se tanata tū ma tana matila hakautauta ki te murivaka.	A man stands with his rod and lands the fish in the canoe end.
Uāīē, uru Tesimata i loto te taumanu,	*Simata* enters the flock of birds,
Ni mapuna mai ki taku katea,	And the fish are on my starboard side,
Ko Heni tū ma tana matila ha kautautaki ana hutia.	Heni stands with his rod and lands the fish in the canoe end.
Uāīē, noho iho se tanata ē i tana hare,	One man stayed at home,
Ha karono iho ki te hakaiō,	Listening to the calls of success,
Tēnā se hakaiō a taku vaka.	The ones coming from my canoe.
Uāīē, noho iho soko Helo ē i tana hare,	Ahelo stayed at home,
Mate iho koe ki te hakaiō,	Recognizing that the shouts came from you,
Tēnā se hakaiō a Tesimata,	The ones coming from *Simata*,
E aro i tana inaho.	Which went in search of its flock of birds.

Not all *tuki* intended for dancing are as syllabic as this example, and many incorporate melisma, particularly at line endings, as shown in example 34, a song composed in 1998 but using an established melodic stereotype. For reasons of economy of space, the notation omits the two final verses.

Ō ka sepu iho taku vaka,	I go out in my canoe,
E uetia iho ko nā tahe nā ē.	Going out in the currents.
I te inaho taku kave nei.	To the fish belonging to my sister.
Ē ka sepu iho ko Tehuaroto nā	Tehuaroto goes out
E uetia iho ko nā tahe nā ē	Out in the currents
I te inaho taku kave nei.	To the fish belonging to my sister.
E se tanata e hano ma tana kave nā ē,	One man went with his sister,
Uruhia ko te hareika, nā ē;	And entered the house of fish;
Ie, Tāsani e hano ma Patoko nā ē,	Tāsani went with Patoko,
Uruhia ko te hareika, nā ē.	And entered the house of fish.
Ie, ko se tanata e aru ma tana inaho nā ē,	A man was calling for his school,
E aru iho ki te hareika, nā ē;	Calling to the house of fish;
Ē, Panono e aru ma tana matila nā ē,	Panono was calling for his school,
Ni aru iho ki Savaiki, nā ē.	Calling to Savaiki.

EXAMPLE 34. A danced *tuki* containing regular melisma.

As mentioned earlier, two danced songs constitute communal favorites since they both are routinely included in parties at Tāloki and Sialeva and also on the *marae* during a *tukumai*. The songs' enduring popularity may be attributed to the social values their poetry continues to endorse, more than a hundred years after their composition in the nineteenth century. The poetry of one of these songs, the *tuki i Nukurekia*, has already been discussed in chapter 1; its music appears in example 35.

Unlike this *tuki*, the second of the favorites is normally identified and referred to by its first line. Takū residents say that its poetic reference to a stone fish trap locates it in the lagoon area off Takū Island and to the period when that island was still inhabited, that is, sometime prior to the 1880s. Its theme, the value of parental advice, is highlighted by recounting the adverse effects of nonconformist behavior; it is the timeless tale of the failure and humiliation of a child who chooses not to heed such advice. The song appears as example 36.

EXAMPLE 35. The music of the *tuki i Nukurekia*.

Ko nau kā sē moe i te pō,   I couldn't sleep at night,
nau ka tautauria te tai.   I was watching the sea.
Tana tereana e kina hota ē   He went to the fish trap,
ko ana manoni e soroia te tai.   his perfume obliterated by the water.
E tana tūana ko nā matāhare,   He stood outside and your father asked;
te vasiri mai a tō tamana a te pō nei [he replied] the night would be stormy.
  hakarehurehu.
E tana tūana ko nā matāhare,   He stood outside and your father asked;
te vasiri mai a tō tamana ā te pō nei [he replied] the rain would be pelting
  ku tō patapata.   down.
Ā te vasiri mai tō tinana ā nei ō kai. Your mother asked then said, "Here's your
                                          food."
Ā te vasiri mai tō tinana ā nei ō taro. Your mother asked then said, "Here's your
                                          taro."[26]

EXAMPLE 36. The second of the two community favorites.

Foreign Songs and Dances

Takū has a longstanding tradition of absorbing foreign artistic material into the local repertoire, to the point where at least two of the founding canoes are said to have embarked on voyages far to the southeast specifically in search of new songs and dances for the entertainment of the Ariki. A few of the dances brought in that era survive, notably the *paki* and the *toki,* the former allegedly from Samoa and the latter possibly also from Samoa. The replacement of sailing canoes by ships did not adversely affect the inward flow of foreign material, and although some dances genres appear to have been discontinued in living memory, there is no evidence that such processes represent anything more than the normal processes of a dynamic artistic tradition.

The *paronu hareika* dance was one casualty of the depopulation of Takū Island in the late nineteenth century. Its sole owner in the early years of this century was an elder called Rousarī, the last resident of that island, who died childless and without an heir. Whatever proficiency Rousarī's contemporaries on Kapeiatu Island may have possessed at that time was outweighed by the absence of any authorized successor and fear of possible consequences if performed independent of the dance owner's approval, invoking the presence of potentially dangerous spirits. Five generations later, the circumstances of that particular *paronu*'s abandonment are still recounted in subdued tones in vestigial respect for those powers who, unnamed and uncounted, maintain their unseen presence. Despite this appearance of discontinuation, portions of the dance were performed in 1999 by family members inside the house of a resident who had died in 1998 and again later that day in a beachfront yard; on both occasions, participants were quite drunk and declined to provide any information about the dance when sober. Another *paronu*, known as *nā tama Kiakia* (the Kiakia people), has no such restrictions, but little is known of its origin.[27]

A series of nineteenth-century drift voyages from outliers situated to the southeast—notably Nukumanu, Peilau, and Liuaniua—eventually resulted in the introduction of sets of *tuki* songs and dances. The sale of the Takū atoll to Emma Forsayth in 1886 and subsequent importation of plantation laborers from elsewhere in the then German New Guinea also marked the start of an enduring social and musical relationship with Nukuria, the outlier situated to the immediate west of Takū, in contrast to the more sporadic contact in the earlier times. Tuiatua (who changed his name on arrival to Tekapu) brought the hour-long set of dreamed *sore* dances carrying his name, as did his contemporary, Vakapū. Tekapu also introduced a *takere* stick-dance, as did Atua and Mahana. In the early 1970s Graham Carson, a European businessman living on Nukuria, hired laborers from Takū to work in his fishery business, resulting in some intermarriage, and knowledge of sets of *tuki* and *kkai* stories from the atoll. Families of persons having a Nukuria ancestral line routinely sing sets of Nukuria *tuki* at their *tukumai;* performance of these sets is distinguished from locally composed *tuki* because an entire set may be sung without interruption even when local compositions are sung in rotation among the family groups represented, two or three from each in turn. More recently, Takū men working at Kaveing, Rabaul, Nissan, Buka, Bougainville and elsewhere in Papua New Guinea have learned local dances and, on return to Takū, have taught them for public performance, typically at a *tukumai* or the annual school concert. Such items tend not to be repeated in successive years and may lie dormant for an extended period of time.

One exception occurred in 1998 and is significant in three respects. The dance was performed by foreigners on Takū rather than in its homeland; only a single performance was given, and it was a dance well known throughout the Pacific.

While engaged in New Zealand–led peace monitoring duties on Bougainville in 1998, Brigadier Roger Mortlock visited Takū enquiring as to the European origin of its better-known name, Mortlock Island. As his all-male group was about to depart, they gave an impromptu and spontaneous performance of New Zealand's best-known Maori *haka,* which residents identified only as a *sea,* a term referring to the lifting of one leg as commonly found in dances at Nukumanu. In 1999 a group from Sialeva who had witnessed the dance gave a rendition of it at the school concert, but with three significant changes: the dancers were women, the performance was intended to be humorous, and many of the words (which had been heard only once on the earlier occasion and were incomprehensible) had been changed. Wearing skirts of young coconut leaves, the women (who included one of the largest on the island) proceeded onto the schoolyard grunting, *"Hū, hū"* and thrusting their arms to one side, before forming a single line and dancing. The combination of obvious incongruities achieved the desired hilarity. (Field notes, 1999)

Accuracy in the transmission of oral tradition is one of the popularized pillars of Polynesian culture as a whole and is well documented, but is typically based on active learning rather than a single exposure to a performance event. Comparison with the Maori poetry reveals moderate, but incomplete, recall from the performance in 1998:

Maori 1998	Takū 1999
Ka mate, ka mate ka ora, ka ora	*Tā mate, tā mate, taora taora*
Tēnei te tanata pūhuruhuru	*Tēnei he tanata*
Nāna i tiki mai whakahiti te rā	
Aue upane, aue upane	*Hūtane hūtane*
Aue upane kaupane whiti te rā.	*Pīpī taura.*

The intended humor presupposed that the audience recollected enough of the sound and sight of the original performance to recognize the contrast afforded by the local version. There are, of course, too many variables and unknown factors to permit hard conclusions from this single instance, but our understanding of Polynesian oral transmission may well benefit from an examination of its processes as well as its products.

In contrast to this single-performance item, a few dances of acknowledged foreign origin remain in the active repertoire where they have been imbued with local notions of ownership and performance protocol, and we now turn to this body of material.

Takere

Two *takere* dances persist on Takū, each performed by stick-wielding men who dance in lines along the two-hundred-meter "main road" to the *marae,* which they occupy for several minutes before retreating, still dancing, back along the road. Unlike dances of local origin, the *takere* are acknowledged as having been brought to Takū from Nukuria.

TAKERE MOANA Tekapu was a close relative of the dance's first owner on Nukuria and assumed ownership of it when he resettled on Takū. Ownership was later transferred patrilineally within Hare Nāoro to Pōpī, then to Pilike and his younger cousin, Āpē. As Āpē himself relates:

> This dance was brought from the ocean. It belonged to spirits and was brought from the ocean. It was later brought and introduced here to this island. I don't understand its associated actions because they belong to spirits. It was brought from the ocean by spirits, not from a land tree but from [an ocean current known as a] "sea tree." The place where they performed was called Tearatahe, and they brought their song to the living world, where we continue to dance it now. When it was introduced, only the sons of chiefs could dance it—not just anybody, only chiefs' sons. The dance was brought to Takū by Tekapu, who brought it to this island and taught us how to dance the song. This song isn't for just anybody to dance for fun, or for someone to come and dance on just any occasion. No, this song is to be danced only on major occasions.

This is currently the most frequently performed dance of foreign origin and, somewhat ironically, it is routinely included in dance programs performed off-island by Takū men and intended for a foreign audience; notable performances have included those on Bougainville to entertain Queen Elizabeth II (1972), on the first arrival at Takū of the MV *Sankamap* (1993), on the visit to Bougainville of the Australian and New Zealand Ministers of Foreign Affairs (1996), and on the visit to Bougainville of Papua New Guinea's Prime Minister (1997). On Takū itself, the dance is frequently performed during *tukumai* and in 1999 it was taught to boys and danced at the school concert for the first time, led by Āpē himself.

Āpē's comments on the unintelligibility of the song poetry is in line with a general view that poetry composed by a spirit is usually unintelligible, except perhaps to immediate family members. Like other stand-alone dances, this *takere* incorporates danced entry and exit sections and features lines of dancers each headed by a *tama haimako* leader chosen for his patrilineal credentials; it is also subject to performance restrictions, though more so in the past than at present.

Despite its foreign origin, the dance retains close links with the spirit world when performed at Takū, and the use of weapons—formerly spears, but now sticks—as dance accessories carries an added risk or danger to the sanctity of the persons of the Ariki and Pure. As Sione Pilike noted,

> If we're going to perform the dance, someone like me should attend and perform, standing at the head of the line, and wearing sacra from the elder's house, Pūtahu's house—that's where I get my sacra so I can go and dance on the *marae*. This done, we go to Avo's *marae*, but not without sacra because we fear the spirits, and they would kill us. The spirits will become angry because we brought the song to that place, and we fear the dance because we use sticks, and the *marae* normally prohibits the use of sticks. For example, [the Pure] Kīpū—you might try to take a stick and injure Kīpū—so that's why it is forbidden. If you do that, Kīpū will drop dead. And

Avo also is a chief. If you try something like that and Kīpū doesn't actually drop
dead, he'll instantly become insane.

Although in later years Pilike was too infirm to dance, he continued to
support performances by singing from the front row of *tautua* ritual assistants. His superior knowledge of the dance was evident even to the last performance before he died: Āpē, current owner of the dance and always one of the
line leaders, routinely turned to the older man while resting for his prompt
with the first words of the next section.

The dancers move in two lines, dancing to the *marae* along the two hundred
meters of Nukutoa's "main road," starting at its southern end. Four sections
incorporate the processional dance, each called simply *takere;* each section is
repeated several times and is followed by a brief rest period. The overall number of repeats is judged so that the dancers arrive at the *marae* on completion
of the final one. Example 37 presents the first of the four sections.

EXAMPLE 37. The *taki* processional section for the *takere moana.*

The three sections that follow are called collectively *taukaro* and start with
a brief period of singing, following which the dancers form quartets and clash
their sticks together in fast sequence; each section ends with the dancers
retreating rapidly in line to the edges of the *marae* as they speak the final lines
of poetry. When referring to individual sections for identification purposes,
people speak the first words of their respective first lines: *He mata ki moana,*
Tū ma hina, and *Tū rona.* The musical content of each section is identical: following the repetition of a short line as the dancers merely stand, the triplet
tempo suddenly increases and the sequence of stick clashing begins (photo
38). Example 38 illustrates the section *Tū mahina.*

According to the dance protocol received from Nukuria, the poetic content of one section calls for the Ariki, spear in hand, to run across the *marae*
on the singing of the lines beginning *Terekia mai ko he tao* (A spear goes running out) but, being prohibited from dancing by dint of his sacred status
while on the *marae,* the Ariki himself does not participate and appoints in
advance one dancer as his representative.

Tū ma·hi — na, tū   ma·hi·na mai te la·ni.   · Tū ma·hi· na, tū·ma·hi·na mai te la·ni.   ·

sticks   (etc.)
Tū ma·hi·na mai te la·ni, ha·ka·uē te ha·ute ha·re·i·ka   rā. Tō te va·e·nu·tu ē, ka tū pe·na·pe·na,   ka

tū pe·na·pe·na, ka   tū pe·na·pe·na.   Ni a·nu pe·na·pe·na Kū nā   to·ro ki te pu·ku a·ru·na,

Nā to·ro ki ra·ra te a·tu ro·ro, a·nu·mi·a te ta·ke·re i va·e moa·na. Ē ka tū pe·na·pe·na,   ni a·nu pe·na·pe·na,

Ē ka tū pe·na·pe·na.   I·ā pe·na·pe·na, i·ā te la·ni ma·ha·ra u·na. Ta·u he ka·ni va·e mo·a·na, ke·ke·mo te ui·la,

pa·ki·si te ha·tu·tu·ri, pi·sa·ke.

EXAMPLE 38. The *Tū mahina* section of the *takere moana*.

PHOTO 38. The *taikaro* section of the *takere,* during which the dancers form quartets and clash their sticks against those of other members of their group. *(Richard Moyle)*

TAKERE OKI The second *takere* was brought to Takū from Nukuria in the early 1900s by two men, Atua and Mahana. Ownership was later transferred to Tehatu, thence to the Pure Marena within the Hare Mania clan. At that time, one of the dance line leaders was a talented man of Hare Māsani clan, and his close and constant association with the dance resulted in a degree of control being vested in that clan. The dance is believed to depict a nineteenth-century incident on Nukuria in which a nephew of the despot Soaʻa tried forcefully, but unsuccessfully, to overthrow his uncle. The language, which is not understood on Takū, is said to be Paga, which originates from New Ireland. As in the other dance, the *takere oki* men proceed along the road to the *marae*, dance in quartets of stick-clashing vigor, then proceed back along the road a short distance, still dancing, to complete the performance. The association with Hare Māsani allows that clan to supply one line leader, and the seniority of that clan's present elder, Kikiva, allows him to lead rehearsals even though his physical infirmity forces him to do so from a chair.

The *taki* processional section is long, incorporating nine sung sections each separated by several seconds as the dancers rest. The singing is slow and has no clear pulse or rhythm. The acknowledged foreign origin of the two *takere* dances and Takū dancers' and audiences' imperfect understanding of the poetry have not deterred the frequent performance or general popularity of these dances. On the contrary, just as their Nukuria owners were incorporated into Takū society through adoption, the dances they brought have themselves been integrated into Takū's own repertoire. Although performance styles and costumes are distinctive, the dances embody the same unison singing and synchronized movement of local compositions; at the same time they retain notions of ownership and line leadership no longer used for contemporary compositions. The inclusion of a boys' performance of the *takere moana* at the 1999 school concert, therefore, represented a break from almost a century of adult performances, but on attaining adulthood those same boys are expected to fill the ranks of dancers, and it is significant that their 1999 performance was held in the schoolyard and not on the *marae*, where strict protocol continues to be observed and where only adults may participate.

Paki

In 1972 Queen Elizabeth II visited Papua New Guinea and spent a brief period at Kieta on Bougainville Island. While there, she was entertained by a program of traditional dances by provincial ethnic groups, including the atolls. For this event Takū men performed what they held most valuable in their repertoire—the *paki*. Although the dance was, by local accounts, well received, it was not performed again for twenty-three years, when it was chosen to be the centerpiece of an afternoon of sponsored dance.[28]

There exists in oral tradition an account that Takū residents assign to the most distant period of existence, when the world as they know it was populated by spirits—that is, prior to the arrival of the first human. This myth relates the journey of the founding canoe *Taoa,* and the principal focus is a dance called *te paki.* The acquisition of a new dance to entertain the Ariki constituted the reason for a voyage far beyond the ambit of normal oceangoing travel. The following is a synopsis given in 1994 by the present elder of Hare Nāoro, Pūtahu Tekapu.

They arrived and landed at Ttuila and immediately carved a canoe out of mahogany. Only mahogany trees grew on the island, and they carved the canoe and joined the two sections together. But then they didn't go down to the sea; the sea said that, if the canoe came down, it would destroy it; the joint was weak on the canoe. They returned and cut another tree and made another join. So they prepared the central section and joined it to the two end sections. Then they set sail, and the ocean said that it was good. They set off and arrived at Savaiki, the first island to appear. They went and brought away their items from Savaiki, a spear and a sword. They departed from Savaiki and found Samoa. They didn't go inland because the chief didn't want to—when they arrived at Samoa the land was covered by night. They moved along and became aware of the singing for the *paki* dance.

Then the chief [Maile] spoke, ordering the sail-rope to be slackened so that they could listen to the song being sung on shore, that is, the *paki.* As soon as the dance was finished, he order the sail-rope to be tightened. They went off, knowing the song. So they went off across the ocean, looking at the *paki* inside their magical coconut shell, and *"paki"* became its name.

They came to Rotuma, and the chief of Rotuma asked that man [ie, the captain] what thing had been brought away from the islands they had been to. The man replied, "I brought a spear and a sword for myself."

"What are they for?"

"They're my weapons."

"What did you bring from Samoa?"

"The *paki.*"

"Sing it so I can hear it."

So the chief sang it. Then the Ariki said, "There's nothing here that I can give you, I can think of nothing to give you, but how about you take away this thing, the *maile* plant." That plant was the gift of the Ariki of Rotuma. And that *maile* was the one planted at the rear of Harehatu [island on Takū], the term for the place is Tua Te Maile [at the rear of Kapeiatu island].

They left Rotuma and came to Taputapu. After Taputapu they came to Niua. And after Niua they went and found Tikopia. When the Ariki of Tikopia asked what he had been able to get, the chief Maile replied, "With these weapons I now have all that I need, and I've also brought a dance."

He sailed on beyond Tikopia and went on to Sikeiana. The island had no reef channel, so *Taoa* simply stood on and off outside the reef. They left Sikeiana and came straight on to Liuaniua. There he dropped off a woman, a woman called Teruehine. They left Teruehina on Liuaniua together with a pig and a weapon, and they also left a chicken. Maile stood on the island and hurled his spear and it landed in the reef flat between Nukutoa and Takū. Then he arrived here and someone on the canoe who was with him died, and he was buried in a hole on the reef flat. They had made landfall at Tenipu Teise [a small reef pool].

He sailed round to the ocean side of the atoll. (On arrival he was unaware that other people were already on the island. The canoe *Tepuraka* had already arrived, but Maile didn't understand how it could have passed him.) He arrived right at the point of the tidal flat and dropped off his woman, Teatuai.

Next morning he bathed and went and visited the cemetery, making a formal visit. When he came onto the flat, he visited his ancestor, then returned. The canoe *Hakautu* arrived later and discovered the woman. The spirits on board argued about who would marry her. She became the wife of Pūkena, Avo's [clan's] spirit. The Ariki became our affine. The woman from *Taoa* who was dropped off became that snake who was buried on the flat; it wasn't really a snake, but a woman.

That [place] Tēppū is now mine, but it once belonged to the Ariki. Pūkena then handed it over to his wife. So, *Taoa* came and finished up here, and that *paki* was taught.

It is probably irrelevant to the myth's cultural value whether it recounts a genuine historical event or an imaginary one. It may be usefully considered an artifact of cultural logic that imposes measurable boundaries on a world beyond living recall, and also to establish a degree of coherent control and order over the dance's origin as a reference point for the blurring and merging of ownership that was to follow. Assuming the accuracy of detail in this account for discussion purposes, it appears that the "Samoa" from which the dance was obtained may not have been Samoa itself, even though this island name is commonly offered by adults as the dance's place of origin. Tutuila and Savai'i are part of Samoa, but there is no Samoan island itself called "Samoa." The dance name itself and the distinctive dance implement from which that name derives both suggest an origin on East Futuna, where the *tā paki* constitutes a similar category of dance. Whatever its specific origin, however, it is significant that current belief firmly identifies the *paki* as a dance from Samoa, in support of which, a poetic line is quoted: *Oa taro niu ē, ku tāia se vaka i Samoa, io nunumake.* Although the meaning of the first and last phrases is unknown, the central phrase translatable as Takū—"a canoe was carved in Samoa"—is adduced as evidence of a Samoan origin.

Mythology records that this was not the only trip on which canoes traveled to Samoa. The founding ancestor who gave his name to the atoll, Takū, lived on Ttuila until his father came and took him to discover a new atoll. After discovering Takū, the son returned to Ttuila to collect swamp taro, coconuts, and people to colonize the new place. In another myth, the second son of Takū also lived on Ttuila with his father and in yet another account, the daughter of Takū, later the founding ancestor of the settlement on Liuaniua, was born on the island of Savaiki. Samoa was also the mythological source of tattooing combs used on Takū. Although the express purpose of the trip to Samoa was to find and bring back a companion dance *(hakasoa mako)* for the dance of the Ariki, neither this myth nor that of the voyages of the Ariki's clan canoe identify that other dance. And, oral tradition records that the Ariki's clan canoe also voyaged out in search of a new dance on one occasion, but it was unsuccessful.

Oral tradition records that, having been brought back to Takū in the canoe of the Noho i Tai clan, the *paki* was deemed to belong to that clan. In the course of succession, it happened that one owner had no sons and was obliged to pass on the dance to his sister's son, whom he adopted and who was of the Noho i Saupuku clan because his mother had married a man of that clan (figure 4). The Noho i Saupuku was then in a position to claim a proprietary interest in the dance. For its part, Te Noho i Tai did not completely relinquish its historical control, but accepted a compromise.

The song was passed to the clan elder for Te Noho i Saupuku, who took it and taught the dance in its entirety to men of the Sikipura group, while the Te Noho i Tai clan continued to retain a degree of ownership. The dual nature of the dance's ownership is reflected in accounts of early performances that use two columns of dancers headed by a senior man from each group. After the move to Nukutoa in the 1930s, the enduring association with the then-dissolved Noho i Tai was also manifest in the elder of that clan (renamed as Hare Nāoro) preparing the sacra that sanction performance and giving them to the head of the co-owning clan, Hare Māsani, before the men moved into position for the procession to the *marae*. After World War One and the subsequent establishment of the two village sections, Tāloki and Sialeva, however, the owner clans lost the proximity of residence they had enjoyed on Takū Island (see figure 5). Hare Nāoro and Hare Māsani represent the two smallest clans, with a total resident population in 1994 of only sixty-five, some 17

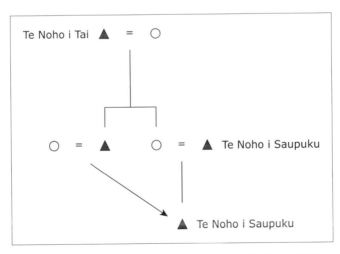

FIGURE 4. The transfer of *paki* ownership from Te Noho i Tai clan to Te Noho i Saupuku clan

percent of the island's total population. From a purely practical point of view, neither clan by itself has sufficient adult males to perform the dance and thus must rely on the approval with the other. It follows also that either clan can veto a performance by simple withdrawal of personnel. Given the likely small population on Takū in precontact times, performance of the *paki* has depended on cooperation between these two clans for a considerable time.

Performances of the *paki* in precontact times are said to have been confined to the six-month period each year during which the spirit Pukena was on show outside his house, and before whom the entire adult population danced each afternoon. The entertainment of Pukena ceased when the atoll was bought by Emma Forsayth in 1886, the population resettled on Kapeiatu island, and Takū itself developed into a copra plantation. Along with the loss of the material representation of their deity, the residents also lost the principal reason for performing the *paki*.

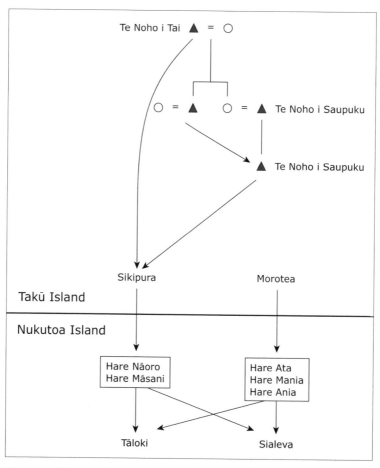

FIGURE 5. The transfer of *paki* ownership to the clans on Nukutoa Island

The infrequent performance of the *paki* in the last thirty years is attributed to a parallel infrequency of occasions of appropriate significance, since "the *paki* is not danced indiscriminately" *(te paki rā ku sē anu vare)*. This statement of principle is matched on a practical level by the need for prior approval from the owner clan heads and a period of some weeks for rehearsal. And there is also the spiritual dimension, since the attendance of the atoll's major deities renders the whole situation potentially dangerous to general health and welfare.[29] There appears to be no recollection of a performance prior to 1972.

At present, the annual celebration of Papua New Guinea's independence, for which the central government provides K500 to the atoll, is the principal secular dance event on Takū, and several hours of dancing are a normal part of these festivities. But because protocol prevents men from participating in any other dance event the same day they perform the *paki,* this dance is not routinely included in the National Independence program.

The word *paki* designates both the dance and the triangular wooden implement that each man holds. The dance itself includes three broad sections, each having its own music: the *taki* entrance procession along the road to the *marae,* the dancing on the *marae,* and the *sari* exit procession back a short distance along the road. The song for the *taki* consists of multiple repeats of a single poetic phrase *Ā ō taro niu ē ō ē ā tarotaro.* Although it is possible to aggregate individual combinations of syllables to form intelligible words, the meaning of the entire phrase is not known. As the lines of dancers slowly advance down the road, they sing this phrase seven times, holding their *paki* implements in the air in brief salute before standing to rest for several seconds; the phrase sequence is repeated as many times as necessary to reach the *marae;* this can take ten minutes, or longer. The singing, which has no clear pulse and tends to be sung in imprecise unison, is as follows (example 39):

EXAMPLE 39. The *taki* processional section of the *paki* dance.

On reaching the *marae,* the men perform for the first time to the beating of the *tuki* slit drum, dancing two sections separated by a few seconds of silence. The poetry of each section consists of a single line repeated many times as the dancers work through their movement sequences, starting as follows (example 40):

EXAMPLE 40. The *marae*-based section of the *paki.*

Once the singing notated above has been completed, the material is repeated, this time much faster. On completion of these sections, a further section known as *te toki* (the axe) is danced (example 41). Opinions differ as to the identity of the *toki,* some claiming that it has "always" been a part of the *paki,* others arguing that it is a separate dance in its own right, brought from Samoa in the mythological era but later grafted onto the *paki.* The dancers formalize their departure from the *marae* in the *sari,* a brief final section whose melody is sung three times.

A 1994 performance of the *paki* was marked by controversy. It gave unprecedented formal prominence to two men who insisted on taking lead positions in the dance lines but whose familiarity with the dance and dancing ability were dubious. The owner clans had no competent drummers of their own and enlisted three men from another clan who claimed no special familiarity with the accompanying rhythms for the dance. The drummers were decidedly

EXAMPLE 41. The *toki* section of the *paki.*

uneasy about their responsibility. The novelty of the performance occasion attracted some fifty dancers, only a few of whom had danced it in 1972. In hindsight, these factors all set the stage for disaster.

On the day of the performance, the dancers donned their dress, formed their four lines, and proceeded down the roadway toward the *marae* some two hundred meters away, where the elders and village had assembled along with the drummers. The dancers paused several times en route as they performed the first sections of the dance, and it immediately became apparent that all was not well. The distance of the drums, the lack of unison beating by the three drummers, the length of the four lines, and the low-pitched singing of the senior dancers in front combined to confuse the dancers at the rear, who sang at a different speed and pitch with all the enthusiasm that comes with ignorance. The dance movements lost their synchrony and as the performance lost its overall unity of sight and sound, it stopped. Loud grumbling from among the ranks of the dancers gave way to accusations and counter-accusations of incompetence, and there was consternation at the blunder among those waiting on the *marae*. The dancers moved silently to the *marae* proper and performed the rest of the dance without further incident but also without their former enthusiasm. Wide criticism followed, in particular, of the standard of drumming, with dancers and spectators alike complaining that the unclear and inconsistent beating had contributed to an unprecedented disaster.

Despite its foreign origin, the *paki* dance is held up as an icon of island artistry and draws its participants from different clans and different residential groupings, in contrast to the dances making up the bulk of the repertoire. The *paki*'s relatively infrequent performance is a measure of its high esteem, since only rarely are the necessary prerequisites met. However, that same infrequency makes its performance potentially vulnerable to change (deliberate or unintentional) and tends to diminish the level of the dancers' competence.

The end of communal residence on Takū Island in the 1890s meant the end to the entertainment of local deities; this in turn removed the sole performance occasion for the *paki*. A dance now celebrated as a national icon and carrying the strictest protocol of any item in the local repertoire was not performed for twenty-three years for lack of a suitable occasion. And when it was danced again, the performance fell apart through lack of preparation. Initial gloom at this failure was eventually replaced by confidence that the next performance, whenever and wherever that may be, will be successful, even though the waters of local politics still require careful navigation. In the meantime, knowledge of the dance has become limited to a few persons, only one of whom is physically capable of leading by example. Two further conflicting forces appear to be operating: performances need to continue, to maintain a supply of competent dancers, but there are no foreseeable occasions when the next performance might occur. The next few years will probably be crucial to the identity and future survival of this dance.

Summary

Dancing on Takū is subject to many pressures and forces. The ongoing need for new *tuki* songs at each *tukumai* presents the poet/composer with an opportunity but also the obligation to create not only songs but danced songs. The existence of musical and poetic stereotypes as well as a relatively small inventory of dance movements help place creation within the capability of many adults; indeed, more than half the adult population has produced at least one *tuki*. In such circumstances, the desire for new material is driven by the need to recognize, via art, a deceased resident's social individuality. This situation contrasts with the motives behind importation of foreign dances that are now a normal part of the program ending the first all-night session of a *tukumai*. Invariably performed to a song in a language sufficiently foreign to be unintelligible to most, if not all, of the audience, the primary emphasis is on the visual effect of new movements and costumes. There is still, however, a link to the deceased since the dances chosen may hail from a geographical location he/she frequented, such as Rabaul or Buka. The period of at least six months between a death and the subsequent *tukumai* is sufficient to select and rehearse such dances. One striking example in 1997 involved the series of *sore* dances brought to the island from Nukuria by Tekapu in the early twentieth century and now known by his own original name: *nā sore Tuiatua*. This set, which is said to have lain dormant for almost fifty years and which took some fifty minutes to perform, was learned by a group of women in two months of concentrated rehearsals.

The discontinuation of the *tānaki* ritual in 1974 parallels the discontinued composition of *llū* travel songs in the late nineteenth century with the community's decimation by epidemic. Both calamities effectively eliminated the sources of new material for several whole categories of song or dance, and the community's response was identical on both occasions—consolidating the then-existing dynamic repertoire into a static collection of more-or-less fixed size. The present performance on the *marae* of *sau*, *manakoho*, and *sore* (as well as *llū* songs) is testament to the communal determination to celebrate their belief in an idyllic life after death and the ability of the powerful dead to communicate these circumstances to the living via danced songs. In the period since 1974 general knowledge of the referential details of the song poetry has contracted, in sharp contrast with other categories of song whose repertoire is living. Present-day performances represent danced tributes to not so much the specific deceased named in the song poetry as to the religious beliefs underpinning the transmissions of those individuals to their families. To some extent, these beliefs are now incorporated in *tuki* songs claimed to have been taught by the dead; but, as noted elsewhere, the private and unverifiable nature of their transmission contrasts with the public transmissions that occurred in the *tānaki*, and skepticism sometimes surrounds present claims.

Denied the means of keeping all categories in its repertoire alive and growing, Takū have resorted to a variety of means to sustain the links between the living and the dead. Further, denied the creative skills of *purotu* performance specialists, the community has responded by using the medium of *tuki* songs and dances to spread compositional responsibilities among its adult members. In its various occurrences and forms, dancing continues to provide an outlet for individual and group expression and for emotional release, all within the larger confines of social solidarity.

Conclusion

On a technical level, Takū's musicking is the act of marshaling voices to sing in unison and linking dance actions to those voices in a manner that produces synchronized sequences of movement. These performance characteristics, together with an expectation of proficiency from all participating individuals, constitute a form of egalitarianism, a behavioral principle that permeates Takū culture as a whole and promotes community survival. This principle is temporarily put aside, but not compromised, when the community joins to acknowledge individual achievement through events such as competitions.

Some elements of Takū's musical style are shared among other outliers, but some appear to be unique to the atoll. One can say that Takū's unison singing of melodies having relatively small vocal range, their minimal use of melisma, occasional shifts of vowels from /a/ to /o/, forceful enunciation, use of short rhythmic figures, and clear pulse from accompanying handclapping or wooden idiophones are common to several outliers, on the basis of present information. Takū is unique in its tradition of the *lū*, with its slow tempo, glissands, and minimal emphasis on rhythm. Split syllables and strong vocal pulsations are also identifiers of Takū singing.

Takū's remote and insular identity ensures that the community is both provider and consumer of its own cultural activity. On informal performance occasions, the boundary between participant and audience is often fluid. Indeed, it is only on the *marae* that an audience is routinely present as a discrete body of adults contributing nothing but their attention, as the act of singing creates discrete groups of producers and consumers and the musicking identifies and affirms groups within the community based on gender, clan affiliation, age, and most recently, religious belief. *Marae* performances also attract the attention of both founding and ancestral spirits, whose anthropomorphic attributes include responsiveness to living modes of interaction, including food offerings, verbal communication, singing, and dancing. But a potential hazard lies in every instance of such contact: any inaccuracy or inappropriateness of the mechanics is believed to result in not just failure to achieve the desired end, but also supernatural retribution in the form of personal disaster. The logic of entrusting the community's spiritual well-being to individuals possessing specialist knowledge is clear. But the widely shared domestic experiences on this small atoll produce a certain leveling of abilities and a consequent absence of specialists; the two obvious exceptions to this are the earned conspicuousness of men skilled at pelagic fishing, and the inherited positions of distinction displayed in ritually charged circumstances. These positions are formalized by their nomenclature and a blend of privilege and responsibility. The purviews of the Ariki, Pure, *tautai, tautua, tauru,* and *purotu* are distinct, but there are areas of overlap and they all share an above-average frequency of contact with the supernatural world. Clan elders do not act for any personal advantage but for the welfare of their respective clans since the spiritual source of their authority is fixed on the atoll itself. And, while the Ariki is the elder of his own clan, his responsibility as Ariki extends to the community as a whole.

The centrality of the sea as Takū's ultimate provider is celebrated in its two dominant representations, as the direct basis of economic sustenance and as the indirect source of personal prestige. In death as in life, the sea dominates thought and action, and statements to this effect are communicated by spirits of the dead to surviving family members as comforting evidence of the continuation beyond mortal life of this fundamentally familiar environment. Takū's residents sing to express essentially positive views of their social and religious worlds. Significant and lasting changes in both worlds occurred in the lifetime of the grandparents of present-day residents, and songs predating those changes are retained in the repertoire more as vehicles of nostalgia than instruments of belief. With or without alcohol, singing functions as an emotional stimulant, generating a spontaneous urge for the greater physical involvement that dancing satisfies, and creating empathy among both singers and dancers. By focusing on images of an idealized life, human-composed songs do not ignore the reality of immediate difficulties and particularly the enduring loss of death. Rather, they offer the relief of perspective in distressing circumstances and provide opportunities for catharsis, by emphasizing how shared grief is both poetically personal (by use of "I" and "my") and positive (by accounts of the successful passage of the soul, and the pride of the family survivors).

The fragility of existence on a small, isolated atoll is well understood by its residents, and the community's survival strategies include mechanisms for the management and control of uncertainty. Takū's residents turn to three sources of general support—interpersonal relationships, personal skills, and the advice and material assistance of personal ancestors in particular and the spirit world in general. At the interpersonal level, communal relationships are channeled through family links, formally sharing responsibilities for child rearing and individual welfare, and informally and voluntarily assisting one another with projects that are beyond immediate individual achievement. Personal skills are learned in the first instance from older family members able and willing to demonstrate; but a parent will provide information to a child only if the child requests it, the request constituting necessary evidence of the child's willingness to learn. Secular knowledge may be gleaned from listening to casual conversations or participating peripherally in a large-scale activity, but the potential risks associated with ritual knowledge require that it be taught on formal, private occasions. Secular and ritual skills alike are precedent-based and innovation is not encouraged in the face of the near-certain success of an existing model. Requests for information are not confined to the living: the sympathetic and influential dead also respond favorably to entreaties. Supernatural intervention is thus considered the entirely reasonable result of an appeal against uncertainty, founded on the assumption that dependable interpersonal relationships continue after death between the spirits of the dead and members of their surviving family. Island residents may appeal privately for such aid but those same people will validate their actions and proclaim their successful outcomes in a public manner—by singing.

What emerges from such patterns of behavior within and outside the performance context? To use a rather simple metaphor, the building blocks of Takū society—its survival strategies, self-sufficiency in material needs, skills in both agriculture and mariculture, practicing a hereditary system of clan-based leadership, enacting interpersonal relationships through egalitarianism and reciprocity, and confronting and managing the unknown through a religious system that incorporates two-way communication and reciprocity—are bound fast by its musicking—an activity that gives artistic expression to all these qualities, confirming their existence, validating them, and even praising them, through communal singing and dance.

The structure of Takū discourse—whether spoken, narrated, or sung—manifests the interlocking principle that repetition precedes innovation, a principle analogous to the progression from the general to the particular in song poetry. The expression of this principle is most precisely defined for singing, in the nomenclature of structural units and the extensive rehearsal of new compositions. Singing and dancing are the stylized presentation of principles that bind the occupants of the 140 houses into a functioning community. Egalitarianism is demonstrated in leader-free unison singing and dancing, historical precedents take the form of melodic stereotypes and stock poetic content, which commonly feature praise for skills on land and sea. These performances affirm social ideals in their specific stories and validate religious beliefs by their praise for ventures successfully concluded through intercession.

Dancing demands a containment of energy, not just an outpouring of it, since the nature, timing, and sequence of movements is determined by an outside force, that of singing. Although no Takū dance functions primarily as an aesthetic display, the aesthetic element in each genre is considered in audience comments and represented generally by the concept of *tihana*. Small's observation is useful in this context: "If the function of musicking is to explore, affirm, and celebrate the concepts of ideal relationships of those taking part, then the best performance must be one that empowers all the participants to do this most comprehensively" (1998, 215). Comprehensive physical involvement is the basis of *tīhana* and, although not all dancers achieve it, this is a physical state that anyone can achieve, at least theoretically. To turn Small's statement around, the nature of *tīhana* appears to confirm that articulation of idealized relationships is a key functional focus of Takū musicking.

Song poetry does not openly speak of functions, but makes abstract ideas concrete through references to the lives and achievements of individual people. Such individuals and their achievements may well be already known to the audience, but they undergo a functional change through sung and danced performance on the *marae* where, in audible and visible form, they are transformed to become a means to broader ends—the legitimation of clan identity and leadership, acknowledgment of the bonds of kinship, acceptance of existing forms of social authority and validation of religious beliefs. A kind of cyclic process operates here, in which the artifact presents a case study of acceptable social principles, but group action restores that artifact to the level of a principle. This process strengthens the whole fabric of Takū society, and the sheer frequency of singing on the island is testimony to the significance of these broader ends.

It is immediately apparent that such a large repertoire can best be retained if an organizing principle at both the compositional and performance levels minimizes the necessity to memorize all the details of a song. The poetic elements in the singing stabilizer and refrain contribute to this organizational structure, as does the binary structure of individual verses. The corresponding musical component allows for variation in syllable counts among verse halves, accommodated by flexibility in the extent of level movement while maintaining a particular rhythmic figure. Additionally, the high incidence of melodic stereotypes in more recent compositions aids the processes of composition and learning. This is not to suggest any resistance to genuinely new melodies; on the contrary, such melodies are readily and approvingly noted, for example, among newly created *tuki* songs at a *tukumai*. Running parallel to these musical characteristics, poetic conformity to established subject matter coexists with the general-to-specific presentation of information across verse halves and performance characteristics that permit cueing. The situation between 1994 and 2000, which appears to represent a growing recourse to stock types, may well be due to discontinuation of the *purotu* specialist. By convention, each new composition contains a combination of the predictable and the novel, the one forming the conceptual anchor and the other the intellectual stimulant. Most modern *tuki* lean toward the former, whereas *tuki* composed by the performance specialists Sāre and Willie, as well as by their predecessors, inclined toward the latter.

Four events that took place in the last two centuries significantly and adversely affected the integrity of local culture and musicking in particular. The late nineteenth century epidemic reduced the population to a figure below that necessary to maintain important dance forms known to exist at that time, of which only a few *sau* still remain. Sale of the atoll and removal of the few survivors from Takū Island to Kapeiatu, where they endured more than thirty years in virtual confinement, caused a significant break from established patterns of residence and religious practice, and severely constrained all forms of musicking. Although the spiritual revelations of Faite Pūtahu restored social cohesion to the newly formed community on Nukutoa, these gains were offset by Ariki Kaiposu's death off-island in 1974, which again threw the community into fear and confusion of a kind that was, quite literally, unprecedented. The deaths of three *purotu* performance specialists, with no replacements twenty years on, denied the community not only a ready supply of new songs and dances but also a high level of teaching and drumming, and a reservoir of knowledge sufficient for reviving compositions long dormant. The informal devolution of *purotu* duties upon Nūnua Posongat appears to have been in effect for the past seven years, but Nūnua's declining health since 1999 has reduced his ability to lead *marae* performances, and his participation at party singing is also sporadic and confined to singing. It would be a fair statement that the combined musical knowledge possessed by Nūnua and his wife Tūhea is unrivalled on the island, and their eventual demise will bring significant losses to the community's repertoire, since neither of them is actively training a successor.

The calamitous events of the past have also affected the position of the Ariki, permanently changing his physical residence from the isolation of Takū Island to incorporation on Nukutoa, permanently removing from religious life the physical images of the deities and the rituals around them his predecessors had led, and narrowing the scope of his activities by a break in the formal transmission of ritual knowledge from officeholder to successor-designate.

Until the mid-1900s, Takū's small population enjoyed effective governance by a few individuals, but the relatively recent creation of additional layers of social authority in the form of the government council and representation within the provincial government and council of elders provide at least the potential for external influence on that governance. A more immediate challenge to existing forms of social authority is the Christian church, whose establishment on neighboring islands was seen as an omen of Takū's own future. The establishment of churches on Takū itself in 1999 was viewed with deep concern by many of the adult population. But, overriding even these concerns is the fate of the island itself.

Takū's future is increasingly uncertain because of the rising sea levels that continue to erode the shorelines of all its islands. Indeed, in recognition of this threat, which is shared by the neighboring atolls, a representative from Francis Ona's "rebel government" on Bougainville visited Takū in 1999, advising that all the residents of the atolls should relocate to Bougainville, where an area of coastal land had already been selected for their resettlement. The Bougainville representative was given a polite but skeptical hearing. The social change such a move would necessarily cause is seen to parallel that following the relocation of Takū Island's small population to Kapeiatu in the 1890s, an era recalled in predominantly negative terms. However, as the very high tides of the northwest trade wind continue to cause trees to fall and abscond with meters of beach frontage, and as waters begin to enter the canoe-building yard at Sialeva and sweep through the wooden barriers erected next to the teachers' houses on the northern coast of Nukutoa, residents can do little more than observe and shake their heads in disbelief. At the time of writing (early 2002), seawater contamination of the taro gardens on Takū Island had begun, a first step in the destruction of the islanders' self-sufficiency. As yet, however, Takū's council has not devised or enacted any island-wide or long-term strategy to meet this unprecedented threat to their lifestyle and future residence, a threat that, ironically, comes from the same source that has, since first colonization, provided them with their principal food supply and shaped their sense of pride and self-identity.

Notes

Chapter 1: Geography and History

1. The atoll was given a variety of names by passing European ships, including "Marcken" in 1616 by Schouten and Le Maire (Sharp 1968, 194); "Cocos Islands" in 1794 by Wilkinson (Jack-Hinton 1969, 324); "New Spice Island" in 1795 by Page (Jack-Hinton 1969, 324); "Governor Hunter" in 1795 by Mortlock (nd); and "Tauu" in 1831–1832 in various American whaling publications (Ward 1967, 7, 239–256). Since Mortlock's assigned name already existed elsewhere in the Pacific, the eventual accepted name for the atoll became "Mortlock Islands," in incorrect creditation of its discovery.

2. Churchill gives the dimensions of these canoes in 1884 as forty-five feet long and five feet deep (1909, 88).

3. Summaries of Takū origin myths are contained in Bladen (1961, 81ff) and Moir (1989, 64–72). Similarities in structure and proper names occur in parallel myths recorded from the other outliers of Nukuria (Parkinson 1897, 105–106; Thilenius 1898, 315), and Peilau and Luaniua (Hogbin 1931, 30; 1941, 113; Woodford 1916, 36–37).

4. Elbert did not publish the results of his 1963 linguistic fieldwork.

5. There is relatively little evidence of extensive contact with islands further west than Nukuria, although Spriggs notes without citation the presence on Takū around 1860 of obsidian spear points from Manus Island, to the distant northwest (1997, 190).

6. There appears to be little corroborative evidence in the published literature of the arrival of Takū vessels at other outliers, although Hogbin notes the arrival of one canoe during his residence of 1927–1928 on Peilau and Liuaniua (1941, 99).

7. Two pronunciations of the island name are in common use on Takū—Nukeria and Nukuria.

8. It appears that Manauī was the sole long-term survivor, rather than the sole occupant, of the canoe (Thilenius 1931, 501). Other men to drift to Takū, apparently also in the nineteenth century, included Pāsia, Amani, and Teneke.

9. Not all contact was peaceable: mythology records at least one attempted seizure of Takū by a pair of warriors from Peilau.

10. Parkinson's reference to sixteen canoes arriving at Takū from Liuaniua at around the same time may be a variant version of the same incident, since Peilau and Liuaniua are situated on the same large atoll (Thilenius 1902, 36).

11. A summary of Peilau's music appears in McLean 1999, 233–239.

12. Alternative names occurring in song poetry include Nivaniva, Lanohau, Liua-liua, and Te Akauroa.

13. Driftings continued into the twentieth century. During his brief visit to the island in 1910, Ernst Sarfert was told of a recent drift arrival from Liuaniua in which, of the canoe's five occupants, only one woman survived (Thilenius 1931, 501).

14. A summary of published references to Liuaniua music is given in Love 1998b.

15. Frequently pronounced Sikeiana, and appearing variously in song poetry as Seana, Seiana, and Tehē.

16. The summary of Sikaiana's musical characteristics given by Donner indicates cognate terms for both song and dance genres but few other details (1998).

17. Oral tradition recalls an unusual hazard arising from travel to Tikopia. In an apparently unprecedented act, Ariki Poehitu himself traveled there, incurring the wrath of those remaining on Takū. They so resented the long absence of their religious leader that they prevailed on the Pure of the day to replace him. On his eventual return, Poehitu was powerless to restore himself to his former position, and he left the island permanently.

18. On a more recent note, the wide but somewhat vague belief in a Samoan colonization origin is also said to have prompted the composer Teinoa Tenehu in 1994 to include in his *hula* song the line *Akoe e tiputipu ma he Sāmoa ē* (You look like a Samoan), praising a local woman's beauty.

19. To some extent, the present-day understanding of pre-European contact with Samoa is clouded by fragmentary knowledge of Samoans on Takū who may have been associated with Emma Forsayth, who was part Samoan. One of her associates is said to have taught an (unnamed and now forgotten) women's dance, and another lived for many years on the island before being repatriated to Samoa, apparently by Forsayth herself.

20. Oral tradition also names island destinations that I have been unable to identify, including Āvai, Sāpai, Topi, Nānoki, and Māuliuli.

21. Parkinson's comment, "In the middle of last century a whaling boat was destroyed, and the whole crew killed" (1999, 233), may possibly be an embellishment of this same incident.

22. A recording of this *tuki* appears on track 4 of the CD *Songs from the Second Float.*

23. The vessel may have been the *Sumatra,* a German vessel engaged in ethnographic collecting in the early 1900s (Buschmann 2001); although the name of its captain, Karl Nauer, appears as the depositor on the register of Leipzig Museum where three spirit figures are now located, it is unclear whether Nauer visited Takū himself or engaged a local collector.

24. "Queen" Emma was "the Samoan/American girl who defied convention and founded a commercial empire in 19th century New Guinea" (Robson 1994, cover note).

25. His headstone is still on the island, lying next to that of Phoebe's second husband.

26. Parkinson had taken a photograph of Ariki Manauī some years earlier on Takū (1911, Table 42); Sarfert's 1910 photo of him on Kapeiatu (Thilenius 1931, table 58) appears here as photo 4 in chapter 1.

27. Calder died in Australia sometime before World War One (Moir 1989, 85). Despite her earlier and later marriages, it is as Mrs Calder ("Mrs Cola") that Phoebe is remembered and referred to today.

28. Goodson is remembered today as Kaisupiko—"Crooked Nose"—so-called from wearing an artificial nose, his own having been shot off, reportedly in a war.

29. Relations with the community reached a nadir when Phoebe Calder was convicted of assault, having struck Ariki Apeo for the "unauthorized" use of a coconut for ritually washing a *parumea* fish he had caught the previous night (Chinnery papers, Chinnery to administrator, 29 Oct 1928, MS 766/5/17).

30. Although the active repertoire includes songs and dances dating to the period of residence on Takū Island, and other compositions dating to the early residence on Nukutoa, there appear to be no surviving songs datable to the forty years of residence on Kapeiatu. At this distance in time, any conclusions would be speculative, but the absence is noteworthy.

31. Funerary rituals were a significant exception, and access to the cemeteries on Takū Island was maintained, including the burial at the chiefly *kava i Kahetau of Ariki Manaui,* the last office holder to rest there.

32. More commonly referred to in shortened form as Laroteone.

33. For more information on the religious aspects of Faite's accomplishments, see chapter 3.

34. Indeed, contemporary accounts merge her identity and that of Laroteone to the point that Faite herself is often spoken of as the *masalai* rather than its embodiment.

35. Acting District Officer P F Sebire "sighted and copied documents re Takū purchase by natives but one, which they claim was for remainder of islands, including Nukutoa and Petasi, lost" (Sebire 1960a). The acceptance of provisional title to Nukutoa and Pētasi was a matter of concern, since it allowed residents "to take and use food and material necessary for their ordinary existence" but not to produce copra (Sebire 1962). Sebire's solution was to recommend that the "small line of palms close to [the] school be given to teachers for their use and [the] remainder used for food, drink, toddy/molasses and building materials by all Mortlocks" (Sebire 1962). But copra making as a school fund-raising scheme was not to proceed, lest the funds be appropriated by the Ariki for his own purposes, as had allegedly occurred on earlier visits.

36. It is widely, though privately, believed that Goodson fathered two children by a married woman while living on Nukutoa, and it seems possible that the timing of his departure after the birth of the second child may have been due to the community's view of his actions. Burns Philp relinquished its interest in Takū in 1966 (*PIM* 1968, 86).

37. In 1952 only Takū and Nukumanu were not declared infected areas within Bougainville District under infectious diseases regulations, hence this precaution (Jackson 1954, 5).

38. A K Jackson's comment in his patrol report of 1953–1954 is typical: "The tendency to wax lyrical in this report is regretted but the bare facts are a matter of wonder and the communities [Takū and Nukumanu] fascinated me. We may be able to assist these people in some ways materially but by and large they have far outstripped us in the pursuit of happiness."

39. Willie Tekapu, one of Takū's song and dance specialists, was among this group and composed a *lū* song known as *te lū te Ākau Apua* to mark the occasion.

40. Report 6 of Patrol Officer T J Leabeater notes an apparent takeover bid by Sieki in the temporary absence of Apeo on Nukuria on the grounds that Apeo's Nukumanu father made him less than a "true Mortlock" and therefore inferior to Sieki

himself. The report notes, however, that a public hearing on the island conducted by Leabeater himself confirmed that the primacy of Apeo's clan (Hare Ata), and that this and the installation of Apeo as its elder were the reasons (subsequently accepted by Leabeater) why the community had not supported Sieki's claim (Leabeater 1954, 2–3). It appears that Sieki's family supported his claim to primacy, since on his grave an engraved plate reads: "Sieki Marena / paramount chief of Takuu / matua [elder] of Tuila / tul tul of Nukutoa / chairman of community government / respected patri- arch & leader / loving father grandfather and great grandfather." A second engraved plate says "Died in his seventieth decade [*sic*] on 10th October 1983."

41. During the 1980s, groups of men moved away from Tāloki and Sialeva and met elsewhere for Saturday drinking and games of darts, forming groups with names such as Hideaway, with a later breakaway group called Crisis; Tuamārama, with a break- away group called Sakasulu (Shaka Zulu, a television series broadcast on Papua New Guinea's local network); and Vaekīkī (Waikiki). These names periodically resurface as the names of dance groups at the annual school concert.

42. Sterilization was also considered as a means of lowering the birth rate (Allen 1958).

Chapter 2: Takū Society as the Locus for Musicking

1. Although Takū exhibits the characteristics of food-foraging groups (after Havi- land 1999, 172)—including the sharing of food among adults, egalitarianism, and generalized exchange—the community "forages" at sea, not because resources at any one location are insufficient for permanent settlement, but for the exactly opposite reason: the abundance of fish stock obviates any need for comprehensive cultivation of the primary food supply, so people can stay close to their food without moving around.

2. This reference is in the *sau Tepā* dance; the spirit of a long-deceased woman dances at the location of the Ariki's house on that island.

3. The sole stated proviso is that each man must bring a material contribution, usu- ally several liters of toddy; if women assemble in the adjacent house, toddy is shared with them.

4. From the *sau taupeara* dance, one of only two *sau* dances for men.

5. The couple was, however, free to adopt one or more children from families already within the *hata*. In the course of tracing family trees during fieldwork, this practice was sometimes identified as the reason why particular couples apparently had no surviving children. The parents of Apeo, Asimi, and Sāre were the first people who, as children, were not killed because their own parents had not paid the *penupenu*.

6. Oral tradition records no comparable relationship with the other principal deity of the island, Oroatu.

7. During his 1885 visit to the island, Parkinson noted the presence of an "upper class" consisting of the "chiefs and their relatives" and carrying the name "Tui" (1999, 230). At the time of the visit, the Ariki was Manauī, himself an Ariki Atui.

8. Two different categories of people are designated by the same term *te pure*. One is the elder for Hare Mania clan and the secular counterpart of the Ariki, and the other is the medium who communicates with the spirit of a recently deceased fellow clan member. Context identifies the appropriate referent. I identify the title by capi- talization.

9. During the period of Moir's residence on Takū (1978–1983), the role of the Pure also included direction of a variety of community matters (Moir 1989, 121). By the 1990s, selection and oversight of such activities had devolved to the community council, of which the Pure was automatically counted a member.

10. According to Moir (1989, 96), Hare Ata clan was elevated from second place to first in recognition of the spiritual supremacy of the Ariki's clan, but Hare Ata's colonization myth, as recorded from Ariki Avo in 1998, identifies his own clan's ancestral canoe *(Hakautu)* as being the first to arrive and therefore establishing superiority.

11. The elders of Hare Nāoro and Hare Ania have no equivalent designation. According to Ariki Avo, *e mē sokoīa* (they are independent) and are *sē hai hakautana* (not part of the proclamation).

12. This term for musical specialist is in widespread use throughout West Polynesia and the outliers (see McLean 1999, 384).

13. In one sense, his voice lives on through that of Nake, who consciously and deliberately imitates Willie's rasping vocal quality.

14. Nūnua pointed out that the *huatana* were not composed by Sāre himself—they were old *tuki*—but that this had been the first occasion in living memory they were publicly performed.

15. Apuku's dual clan affiliation arose from incorporation within both the adoptive and birth clans of his own adopted father.

16. The practice of catching oil fish (*Ruvettus* sp) was discontinued in the late nineteenth century apparently because of the associated difficulties and dangers (Parkinson 1999, 234). The new method of capture introduced by these two master fishermen is still in use.

17. There are reported instances where arguments have occurred when a composer was asked to change the name of a mourner in the poetry of a new *tuki* to that of someone closely related to the requester. Such requests are normally denied.

18. In 1996, for example, all available men and boys of Hare Mania traveled to Nukurēkia as an escort to Apava Pūō on the occasion of the death of his wife. Depositing him on the island in the company of a few older men, the others departed for a whole day and night of fishing on nearby reefs and channels. By contrast, in 1999, in order to entertain Pūtahu Tekapu on the occasion of the death of his nephew Possiri, a large group of men, women, and children undertook a mass fish drive on the reef area adjacent to Nukurēkia, taking more than five hundred large fish to that island to cook and eat. Because of Pūtahu's status—the oldest man on the island and the elder of Hare Nāoro—the group consisted of not just Hare Nāoro personnel but all men possessing an outboard motor (and Pūtahu's son Ahelo donated petrol).

19. Within living memory, performance of the dance has also been known to follow the return of an exceptionally successful tuna-fishing expedition.

20. Use of the present tense in the above description needs qualification: although the *sau taupeara* dance in particular is still known by older men and although male mourners from Hare Māsani and Hare Nāoro are still taken to Nukurekia as a diversion to their grief, the dance has not been performed for several years, men preferring to return straight home to cook and eat the fish they caught during the previous night. The song of the *sau taupeara* dance was, however, performed in 2000 for the celebration of the birth of a first-born child.

21. The term *areha* (tour) is commonly applied to this procession; *kkaukkau* is more specific but less frequently used.

22. Although this account summarizes the mythological basis for the close rela-

tionship and is considered precedent for present action, two further events in the historical past have strengthened the bond. Pāsia, a man who drifted to Takū from Nukumanu several generations ago, was adopted into Hare Ania and later married Ariki Apeo's wife's mother, Taura, before becoming the clan elder, thus positioning himself within the Ariki's own family. And the mother of the present Hare Ania elder, Pāsia Piri, was adopted by Ariki Apeo. The two clans are thus linked both corporately on the grounds of mythology and personally on the grounds of descent.

23. Prizes are in fact awarded, but these are of relatively little value in themselves; formerly they consisted of giant taro and now include mainly laplaps, tobacco, nylon line, and tinned food.

24. This mat is normally woven by an immediate family member before the death and stored until needed. The element of shame attached to a family's unpreparedness in this respect is foremost in stories of the sudden and unexpected deaths of residents.

25. Mourners may also or alternatively wear a length of cotton as a belt; this too is the *tau* or simply the *maro*.

26. The Ariki then takes the victim out fishing at sea to demonstrate his full recovery, although such a trip may be token if the victim is still convalescing after the five-day period.

27. The related term *taka ilāmotu* is used in a reciprocal sense to refer to a man's nieces and nephews (sister's daughter, sister's son). The significance of this relationship with Polynesia is well attested; see, for instance, within outlier societies Tikopia (Firth 1967a, 23); Bellona (Monberg 1991, 17); and Anuta (Feinberg 1981, 46).

28. Complementary fishing competitions are *te sī haiavana,* and *te paretua* in which men and their wives compete together.

29. The practice extends to English-language terms. Utterance of the name Kano was deemed to be too close in sound to the English word "canoe," so the family substituted *vaka* (canoe) for the personal name; similarly, avoidance of the name Tefatu was accomplished by the substitution of the English translation of that very word, "Stone."

30. Firth speaks of the youngest child in a Tikopia family earning the greatest parental affection (1957, 153), and Samoan and Tongan oral tradition is full of fictional instances of special treatment afforded to such a child (see Moyle 1981, 1995, 1998).

31. The successful fisherman is morally obliged by his community to distribute a large catch; anyone who declines to do so is criticized privately as arrogant *(haka-tanata).*

32. An identical procedure is recorded from the Polynesian outlier Kapingamarangi (Emory 1965, 144).

33. Thomas identifies egalitarianism as an operating principle on Tokelau (1996, 158).

34. In activities held to require participants to be skillful *(mariu),* those deriving from a teacher-pupil relationship appear to be founded on the premise that a pupil should never attempt to usurp the superior position of his teacher. Although no instances from Takū were related, one celebrated case at Peilau is preserved in song. Incensed when his former pupil Pipitau defeated him at a fishing competition, master fisherman Teara killed him and returned the body to shore as if it were a fish.

35. Canoe races additionally provide a clear balance of privilege and responsibility, since the winner of one race automatically becomes the sponsor for the next.

36. The total catch from a *paretua* competition held in 1998 was 2,311 fish, which were duly divided into forty-six allotments for each of the forty-six participating couples. The process took some fifteen minutes and was accomplished with only occasional adjustments and no verbal disagreement. On all such occasions, consensus precedes removal.

37. Mourners usually sit with heads bowed for the first half hour or so of singing and, although they accept cups of alcohol when offered, they do not voluntarily stand and dance. The initiative for incorporating them into the dancing comes from an affine, who walks across the house and taps a mourner on the thigh or side as an invitation to stand and dance, sometimes adding the call *masike* (stand up); the invitation is invariably accepted.

38. At the January 1999 *tukumai* for a total of eleven deceased persons, no set number of taro per family was announced, but women took pains to ensure that each basket laid out for display was filled to approximately the same level before moving en masse to empty them onto the pile.

39. The recent practice of holding *tukumai* in December for all residents dying during that year has, however, caused variation in the mourning period from one individual to another. A series of *tukumai* planned for late 1998 was delayed on the death of another resident mid-year; Ariki Avo declared that the deceased's family wanted to be able to grow a quantity of taro for the rituals, and he consequently announced a postponement of two months. By contrast, the *tukumai* for a woman who died off-island in late December 1998, only weeks before the planned start of this postponed round of *tukumai,* was delayed for a whole year.

40. A stillborn baby is buried immediately, usually inside the parental house, and without ceremony. The successor to a dead elder is required to signal the transfer of authority by crawling over the corpse as it lies in state on Takū Island.

41. *Ruvettus pretiosus,* the oil fish, is caught on the open ocean only at night; see Hooper 1991.

42. The details and sequence of these ritual actions, as well as the particular type of leaves or seaweed used, vary among the island's clans, as do the names for specific actions.

43. By 1999 only one tuna canoe routinely used its sail; the others were powered by outboard motor, whose sound drowned the singing until the motor was cut on its final approach to the shore.

44. Each church also possesses locally composed hymns, which, among other things, call on Christ to "save Nukutoa" *(hakasao Nukutoa)* and "return soon to Nukutoa" *(hakavave maia ki Nukutoa).* Linguistically, such expressions represent a form of self-reference different from that of secular discourse, in which the island is referred to as "this land" *(te henua nei)* and may possibly be an early indicator of an emergent social division.

45. This practice ceased in 1998 on order of the Ariki out of concern over the financial cost.

46. On the restoration of ideal conditions following rain or interpersonal tensions, the *marae* is said to be *fui* (cleansed).

47. There is, therefore, dual abandonment associated with death—of both the deceased's material possessions and his or her intellectual property (ie, the *llū*). In this respect, the *llū* are believed to be more closely identified with each clan member than any other category of song, and no other songs appear to be subject to a ban after death.

Chapter 3: Religious Contexts of Music

1. Because much of the English-language vocabulary for categories of supernatural beings is strongly Christian-orientated, and because there are types of beings on Takū for which no English term appears appropriate, I have relied heavily on the terms "spirit" and "deity" as generic glosses for the objects of religious belief and tried to avoid any ambiguity through contextualization of my remarks.

2. By contrast, access to personal ancestors *(tipuna)* via invocation to ensure success in specific endeavors is an option available to all men.

3. Monberg notes a similar situation on the outlier of Bellona (1991, 31).

4. As Goodson reported to Chinnery in 1928, "There were too many spiritualistic seances in [Apeo's] family to be pleasant" (Chinnery papers, Goodson to Chinnery, Mortlock Papers, 18 March 1928).

5. During Kaiposu's absence and after his eventual death at Kieta, his nephew Nes Mōmoa became caretaker occupant of Hare Ata, but Nes was so fearful of the supernatural consequences of his uncle's death that he refused even to go to Vaihare or preside over the funerary rituals of residents dying soon thereafter. In his capacity as Pure and thereby overseer of the cemetery, Pūō officiated in Nes's place.

6. There is always the theoretical possibility that a medium will be contacted at some other time and, recognizing such a possibility, he or she is always accompanied by at least one minder who will note and later pass on anything said.

7. The nature of formal social divisions during the forty-year period of residence on Kapeiatu is unknown but, although a cleared area provided a locus for social dancing, there appears to have been no functioning *marae,* a situation that would necessarily have curtailed the activities of any *tautua* at that time.

8. Maintenance of individual doorways and their adjacent wall and roof panels in the house of each *mātua* is the responsibility of designated families.

9. For example, among the outliers, Tikopia (Firth 1967a, 25–28) and Bellona (Monberg 1991).

10. In line with missionizing practice elsewhere in Polynesia, the term *atua* has been appropriated by Takū's Christians to refer to the Christian God when using the indigenous language. However, preaching and proselytizing tend to use Tok Pisin.

11. These locations are well known, and posts from two of the houses are still in existence, but the sites are overgrown and unused.

12. Only one exception appears to have occurred in living memory: the sudden and permanent blindness of a young girl was attributed to her having accidentally seen a passing spirit.

13. Passive knowledge "enables a person to understand and respond to something without being capable of reproducing it" (Brinner 1995, 35). Much passive knowledge on Takū surrounds the act of making contact with the supernatural. The knowledge that many adults possess of the clan elders' invocations performed on the *marae* in time of communal need or ritual utterances by individual men during fishing, for example, exemplifies passive knowledge circumscribed along clan lines.

14. The invocation's association with fishing is sufficiently strong that a man will not indiscriminately call on his ancestors while on shore, lest they tire of listening and disregard calls made in earnest at sea.

15. An anecdotal account exists of Pakeva coming ashore each night to an assignation with a local man, and subsequently rewarding his amorous performances with catches of prodigious size.

16. Local fables *(kkai)* refer to unions between humans or animals and supernatural partners; this principle is not unique.

Don Niles has drawn my attention to the fact that the word *masalai* carries a similar meaning in Tok Pisin, raising the possibility of a foreign origin for this category of this spirit on Takū (pers comm). Mihalic defines it as a word of New Hanover Island origin meaning "the spirits thought to inhabit streams, rocks, trees, whirlpools, whirlwinds, eddies, and such like," (1971, 131), but Ross is unable to ascribe a geographical origin (1992, 380). The issue therefore remains intriguing, theoretically possible, but unproven.

17. When translating song poetry, an element of uncertainty may surround the precise referent of the term; for ease of reference, *tipuna* has been glossed as "grandfather" where the relationship is father's father, and "ancestor" where the relationship spans more than two generations. It appears that genealogically distant links qualify for inclusion as *tipuna* if a close relationship existed while the older individual was still alive. Nūnua, for example, claims Rousarī as his *tipuna* because of time spent with the old man on Takū, even though their relationship is genealogically distant. He is Nūnua's MBWMMB.

18. Ancestral spirits are believed to be invisible. On one occasion in 1998, however, Apava entered Sialeva during a regular drinking session and announced that he had seen a *mouri*—*te mouri te henua nei* (the spirit of someone from this island) that same morning in his house. (Mouri refers to spirits of the dead in a more general sense.) It was, he added, someone who had died from malaria. The normally noisy gathering fell silent and heard him out but did not ask many questions.

19. Although the term is synonymous with *mouri,* it alone appears to be used in this particular context.

20. Safert detailed practices in Nukumanu and Luainiua similar in some respects to those of Takū (Thilenius 1931, 348ff).

21. To borrow Wilber's phrase (1996, 322).

22. As on Bellona (Monberg 1991, 411), there appear to be no exclusively female rituals.

Chapter 4: Processes of Takū Music

1. Taken there to get national government endorsement of Kaiposu's status as Ariki.

2. Sione Pilike died in 2000.

3. In the 1970s, Nūnua composed a *tuki* in praise of the canoe *Mauakena,* in which he broke with tradition and openly acknowledged the mechanized means of local water transport; the singing stabilizer of the song was *Turekina te gear te motor nei, kau atu ki tana go ahead nei* (I put the outboard into gear and ran it at full speed). Nicknamed the "outboard *tuki,*" the song remained several years in the active repertoire, but no other poet has imitated this innovation.

4. The shared elements embody a representation of Takū cultural thinking that, for example, finds nothing contradictory in the Ariki officiating on the *marae* wearing traditional emblems on his head, neck, and arms, but basketball shorts around his waist. By contrast, private ridicule was directed at a man who was unable to memorize a fishing incantation and resorted to reading it aloud from a piece of paper while on the ocean.

5. There is no evidence of competition among composers for the right to provide a new song honoring such an event.

6. Apava's withdrawal from active participation in community matters stems from his failure to be nominated as Pure on the death of his father. Before he died, Pure Temarena stated that his son Sieki was at that time too inexperienced to succeed him immediately, and stipulated that his brother Pūō would be the next Pure but that, on the death of Pūō, the title would pass to Sieki. Temarena was within his rights to make such a decision, but Apava, who was Pūō's son, believed he had been unrightfully deprived of the Pure title and in protest withdrew from active community affairs.

7. A degree of assistance may be necessary to attain full participation. At a *hāunu* party at Tāloki in 1998, Nake Tepaia, a mourner in whose honor the event had been organized, tried three times to begin a *tuki* but his voice was drowned out by those of the other men as they innocently followed the lead of another man having a louder voice than Nake's. Eventually, Hareata, an organizer of the event, noticed Nake's plight and, after the next song had finished, he called out to Nake to begin his own song, whereon the entire gathering joined in enthusiastically.

8. An act that may, in the face of criticism, be defended by the dancer as a response to the poor performance of those in front of him.

9. Although such an arrangement is given prior consent by participants, it sometimes happens that an overenthusiastic group may attempt to sing more than its allocated number in a given round; this breach is met by immediate complaint from other groups, which is enough to bring the singing to stop.

10. At a *tukumai* in 1999 several mediums participated in the dancing, to the initial concern of residents who called to them to sit down. Senior men intervened, with repeated shouts of *E tana!* (It's permitted!), and the mediums thereafter participated without attracting further comment.

11. This sitting arrangement may be in response to the fierceness of the afternoon sun, since a degree of shade is offered to women in that location, as opposed to that of the elders who are obliged to remain in the sun for the entire duration of the dancing, some two hours.

12. A form of poetic cueing is reported from the outlier of Bellona (Rossen 1987, 2, 34).

13. "Singing stabilizer," a direct translation of the term *hakamauhua*, refers to the usually short line of text that immediately follows each verse part of a *tuki* song in the manner of a sub-refrain, since the refrain proper *(hati)* occurs only at the end of each complete verse, that is, after the *hakamauhua*, which follows the second verse part. More details are given in the foreword.

14. The *tuki i Nukurekia* is one of the few songs that men and women regularly sing at their respective houses at Tāloki and Sialeva; indeed, it was sung by women at Tāloki on two consecutive days without comment in 1999. In terms of frequency of performance, it represents the community's most popular item; the song's origin and poetry have already been discussed. Despite the passing of 160 years since the song's composition and despite the negative associations of the event that instigated it (two residents were killed), the poetic narrative endures as an essentially positive statement, perhaps the most poignant expression of community solidarity and the eventual triumph of the Ariki's powers in the oral tradition (see example 35). The second song is a *tuki* identified by its first line, *Nau ka sē moe i te pō* (I didn't sleep at night), and it relates a young man's comeuppance after disregarding parental advice. Here, too,

the composition represents a positive assertion of social values still valid more than a century after its creation; the song is notated as example 36. A form of poetic cueing is reported from the outlier of Bellona (Rossen 1987, 2, 34).

15. Also known as *nā tuki ē ppā*.

16. The Museum für Völkerkunde in Hamburg has a wooden slit drum (Nr. 12 135,143) considered of Takū provenance, but whose details are problematic. Four meters long, thirty-six centimeters high, and with several fish figures carved along its length, it is clearly very different in size and appearance from all other known drums of local creation. The museum register gives no information on the date of accession or the identity of the collector. Thilenius's account of Sarfert's brief museum-sponsored visit to Takū in 1910 makes no mention of seeing or procuring a drum (1931, 451), although other artifacts are listed, and his only reference to the instrument is contained in a footnote (1931, 356). Since the local population at the time of the visit was only sixteen (see Thilenius 1931, table 58), and living under very restricted conditions on Kapeiatu Island, it appears unlikely that the drum was in use at that time or was even on that particular island. Don Niles, a Papua New Guinea music specialist and head of the Institute of Papua New Guinea Studies, notes that the instrument is unlike anything else reported from the region (pers comm). From these pieces of information, it appears possible that the drum was wrongly attributed to Takū. Using Thilenius' information, Fischer also attributed the instrument to Takū without comment (1983, 31).

17. The absence since 1974 of recent women's dances conveyed from the dead, in particular *sau* and *manakoho*, has resulted in the regular repetition of a relatively small repertoire of such dances. By this repetition, more women have learned them to a level of proficiency than would probably otherwise be the case.

18. Avo told me it was his understanding that an Ariki was permitted to dance, but only on the *marae* and only as a solo performance, adding that such an occasion had not occurred during his lifetime.

Chapter 5: The Nature of Takū Song

1. A widely reported feature of Polynesian song poetry is an avoidance of directness, poets opting instead for an allusive frame of reference that goes around a subject without necessarily touching on the central point (see, eg, Moyle 1987, 48–49; Pukui and Korn 1973; Elbert and Mahoe 1982, 15–19).

2. There is, however, a stereotyped image of a person choosing to sit alone, meditating on the recent death of a loved one, covered by the term *hakāroha*, which in this context glosses as "sorrowing."

3. Several Nukumanu *hula* and *lani* are in Takū's own repertoire, and Takū composers have occasionally created new specimens in the Nukumanu language.

4. Feinberg notes a similar major poetic focus on the Polynesian outlier of Anuta (1988a, 185).

5. Firth reports a parallel poetic situation on Tikopia (1985, 606).

6. As noted elsewhere, verses referring to the sea deity Pākeva consist of a single repeated line; no pattern in the subject matter is discernible for other single-line verses.

7. Immediately before a performance in 2000 of the *sau Horau* dance on the *marae*,

Tūhea Nūnua reminded the women participants, "In this dance, the opening line is sung [identically] twice" *(Sau nei e vvorovoro rua).*

8. The plural form of *lū* is *llū*, as noted in chapter 2.

9. For reasons of economy of space, I have transcribed here only the song's first minutes, but these illustrate the pattern followed in all subsequent verses. The entire performance lasts some twenty minutes.

10. Because of his knowledge and seniority, Nes was asked to act as interim Ariki following the death of Ariki Kaiposu in 1974, but he declined.

11. A recording of a *lū* appears on track 6 of the CD *Songs from the Second Float.*

12. The POLLEX (Comparative Polynesian Lexicon) lists cognate forms of the word having musical connotations in East Futuna, Kapingamarangi, Maori, Nukuoro, Ontong Java, Samoa, Tahiti, Tikopia, and Tonga.

13. On one remarkable occasion at Sialeva in 1999, a total of some thirty men formed four impromptu groups and, for a period of half an hour, simultaneously sang four different kinds of songs—*tuki, lani, rue,* and *hula*—in total toddy-assisted indifference to their surroundings.

14. A recording of this *lani* appears on track 8 of the CD *Songs from the Second Float.*

15. In his spoken announcement on tape, Elbert himself identifies the bracket of songs as *uru* and *uru sakasiri* (swearing *uru*); I was unable to confirm the genre name from my own informants.

16. Elsewhere in Polynesia, sexually explicit songs were associated with religious rites in the pre-missionary era, reportedly sung to obtain abundance from Tahitian gods of fertility (Moulin 1979, 20), or to arouse the generative energy of Marquesan ancestors (Rossen and Colbert 1981, 451).

17. It is said that such songs have been sung in living memory, and with similar intention, when drift logs were being hauled from the lagoon onto dry land for carving into canoes. The group's inability to make a log budge was interpreted as evidence of *tipua* interference that could be stopped only by recourse to scandalously offensive language.

18. A summary of the principal characteristics of Takū's songs appears in table 3.

Chapter 6: The Nature of Takū Dance

1. Song and dance nomenclature tends to follow a linguistic formula: [genre] + [canoe/proper name/poetic topic]; for example, *te tuki pakū Sakaina* (the shark-catching song of the canoe *Sakaina*); *te Sau Moehiti* (the *sau* dance sent back by Moehiti); *te tuki kapi* (the resolution song).

2. That is, father, father's brothers, and mother's brothers.

3. According to Tūhea Nūnua, women should start each verse with an inward two-arm movement she called *uhi* (covering) before opening out the arms to the *sava*, but it is evident that not all younger dancers are doing this.

4. During the brief rest period between sections of a *sau*, during which the dancers sit, their lines of formation are clearly evident in the smooth patches they leave behind, the feet having brushed aside the coral sand forming the island's surface.

5. A few individual *sau* also contain uniquely named sections, such as *usu (sau Tereimua, sau Moehiti); sivasiva (sau Horau); hakatū te Ika (sau Horau);* and *hakatere (sau te Masaurani).*

6. A recording of part of a *sau* appears on track 7 of the CD *Songs from the Second Float*.

7. Although women have danced *tuki* for at least the past seventy years, the dance was reserved for men earlier in the twentieth century, apparently prior to the community's move from Kapeiatu to Nukutoa.

8. An example of a *rue* appears on track 1 of the CD *Songs from the Second Float*.

9. The oldest dances are also glossed as *nā sau te hata* (dances of the *hata*), a reference to the social institution that ceased some five generations ago; see chapter 2.

10. The *sava* action is also used extensively in *tuki* dances, during poetic lines whose references are nonspecific. The *toetoe* foot movement is also a prominent feature of *tuki* dances.

11. Proceeding along the southern reef entailed swimming two reef passages, which men say they did with some trepidation because of the ever-attendant sharks. A small fleet of canoes accompanying the two groups carried the principal mourners.

12. Ariki Avo related a similar tour he had participated in during his youth by swimming (rather than walking) to Nukurekia and back on the following day. Unfortunately, the effort quite exhausted the men, who were unable to dance on their return to Nukutoa.

13. A 1996 performance represented the discretion accorded to Ariki Avo because of family associations during a *tukumai* for his niece, and a further performance occurred in 1999 during the *tukumai* for his brother.

14. A recording of part of this *manakoho* appears on track 3 of the CD *Songs from the Second Float*.

15. Nūnua once commented that there existed *nā sore e hatu, nā sore nā aitu* (those humanly composed and those brought from spirits) but, regrettably, did not elaborate.

16. Pūtahu Tehatu commented that, in former times, performance of some *sore* could generate rain and others could stop it but, through fear of supernatural retribution for lack of knowledgeable leaders, no performances for either purpose had occurred for many years. I was unable to obtain corroboration of this view.

17. For a discussion of the poetry of this song, see p. 119.

18. See further details on the composition of *hula* songs on p. 141.

19. A recording of a *hula* appears on track 10 of the CD *Songs from the Second Float*.

20. Through long exposure to performances, many men are familiar with the *toha* in the local repertoire, but the only occasion on which they dance is after a fishing competition for married couples. Couples, either singly or in small groups, perform surrounded by women and children eager to ridicule any self-consciousness or errors (see photo 24).

21. A recording of a *toha* appears on track 9 of the CD *Songs from the Second Float*.

22. I am unable to provide a translation of the term *huatana*. Cognate forms of the word in Tikopia (*fuatanga* [Firth 1985, 136]) and Anuta (*puatanga* [Feinberg 1998, 857]) designate a funeral lament, although this is not the case on Takū at present.

23. Nukuria's language is cognate with Takū's.

24. Among my recorded collection, such sets total three, five, six, and eleven songs.

25. Tehīlau here is the poetic version of the name Teheilau.

26. A recording of this *tuki* appears on track 5 of the CD *Songs from the Second Float*.

27. A recording of part of this *paronu* appears on track 11 of the CD *Songs from the Second Float*.

28. The name *paki* applies to both the dance and the wooden implement each dancer carries.

29. For a 1994 performance at least two men were given white *vasi pāpā* necklets by the elder of Hare Māsani as protection against such deities. It is believed that the act of moving in procession toward the *marae* attracts the island's *aitu* to the *marae*. Other dancers were given sacra by their clan elders.

Glossary of Takū Terms

aitu	a category of spirit; spirit medium
anu	generic term for dance (verb and noun)
Ariki	Takū's spiritual leader and ex officio elder of Hare Ata clan
atua	a category of spirit
āuna	dance action
ava	reef channel
firipoi	a swiveling foot movement characteristic of the *toha* dance
haikavanatia	spirit seduction
haikave	opposite sex "cousin"
haimātua	nuclear family
hakaffiti nā hekau	the exchange of bags of belongings as part of funeral rites
hakamārama te tinnae	ritual of purification for a new mother
hakamaseu	"disbandment" dance and song session after mortuary rites
hakamauhua	"singing stabilizer": the poetic line occurring immediately after each of the two lines typically constituting a song verse
hākapu	bodily sanctity
hakasoro	night fishing for oil fish
hakatū	"foundation": the slow section of a *sau* dance
hare	house; term for a clan after the community shifted to Nukutoa Island, replacing *noho*
hare ākina	linked kindred
hareinoa	namesake
hare tapu	"sacred house": the house of a clan elder
hata	a social grouping practiced when the community lived on Takū Island
hati	refrain: the one or two poetic lines sung between verses (*puku*) of a song
hatu	compose a song or dance
hau	ritual of lashing a new outrigger and float to a newly carved canoe
hāunu	parties for mourners

henua	island, "home"; also the necklet placed on a corpse
hinaona	collective term for the affines of the generation above one's spouse
hoe	women's dance using paddles
hua	sing; also *huahua*
hula	a female dance, introduced from Nukumanu
ikatau	"prestige fish": certain species of pelagic shark, tuna, and marlin
ilāmotu	relationship term: mother's brother
kaina	the large pile of taro collected for display and distribution on the first day of the *tukumai* ritual
kaisuru	an object rendered sacred through invocation and worn or used to optimize success in a particular activity; rituals in general; the body of religious knowledge and activities of a clan elder
kanokano	giant taro
kareve	toddy; an alcoholic beverage made from the sap of a coconut palm
karile	porpoise teeth (bride-wealth)
kavai	an invocation used to help achieve a desired goal or avoid an unwanted outcome
kkai	a fable, a fictional story including one or more short songs
lani	a category of song sung in two parts (also known as *rani*)
llea	be in a state of altered consciousness during which a medium conveys information from the spirit of a dead relative
lū (plural *llū*)	a category of song; most *llū* relate to prehistoric voyaging
mako	generic term for song
manakoho	a women's dance, obtained from the spirit of a dead resident
manava	grandpatrilineal kin
marae	an unbounded area adjacent to the Ariki's house where all community rituals are held
manu	an obsolete dance
masalai	a category of spirit (spirit child)
masaurani	a category of spirit
mātua	a clan elder; both the Ariki and Pure are elders in their own right
minilua (plural *mminilua*)	protective pandanus leaf necklet for ritual assistants
motu	a small island, usually uninhabited
mouri	a category of spirit; the spirit of a deceased resident
niho	tooth; whale tooth; type of shell adze
noho	the term for a clan when the community lived on Takū Island; later replaced by *hare*
noti	the emblem of the founding spirit, Pukena: a conical wooden head decoration worn by the Ariki on ritual occasions
ororua	obsolete dance category

paki	a men's dance believed to have been brought to Takū from Samoa in the mythological era
pakū	ocean fishing for shark using a hand-line
paretua	fishing competition for married couples
pārina	house(s) of mourning, in which close relatives of a deceased resident stay until the *tukumai* ritual
pāronu	an ancient dance category rarely performed
penupenu	bride-wealth
puku	a song verse, normally in two sections, each followed by the *hakamauhua*
Pure	the second highest ranking man, and elder of Hare Mania clan
puru	adopt; adoption
purotu	a performance specialist who created poetry, music, and dance movements on behalf of his clan
rani	see *lani*
rima sava	obsolete term for the ritual assistant to the Ariki
rue	a male dance
sakitao	a female dance, obtained from the spirit of a dead resident
sau	a female dance, obtained from the spirit of a dead resident; a category of spirit whose audible singing presages an imminent death
sava	the dance position in which the arms are outstretched on either side of the body
sī	a method of catching tuna in which men stand in a canoe and wield stout rods
soa puku	companion verse
sore	a female dance, obtained from the spirit of a dead resident
ssako	collective name for affines who assist in predefined ways during a ritual
taka	system of sponsorship; sponsor
takapau	coconut leaf mat used for sleeping or wrapping a corpse
takere	a male dance using sticks
takitaki	"processional": the fast section of a *sau* dance
taku	an invocation to clan spirits performed on the *marae* by a clan elder
tama haimako	leader of a dance line
tama hakasere	"special child": an institutionalized favorite child within a family; now obsolete
tānaki	the ten-day ritual during which a song from a dead resident was relayed via a spirit medium and learned for performance on the *marae*
taora	first pregnancy ritual
tarikai	pre-marriage ritual
taupeara	youth, unmarried man
taupu	girl, unmarried woman
tauru	male ritual assistant

tautai	the man in charge of a canoe fishing for a prestige fish *(ikatau);* master fisherman
tautua	male ritual assistant to a clan elder
telā vasi	the "other side": the realm of the afterworld
tīhana	litheness, the primary physical attribute of a superior dancer
tīhuna	master canoe builder
tipua	a category of troublesome spirit
tipuna	person of grandparental status; ancestor
toaha	inner complex of women's gardens
toha	a female dance characterized by a sudden increase in tempo in the latter stages, and dancers holding their heads down and using *firipoi* foot movements
toki	ceremonial adze forming part of bride-wealth
tokonaki	reciprocal behavior
tuata	canoe race
tuki	a song, either sung alone or having its own dance, in praise of a recently deceased resident and first performed at a *tukumai* ritual; slit drum
tuki hakasoro	a song praising success in catching the oil fish (*Ruvettus* sp)
tuki heiva	formal occasion for women to demonstrate ritual knowledge
tuki pakū	a song in praise of shark fishing during which men beat *(pakū)* their paddles against the canoe hull
tuki sī	a song in praise of success in tuna fishing using the *sī* technique
tuki tihuna	a song in praise of canoe building
tukumai	five-day commemorative ritual for a recently deceased resident
tukutuku manava	death necklet placed to ensure the body will remain still
ui	a category of women's dance sent back from the dead
uru	an obsolete category of song containing sexually explicit references designed to distract malevolent spirits
uta	middle south doorway of elder's house, site for curing
vaka	outrigger canoe
vaka sī	large canoe designed to catch tuna using the method known as *sī*
vasi	side; matrilineal and patrilineal divisions of a clan
vvoro	song opener: the poetic line, often immediately repeated, that commences a song. In some songs, the poetic content is identical to that of the refrain *(hati).*

Bibliography

Allen, W D
   1958   Report, 31 October. Patrol notes to Village Book 1. National Archives of Papua New Guinea, Waigani.

Averill, Gage
   1999   Bell Tones and Ringing Chords: Sense and Sensation in Barbershop Harmony. *The World of Music* 41 (1): 37–51.

Baily, F G
   1991   *The Prevalence of Deceit*. Ithaca, NY: Cornell University Press.

Bayliss-Smith, Tim
   1978   Changing Patterns of Inter-island Mobility in Ongtong Java Atoll. *Archaeological and Physical Anthropology in Oceania* 13 (a): 40–73.

Besnier, Niko
   1994   The Truth and Other Irrelevant Aspects of Nukulaelae Gossip. *Pacific Studies* 17 (3): 1–39.

Biebuyck-Goetz, Brunhilde
   1977   This is the Dyin' Truth: Mechanisms of Lying. *Journal of the Folklore Institute* 14:73–95.

Bladen, Gordon
   1961   The Mortlock Islands. *Journal of the Public Service, Territory of Papua and New Guinea* 3:79–82.

Boag, A D, and R E Curtis
   1959   Agriculture and Population in the Mortlock Islands. *Papua and New Guinea Agriculture Journal* 12 (1): 20–27.

Brinner, Benjamin
   1995   *Knowing Music, Making Music: Javanese Gamelan and the Theory of Musical Competence and Interaction*. Chicago: University of Chicago Press.

Burrows, Edwin G
   1963   *Flower in My Ear: Arts and Ethos of Ifaluk Atoll*. Seattle: University of Washington Press.

Buschmann, Rainer
   2001   Karl Nauer and the Politics of Collecting Ethnographic Objects in German New Guinea. *Pacific Arts* 21/22: 93–102.

Central Court of the Territory of New Guinea
   1973   *Custodian of Expropriated Property and Phoebe Kroening v Commissioner of Native Affairs (re Mortlock Islands)* [1930]. *Papua New Guinea Law Reports* 1971–1972, 621–657. Sydney: Law Book Co.

Chinnery Papers
  1897–1971   Papers of Ernest William Pearson Chinnery, 1897–1971. Australian
                 National Library, NLA MS 766.
Churchill, W
  1909   The Dying People of Tauu. *Bulletin of the American Geographic Society* 41:86–
            92.
Commonwealth of Australia
  [1958]   Census of the Commonwealth of Australia, 30th June 1954. Vol VII, Terri-
            tories, detailed tables. Canberra: Commonwealth Bureau of Census and
            Statistics.
Donner, William
  1998   Sikaiana. In Kaeppler and Love 1998, 844–848.
Elbert, Samuel H
  1963a   Mortlock Islands. Memorandum to the District Commissioner, Bougainville
            District, Territory of Papua and New Guinea. 8 April. National Archives of
            Papua New Guinea, Waigani.
  1963b   Audio recordings made on Takū. Audio Archives, Bernice P Bishop Museum,
            Honolulu.
Feinberg, Richard
  1981   *Anuta: Social Structure of a Polynesian Island.* Lāʻie, Hawaiʻi: Institute for Poly-
            nesian Studies.
  1988a   *Polynesian Seafaring and Navigation: Ocean Travel in Anutan Culture and Society.*
            Kent, OH: Kent State University Press.
  1988b   Socio-spatial Symbolism and the Logic of Rank on Two Polynesian Outliers.
            Ethnology 27: 291–310.
  1998   Anuta. In Kaeppler and Love 1998, 856–861.
Finnegan, Ruth
  1990   Introduction: or, Why the Comparativist Should Take Account of the South.
            Oral Tradition 5 (2/3): 159–184.
Firth, Raymond
  1967   *The Work of the Gods in Tikopia.* London: The Athlone Press.
  1985   *Tikopia-English Dictionary/Taranga Fakatikopia ma Taranga Fakainglisi.* With
            special assistance from Ishmael Tuki, Pa Rangiaco. Auckland: Auckland
            University Press; Oxford: Oxford University Press.
  1990   *Tikopia Songs: Poetic and Music Art of a Polynesian People of the Solomon Islands.*
            With Mervyn McLean. Cambridge: Cambridge University Press.
Fischer, Hans
  1983   *Sound-Producing Instruments in Oceania.* English translation of 1958 German
            edition. Translated by Phillip W Holzknecht, edited by Don Niles. Boroko,
            PNG: Institute of Papua New Guinea Studies.
Friederici C
  1912   *Wissenschaftliche Ergebnisse einer amtlichen Forschungsreise nach dem Bismark-
            Archipel im Jahre 1908.* Vol 2. Berlin: E S Mittler & Son.
Gilsenan, Michael
  1976   Lying, Honor and Contradiction. In *Transaction and Meaning: Directions in
            the Anthropology of Exchange and Symbolic Behavior,* edited by Bruce Kapferer,
            191–219. Philadelphia: ISHI Press.
Goldman, Irving
  1970   *Ancient Polynesian Society.* Chicago: University of Chicago Press.

Goldman, Laurence R
  1995   The Depths of Deception: Cultural Schemas of Illusion in Huli. In *Papuan
          Borderlands,* edited by Aletta Biersack, 111–138. Ann Arbor: University of
          Michigan Press.
Handy, E S Craighill
  1927   *Polynesian Religion.* Bulletin 34. Honolulu: Bernice P Bishop Museum.
Haviland, William A
  1999   *Cultural Anthropology.* Ninth Edition. Fort Worth, TX: Harcourt Brace Col-
          lege.
Hoëm, Ingjerd, Even Hovdhaugen, and Arnfinn Muruik Vonen
  1992   *Kupu mai te Tūtolu: Tokelau Oral Literature.* Oslo: Scandanavian University
          Press.
Hogbin, H Ian
  1931   Tribal Ceremonies at Ontong Java. *Journal of the Royal Anthropological Institute*
          61:27–55.
  1941   "Polynesian" Colonies in Melanesia. In *Polynesian Anthropological Studies.*
          Memoirs of the Polynesian Society 17:97–118. New Plymouth, NZ: Thomas Avery
          & Sons.
Hooper, Robin
  1991   Denizens of the Deep: The Semantic History of Proto-Polynesian *Palu.
          In *Man and a Half: Essays in Pacific Anthropology and Ethnobiology in Honour
          of Ralph Bulmer,* edited by Andrew Pawley, 119–127. Auckland: Polynesian
          Society.
Howard, Irwin
  1981   Proto-Ellicean. In *Studies in Pacific Languages and Cultures in Honour of Bruce
          Biggs,* edited by Jim Hollyman and Andrew Pawley, 101–118. Auckland: Lin-
          guistic Society of New Zealand.
Huntsman, Judith
  1990   Fiction, Fact and Imagination: A Tokelau Narrative. *Oral Tradition* 5 (2/3):
          283–315.
Jack-Hinton, Colin
  1969   *The Search for the Islands of Solomon, 1567–1838.* Oxford: Clarendon Press.
Jackson, A K
  1954   Patrol Report No. 3 of 1953/1954 to the District Commissioner, Bougain-
          ville District. National Archives of Papua New Guinea, Waigani.
Kaeppler, Adrienne L, and J W Love, editors
  1998   *The Garland Encyclopedia of World Music Volume 9: Australia and the Pacific
          Islands.* New York: Garland Publishing Group.
Kirch, Patrick Vinton
  1984   *The Evolution of Polynesian Chiefdoms.* Cambridge: Cambridge University
          Press.
Kirch, Patrick Vinton, and Roger C Green
  2001   *Hawaiki, Ancestral Polynesia: An Essay in Historical Anthropology.* Cambridge:
          Cambridge University Press.
Kubik, Gerhard
  2000   Interconnectedness in Ethnomusicological Research. *Ethnomusicology* 44
          (1): 1–14.
Leabeater, T J
  1954   Territory of Papua New Guinea, District of Bougainville, Buka Passage Sub-

district. Patrol Report No 6 of 1953/1954. National Archives of Papua New Guinea, Waigani.

Lieber, Michael D

1994   *More than a Living: Fishing and the Social Order on a Polynesian Atoll.* Boulder, CO: Westview Press.

Love, J W

1998a   Sonics. In Kaeppler and Love 1998, 325–328.

1998b   Liuangiua. In Kaeppler and Love 1998, 842–844.

Macintosh, N W G

1958   Infanticide in the Mortlock Islands and the Identification of Infant Skeletons. *Oceania* 28 (3): 208–221.

Mahina, 'Okusitino

1993   The Poetics of Tongan Traditional History, Tala-e-Fonua. *Journal of Pacific History* 28 (1): 109–121.

Marck, Jeff

2000   *Topics in Polynesian Language and Culture History.* Canberra: Pacific Linguistics 504.

Markham, Albert Hastings

1970   *The Cruise of the Rosario amongst the New Hebrides and Santa Cruz Islands.* Facsimile reprint edition. London: Dawson. Originally published in London: Low, Marston, Low & Searle, 1873.

McClary, Susan

1987   The Blasphemy of Talking Politics during Bach Year. In *Music and Society: The Politics of Composition, Performance and Reception,* edited by Richard Leppert and Susan McClary, 63–104. Cambridge: Cambridge University Press.

McLean, Mervyn

1990   Musical Analysis. In *Tikopia Songs: Poetic and Music Art of a Polynesian People of the Solomon Islands,* edited by Raymond Firth, 105–124. Cambridge: Cambridge University Press.

1994   *Diffusion of Musical Instruments and Their Relation to Language Migrations in New Guinea.* Boroko, PNG: The National Research Institute.

1999   *Weavers of Song: Polynesian Music and Dance.* Auckland: Auckland University Press.

Mihalic, Frank

1971   *The Jacaranda Dictionary and Grammar of Melanesian Pidgin.* Milton, QLD: Jacaranda Press.

Mitchell, Robert W, and Nicholas S Thompson

1986   *Deception: Perspectives on Human and Nonhuman Deceit.* Albany: State University of New York Press.

Moir, Barbara G

1989   Mariculture and Material Culture of Takuu Atoll: Indigenous Cultivation of Tridacna Gigas (Mollusca: Bivalvia) and Its Implications for Pre-European Technology, Resource Management, and Social Relations on a Polynesian Outlier. PhD thesis, University of Hawai'i.

1998   Takuu. In Kaeppler and Love 1998, 838–842.

Monberg, Torben

1991   *Bellona Island Beliefs and Rituals.* Pacific Islands Monograph Series 9. Honolulu: University of Hawai'i Center for Pacific Islands Studies and University of Hawai'i Press.

Mortlock, James
    nd   A Journal of the Proceedings of the Ship *Young William* in a Voyage from
            London to Port Jackson and China and back to London Commencing 11th
            Sept 1794 ending the 4th Aug 1796 by James Mortlock, Master. Manuscript
            in the series microfilmed by the Australian Joint Copying Project, Microfilm
            M1622.

Moulin, Jane Freeman
    1979   *The Dance of Tahiti.* Papeete: Gleizal.

Moyle, Richard M
    1981   *Fagogo: Fables from Samoa in Samoan and English.* Auckland: Auckland Univer-
            sity Press.

    1987   *Tongan Music.* Auckland: Auckland University Press.

    1995   *Fananga: Fables from Tonga in Tongan and English.* Vol 1. Nuku'alofa: Taulua
            Press.

    1998   *Fananga: Fables from Tonga in Tongan and English.* Vol 2. Nuku'alofa: Taulua
            Press.

    2002   Nūnua Posongat (Obituary). *SEM Newsletter* 36 (4): 20–21.

    2003   *Nā kkai Takū: Takū's Musical Fables.* English translations by Natan Nake and
            Tekaso Laroteone. Apwitihire: Studies in Papua New Guinea Musics, 7.
            Boroko [Port Moresby]: Institute of Papua New Guinea Studies.

Orbell, Margaret
    1991   *Waiata: Maori Songs in History.* Auckland: Reed.

Parkinson, R H R
    1897   Zur Ethnologie der Ongtong-Java und Tasman-Inseln. *Internationales Archive
            für Ethnographie* 10:104–118, 137–151.

    1911   *Dreissg Jahre in der Südsee.* Stuttgart: Strecker & Schröder.

    1999   *Thirty Years in the South Seas.* Translation of *Dreissig Jahre in der Südsee.* Edited
            by B Ankerman; translated by John Dennison; translation edited by J Peter
            White. Honolulu: University of Hawai'i Press. Originally published in
            Bathurst: Crawford House, 1911.

PIM, Pacific Islands Monthly
    1968   Spotlight on the Mortlocks and Tasmans. *Pacific Islands Monthly* 38 (Febru-
            ary): 85–87.

Pond, Wendy
    1980   Lakalaka Feke. *Faikava* 5:10–15.

    1982   A Lyric Song. *Faikava* 7:22–28.

    1983   The Tafahi Eke. *Faikava* 9:31–37.

Pukui, Mary K, and Alfons L Korn
    1973   *The Echo of Our Song: Chants and Poems of the Hawaiians.* Honolulu: University
            of Hawai'i Press.

Robson, R W
    1994   *Queen Emma: The Samoan-American Girl Who Founded an Empire in 19th Century
            New Guinea.* Revised edition. Coorparoo, QLD: Robert Brown & Associates.
            Originally published in Sydney: Pacific Publications; San Francisco, Tri-
            Ocean Books, 1965.

Ross, Malcolm
    1992   The Sources of Austronesian Lexical Items in Tok Pisin. In *The Language
            Game: Papers in Memory of Donald C. Laycock,* edited by Tom Dutton, Malcolm

Ross, and Darrell Tryon, 361–384. Pacific Linguistics C110. Canberra: Australian National University.

Rossen, Jane Mink

1987   *Songs of Bellona Island.* 2 vols. Copenhagen: Forlaget Kragen.

Rossen, Jane Mink, and Margaret Mink Colbert

1981   Dance of Bellona, Solomon Islands: A Preliminary Study of Style and Concept. *Ethnomusicology* (25) 3: 447–466.

Sahlins, Marshall D

1958   *Social Stratification in Polynesia.* Seattle: University of Washington Press.

Schouten W C

1968   *A Wonderfull Voiage Round about the World.* Facsimile reproduction. New York: Da Capo. Originally published in London, 1619.

Sebire, P F [Acting District Officer]

1960a   Report 20–27 May. Patrol notes to Village Book 1. National Archives of Papua New Guinea, Waigani.

1960b   Report 14 August. Patrol notes to Village Book 1. National Archives of Papua New Guinea, Waigani.

1962   Report 17–19 April. Patrol notes to Village Book 1. National Archives of Papua New Guinea, Waigani.

Sharp, Andrew

1968   *The Voyages of Abel Janszoon Tasman.* London: Clarendon Press.

Shineberg, Dorothy, editor

1971   *The Trading Voyages of Andrew Cheyne, 1841–1844.* Canberra: Australian National University Press.

Shore, Bradd

1996   *Culture in Mind: Cognition, Culture, and the Problem of Meaning.* New York: Oxford University Press.

Small, Christopher

1998   *Musicking: The Meanings of Performing and Listening.* Hanover, NH: Wesleyan University Press.

Spencer, Margaret Cumpstan

[1967] *Doctor's Wife in Rabaul.* London: Robert Hale.

Spriggs, Matthew

1997   *The Island Melanesians.* Oxford: Blackwell Publishers.

Thilenius, G

1898   Nordwest-Polynesier. *Globus* 74 (20): 313–315.

1902   *Ethnographische Ergebnisse aus Melanesien.* Halle: Druck von Ehrhardt Karras, Halle a. S.

1931   *Ergebnisse der Südsee-Expedition, 1908–1910.* Vol 12. Hamburg: Friederichsen, De Gruyter.

Thomas, Allan

1992   Songs as History: A Preliminary Assessment of Two Songs of the Recruiting Era Recently Recorded in West Futuna, Vanuatu. *Journal of Pacific History* 27 (2): 229–236.

1996   *New Song and Dance from the Central Pacific: Creating and Performing the Fātele of Tokelau in the Islands and in New Zealand.* Dance and Music Series 9. Stuyvesant, NY: Pendragon Press.

Thomas, Allan, Ineleo Tuia, and Judith Hunstman, editors
   1990   *Songs and Stories of Tokelau: An Introduction to the Cultural Heritage.* Welling-
          ton, NZ: Victoria University Press.

Ward, R Gerard
   1967   *American Activities in the Central Pacific, 1790–1870.* 8 vols. Ridgewood, NJ:
          The Gregg Press.

Wilber, Ken
   1996   *A Brief History of Everything.* Boston: Shambhala.

Woodford, Charles M
   1916   On Some Little-known Polynesian Settlements in the Neighbourhood of the
          Solomon Islands. *The Geographic Journal* 48:26–54.

Index

About the Author

Richard Moyle is director of Pacific Studies and director of the Archive of Maori and Pacific Music at the University of Auckland. He has spent almost ten years of fieldwork in the Pacific and Aboriginal Australia and is the author of many books on the music, oral traditions, and history of the region.

Production Notes for *Moyle / Songs from the Second Float*

Designed by Paul Herr with New Baskerville text
and display in Palatino

Composition by Josie Herr

Printing and binding by The Maple-Vail Book
Manufacturing Group

Printed on 55# Glatfelter Offset D37, 360 ppi

Tokyo
JAPAN
CHINA
Kure
Midway
International Dateline
Wake
NORTHERN MARIANA ISLANDS
Saipan
GUAM
MARSHALL ISLANDS
Ratak Chain
Rālik Chain
Kuwajleen
Mājro
Manila
PHILIPPINES
Yap
Chuuk
Pohnpei
Kosrae
Sunday
Saturday
PALAU
FEDERATED STATES OF MICRONESIA
Tarawa
Gilbert Islands
K I R I B
NAURU
Banaba
Phoe
equator
TAKŪ
New Ireland
Bougainville
PAPUA
PAPUA NEW GUINEA
New Britain
SOLOMON ISLANDS
TUVALU
TOKEL
Santa Cruz Islands
Guadalcanal
Rotuma
Wallis & Futuna
SAMOA
FIJI
VANUATU
Vanualevu
Vitilevu
Lau Group
TON
Loyalty Islands
Coral Sea
NEW CALEDONIA
AUSTRALIA
Brisbane
Norfolk
Kermadec Islands
Sydney
Tasman Sea
Auckland
NEW ZEALAND
Chath Isla
175°E
160°E
145°E
130°E
115°E